MY ATTAINMENT
OF THE POLE

Frederick A Cook

MY ATTAINMENT OF THE POLE

*Being the Record of the Expedition
That First Reached the Boreal Center,
1907-1909. With the Final Summary of the Polar Controversy*

By

DR. FREDERICK A. COOK

New Introduction by Robert M. Bryce

Cooper Square Press

First Cooper Square Press edition 2001

This Cooper Square Press paperback edition of *My Attainment of the Pole* is an unabridged republication of the revised 1913 edition of the work originally published in 1911 and here supplemented with a new introduction by Robert M. Bryce

Published by Cooper Square Press
An Imprint of the Rowman & Littlefield Publishing Group
150 Fifth Avenue, Suite 911
New York, New York 10011

Distributed by National Book Network

Library of Congress Cataloging-in-Publication Data

Cook, Frederick Albert, 1865–1940
  My attainment of the pole / Frederick A. Cook.
      p. cm.
    Originally published: New York : M. Kennerley, c1913.
    ISBN 0-8154-1137-5 (pbk. : alk. paper)
      1. Cook, Frederick Albert, 1865–1940— Journeys— Arctic regions. 2. Arctic regions— Discovery and exploration. 3. North Pole— Discovery and exploration. I. Title.

G670 1908.C7 C66 2001
919.804'092— dc21

                                        00-065632

⊖™ The paper used in this publication meets the minimum requirements of American National Standard for Information Sciences— Permanence of Paper for Printed Library Materials, ANSI/NISO Z39.48–1992.
Manufactured in the United States of America.

INTRODUCTION TO THE COOPER SQUARE PRESS EDITION

In September 1909, the name of Frederick Albert Cook was on the lips of the entire civilized world. Some said he was the greatest of heroes; others said he was the greatest of scoundrels. To this day, he remains the most controversial figure in the history of exploration.

Cook, the son of German immigrants, was born on June 10, 1865, in the upstate New York hamlet of Hortonville. His father, a country doctor, died shortly before Cook turned five years old. For financial reasons, the family moved, first to Port Jervis and finally settled in Brooklyn in 1878, where young Fred Cook showed great enterprise working as a job printer, rent collector, and vegetable vendor. After graduation from public school, he entered Columbia University, supporting himself with a milk route. He then transferred to New York University, where he received his medical degree in 1890. That same year, the death of his young wife while giving birth to a still-born daughter drove him to seek escape. He found that escape in a newspaper ad placed by Lieutenant Robert E. Peary, who was seeking a surgeon for his first full-scale Arctic expedition. Peary's object was to cross the Greenland icecap, from west to east.

Cook was chosen by Peary and earned Peary's praise during the expedition for his medical ability and coolness under adversity. Despite the success of the trip, Cook decided against returning to Greenland with Peary when Peary denied him the right to publish his observations of the Inuit, whose medical and social peculiarities set Cook to thinking in new ways. Instead, Cook chaperoned the son of a rich Yale professor to Greenland on the yacht *Zeta*, where he began to lay plans for an expedition to Antarctica. He hoped to finance it by a series of lectures at which he exhibited two Labrador "Eskimo" children whose parents gave him permission to take them to the United States.

When these lectures failed to bring in the needed cash, he organized a "tourist excursion" to Greenland. The voyage attracted well-heeled Ivy Leaguers and their illustrious professors but was plagued by disaster. The iron steamer *Miranda*—which Cook had been warned was not appropriate for ice work—struck an iceberg, but was not fatally holed. After repair, she reached Greenland only to rip out her bottom on a sunken reef near Sukkertoppen. Cook accompanied a boat sailed by an expert Inuit pilot and Danish-Inuit crew ninety miles north to Holsteinborg, where he secured the aid of the Gloucester fishing vessel *Rigel*. The vessel accompanied the crippled *Miranda* as she struggled to reach home. When the *Miranda* foundered in Davis Strait, all aboard were safely transferred to the *Rigel*. Cook cleared little money over his expenses from this voyage.

Unable to secure backing for his own forward-looking plans to explore Antarctica, Cook accepted the position of surgeon on the Belgian Antarctic Expedition, organized by Adrien de Gerlache, which sailed from Anvers in August 1897. The expedition ship, *Belgica*, became the first to winter in the Antarctic pack when she was caught in the ice of the Bellinghausen Sea for thirteen months and a day. During that time, a medical crisis developed among the crew, who showed signs of incipient scurvy. Cook rose to the challenge. Taking his cue from the antiscorbutic effects of the raw-meat diet he had observed among Greenland's Inuit, Cook had the crew eat lightly cooked seal and penguin steaks, from which they obtained the nutrients needed to stem the progress of the disease.

During the polar night of seventy days, Cook observed other physical and mental effects, which he correctly attributed to the absence of the sun. He devised a crude form of the same light therapy now used to treat what has come to be known as "seasonal affective disorder." Cook alleviated this disorder's debilitating effects by placing the afflicted crewmembers before an open fire.

After the safe return of the *Belgica* in 1899, Cook was honored with the Order of Leopold I by the Belgian king and published the only account of the voyage in English, *Through the First Antarctic Night*. While in Europe to help arrange publication of the results of the expedition, he became interested in mountain climbing through conversations with Edward Whymper and other alpinists. Upon returning to the United States, Cook helped found the American Alpine Club and then led the second attempt to climb Mt. McKinley in Alaska, the highest peak in North America, in 1903. He failed in this goal, but his expedition completely circumnavigated the McKinley group, exploring previously uncharted territory, made several important discoveries, and reached the coast by means of a harrowing raft trip down a glacial river.

In 1906 Cook returned to Alaska to try again. After a fruitless summer of reconnoitering, he appeared to have given up any attempt to climb the mountain by a new route from the south. However, in late August, he took Edward Barrill, one of his packers, on what he said was a reconnaissance for a future attempt. A month later, Cook returned to announce that they had hit upon a totally unknown route up a large glacier, found a workable ridge, and reached the summit on September 16, 1906. As a result, Cook was elected second president of the Explorers Club of New York and earned the financial backing of a millionaire sportsman for his most cherished ambition: a try at the North Pole.

Cook left Gloucester, Massachusetts, in July 1907, wintered with Rudolph Franke at Annoatok in northern Greenland, and struck out for the Pole soon after polar dawn in late February 1908. He was not heard from again until September 1, 1909, when he wired from the Shetland Islands that he and two young Eskimo hunters had reached the North Pole on April 21, 1908, but—unable to regain their outward food caches—had been compelled to winter on North Devon Island before returning to their base in Greenland in the spring of 1909. This unexpected news caused a worldwide press sensation.

Cook reached civilization again in Copenhagen, Denmark, touching off a frenzy of adulation, which ended in Cook being heaped with honors. The drama increased when, during the celebrations, word arrived from Labrador that Peary, after twenty-three years of intermittent attempts, had reached the North Pole on April 6, 1909. A few days later, Peary intimated that Cook's story should not be taken seriously and, before the week was out, declared that his rival had simply "handed the world a gold brick." Thus began "The Polar Controversy," which has become the greatest geographical dispute of all time. It was front-page news every day for the better part of four months, and even today, a small group of ardent advocates of each man still insists that they champion the true discoverer.

Cook was the public's initial favorite because of his modest and gentlemanly demeanor in the face of bitter attacks that Peary made—attacks which made Peary seem like nothing more than a very poor loser. But before long, a skillful press campaign mounted by Peary's backers began to undermine Cook's credibility.

First, members of Peary's expedition swore they had interviewed Cook's Inuit companions while still in Greenland. The Inuit hunters were said to have denied that they had ever been out of sight of land on Cook's recent attempt and therefore never came closer than hundreds of miles to the Pole. Next, the only witness to Cook's Alaskan feat swore out an affidavit stating that the doctor's claimed ascent of McKinley was merely a hoax arranged by Cook with his complicity. Finally, two men came forward to swear additional affidavits saying that Cook had hired them to manufacture a set of faked astronomical observations in proof of his having been at the Pole. When Cook's polar "proofs" were examined by a University of Copenhagen committee, to whom he had promised them while in Denmark, it found no trace of the allegedly forged observations among them. But it also could not find in them "any proof whatsoever of Dr. Cook having reached the North Pole."

The negative verdict of the committee—judges whom Cook had chosen himself—instantaneously branded him in the press as the "American Munchausen," and a "monster of duplicity." This, coupled with Cook's apparent flight from the country, was taken as an admission of guilt and convinced many that their recent hero was nothing more than a contemptible cheat. At the same time, it allowed Peary to step forward unopposed to claim the prize he had sought for so long: the everlasting fame that belonged to the discoverer of the North Pole.

For nearly a year, no one learned the whereabouts of his discredited rival. Then Cook resurfaced in London, saying he would soon return to reassert his claim and give "a full answer to everything in my own time." Secret meetings with writer T. Everett Harry, who was working as the agent for magazine publisher Benjamin Hampton, resulted in a contract for Cook to write a series of articles timed to coincide with his return to the United States in late 1910. With this contract, Hampton hoped to recoup the immense losses he suffered from his publication of the serialized version of "Peary's Own Story" that had appeared in his magazine earlier that year. The series had earned back little of the phenomenal $40,000 (the equivalent of $500,000 in 2001 dollars) that Hampton had paid Peary—a deal that had placed him on the brink of bankruptcy.

Hampton had hoped to get Cook to tell the inside story of his faked claim to the North Pole, but when the explorer still insisted he had been reasonably close to his goal, Hampton took advantage of the terms of Cook's contract, which stipulated "no editorial guarantees, what-soever." The publisher had statements inserted into the first article that implied Cook's polar claim was the result of temporary insanity brought on by the incredible hard-ships he had suffered in the Arctic. *Hampton's Magazine* billed the article "Dr. Cook's Confession," but the bal-ance of Cook's series, in which Cook more or less reas-serted his claim, was left untouched. The inconsistency between title and subject matter was taken for insincerity and brought hoots of derision from the press and worse than indifference from the public, thus guaranteeing an-other costly publishing fiasco for *Hampton's* and driving it into receivership within two years.

A stenographer at *Hampton's* identified T. Everett Harry as the author of "Dr. Cook's Confession." Harry later denied that he wrote the "insanity" insertions but acknowledged that he had "collaborated" with Cook to write the *Hampton's* series itself. However, although the plea of "insanity" to explain Cook's actions may have been inserted, the whole series had frequent recourse to psychological imagery. Because Harry was interested in psychic phenomenon, and because the numerous refer-ences to psychological concepts and the workings of the unconscious mind provide a link between the "confes-sion" and the balance of the series, the psychological tone may have been part of Harry's collaboration.

Cook renounced his *Hampton's* articles as fabrica-tions: "Imagine my amazed indignation when, on reach-ing the shores of my native country, I found that the magazine which was running my articles, in which I hoped to explain myself, had blazoned the sensation-pro-voking lie over its cover, 'Dr. Cook's Confession'! I had made no confession. I had made the admission that I was uncertain as to having reached the exact mathematical pole."

Shortly after his return, Cook launched a shrewd campaign designed to reestablish his claim and throw the blame for his discredit on a moneyed conspiracy by what he called "The Arctic Trust" that backed Peary. To this end, he went to Chicago and cast himself in the lead of a self-financed melodramatic film intended to dramatize Peary's maltreatment of him. He appeared with it on the vaudeville stage and made shocking allegations, implying that Peary had sired children with an Inuit mistress while on his expeditions. Cook also planned to publish a book that would not only contain an account of his polar attainment, but would expose the conspiracy he said was arrayed against him. He had tried to do this in his *Hampton's* articles, but all references to Peary had been deleted before publication.

Cook hired T. Everett Harré, as Harry now styled himself, to rework his material and represent it to various publishers. Harré had a difficult task. Cook's stock was so low that no publisher would touch it. When Harré exhausted all prospects, Cook established the Polar Publishing Company to publish his narrative and manage the series of lectures he planned to give once it was released.

The newspapers, which knew nothing of Hampton's tampering with the Cook series, simply could not fathom how he could be claiming the Pole once again. Nevertheless, the Polar Publishing Company's letterhead boldly proclaimed Dr. Cook's book, *My Attainment of the Pole* as "the sensation of the decade—eagerly awaited for two

years." When it appeared, on August 1, 1911, it proved
less than that to most reviewers.

The *New York Times,* which had backed Peary in his
dispute with Cook, dismissed the book as a total fantasy.
Less biased reviewers found the book filled with bombas-
tic language and inexplicable mistakes. Still, one acknowledged that "the volume, as a speech for the
defense, makes out a superficially plausible case; but . . .
whether the author is trying to delude the public or has
succeeded in deluding himself . . . delusion is the preva-
lent atmosphere of the whole affair."

One reviewer especially objected to the material
aimed at Peary:

> The attack on Peary strikes an impartial reader as
> the real object of the book . . . [and it] fails on
> account of its very intensity. . . . Cook has now re-
> vealed to us . . . his animosity against Peary. We
> know that it is universally recognized that, whatever
> may be his faults of taste, Peary is a man of high
> character and honorable conduct; and the malig-
> nant and unjustifiable attack made upon him recoils
> upon his assailant.

Despite its generally negative reception, Cook set off
on a tour of the western United States to promote the new
book. His lectures were sympathetically received and
were a considerable success, but failed to move many
books at a pricey three dollars per copy (about forty-eight
dollars in 2001).

In 1912, Cook published a second edition of his
book through Harré's publisher, Mitchell Kennerley, and

brought out a revised edition in 1913 containing additional material in a printing of 60,000 copies. The present volume is a facsimile of this third edition and makes Cook's text available for the first time since that printing.

For six years Cook made his living as an attraction on the lyceum and vaudeville circuits with illustrated talks on his polar attainment and his subsequent persecution at the hands of Peary's Arctic Trust. During that time, he spoke to millions and sold copies of *My Attainment of the Pole* to many of them at one dollar apiece (sixteen dollars today). Through his lectures and his book he convinced many that he was, indeed, the discoverer of the North Pole and a very wronged man.

Like Peary's book, *The North Pole*, Cook's book has a curious history, and, also like his rival's account, the amount the ascribed author actually wrote is in severe doubt. The two also share a common origin in the articles that originally appeared under their names in *Hampton's Magazine*.

Although Cook professed to be distraught over the tampering that *Hampton's* had done, he confirmed that little had been inserted: "The articles that eventually appeared in *Hampton*'s, with the exception of unauthorized editorial changes and excisions of vitally important matter concerning Mr. Peary, were practically the same as planned in London." This must be true since a comparison shows that their content, with the exception of the last installment, which was never reused, is either identical to passages that are found in *My Attainment of the Pole* or only slightly different, and what isn't identical matches the book in substance if not in wording.

Dr. Cook proclaimed in his original introduction to

My Attainment of the Pole, "I was relieved of much of the routine editorial work by Mr. T. Everett Harry. By his ceaseless study of the subject and his rearrangement of material, a book of better literary workmanship has been made" This was changed in subsequent editions to read, "by whose handling of certain purely adventure matter a book of better literary workmanship has been made." This change—one of the few made to the text among the three editions—is curious. Perhaps it was designed to obscure Harré's true contribution to the book's content by limiting his role in its creation to "purely adventure matter."

One reviewer of *My Attainment of the Pole* suspected that Harré's contribution explained a number of its peculiar features when compared with Cook's former writings. The reviewer objected to the book's turgid style and to the ignorance or misuse of the English language it contained, remarking that if Dr. Cook's claim that "a book of better literary workmanship has been made" was true, then "what its earlier embryonic condition must have been staggers the imagination, for even after all Mr. Harry's care the literary workmanship not unfrequently suggests the collaboration of a learned Babu." The reviewer rated the book as "at best what Tennyson called 'confessions of a second-rate sensitive mind.' "

Along with these crudities and excesses, he noticed a number of errors not to be expected of an experienced Arctic explorer or well-schooled physician: a "walrus" was described as if it were a narwhal [p. 125] and physiological absurdities such as "the iris was reduced to a mere pinhole" were recorded.

Rather than scientific proof of Cook's attainment, the

reviewer said, the book contained "an unfailing stream of that fervid enthusiasm, that gushing rhetoric, those iridescent descriptions, which have always furnished such convincing proof of the sterling purity of the doctor's soul," and concluded that "the efforts in this book, published long after the events, to make out a plausible case, have failed, and so egregiously as to inspire a doubt whether they are actually the work of the man who figures as the explorer and author."

By implication, Harré is the man responsible for the "wordy rubbish" to which Cook signed his name. Similarly, the poet Elsa Barker had written most of Peary's book. Could Cook, like Peary, have entrusted the book upon which his claim would hinge to a ghostwriter?

Harré characterized his part by saying he "undertook the editorial revision of all [of Cook's] material on his Polar exploit for book publication." Even a brief passage from any of Harré's subsequent books will convince anyone that Harré was capable of the sort of literary excess that dismayed the perceptive critic. Nevertheless, most of the main elements of *My Attainment of the Pole* originated with Cook. Many were outlined in practically the same terms in his extant polar notebooks (now in the Library of Congress), including a list of many of the vivid color images that mark the book's descriptions.

At least a few passages in Cook's *Through the First Antarctic Night*, which was well received by its critics, show the same tendency to excess as *My Attainment of the Pole*. There are a number of other points by which a common author of the two books can be recognized. Little of the substance, then, and certainly not all of the extravagance of *My Attainment of the Pole* are the work of T. Everett Harré.

Cook knew that, to be successful, a story had to capture the imagination of its intended audience. "Apply as far as possible principles of experience in such a way that the common man grasps it," he advised. "A book must live by the emotional impress it delivers," he believed. "If it fails to blend with the reader's mentality and does not supply a ferment to produce a wine of action, it is itself potentially dead. How can the printed page live is ever the author's study."

In Harré, Cook found an editor in tune with his ideas about writing, who had a knack for sometimes excessive but sometimes mesmerizing descriptions. It is possible that if Cook was the unscrupulous knave some have made him out to be, he would not let a little thing like Harré's authorship of "Dr. Cook's Confession" stand in the way of obtaining the services of such a man.

If there is some question as to just how much of the book's literary style—which has either enthralled or appalled its readers—is Cook's responsibility, there can be no doubt that the considerable portions of the book devoted to the Polar Controversy are his alone. Many have scoffed at *My Attainment of the Pole* for its color-drenched descriptions and its aggressive attacks on Peary and the exploring establishment that ostracized Cook. But those who have proclaimed Cook's narrative an outrageous fraud while embracing Peary's confused *The North Pole* with its far more implausible story, have missed the true intent of Cook's book.

Even though it professes to be "the final proof of Dr. Cook's polar attainment," *My Attainment of the Pole* was not in any way intended to convince the scientific community, which had already rejected his claims. The book was aimed squarely at supplying "a ferment to produce a wine of action" to intoxicate the minds of the masses and to raise the possibility in those minds that Cook had actually reached the Pole, despite what the scientists thought.

As he says on the book's closing page:

> My case rests, not with any body of armchair explorers or kitchen geographers, but with Arctic travelers who can see beyond the mist of selfish interests, and with my fellow-countrymen, who breathe normal air and view without bias the large open fields of honest human endeavor.
>
> In this book I have stated my case, presented my proofs. As to the relative merits of my claim, and Mr. Peary's, place the two records side by side. Compare them. I shall be satisfied with your decision.

Cook had no qualms about inviting this comparison. He knew the narrative contained in Peary's *The North Pole* was absurd but best left unquestioned, since the comparison that he suggested made his claims seem all the more plausible. In an unguarded moment, however, he had already dismissed it by saying: "Can it be believed that Peary, with his Negro associate, Henson, could have travelled north 135 miles over an unbroken trail and south 135 miles, making 270 miles in four [*sic*] days, less the time spent in observations? Why, he could not have done it without an aeroplane." It was perhaps this knowledge—that Peary's story was no truer than his—that justified, in Cook's mind, his bitter attacks upon Peary. It convinced Cook that Peary would never fight back, and assured Cook that he would be allowed to live comfortably as a lecturer denouncing the limitless conspiracy of "The Arctic Trust."

Cook once described the central desire of an Inuit's life: "The real pivot upon which all his efforts are based is the desire to be rated well among his colleagues. . . . Is not this also the inspiration of all the world?" It was Cook's inspiration, that and the desire of any man not to be forgotten. Cook knew the truth about human immortality: that as long as just one living person remembers you, you are immortal, and as long as that one believes in your goodness, you are in heaven, not hell. And there are good reasons, based on the contents of *My Attainment of the Pole,* for belief in Frederick A. Cook and his ultimate salvation, if one only makes the right interpretations and has faith.

Lending additional strength to those who still believe today are those harsh charges leveled against Peary on the pages of Cook's book, which convinced many of its original readers that a moneyed conspiracy had robbed Cook of his honor, while blurring the fact that his own lack of proof was actually the cause of the rejection of his claims. Some of these charges, widely dismissed at the time of their writing, now have been shown to be true, and most of the rest have at least some plausible basis.

My Attainment of the Pole is, then, a polemic—not for scientific vindication, but for popular belief—and a magnificent one, couching its true intent in the beguiling story at its core.

Since its first appearance, *My Attainment of the Pole* has been considered by most to be beneath criticism, so there has been little attempt to analyze it on the scale devoted to debunking Peary's narrative in *The North Pole*. The only real attempt before the publication of my book, *Cook & Peary: The Polar Controversy, Resolved* (based on Cook's personal papers), was made by Representative Henry Helgesen of North Dakota, who had published a number of speeches attacking Peary's claim in the *Congressional Record*. Actually, E. C. Rost, who had been working as Cook's congressional lobbyist, had authored all of Helgesen's speeches, but Rost had fallen out with the doctor because of long-overdue back wages. Rost got even on September 4, 1916, when Helgesen announced that he would place in the *Congressional Record* still more remarks on the North Pole question. But this time the subject would not be Peary's credibility; it would be Cook's.

Helgesen related how he had written to Cook asking whether he still considered the information contained in his book "the test of an explorer's claims," as Cook had said in its preface. Cook replied in the affirmative, and Rost took him up on it. In twenty-eight pages of fine print, Rost closely analyzed Cook's book and pointed out numerous minor errors, discrepancies of dates, internal inconsistencies, and contradictions.

He compared it to statements by Cook's backer, John R. Bradley, and those statements in the book published by his only white companion, Rudolph Franke, and found many more incongruities. Most telling were his analyses of other explorers' narratives, which showed how Cook might have used them as a basis to embroider a

fanciful story of his journey to the Pole and back. Rost
pointed out discrepancies in lunar phases that apparently
had been erroneously taken from an almanac for 1908
rather than 1907. He scrutinized Cook's photographs and
disparaged the shadow data Cook said convinced him he
had reached the Pole. He derided the lack of any observations for magnetic variation and the inadequacy of certain features of Cook's claimed observations for longitude
and latitude. He theorized a rationale for all of Cook's
"discoveries" along the way to the Pole, and he questioned Cook's veracity throughout—up to and including
his accounts of the events at Annoatok upon his return—
using the account in a book written by Harry Whitney,
who had witnessed Cook's return, as a comparison.

Considering that Cook had had plenty of time, three
serial accounts, and three editions of his book to correct
any unintentional errors, Rost had Helgesen sum up the
evidence that he gave: "After a careful, analytical reading of Cook's book, remembering that the material contained in this book has been revised by Cook six times
. . . is it possible for anyone who gives this matter any
thought or study at all to believe that Dr. Cook ever attained or remotely approached the North Pole?"

One of the most significant parts of Rost's analysis
had to do with Cook's errors in astronomical observations.
He called attention to suspicious revisions made between
the first edition of *My Attainment of the Pole* and subsequent editions that could not be explained away as typo-
graphical. The revisions as presented in the third edition
[chapter 17, p. 257 and 274] gave the same, required
results as those in the first while neatly correcting a fatal
internal mathematical error the originals contained that

brought into question the observer's basic competence with navigational instruments. Rost deduced from this that Cook had intentionally adjusted the observations to correct this fatal error: "If Dr. Cook was as clever in making observations as in correcting the errors after they were brought to his attention," Rost concluded, "he would be able to more convincingly demonstrate that he really knew anything about his geographical position during the various stages of his so-called 'Polar journey,' as his observations prove that he was either deplorably ignorant or inexcusably careless in making his observations, we can place no more reliance upon them than we can upon Peary's."

Many other curiosities result from a close examination of the technical aspects of Cook's narrative. To mention just one, Cook tried to prove he knew he was at the Pole by the constancy of the length of a man's shadow throughout any given day. He illustrated this concept by a "shadow dial" [chapter 20, p. 308]. A sharp-eyed reviewer noticed his mistake: "That diagram shows the shadow coming back to the same position after twelve hours, not twenty-four. The man was so supremely careless in preparing the book by which he desired to be judged that he actually allowed a blunder of this sort to pass. We can hardly believe that he could have allowed it to pass if the shadow game had ever been played."

Nonetheless, Cook always maintained that the proof of his claim lay in the narrative content of *My Attainment of the Pole*. In 1917, an early analyst found Cook's narrative consistent and pronounced it "unimpeachable." But much of it has since been impeached by the knowledge

of the central Arctic Ocean basin accumulated since
Cook wrote his book and some by the inconsistencies
pointed out in the Helgesen-Rost analysis, which have
proven to be very significant with the opening of Cook's
papers in 1990. For instance, Rost's theory that Cook set
back his departure date one week from the date he actually started toward the Pole to improve the plausibility of
his narrative's timetable is strongly supported by the content of the explorer's original notebooks.

But unlike defenses of Peary's claim, most of the
defenses of Cook's claim center on his polar narrative.
The book's defenders contend that it describes physical
features that only a person who had actually made the
journey could have known about, since no one had ever
been there before. Therefore, they argue that Cook had
observed these things firsthand and must have at least
reached the near vicinity of the North Pole.

Cook described two islands lying at about 85 degrees north, which he named Bradley Land. These islands, like Peary's "Crocker Land," do not exist, yet
Cook's supporters have tried to resuscitate his credibility
by linking "Bradley Land" to a discovery made in the
Arctic since Cook's death.

After World War II, aerial reconnaissance revealed
a number of large tabular bergs drifting slowly clockwise
in the Arctic basin north of Ellesmere Island. Several
Arctic researchers and scientists have suggested these
so-called "ice islands"—breakaway pieces of its ancient
ice shelf—are probably what Cook mistook for "Bradley
Land," and Cook's advocates have repeated these statements to support the doctor's claim.

Ice islands are no more than one hundred to two

hundred feet thick, total. They are nearly flat with only
rolling undulations and rise only about twenty-five feet
above sea level. However, Cook gave this description of
"Bradley Land": "The lower coast resembled Heiberg
Island, with mountains and high valleys. The upper coast
I estimated as being about one thousand feet high, flat,
and covered with a thin sheet of ice" [chapter 16]. Cook's
"Bradley Land" therefore does not remotely resemble an
ice island, or even an ice island magnified by mirage.

Even the two pictures Cook published of the high,
mountainous land he called "Bradley Land" do nothing
to support his proposed discovery [chapter 16, opposite
pp. 236 and 237, top panels]. His Inuit companions are
reported to have said these pictures were of two small
islands off the northwest coast of Axel Heiberg Land; others believe they are of the coast of Heiberg Island itself,
though the pictures have never been duplicated.

A far better candidate for an ice island is the "Glacial Island" Cook said he crossed between the 87th and
88th parallels. His description of it fits almost exactly the
ice islands now known to drift within two degrees of the
Pole—exactly where Cook says he crossed the "Glacial
Island" [chapter 18]. But his photograph of it, like that
of "Bradley Land," has proven fraudulent [chapter 16,
opposite p. 236 central panel].

The Arctic explorer Wally Herbert found a differ-
ently cropped lantern slide of this picture among Cook's
photographic material donated to the Library of Congress.
It shows substantial, rocky land on the right-hand mar-
gin—an impossibility at the reported position of the
"Glacial Island."

But how could Cook have dreamed up an ice island

before any had been discovered? There were precedents. Norwegian explorer Fridtjof Nansen mentions in his book, *Farthest North*, that he passed over undulating country covered with snow far at sea. In *Nearest the Pole*, Peary described crossing "several large level old floes, which my Eskimos at once remarked, looked as if they did not move even in summer," and "several berg-like pieces of ice discolored with sand were noted."

Many of the features and incidents described along Cook's route from his place of departure to his "Glacial Island" will sound familiar to anyone who has studied the previous writings of Cook and Peary. The distortions of the sun at low altitudes and the descriptions of ice flowers forming along new ice can be found in *Through the First Antarctic Night*. The sudden storm on the pack ice has a close parallel in a "hurricane" at Annoatok described in Cook's winter diary of 1907–8. The collapse of the igloo on the Arctic pack is very similar to the collapse of an igloo in 1892—as described in Peary's *Northward Over the "Great Ice"*—and Cook's crossing of the Big Lead shares much with Peary's description of that same accomplishment in *Nearest the Pole*.

As for conditions at the Pole itself, though not definitely known in 1908, there was general agreement after the discoveries of Nansen aboard the drifting *Fram* in the mid-1890s that there was no land in the immediate vicinity of the Pole. Cook held this view himself. "The North Pole is in the center of an imprisoned sea of ice," he wrote in 1904. In fact, nearly every observation contained in his narrative is firmly grounded in the scientific theory of his time, whether correct or incorrect.

At the Pole, Cook set the thickness of the ice at sixteen feet, a very common measurement in the central polar basin cited in other narratives, including Nansen's. Cook correctly said the ice drifted southeast over the Pole, but this might have been deduced from the drift course of the *Fram*.

About the only original scientific observation Cook published was to say that his magnetic compass pointed south toward the magnetic pole along the 97th meridian when he was at the North Pole. We now know from computer models that in 1908 the magnetic compass would have pointed along meridian 133 degrees 28.8 minutes west, plus or minus 0.5 degrees. This leads to the logical conclusion that Cook did not actually determine magnetic declinations. If he had done so, he would not have claimed that the compass pointed south along the 97th west meridian. Furthermore, there is no mention in his surviving notebooks that he made any such calculations, nor is there any observational record for magnetic declination among his papers.

Cook also places the temperature at the Pole ten degrees higher than the temperature south of it, which is in line with a long-held but incorrect contemporary scientific theory that the temperature rises nearer the Pole because of the constancy of sunlight.

Contemporaneous scientific theory also led Cook to believe that each pole was depressed about thirteen miles to compensate for a perceived equatorial bulge of twenty-six miles. Today, satellites have revealed that instead of a depression, the earth bulges slightly at the North Pole—sixty-two feet higher than if the earth were a perfect sphere. Given the theories of his time, however, perhaps Cook's only obvious gaffe came in his description of the movements of the sun at the Pole—a concept, like celestial navigation and geomagnetism, that requires a grasp of mathematical concepts. Such concepts always gave Cook trouble.

Cook originally described his observations of the sun at the North Pole like this: "In two days' observations it was determined that the sun circled the horizon always at the same elevation, from which resulted the only possible proof that the pole was actually reached."

Of course, the sun does not do this at all, but actually rises spirally, higher and higher, until June 21; then it begins to sink spirally until September 22, when it sets. On April 21 and 22 the sun would have appeared to rise, respectively, 20′ 33 seconds and 20′ 21 seconds daily, but Cook did not include this in his reports until the publication of his book in 1911 [chapter 20].

Moreover, many of Cook's more commonplace scientific observations about the central Arctic Ocean have proven incorrect. Cook says it was "a dead world of ice" [chapter 20]. This was the popular view at the time, but the Arctic pack is not a "sterile sea," nor has it been so reported by travelers toward the Pole since 1908. Polar bears have been seen above the 88th parallel. Since bears sit at the top of the Arctic's food pyramid, their presence implies a complete chain of life below them.

In 1914, the *Scottish Geographical Magazine* summed up all the observations of Cook's polar narrative and found in them nothing startlingly original:

With a knowledge of Peary's Crocker Land, found in 1906, Peary's land ice near 86 degrees N., found the same year, and the experience in polar travel, which Dr. Cook certainly had, both in the Arctic and Antarctic, we submit that an imaginative man, taking into account probabilities, had an easy task in writing the story, and surely any man of even average education could write of the pole as "an endless field of purple snows. No life. No land." The more plausible hypothesis is that Cook never traveled as far north as the alleged Crocker Land, but turned back at or about the Big Lead and, unwilling to admit defeat in the project which he asserts was his life's ambition, proceeded to write his story from the data previously outlined by Peary.

On his return journey, Cook said, he was unable to reach his outward caches because an unknown current drifted him far to the west. Eventually it became known that a westward-flowing current does pass through the area that Cook would have traversed on his described return route. This has been advanced as positive evidence of the authenticity of his narrative. But he might have discovered it by a journey of less than one hundred miles to the northwest, which is exactly the extent of his journey indicated in his original notebooks. (On just such a journey in 1914 Peary's protégé, Donald MacMillan, noted a strong tide or current at the place he turned back.) Or, it could have been just a lucky expedient, since Cook's story made it necessary that he be carried west to explain his inability to reach Axel Heiberg Land and his subsequent absence over the next winter.

Cook devotes a considerable part of *My Attainment of the Pole* to describing the winter he spent with his two Inuit companions at Cape Sparbo [chapter 24]. Cook claimed that he was without civilized food or ammunition to obtain game and survived only by reviving the techniques of the Stone Age hunter. Many who have vehemently denied that he reached the North Pole have been willing to acknowledge his winter on Devon Island as one of the greatest of all Arctic survival stories. But even this enthralling story collapses upon analysis of Cook's original diaries now at the Library of Congress. According to them, Cook arrived at Sparbo with considerable food and ammunition, wintered in a snug standard Inuit stone igloo in a far milder climate than northern Greenland, and was surrounded by ample game that he slaughtered at will.

Other important details of Cook's narrative also suffer on close analysis, though less so than Peary's. One of the main charges against Peary concerns the incredible speed he claimed to travel at during the unwitnessed part of his polar journey. Cook's travel times look conservative by comparison, yet Cook's progress to the Pole, at an average of more than fifteen miles a day, is far faster than Cook himself estimated was possible before he attempted it. No dogsled journey to the Pole, before or since—even ones that were resupplied en route, and so did not need to haul all supplies to the Pole and back again—has ever approached anything like it. In fact, until 1995, no surface expedition of any kind had reached the North Pole and returned to any point of land unresupplied in any amount of time.

All of Cook's pictures purporting to illustrate his climb of Mount McKinley in 1906 have been shown to be misrepresentations or out-and-out fakes, such as the one he claimed showed his climbing partner standing on the summit of the mountain itself. My recovery of an original uncropped print of this picture in 1994 proved irrefutably that it was taken on an insignificant outcrop of rock barely 5,000 feet high and nineteen miles from the true summit, which is more than 20,000 feet high, just as Cook's critics have alleged for decades. His polar pictures fare little better upon analysis. In chapter 20, [opposite pp. 300–1] Cook's two pictures representing his igloo at the North Pole contain little detail and no discernible shadows. Cook attributed their washed-out appearance to the actinic light at the Pole, which caused a "blue haze over everything" and a diffuse effect on the film.

Yet a photograph of the same igloo in Rudolph Franke's book is not spoiled by "actinic light." The existence of a clear photograph of this igloo tends to show that the polar igloo picture, too, is a fake, since it destroys the reason that Cook gave for the lack of definition in the ones he printed.

Donald MacMillan reported that one of Cook's Inuit companions told him that this "polar igloo" was built near Cape Faraday on the eastern shore of Ellesmere Land in the spring of 1909. By that time, Cook had abandoned one of his sledges and all of his dogs. No dogs and a portion of only one sledge are visible in either of Cook's polar igloo photographs, though he claimed to have two sledges and dogs at the Pole.

Other photographs indicate misrepresentation as well, when compared with original prints now in the Library of Congress. The original of the photo opposite page 172 shows definite shadows of measurable objects, none of which are long enough for even the highest sun angle Cook would have experienced on the outward trip— twelve degrees. This picture must have been taken when the sun would have been at a far higher angle than implied by its position in the text.

Proponents have often pointed to one of Cook's photos as evidence in his favor. "Mending near the Pole" (chapter 18, opposite page 269) has shadows appropriate to a sun angle of twelve degrees, but this could be a coincidence or even an easily faked deception, which in isolation proves nothing.

But the most damaging evidence comes from Cook's own hands in the form of the diaries and notebooks he kept during his 1907–9 expedition. They show every indication that Cook's tale is true only to a point, and that point lies more than 400 miles short of the North Pole. The rest is a fabrication based on Cook's real experiences and embroidered with his extensive knowledge of other Arctic narratives and the scientific opinion of his day. Even his so-called Original Field Notes (partially published in the appendix to this book) do not match the events recorded for some of the same days in his original diary of the polar journey, which I recovered from Copenhagen in 1993. At different places in his other notebooks he gives different latitudes for his position on specific dates, different dates for key events, even different dates for his arrival at the North Pole—all indicating that his account was a story in the making until it was set down in final form in the *New York Herald* upon his return from the Arctic in September 1909.

There can be no legitimate justification for these discrepancies—especially the failure of dates and latitudes to match the original field notes—if those notes were genuine. Rather, the inconsistencies of his own account of the events of his expedition, written in his own hand in his contemporaneous notebooks kept on his polar journey, are the badges of fraud.

Cook was a remarkable man in many ways, with many real accomplishments to his credit, but he was never satisfied with his real experiences, remarkable as they were. He always wanted more and knew how to embellish even remarkable experiences to make them extraordinary, and to do so in a way that would convince his audience that they were completely plausible. There are ample examples of such embellishments in *My Attainment of the Pole*.

As one German reviewer of the book remarked: "The contents of the book have held us chained from beginning to end. The descriptions are simple and modest and so natural. It can be no lie what this man lets us experience, and even if it is a lie, it has earned a place in every library."

With this first republication in eighty-eight years, Dr. Frederick A. Cook's *My Attainment of the Pole* has the opportunity to earn that place once again.

ROBERT M. BRYCE
Monrovia, Maryland
August 2000

In the wake of the 1997 publication of his monumental study, *Cook & Peary, the Polar Controversy Resolved*, **ROBERT M. BRYCE** is widely regarded as the leading authority on the controversy surrounding the rival claims of Frederick Cook and Robert Peary to have been the first man to have reached the North Pole. He has been a scholar of the subject for more than twenty-five years and has studied extensively the original diaries and personal papers of both explorers. His discovery of a copy of Cook's original polar notebook in Denmark was a major blow to Cook's credibility, as it contained important evidence that his claim to have reached the North Pole on April 21, 1908, was a hoax. His recovery of an original print of the photograph claimed by Cook to have been made at the summit of Mt. McKinley in 1906 made national news in 1998. The picture proved to be a deception, taken nearly twenty miles from the mountain's summit, adding immeasurably to the overwhelming evidence that Cook's assertion to have been first to summit the highest peak in North America was another of his fantasies. Likewise, his examination of Peary's papers brought much new evidence to light that supports the widening consensus that Peary's claim to have discovered the North pole on April 6, 1909, was also a hoax.

To the Pathfinders

To the Indian who invented pemmican and snowshoes;
To the Eskimo who gave the art of sled traveling;
To this twin family of wild folk who have no flag
Goes the first credit.
To the forgotten trail makers whose book of experience
        has been a guide;
To the fallen victors whose bleached bones mark steps
        in the ascent of the ladder of latitudes;
To these, the pathfinders—past, present and future—
I inscribe the first page.
In the ultimate success there is glory enough
To go to the graves of the dead and to the heads
        of the living.

THE PRESENT STATUS OF THE POLAR CONTROVERSY

DR. COOK IS VINDICATED. HIS DISCOVERY OF THE NORTH POLE IS ENDORSED BY THE EXPLORERS OF ALL THE WORLD.

In placing Dr. Cook on the Chautauqua platform as a lecturer, we have been compelled to study the statements issued for and against the rival polar claims with special reference to the facts bearing upon the present status of the Polar Controversy.

Though the question has been argued during four years, we find that it is almost the unanimous opinion of arctic explorers today, that Dr. Cook reached the North Pole on April 21, 1909.

With officer Peary's first announcement he chose to force a press campaign to deny Dr. Cook's success and to proclaim himself as the sole Polar Victor. Peary aimed to be retired as a Rear-Admiral on a pension of $6,000 per year. This ambition was granted; but the American Congress rejected his claim for priority by eliminating from the pension bill the words "Discovery of the Pole." The European geographical societies, forced under diplomatic pressure to honor Peary, have also refused him the title of "Discoverer." By a final verdict of the American government and of the highest European authorities, Peary is therefore denied the assumption of being the discoverer of the Pole, though his claim as a re-discoverer is allowed. The evasive inscriptions on the Peary medals prove this statement.

Following the acute excitement of the first announcement, it seemed to be desirable to bring the question to a focus by submitting to some authoritative body for decision. Such an institution, however, did not exist. Previously, explorers had been rated by the slow process of historic digestion and assimilation of the facts offered, but it was thought that an academic examination would meet the demands. Officer Peary first submitted his case to a commission appointed by the National Geographic Society of Washington, D. C. This jury promptly said that in their "opinion" Peary reached the Pole on April 6, 1909; but a year later in congress the same men unwillingly admitted that in the Peary proofs there was no positive proof.

Dr. Cook's data was sent to a commission appointed by the University of Copenhagen. The Danes reported that the material presented was incomplete and did not constitute positive proof. This verdict, however, did not carry the interpretation that the Pole had not been reached. The Danes have never said, as they have been quoted by the press, that Dr. Cook did not reach the Pole; quite to the contrary, the University of Copenhagen conferred the degree of Ph. D. and the Royal Danish Geographical Society gave a gold medal, both in recognition of the merits of the Polar effort.

This early examination was based mostly upon the nautical calculations for position, and both verdicts when analyzed gave the version that in such observations there was no positive proof. The Washington jury ventured an opinion. The Danes refused to give an opinion, but showed their belief in Dr. Cook's success by conferring honorary degrees.

[A]

It is the unfair interpretation of the respective verdicts by the newspapers which has precipitated the turbulent air of distrust which previously rested over the entire Polar achievement. All this, however, has now been cleared by the final word of fifty of the foremost Polar explorers and scientific experts.

In so far as they were able to judge from all the data presented in the final books of both claimants the following experts have given it as their opinion that Dr. Cook reached the Pole, and that officer Peary's similar report coming later is supplementary proof of the first victory:

General A. W. Greely, U. S. A., commander of the Lady Franklin Bay Expedition, who spent four years in the region under discussion.

Rear Admiral W. S. Schley, U. S. N., commander of the Greely Relief Expedition.

Capt. Otto Sverdrup, discoverer of the land over which Dr. Cook's route was forced.

Capt. J. E. Bernier, commanding the Canadian Arctic Expeditions.

Prof. G. Frederick Wright, author of the "Ice Age of North America."

Capt. E. B. Baldwin, commanding the Baldwin-Ziegler Expedition.

Prof. W. H. Brewer for 16 years president of the Arctic Club of America.

Prof. Julius Payer of the Weyprecht-Payer Expedition.

Prof. L. L. Dyche, member of various Peary and Cook Expeditions.

Mr. Maurice Connell, Greely Expedition, and U. S. Weather Bureau.

Capt. O. C. Hamlet, U. S. A. Arctic Revenue Service.

Capt. E. A. Haven, Baldwin-Ziegler Expedition.

Mr. Andrew J. Stone, Explorer of North Coast of America.

Mr. Dillon Wallace, Labrador Explorer.

Mr. Edwin Swift Balch, author of "The North Pole and Bradley Land."

Captains Johan Menander, B. S. Osbon and Thomas F. Hall.

Messrs. Henry Biederbeck, Frederick B. Wright, F. F. Taylor, Ralph H. Cairns, Theodore Lerner, M. Van Ryssellberghe, J. Knowles Hare, Chas. E. Rilliet, Homer Rogers, R. C. Bates, E. C. Rost, L. C. Bement, Clarence Wychoff, Alfred Church, Archibald Dickinson, Robert Stein, J. S. Warmbath, Geo. B. Butland, Ralph Shainwald, Henry Johnson, S. J. Entrikin, Clark Brown, W. F. Armbruster, John R. Bradley, Harry Whitney and Rudolph Franke.

Drs. T. F. Dedrick, Middleton Smith, J. G. Knowlton, H. J. Egbert, W. H. Axtell, A. H. Cordier and Henry Schwartz.

Judge Jules Leclercq, and Prof. Georges Lecointe, Secretary of the International Bureau of Polar Research.

Thus endorsed by practically all Polar Explorers, Dr. Cook's attainment of the Pole and his earlier work of discovery and exploration is farther established by the following honorary pledges of recognition. (These are now in the possession of Dr. Cook, the press reports to the contrary being untrue).

By the King of Belgium, decorated as Knight of the Order of Leopold.

By the University of Copenhagen in conferring the degree of Ph. D.

By the Royal Danish Geographical Society, presentation of a gold medal

By the Arctic Club of America, presentation of a gold medal.

By the Royal Geographical Society of Belgium, presentation of a gold medal.

By the Municipality of the City of Brussels, presentation of a gold medal.

By the Municipality of the City of New York, with the ceremony of presenting the keys and offering the freedom of the city.

Without denying officer Peary's success, we note that his case rests upon the opinion of three of his official associates in Washington. Three men acting for a society financially interested—three men who have never seen a piece of Polar ice — have given it as their "opinion" that Mr. Peary (a year later than Dr. Cook) reached the Pole. By many this was accepted as a final verdict of experts for Peary. But are such men dependable experts?

Dr. Cook now offers in substantiation of his work the support and the final verdict of fifty of the foremost explorers and scientific experts. Each in his own way has during the past four years examined the polar problem and pronounced in favor of Dr. Cook.

He is therefore vindicated of the propaganda of insinuation and distrust which his enemies forced, and his success in reaching the Pole is conceded and endorsed by his own peers.

In his book, "My Attainment of the Pole," Dr. Cook offers with thrilling vividness a most remarkable series of adventures in the enraptured wilderness at the top of the globe. And in his lectures he takes his audience step by step over the haunts of northernmost man and beyond to the sparkling sea of death at the pole. Above all he leaves in the hearts of his listeners the thrills of a fresh vigor and a new inspiration, which opens the way for other worlds to conquer. By his books and by his lectures, Dr. Cook seeks justice at the bar of public opinion, and three million people have applauded his effort on the platform. One hundred thousand people will read his book during the coming year. We are inclined to agree with Capt. E. B. Baldwin and other Arctic explorers who say —"Putting aside the academic and idle argument of pin-point accuracy, the North Pole has been honestly reached by Dr. Cook, three hundred and fifty days before any one else claimed to have been there."

May 22, 1913.

THE CHAUTAUQUA MANAGERS' ASSOCIATION,
ORCHESTRA BUILDING, CHICAGO.

Chas. W. Ferguson, Pres.   A. L. Flude, Sec'y.

PREFACE

This narrative has been prepared as a general outline of my conquest of the North Pole. In it the scientific data, the observations, every phase of the pioneer work with its drain of human energy has been presented in its proper relation to a strange cycle of events. The camera has been used whenever possible to illustrate the progress of the expedition as well as the wonders and mysteries of the Arctic wilds. Herein, with due after-thought and the better perspective afforded by time, the rough field notes, the disconnected daily tabulations and the records of instrumental observations, every fact, every optical and mental impression, has been re-examined and re-arranged to make a concise record of successive stages of progress to the boreal center. If. I have thus worked out an understandable panorama of our environment, then the mission of this book has served its purpose.

Much has been said about absolute geographic proof of an explorer's work. History demonstrates that the book which gives the final authoritative narrative is the test of an explorer's claims. By it every traveler has been measured. From the time of the discovery of America to the piercing of darkest Africa and the open-

ing of Thibet, men who have sought the truth of the
claims of discovery have sought, not abstract figures,
but the continuity of the narrative in the pages of the
traveler's final book. In such a narrative, after due
digestion and assimilation, there is to be found either
the proof or the disproof of the claims of a discoverer.

In such narratives as the one herewith presented,
subsequent travelers and other experts, with no other
interests to serve except those of fair play, have critically examined the material. With the lapse of time
accordingly, when partisanship feelings have been
merged in calm and conscientious judgment, history has
always finally pronounced a fair and equitable verdict.

In a similar way my claim of being first to reach
the North Pole will rest upon the data presented between the covers of this book.

In working out the destiny of this Expedition, and
this book which records its doings, I have to acknowledge my gratitude for the assistance of many people:
First among those to whom I am deeply indebted is
John R. Bradley. By his liberal hand this Expedition
was given life, and by his loyal support and helpfulness
I was enabled to get to my base of operations at Annoatok. By his liberal donations of food we were enabled to
live comfortably during the first year. To John R.
Bradley, therefore, belong the first fruits of the Polar
conquest.

A tribute of praise must be placed on record for
Rudolph Francke. After the yacht returned, he was
my sole civilized helper and companion. The faithful
manner in which he performed the difficult duties as-
signed to him, and his unruffled cheerfulness during the

trying weeks of the long night, reflect a large measure
of credit.

The band of little people of the Farthest North
furnished without pay the vital force and the primitive
ingenuity without which the quest of the Pole would be
a hopeless task. These boreal pigmies with golden
skins, with muscles of steel, and hearts as finely human
as those of the highest order of man, performed a task
that cannot be too highly commended. The two boys,
Ah-we-lah and E-tuk-i-shook, deserve a place on the tab-
let of fame. They followed me with a perseverance
which demonstrates one of the finest qualities of savage
life. They shared with me the long run of hardship;
they endured without complaint the unsatisfied hunger,
the unquenched thirst, and the maddening isolation, with
no thought of reward except that which comes from an
unselfish desire to follow one whom they chose to regard
as a friend. If a noble deed was ever accomplished,
these boys did it, and history should record their heroic
effort with indelible ink.

At the request of Mrs. Cook, the Canadian Government sent its ship, the "Arctic," under Captain Bernier, with supplementary supplies for me, to Etah.
These were left under the charge of Mr. Harry Whitney. The return to civilization was made in comfort,
by the splendid manner in which this difficult problem
was carried out. To each and all in this combination I
am deeply indebted.

With sweet memories of the warm hospitality of
Danes in Greenland, I here subscribe my never-to-be-
forgotten appreciation. I am also indebted to the
Royal Greenland Trading Company and to the United

S. S. Company for many favors; and, above all, am I grateful to the Danes as a nation, for the whole-souled demonstrations of friendship and appreciation at Copenhagen.

In the making of this book, I was relieved of much routine editorial work by Mr. T. Everett Harry, associate editor of Hampton's Magazine, who rearranged much of my material, and by whose handling of certain purely adventure matter a book of better literary workmanship has been made.

I am closing the pages of this book with a good deal of regret, for, in the effort to make the price of this volume so low that it can go into every home, the need for brevity has dictated the number of pages. My last word to all—to friends and enemies—is, if you must pass judgment, study the problem carefully. You are as capable of forming a correct judgment as the self-appointed experts. One of Peary's captains has said "that he knew, but never would admit, that Peary did not reach the Pole." Rear Admiral Chester has said the same about me, but he "admits" it in big, flaming type. With due respect to these men, in justice to the cause, I am bound to say that these, and others of their kind, who necessarily have a blinding bias, are not better able to judge than the average American citizen.

If you have read this book, then read Mr. Peary's "North Pole." Put the two books side by side. When making comparisons, remember that my attainment of the Pole was one year earlier than Mr. Peary's claim; that my narrative was written and printed months before that of Mr. Peary; that the Peary narrative is such that Rear Admiral Schley has said—"After reading the published accounts daily and critically of both claimants, I was forced to the conclusion from their striking similarity that each of you was the eye-witness of the other's success. Without collusion, it would have been impossible to have written accounts so similar."

This opinion, coming as it does from one of the highest Arctic and Naval authorities, is endorsed by practically all Arctic explorers. Captain E. B. Baldwin goes even further, and proves my claim from the pages of Peary's own book. Governor Brown of Georgia, after a critical examination of the two reports, says, "If it is true, as Peary would like us to believe, that Cook has given us a gold brick, then Peary has offered a paste diamond."

Since my account was written and printed first, the striking analogy apparent in the Peary pages either proves my position at the Pole or it convicts Peary of using my data to fill out and impart verisimilitude .to his own story of a second victory.

Much against my will I find myself compelled to uncover the dark pages of the selfish unfairness of rival interests. In doing so my aim is not to throw doubt and distrust on Mr. Peary's success, but to show his incentive and his methods in attempting to leave the sting of discredit upon me. I would prefer to close my eye to a long series of wrong doings as I have done in the passing years, but the Polar controversy cannot be understood unless we get the perspective of the man who has forced it. Heretofore I have allowed others to expend their argumentative ammunition. The questions which I have raised are minor points. On the main question of Polar attainment there is not now room for doubt. The Pole has been honestly reached—the American Eagle has spread its wings of glory over the world's top. Whether there is room for one or two or more under those wings, I am content to let the future decide.

FREDERICK A. COOK.

The Waldorf-Astoria,
     New York, June 15, 1911.

TABLE OF CONTENTS

LIST OF ILLUSTRATIONS

My Attainment of the Pole

I.

THE POLAR FIGHT

On April 21, 1908, I reached a spot on the silver-shining desert of boreal ice whereat a wild wave of joy filled my heart. I can remember the scene distinctly—it will remain one of those comparatively few mental pictures which are photographed with a terribly vivid distinctness of detail, because of their emotional effect, during everyone's existence, and which reassert themselves in the brain like lightning flashes in stresses of intense emotion, in dreams, in the delirium of sickness, and possibly in the hour of death.

I can see the sun lying low above the horizon, which glittered here and there in shafts of light like the tip of a long, circular, silver blade. The globe of fire, veiled occasionally by purplish, silver-shot mists, was tinged with a faint, burning lilac. Through opening cracks in the constantly moving field of ice, cold strata of air rose, deflecting the sun's rays in every direction, and changing the vision of distant ice irregularities with a deceptive perspective, as an oar blade seen in the depth of still water.

Huge phantom-shapes took form about me; they were nebulous, their color purplish. About the horizon moved what my imagination pictured as the ghosts of dead armies—strange, gigantic, wraith-like shapes whose heads rose above the horizon as the heads of a giant army appearing over the summits of a far-away mountain. They moved forward, retreated, diminished in size, and titanically reappeared again. Above them, in the purple mists and darker clouds, shifted scintillantly waving flashes of light, orange and crimson, the ghosts of their earthly battle banners, wind-tossed, golden and bloodstained.

I stood gazing with wonder, half-appalled, forgetting that these were mirages produced by cold air and deflected light rays, and feeling only as though I were beholding some vague revelation of victorious hosts, beings of that other world which in olden times, it is said, were conjured at Endor. It seemed fitting that they should march and remarch about me; that the low beating of the wind should suddenly swell into throbbing martial music. For that moment I was intoxicated. I stood alone, apart from my two Eskimo companions, a shifting waste of purple ice on every side, alone in a dead world—a world of angry winds, eternal cold, and desolate for hundreds of miles in every direction as the planet before man was made.

I felt in my heart the thrill which any man must feel when an almost impossible but dearly desired work is attained—the thrill of accomplishment with which a poet must regard his greatest masterpiece, which a sculptor must feel when he puts the finishing touch to inanimate matter wherein he has expressed consummately a living thought, which a conqueror must feel when he has mastered a formidable alien army. Stand-

ing on this spot, I felt that I, a human being, with all
of humanity's frailties, had conquered cold, evaded
famine, endured an inhuman battling with a rigorous,
infuriated Nature in a soul-racking, body-sapping
journey such as no man perhaps had ever made. I
had proved myself to myself, with no thought at the
time of any worldy applause. Only the ghosts about
me, which my dazzled imagination evoked, celebrated
the glorious thing with me—a thing in which no human
being could have shared. Over and over again I repeated to myself that I had reached the North Pole,
and the thought thrilled through my nerves and veins
like the shivering sound of silver bells.

That was my hour of victory. It was the climac-
teric hour of my life. The vision and the thrill, despite
all that has passed since then, remain, and will remain
with me as long as life lasts, as the vision and the thrill
of an honest, actual accomplishment.

That I stood at the time on the very pivotal pin-
point of the earth I do not and never did claim; I may
have, I may not. In that moving world of ice, of constantly rising mists, with a low-lying sun whose rays
are always deflected, such an ascertainment of actual
position, even with instruments in the best workable
condition, is, as all scientists will agree, impossible.
That I reached the North Pole approximately, and
ascertained my location as accurately, as painstakingly,
as the terrestrial and celestial conditions and the best instruments would allow; that I thrilled with victory,
and made my claim on as honest, as careful, as scientific
a basis of observations and calculations as any hum-
being could, I do emphatically assert. That an

in reaching this region, could do more than I did to ascertain definitely the mathematical Pole, and that any more voluminous display of figures could substantiate a claim of greater accuracy, I do deny. I believe still what I told the world when I returned, that I am the first white man to reach that spot known as the North Pole as far as it is, or ever will be, humanly possible to ascertain the location of that spot.

Few men in all history, I am inclined to believe, have ever been made the subject of such vicious attacks, of such malevolent assailing of character, of such a series of perjured and forged charges, of such a widespread and relentless press persecution, as I; and few men, I feel sure, have ever been made to suffer so bitterly and so inexpressibly as I because of the assertion of my achievement. So persistent, so egregious, so overwhelming were the attacks made upon me that for a time my spirit was broken, and in the bitterness of my soul I even felt desirous of disappearing to some remote corner of the earth, to be forgotten. I knew that envy was the incentive to all the unkind abuses heaped upon me, and I knew also that in due time, when the public agitation subsided and a better perspective followed, the justice of my claim would force itself to the inevitable light of truth.

With this confidence in the future, I withdrew from the envious, money-waged strife to the calm and restfulness of my own family circle. The campaign of infamy raged and spent its force. The press lined up with this dishonest movement by printing bribed, faked and forged news items, deliberately manufactured by my enemies to feed a newspaper hunger for sensation.

In going away for a rest it did not seem prudent to take the press into my confidence, a course which resulted in the mean slurs that I had abandoned my cause. This again was used by my enemies to blacken my character. In reality, I had tried to keep the ungracious Polar controversy within the bounds of decent, gentlemanly conduct; but indecency had become the keynote, and against this, mild methods served no good purpose. I preferred, therefore, to go away and allow the atmosphere to clear of the stench stirred up by rival interest; but while I was away, my enemies were watched, and I am here now to uncover the darkest campaign of bribery and conspiracy ever forged in a strife for honor.

Now that my disappointment, my bitterness has passed, that my hurt has partly healed, I have determined to tell the whole truth about myself, about the charges made against me, and about those by whom the charges were made. Herein, FOR THE FIRST TIME, I will tell how and why I believed I reached the North Pole, and give fully the record upon which this claim is based. Only upon such a complete account of day-by-day traveling and such observations, can any claim rest.

Despite the hullabaloo of voluminous so-called proofs offered by a rival, I am certain that the unprejudiced reader will herein find as complete a story, and as valuable figures as those ever offered by anyone for any such achievement in exploration as mine. Herein, for the first time, shall I answer *in toto* all charges made against me, and this because the entire truth concerning these same charges I have not succeeded in giving the world through other channels. Because of the power of those who arrayed themselves against me, I found the columns of the press closed to much that I wished to say; articles which I wrote for publication underwent editorial excision, and absolutely necessary explanations, which in themselves attacked my assailants, were eliminated.

Only by reading my own story, as fully set down herein, can anyone judge of the relative value of my claim and that of my rival claimant; only by so doing can anyone get at the truth of the plot made to discredit me; only by doing so can one learn the reason for all of my actions, for my failure to meet charges at the time they were made, for my disappearing at a time when such action was unfairly made to confirm the worst charges of my detractors. That I have been too charitable with those who attempted to steal the justly deserved honors of my achievement, I am now convinced; when desirable, I shall now, having felt the smarting sting of the world's whip, and in order to justify myself, use the knife. I shall tell the truth even though it hurts. I have not been spared, and I shall spare no one in telling the unadorned and unpleasant story of a man who has been bitterly wronged, whose character has been assailed by bought and perjured affidavits, whose life before he returned from the famine-land of ice and cold—the world of his conquest—was endangered, designedly or not, by a dishonest appropriation of food supplies by one who afterwards endeavored to steal from him his honor, which is more dear than life.

To be doubted, and to have one's honesty assailed,

has been the experience of many explorers throughout history.   The discoverer of our own continent, Christopher Columbus, was thrown into prison, and another, Amerigo Vespucci, was given the honor, his name to this day marking the land which was reached only through the intrepidity and single-hearted, single-sustained confidence of a man whose vision his own people doubted.   Even in my own time have explorers been assailed, among them Stanley, whose name for a time was shrouded with suspicion, and others who since have joined the ranks of my assailants.   Unfortunately, in such cases the matter of proof and the reliability of any claim, basicly, must rest entirely upon the intangible evidence of a man's own word; there can be no such thing as a palpable and indubitable proof.   And in the case when a man's good faith is aspersed and his character assailed, the world's decision must rest either upon his own word or that of his detractors.

Returning from the North, exhausted both in body and brain by a savage and excruciating struggle against famine and cold, yet thrilling with the glorious conviction of a personal attainment, I was tossed to the zenith of worldly honor on a wave of enthusiasm, a world-madness, which startled and bewildered me.   In that swift, sudden, lightning-flash ascension to glory, which I had not expected, and in which I was as a bit of helpless drift in the thundering tossing of an ocean storm, I was decorated with unasked-for honors, the laudations of the press of the world rang in my ears, the most notable of living men hailed me as one great among them.   I found myself the unwilling and uncomfortable guest of princes, and I was led forward to receive the gracious hand of a King.

Returning to my own country, still marveling that such honors should be given because I had accomplished what seemed, and still seems, a merely personal achievement, and of little importance to anyone save to him who throbs with the gratification of a personal success, I was greeted with mad cheers and hooting whistles, with bursting guns and blaring bands. I was led through streets filled with applauding men and singing children and arched with triumphal flowers. In a dizzy whirl about the country—which now seems like a delirious dream—I experienced what I am told was an ovation unparalleled of its kind.

Coincident with my return to civilization, and while the world was ringing with congratulations, there came stinging through the cold air from the North, by wireless electric flashes, word from Mr. Peary that he had reached the North Pole and that, in asserting such a claim myself, I was a liar. I did not then doubt the good faith of Peary's claim; having reached the boreal center myself, under extremely favorable weather conditions, I felt that he, with everything in his favor, could do as much a year later, as he claimed. I replied with all candor what I felt, that there was glory enough for two. But I did, of course, feel the sting of my rival's unwarranted and virulent attacks. In the stress of any great crisis, the average human mind is apt to be carried away by unwise impulses.

Following Mr. Peary's return, I found myself the object of a campaign to discredit me in which, I believe, as an explorer, I stand the most shamefully abused man in the history of exploration. Deliberately planned, inspired at first, and at first directed, by Mr. Peary from the wireless stations of Labrador, this campaign was consistently and persistently worked out by a powerful and affluent organization, with unlimited money at its command, which has had as its allies dishonest pseudo-scientists, financially and otherwise interested in the success of Mr. Peary's expedition. With a chain of powerful newspapers, a financial backer of Peary led a campaign to destroy confidence in me. I found myself in due time, before I realized the importance of underhand attacks, in a quandary which baffled and bewildered me. Without any organization behind me, without any wires to pull, without, at the time, any appreciable amount of money for defence, I felt what anyone who is not superhuman would have felt, a sickening sense of helplessness, a disgust at the human duplicity which permitted such things, a sense of the futility of the very thing I had done and its little worth compared to the web of shame my enemies were endeavoring to weave about me.

One of the remarkable things about modern journalism is that, by persistent repetition, it can create as a fact in the public mind a thing which is purely immaterial or untrue. Taking the cue from Peary, there was at the beginning a widespread and unprecedented call for "proofs," which in some vague way were to consist of unreduced reckonings. Mr. Peary had his own—he had buried part of mine. I did not at the time instantly produce these vague and obscure proofs, knowing, as all scientists know, that figures must inevitably be inadequate and that any convincing proof that can exist is to be found only in the narrative account of such a quest. I did not appreciate that in the public mind, because of the newspapers' criticisms, there was growing a demand for this vague something. For this reason, I did not consider an explanation of the absurdity of this exaggerated position necessary.

Nor did I appreciate the relative effect of the National Geographic Society's "acceptance" of Mr. Peary's so-called "proofs" while mine were not forthcoming. I did not know at the time, what has since been brought out in the testimony given before the Naval Committee in Washington, that the National Geographic Society's verdict was based upon an indifferent examination of worthless observations and a few seconds' casual observation of Mr. Peary's instruments by several members of the Society in the Pennsylvania Railroad Station at Washington. With many lecture engagements, I considered that I was right in doing what every other explorer, including Mr. Peary himself, had done before me; that is, to fulfill my lecture and immediate literary opportunities while there was a great public interest aroused, and to offer a narrative of greater length, with field observations and extensive scientific data, later.

Following the exaggerated call for proofs, there began a series of persistently planned attacks. So petty and insignificant did many of them seem to me that I gave them little thought. My speed limits were questioned, this charge being dropped when it was found that Mr. Peary's had exceeded mine. The use by the newspaper running my narrative story of photographs of Arctic scenes—which never change in character— that had been taken by me on previous trips. was held up as visible evidence that I was a faker! Errors which

crept into my newspaper account because of hasty preparation, and which were not corrected because there
was no time to read proofs, were eagerly seized upon,
and long, abstruse and impressive mathematical dis-
sertations were made on these to prove how unscrupulous and unreliable I was.

The photograph of the flag at the Pole was put
forth by one of Mr. Peary's friends to prove on *prima
facie* evidence that I had faked. Inasmuch as the original negative was vague because of the non-actinic light
in the North, the newspaper photographers retouched
the print and painted on it a shadow as being cast from
the flag and snow igloos. This shadow was seized upon
avidly, and after long and learned calculations, was
cited as showing that the picture was taken some five
hundred miles from the Pole.

A formidable appearing statement, signed by various members of his expedition, and copyrighted by the
clique of honor-blind boosters, was issued by Mr.
Peary. In this he gave statements of my two Eskimo
companions to the effect that I had not gotten out of
sight of land for more than one or two "sleeps" on my
trip. I knew that I had encouraged the delusion of my
Eskimos that the mirages and low-lying clouds which
appeared almost daily were signs of land. In their ignorance and their eagerness to be near land, they believed this, and by this innocent deception I prevented
the panic which seizes every Arctic savage when he finds
himself upon the circumpolar sea out of sight of land. I
have since learned that Mr. Peary's Eskimos became
panic-stricken near the Big Lead on his last journey
and that it was only by the life-threatening announce-

ment to them of his determination to leave them alone
on the ice (to get back to land as best they might or
starve to death) that he compelled them to accompany
him.

In any case, I did not consider as important any
testimony of the Eskimos which Mr. Peary might cite,
knowing as well as he did that one can get any sort of
desired reply from these natives by certain adroit questioning, and knowing also that the alleged route on his
map which he said they drew was valueless, inasmuch as
an Eskimo out of sight of land and in an unfamiliar
region has no sense of location. I felt the whole statement to be what it was, a trumped-up document in
which my helpers, perhaps unwittingly, had been
adroitly led to affirm what Mr. Peary by jesuitical and
equivocal questioning planned to have them say, and
that it was therefore unworthy of a reply.

I had left my instruments and part of the unreduced reckonings with Mr. Harry Whitney, a fact
which Mr. Whitney himself confirmed in published
press interviews when he first arrived—in the heat of the
controversy and after I left Copenhagen—in Sidney.
When interviews came from Mr. Peary insinuating
that I had left no instruments in the North, this
becoming a definite charge which was taken up
with great hue and cry, I bitterly felt this to be
a deliberate untruth on Mr. Peary's part. I have since
learned that one of Mr. Peary's officers cross-questioned
my Eskimos, and that by showing them Mr. Peary's
own instruments he discovered just what instruments I
had had with me on my trip, and that by describing the
method of using these instruments to E-tuk-i-shook and

RUDOLPH FRANCKE IN ARCTIC COSTUME

MIDNIGHT—"A PANORAMA OF BLACK LACQUER AND SILVER."

Ah-we-lah, Bartlett learned from them that I did take observations. This information he conveyed to Mr. Peary before his expedition left Etah for America, and this knowledge Mr. Peary and his party, deliberately and with malicious intent, concealed on their return. At the time I had no means of refuting this insinuation; it was simply my word or Mr. Peary's.

I had no extraordinary proofs to offer, but, such as they were, I now know, by comparison with the published reports of Mr. Peary himself, they were as good as any offered by anyone. I was perhaps unfortunate in not having, as Mr. Peary had, a confederate body of financially interested friends to back me up, as was the National Geographic Society.

Not satisfied with unjustly attacking my claim, Mr. Peary's associates proceeded to assail my past career, and I was next confronted by an affidavit made by my guide, Barrill, to the effect that I had not scaled Mt. McKinley, an affidavit which, as I later secured evidence, had been bought. A widely heralded "investigation" was announced by a body of "explorers" of which Peary was president. One of Colonel Mann's muck-rakers was secretary, while its moving spirit was Mr. Peary's press agent, Herbert L. Bridgman. In a desperate effort to help Peary, a cowardly side issue was forced through Professor Herschell Parker, who had been with me on the Mt. McKinley trip but who had turned back after becoming panic-stricken in the crossing of mountain torrents. Mr. Parker expressed doubt of my achievements because he differed with me as to the value of the particular instrument to ascertain altitude which I, with many other mountain climbers, used. I had offered all possible proofs as to having climbed the mountain, as full and adequate proofs as any mountaineer could, or ever has offered.

I resented the meddlesomeness of this pro-Peary group of kitchen explorers, not one of whom knew the first principles of mountaineering. From such an investigation, started to help Peary in his black-hand effort to force the dagger, with the money power easing men's conscience—as was evident at the time everywhere—no fair result could be expected. And as to the widely printed Barrill affidavit—this carried on its face the story of pro-Peary bribery and conspiracy. I have since learned that for it $1,500 and other considerations were paid. Here was a self-confessed liar. I did not think that a sane public therefore could take this underhanded pro-Peary charge as to the climb of Mt. McKinley seriously. Indeed, I paid little attention to it, but by using the cutting power of the press my enemies succeeded in inflicting a wound in my side.

I was thus plunged into the bewildering chaos which friends and enemies created, and swept for three months through a cyclone of events which I believe no human being could have stood. Before returning, I felt weakened mentally and physically by the rigors of the North, where for a year I barely withstood starvation. I was now whirled about the country, daily delivering lectures, greeting thousands of people, buffeted by mobs of well-meaning beings, and compelled to attend dinners and receptions numbering two hundred in sixty days. The air hissed about me with the odious charges which came from every direction. I was alone, helpless, without a single wise counsellor, under the charge of the enemies' press, mud-charged guns fired from every point of the compass. Unlimited funds were being consumed in the infamous mill of bribery.

I had not the money nor the nature to fight in this kind of battle—so I withdrew. At once, howls of execration gleefully rose from the ranks of my enemies; my departure was heralded gloriously as a confession of imposture. Advantage was taken of my absence and new, perjured, forged charges were made to blacken my name. Far from my home and unable to defend myself, Dunkle and Loose swore falsely to having manufactured figures and observations under my direction. When I learned of this, much as it hurt me, I knew that the report which I had sent to Copenhagen would, if it did anything, disprove by the very figures in it the malicious lying document published in the New York *Times*. This, combined with the verdict rendered by the University of Copenhagen—a neutral verdict which carried no implication of the non-attainment of the Pole, but which was interpreted as a rejection—helped to stamp me in the minds of many people as the most monumental impostor the world has ever seen.

I fully realized that under the circumstances the only verdict of an unprejudiced body on any such proofs to such a claim must be favorable or neutral. The members of the University of Copenhagen who examined my papers were neither personal friends nor members of a body financially interested in my quest. Their verdict was honest. Mr. Peary's Washington verdict was dishonest, for two members of the jury admitted a year later in Congress, under pressure, that in the Peary data there was no absolute proof.

By the time I determined to return to my native country and state my case, I had been placed, I am certain, in a position of undeserved discredit unparalleled in history. No epithet was too vile to couple with my name. I was declared a brazen cheat who had concocted the most colossal lie of ages whereby to hoax an entire world for gain. I was made the subject of cheap jokes. My name in antagonistic newspapers had become a synonym for cheap faking. I was compelled to see myself held up gleefully as an impostor, a liar, a fraud, an unscrupulous scoundrel, one who had tried to steal honors from another, and who, to escape exposure, had fled to obscurity.

All the scientific work which scientists themselves had accepted as valuable, all the necessary hardships and the inevitable agonies of my last Arctic journey were forgotten; I was coupled with the most notorious characters in history in a press which panders to the lowest of human emotions and delights in men's shame. When I realized how egregious, how frightful, how undeserved was all this, my soul writhed; when I saw clearly, with the perspective which only time can give, how I, stepping aside, in errors of confused judgment which were purely human, had seemingly contributed to my unhappy plight, I felt the sting of ignominy greater than that which has broken stronger men's hearts.

For the glory which the world gives to such an accomplishment as the discovery of the North Pole, I care very little, but when the very result of such a victory is used as a whip to inflict cuts that mark my future destiny, I have a right to call a halt. I have claimed no national honors, want no medals or money. My feet stepped over the Polar wastes with a will fired only by a personal ambition to succeed in a task where all the higher human powers were put to the test of fitness. That victory was honestly won. All that the achievement ever meant to me—the lure of it before I achieved it, the only satisfaction that remains since—is that it is a personal accomplishment of brain and muscle over hitherto unconquered forces, a thought in which I have pride. From the tremendous ovations that greeted me when I returned to civilization I got not a single thrill. I did thrill with the handclasp of confident, kindly people. I still thrill with the handclasp of my countrymen.

Insofar as the earthly glory and applause are concerned, I should be only too glad to share them, with all material accruements, to any honest, manly rivals—those of the past and those of the future. But against the unjust charges which have been made against me, against the aspersions on my personal integrity, against the ignominy with which my name has been besmirched, I will fight until the public gets a normal perspective.

I have never hoaxed a mythical achievement. Everything I have ever claimed was won by hard labor, by tremendous physical fortitude and endurance, and by such personal sacrifice as only I, and my immediate family, will ever know.

For this reason, I returned to my country in the latter part of 1910, as I always intended to do, after a year's rest. By this time I knew that my enemies would have said all that was possible about me; the excitement of the controversy would have quieted, and I should have the advantage of the last word.

In the heat of the controversy, only just re-

turned in a weakened condition from the North, and
mentally bewildered by the unexpected maelstrom of
events, I should not have been able, with justice to myself, to have met all the charges, criminal and silly,
which were made against me. Even what I did say
was misquoted and distorted by a sensational press
which found it profitable to add fuel to the controversy.
Sometimes I feel that no man ever born has been so
variedly, so persistently lied about, misrepresented,
made the butt of such countless untruths as myself.
When I consider the lies, great and small, which for
more than a year, throughout the entire world, have
been printed about me, I am filled almost with hopelessness. And sometimes, when I think how I have
been unjustly dubbed as the most colossal liar of history, I am filled with a sort of sardonic humor.

Returning to my country, determined to state my
case freely and frankly, and making the honest admission that any claim to the definite, actual attainment of
the North Pole—the mathematical pin-point on which
the earth spins—must rest upon assumptions, because
of the impossibility of accuracy in observations, I found
that this admission, which every explorer would have
to make, which Mr. Peary was unwillingly forced to
make at the Congressional investigation, was construed
throughout the country and widely heralded as a "confession," that garbled extracts were lifted from the
context of my magazine story and their meaning distorted. In hundreds of newspapers I was represented
as confessing to a fraudulent claim or as making a plea
of insanity. A full answer to the charges made against
me, necessary in order to justly cover my case, because

of the controversial nature of certain statements which involved Mr. Peary, was prohibited by the contract I found it necessary to sign in order to get any statement of a comparatively ungarbled sort before a public which had read Mr. Peary's own account of his journey.

I found the columns of the press of my country closed to the publication of statements which involved my enemies, because of the unfounded prejudice created against me during my absence and because of the power of Mr. Peary's friends. It is almost impossible in any condition for anyone to secure a refutation for an unfounded attack in the American papers. With the entire press of the country printing misstatements, I was almost helpless. The justice, kindliness and generous spirit of fair dealing of the American people, however, was extended to me—I found the American people glad—nay, eager—to listen.

It is this spirit which has encouraged me, after the shameful campaign of opprobrium which well-nigh broke my spirit, to tell the entire and unalterable truth about myself and an achievement in which I still believe—in fairness to myself, in order to clear myself, in order that the truth about the discovery of the North Pole may be known by my people and in order that history may record its verdict upon a full, free and frank exposition. I do not address myself to any clique of geographers or scientists, but to the great public of the world, and herein, for the first time, shall I give fully whatever proofs there may be of my conquest. Upon these records must conviction rest.

Did I actually reach the North Pole? When I returned to civilization and reported that the boreal center had been attained, I believed that I had reached the spot toward which valiant men had strained for more than three hundred years. I still believe that I reached the boreal center as far as it is possible for any human being to ascertain it. If I was mistaken in approximately placing my feet upon the pin-point about which this controversy has raged, I maintain that it is the inevitable mistake any man must make. To touch that spot would be an accident. That any other man has more accurately determined the Pole I do deny. That Mr. Peary reached the North Pole—or its environs—with as fair accuracy as was possible, I have never denied. That Mr. Peary was better fitted to reach the Pole, and better equipped to locate this mythical spot, I do not admit. In fact, I believe that, inasmuch as the purely scientific ascertainment is a comparatively simple matter, I stood a better chance of more scientifically and more accurately marking the actual spot than Mr. Peary. I reached my goal when the sun was twelve degrees above the horizon, and was therefore better able to mark a mathematical position than Mr. Peary could have with the sun at less than seven degrees. Mr. Peary's case rests upon three observations of sun altitude so low that, as proof of a position, they are worthless.

Besides taking observations, which, as I shall explain in due course in my narrative, cannot be adequate, I also ascertained what I believed to be my approximate position at the boreal center and en route by measuring the shadows each hour of the long day. Inasmuch as one's shadow decreases or increases in length as the sun rises toward the meridian or descends, at the boreal center, where the sun circles the entire horizon at practically the same height during the entire day, one's shadow in this region of mystery is of the same length. In this observation, which is so simple that a child may understand it, is a sure and certain means of approximately ascertaining the North Pole. I took advantage of this method, which does not seem to have occurred to any other Arctic traveler, and this helped to bring conviction.

I shall in this volume present with detail the story of my Arctic journey—I shall tell how it was possible for me to reach my goal, why I believe I attained that goal; and upon this record must the decision of my people rest. I shall herein tell the story of an unfair and unworthy plot to ruin the reputation of an innocent man because of an achievement the full and prior credit of which was desired by a brutally selfish, brutally unscrupulous rival. I shall tell of a tragedy compared with which the North Pole and any glory accruing to its discoverer pales into insignificance—the tragedy of a spirit that was almost broken, of a man whose honor and pride was cut with knives in unclean hands.

When you have read all this, then, and only then, in fairness to yourself and in fairness to me, do I ask you to form your opinion. Only by reading this can you learn the full truth about me, about my claim and about the plot to discredit me, of the charges made against me, and the reason for all of my own actions. So persistent, so world-wide has been the press campaign made by my enemies, and so egregious have the charges seemed against me, so multitudinous have the lies, fake stories, fake interviews, fake confessions been, so blatant have rung the hideous cries of liar, impostor, cheat and fraud, that the task to right myself, explain myself, and bring the truth into clean relief has seemed colossal.

To return to my country and face the people in view of all that was being said, with my enemies exultant, with antagonistic press men awaiting me as some beast to be devoured, required a determined gritting of the teeth and a reserve temperament to prevent an undignified battle.

For against such things nature dictates the tactics of the tiger. I faced my people, I found them fair and kindly. I accused my enemies of their lies, and they have remained silent. Titanic as is this effort of forcing fair play where biased abuse has reigned so long, I am confident of success. I am confident of the honesty and justice of my people; of their ability spiritually to sense, psychically to appreciate the earmarks of a clean, true effort—a worthy ambition and a real attainment.

INTO THE BOREAL WILDS

II

OVER THE ARCTIC CIRCLE

On July 3, 1907, between seven and eight o'clock in the evening, the yacht, which had been renamed the *John R. Bradley,* quietly withdrew from the pier at Gloucester, Massachusetts, and, turning her prow oceanward, slowly, quietly started on her historic journey to the Arctic seas.

In the tawny glow of sunset, which was fading in the western sky, she looked, with her new sails unfurled, her entire body newly painted a spotless white, like some huge silver bird alighting upon the sunshot waters of the bay. On board, all was quiet. I stood alone, gazing back upon the picturesque fishing village with a tender throb at my heart, for it was the last village of my country which I might see for years, or perhaps ever.

Along the water's edge straggled tiny ramshackle boat houses, dun-colored sheds where fish are dried, and the humble miniature homes of the fisherfolk, in the

windows of which lights soon after appeared. On the
bay about us, fishing boats were lazily bobbing up and
down; in some, old bearded fishermen with broad hats,
smoking clay and corncob pipes, were drying their
seines. Other boats went by, laden with wriggling,
silver-scaled fish; along the shore I could still see tons
of fish being unloaded from scores of boats. Through the
rosy twilight, voices came over the water, murmurous
sounds from the shore, cries from the sea mixed with
the quaint oaths of fisherfolk at work. Ashore, the boys
of the village were testing their firecrackers for the morrow; sputtering explosions cracked through the air.
Occasionally a faint fire rocket scaled the sky. But no
whistles tooted after our departure. No visiting crowds
of curiosity-seekers ashore were frenziedly waving us
good-bye.

An Arctic expedition had been born without the
usual clamor. Prepared in one month, and financed by
a sportsman whose only mission was to hunt game
animals in the North, no press campaign heralded our
project, no government aid had been asked, nor had
large contributions been sought from private individuals to purchase luxuries for a Pullman jaunt of a large
party Poleward. For, although I secretly cherished the
ambition, there was no definite plan to essay the North
Pole.

At the Holland House in New York, a compact
was made between John R. Bradley and myself to
launch an Arctic expedition. Because of my experience, Mr. Bradley delegated to me the outfitting of the
expedition, and had turned over to me money enough
to pay the costs of the hunting trip. A Gloucester

fishing schooner had been purchased by me and was refitted, covered and strengthened for ice navigation. To save fuel space and to gain the advantage of a steamer, I had a Lozier gasoline motor installed. There had been put on board everything of possible use and comfort in the boreal wild. As it is always possible that a summer cruising ship is likely to be lost or delayed a year, common prudence dictated a preparation for the worst emergencies.

So far as the needs of my own personal expedition were concerned, I had with me on the yacht plenty of hard hickory wood for the making of sledges, instruments, clothing and other apparatus gathered with much economy during my former years of exploration, and about one thousand pounds of pemmican. These supplies, necessary to offset the danger of shipwreck and detention by ice, were also all that would be required for a Polar trip. When, later, I finally decided on a Polar campaign, extra ship supplies, contributed from the boat, were stored at Annoatok. There, also, my supply of pemmican was amplified by the stores of walrus meat and fat prepared during the long winter by myself, Rudolph Francke and the Eskimos.

As the yacht slowly soared toward the ocean, and night descended over the fishing village with its home lights glimmering cheerfully as the stars one by one flecked the firmament with dots of fire, I felt that at last I had embarked upon my destiny. Whether I should be able to follow my heart's desire I did not know; I did not dare hazard a guess. But I was leaving my country, now on the eve of celebrating its freedom, behind me; I had elected to live in a world of ice

and cold, of hunger and death, which lay before me—
thousands of miles to the North.

Day by day passed monotonously; we only occasionally saw writhing curves of land to the west of us;
about us was the illimitable sea.   That I had started on
a journey which might result in my starting for the
Pole, that my final chance had come, vaguely thrilled
me.   Yet the full purport of my hope seemed beyond
me.   On the journey to Sydney my mind was full.   I
thought of the early days of my childhood, of the strange
ambition which grew upon me, of my struggles, and the
chance which favored me in the present expedition.

In the early days of my childhood, of which I now
had only indistinct glimmerings, I remembered a restless surge in my little bosom, a yearning for something
that was vague and undefined.   This was, I suppose,
that nebulous desire which sometimes manifests itself in
early youth and later is asserted in strivings toward
some splendid, sometimes spectacular aim.   My boyhood was not happy.   As a tiny child I was discon-
tented, and from the earliest days of consciousness I
felt the burden of two things which accompanied me
through later life—an innate and abnormal desire for
exploration, then the manifestation of my yearning, and
the constant struggle to make ends meet, that sting of
poverty, which, while it tantalizes one with its horrid
grind, sometimes drives men by reason of the strength
developed in overcoming its concomitant obstacles to
some extraordinary accomplishment.

As a very small boy, I remember being fascinated
by the lure of a forbidden swimming pool.   One day,
when but little over five, I, impelled to test the depth,

plunged to the center, where the water was above my head, and nearly lost my life. I shall never forget that struggle, and though I nearly gave out, in that short time I learned to swim. It seems to me now I have been swimming and struggling ever since.

Abject poverty and hard work marked my school days. When quite a boy, after the death of my father, I came to New York. I sold fruit at one of the markets. I saved my money. I enjoyed no luxuries. These days vividly occur in my mind. Later I engaged in a dairy business in Brooklyn, and on the meager profits undertook to study medicine.

At that time the ambition which beset me was undirected; it was only later that I found, almost by accident, what became its focusing point. I graduated from the University of New York in 1890. I felt (as what young man does not?) that I possessed unusual qualifications and exceptional ability. An office was fitted up, and my anxiety over the disappearing pennies was eased by the conviction that I had but to hang out my shingle and the place would be thronged with patients. Six months passed. There had been about three patients.

I recall sitting alone one gloomy winter day. Opening a paper, I read that Peary was preparing his 1891 expedition to the Arctic. I cannot explain my sensations. It was as if a door to a prison cell had opened. I felt the first indomitable, commanding call of the Northland. To invade the Unknown, to assail the fastness of the white, frozen North—all that was latent in me, the impetus of that ambition born in childhood, perhaps before birth, and which had been stifled and starved, surged up tumultuously within me.

I volunteered, and accompanied Peary, on this, the expedition of 1891-92, as surgeon. Whatever merit my work possessed has been cited by others.

Unless one has been in the Arctic, I suppose it is impossible to understand its fascination—a fascination which makes men risk their lives and endure inconceivable hardships for, as I view it now, no profitable personal purpose of any kind. The spell was upon me then. It was upon me as I recalled those early days on the *Bradley* going Northward. With a feeling of sadness I realize that the glamor is all gone now.

On the Peary and all my subsequent expeditions I served without pay.

On my return from that trip I managed to make ends meet by meager earnings from medicine. I was nearly always desperately hard pressed for money. I tried to organize several coöperative expeditions to the Arctic. These failed. I then tried to arouse interest in Antarctic exploration, but without success. Then came the opportunity to join the Belgian Antarctic Expedition, again without pay.

On my return I dreamed of a plan to attain the South Pole, and for a long time worked on a contrivance for that end—an automobile arranged to travel over ice. Financial failure again confronted me. Disappointment only added to my ambition; it scourged me to a determination, a conviction that—I want you to remember this, to bear in mind the mental conviction which buoyed me—I must and should succeed. It is always this innate conviction which encourages men to exceptional feats, to tremendous failures or splendid, single-handed success.

A summer in the Arctic followed my Antarctic trip, and I returned to invade the Alaskan wilds. I succeeded in scaling Mt. McKinley. After my Alaskan expeditions, the routine of my Brooklyn office work seemed like the confinement of prison. I fretted and chafed at the thought. Let me have a chance, and I would succeed. This thought always filled my mind. I convinced myself that in some way the attainment of one of the Poles—the effort on which I had spent sixteen years—would become possible.

I had no money. My work in exploration had netted me nothing, and all my professional income was soon spent. Unless you have felt the goading, devilish grind of poverty hindering you, dogging you, you cannot know the mental fury into which I was lashed.

I waited, and fortune favored me in that I met Mr. John R. Bradley. We planned the Arctic expedition on which I was now embarked. Mr. Bradley's interest in the trip was that of a great sportsman, eager to seek big game in the Arctic. My immediate purpose was to return again to the frozen North. The least the journey would give me was an opportunity to complete the study of the Eskimos which I had started in 1891.

Mr. Bradley and I had talked, of course, of the Pole; but it was not an important incentive to the journey. Back in my brain, barely above the subconscious realm, was the feeling that this, however, might offer opportunity in the preparation for a final future determination. I, therefore, without any conscious purpose, and with my last penny, paid out of my purse for extra supplies for a personal expedition should I leave the ship.*

Aboard the *Bradley,* going northward, my plans were not at all definite. Even had I known before leaving New York that I should try for the Pole, I should not have sought any geographical license from some vague and unknown authority. Though much has since been made by critics of our quiet departure, I always felt the quest of the Pole a personal ambition[†], a crazy hunger I had to satisfy.

Fair weather followed us to Sydney, Cape Breton.

----

* Accused of being the most colossal liar of history, I sometimes feel that more lies have been told about me than about anyone ever born. I have been guilty of many mistakes. Most men really true to themselves admit that. My claim to the North Pole may always be questioned. Yet, when I regard the lies great and small attached to me, I am filled almost with indifference.

As a popular illustration of the sort of yarns that were told, let me refer to the foolish fake of the gum drops. Someone started the story that I expected to reach the Pole by bribing the Eskimos with gum drops—perhaps the idea was that I was to lure them on from point to point with regularly issued rations of these confections.

Wherever I went on my lecture tour after my return to the United States, much to my irritation I saw "Cook" gum drops conspicuously displayed in confectionery store windows. Hundreds of pounds of gum drops were sent to my hotel with the compliments of the manufacturers. On all sides I heard the gum-drop story, and in almost every paper read the reiterated tale of leading the Eskimos to the Pole by dangling a gum drop on a string before them. I never denied this, as I never denied any of the fakes printed about me. The fact is, that I never heard the gum-drop yarn until I came to New York. We took no gum drops with us on our Polar trip, and, to my knowledge, no Eskimo ate a gum drop while with me.

----

†Among the many things which the public has been misled into believing is that Mr. Bradley and I together connived the trip for the purpose of essaying this quest of the Pole. The fact is, not until I reached Annoatok, and saw that conditions were favorable for a long sledge journey, did I finally determine to make a Poleward trip; not until then did I tell my decision definitely to Mr. Bradley.

One of the big mistakes which has been pounded into the public mind is that the proposed Polar exploit was expensively financed. It did cost a great deal to finance the planned hunting trip. Mr. Bradley's expenses aggregated, perhaps, $50,000, but my journey Northward, which was but an extension of this yachting cruise, cost comparatively little.

From this point we sailed over the Gulf of St. Lawrence, then entered the Straits of Belle Isle at a lively speed. On a cold, cheerless day in the middle of July we arrived at Battle Harbor, a little town at the southeastern point of Labrador, where Mr. Bradley joined us. He had preceded us north, by rail and coasting vessels, after watching a part of the work of outfitting the schooner.

On the morning of July 16 we left the rockbound coast of North America and steered straight for Greenland. In this region a dense and heavy fog almost always lies upon the sea. Then nothing is visible but slow-swaying gray masses, which veil all objects in a shroud of ghostly dreariness. Through the fog can be heard the sound of fisher-boat horns, often the very voices of the fishermen themselves, while their crafts are absolutely hidden from view. On this trip, however, from time to time, great fragments of fog slowly lifted, and we saw, emerging out of the gray mistiness, islands, bleak and black and weathertorn, and patches of ocean dotted with scores of Newfoundland boats, which invade this region to fish for cod. We entered the Arctic current, and breasting its stream, a fancy came that perhaps this current, flowing down from out of the mysterious unknown, came from the very Pole itself.

Continuing, we entered Davis Straits, where we encountered headwinds that piled up the water in great waves. It was a good test of the sailing qualities of the *Bradley,* and well did the small craft respond.

Long before the actual coast line of Greenland could be seen we had a first glimpse of the beauties that these northern regions can show. Like great sapphires, blue ice floated in a golden sea; towering masses of crystal rose gloriously, dazzling the eye and gladdening the heart with their superb beauty. The schooner sailed into this wonderful yellow sea, which soon became a broad and gleaming surface of molten silver. Although this striking beauty of the North, which it often is so chary of displaying, possesses a splendor of color equal to the gloriousness of tropical seas, it always impresses one with a steely hardness of quality suggestive of the steely hardness of the heart of the North. And it somehow seemed, curiously enough, as if all this wonderful glitter was a shimmering reflection from the ice-covered mountains of the Greenland interior, although the mountains themselves were still invisible.

We swung from side to side, dodging icebergs. We steered cautiously around low-floating masses, watching to see that the keel was not caught by some treacherous jutting spur just beneath the water-line. Through this fairyland of light and color we sailed slowly into a region rich in animal life, a curious and striking sight. Seals floundered in the sunbeams or slumbered on masses of ice, for even in this Northland there is a strange commingling and contrast of heat and cold. Gulls and petrels darted and fluttered about us in every direction, porpoises were making swift and curving leaps, even a few whales added to the magic and apparent unreality of it all.

At length the coast showed dimly upon the horizon, veiled in a glow of purple and gold. The wind freshened, the sails filled, and the speed of the schooner increased. We were gradually nearing Holsteinborg, and the course was set a point more in towards shore. The land was thrown into bold relief by the brilliancy of lights and shadows, and in the remarkably clear air it seemed as if it could be reached in an hour. But this was an atmospheric deception, of the kind familiar to those who know the pure air of the Rocky Mountains, for, although the land seemed near, it was at least forty miles away. The general color of the land was a frosty blue, and there were deep valleys to be seen, gashes cut by the slow movement of centuries of glaciers, with rocky headlands leaping forward, bleak and cold. It appeared to be a land of sublime desolation.

The course was set still another point nearer the coast; the wind continued fair and strong; and, with every possible stitch of canvas spread, the schooner went rapidly onward.

We saw rocky islands, drenched by clouds of spray and battered by drifting masses of ice. There the eider duck builds its nest and spends the brief summer of the Arctic. We saw dismal cliffs, terra cotta and buff in color, in the crevasses of which millions of birds made their homes, and from which they rose, frightened, in dense clouds, giving vent to a great volume of clamorous hoarseness.

Through our glasses we could see a surprising sight in such a land—little patches of vegetation, seal brown or even emerald green. Yet, so slight were these patches of green that one could not but wonder what freak of imagination led the piratical Eric the Red, one thousand years ago, to give to this coast a name so suggestive of luxuriant forests and shrubs and general lushness of growth as "Greenland." Never, surely, was there a greater misnomer, unless one chooses to regard the old-time Eric as a practical joker.

Between the tall headlands there were fiords cutting far into the interior; arms of the sea, these, winding and twisting back for miles. Along these quiet landlocked waters the Eskimos love to hunt and fish, just as their forefathers have done for centuries. Shaggy looking fellows are these Eskimos, clothed in the skins of animals, relieved by dashes of color of Danish fabric, most of them still using spears, and thus, to outward appearance, in the arts of life almost like those that Eric saw.

Although this rugged coast, with its low-lying islands, its icebergs and floating icefields, its bleak headlands, its picturesque scenes of animal life, is a continuous delight, it presents the worst possible dangers to navigation, not only from reefs and under-water ice, but because there are no lighthouses to mark permanent danger spots and because signs of impending storm are ever on the horizon. While navigating the coast, our officers spent sleepless nights of anxiety; but the shortening of the nights and lengthening of the days, the daily night brightening resulting from the northerly movement, combined with an occasional flash of the aurora, gradually relieved the tension of the situation.

By the time the island of Disco rose splendidly out of the northern blue, the Arctic Circle had been crossed, and a sort of celestial light-house brightened the path of the schooner. Remaining on deck until after midnight, we were rewarded by a sight of the sun magnified to many times its normal size, glowing above the rim of the frosty sea. A light wind blew

gently from the coast, the sea ran in swells of gold, and
the sky was streaked with topaz and crimson.

Bathed in an indescribable glow, the towering
sides of the greatest icebergs showed a medley of ever-
changing, iridescent colors. The jutting pinnacles of
others seemed like oriental minarets of alabaster fretted
with old gold. Here and there, as though flung by an
invisible hand from the zenith, straggled long cloud rib-
bons of flossy crimson and silver. Gradually, im-
perially, the sun rose higher and flushed sky and sea
with deeper orange, more burning crimson, and the
bergs into vivid ruby, chalcedony and chrysophase
walls. This suddenly-changing, kaleidoscopic whirl of
color was rendered more effective because, in its midst,
the cliffs of Disco rose frowningly, a great patch of
blackness in artistic contrast. A pearly vapor now
began to creep over the horizon, and gradually spread
over the waters, imparting a gentle and restful tone of
blue. This gradually darkened into irregular shadows;
the brilliant color glories faded away. Finally we retired to sleep with a feeling that sailing Poleward was
merely a joyous pleasure journey over wonderful
and magic waters. This, the first glorious vision of
the midnight sun, glowed in my dreams—the augury of
success in that for which my heart yearned. The glow
never faded, and the weird lure unconsciously began to
weave its spell.

Next morning, when we went on deck, the schooner
was racing eastward through heavy seas. The terraced
cliffs of Disco, relieved by freshly fallen snow, were but
a few miles off. The cry of gulls and guillemots
echoed from rock to rock. Everything was divested of

the glory of the day before. The sun was slowly rising among mouse-colored clouds. The bergs were of an ugly blue, and the sea ran in gloomy lines of ebony. Although the sea was high, there was little wind, but we felt that a storm was gathering and sought to hasten to shelter in Godhaven—a name which speaks eloquently of the dangers of this coast and the precious value of such a harbor.

As we entered the narrow channel, which turns among low, polished rocks and opens into the harbor, two Eskimos in kayaks came out to act as pilots. Taking them aboard, we soon found a snug anchorage, secure from wind and sea. The launch was lowered, and in it we left the schooner for a visit to the Governor.

Coming up to a little pier, we were cordially greeted by Governor Fenker, who escorted us to his home, where his wife, a cultivated young Danish woman, offered us sincere hospitality.

The little town itself was keenly alive. All the inhabitants, and all the dogs as well, were jumping about on the rocks, eagerly gazing at our schooner. The houses of the Governor and the Inspector were the most important of the town. They were built of wood imported from Denmark, and were covered with tarred paper. Though quite moderate in size, the houses seemed too large and out of place in their setting of ice-polished rocks. Beyond them were twenty Eskimo huts, nearly square in shape, constructed of wood and stone, the cracks of which were filled tightly with moss.

We deferred our visit to the native huts, and invited Governor Fenker and his wife to dine aboard the schooner. The surprise of the evening for these two guests was the playing of our phonograph, the tunes of which brought tears of homesickness to the eyes of the Governor's gentle wife.

Anywhere on the coast of Greenland, the coming of a ship is always one of the prime events of the season. So uneventful is life in these out-of-the-way places that such an arrival is the greatest possible social enlivener. The instant that the approach of our schooner had been noted, the Eskimo girls—queer little maids in queer little trousers—decided upon having a dance, and word was brought us that everyone was invited to take part. The sailors eagerly responded, and tumbled ashore as soon as they were permitted, leaving merely enough for a watch on board ship. Then, to the sound of savage music, the dance was continued until long after midnight. A curious kind of midnight dance it was, with the sun brightly shining in a night unveiled of glitter and color glory. The sailors certainly found pleasure in whirling about, their arms encircling fat and clumsy waists. They did admit, however, when back on board the schooner, that the smell of the furs within which the maidens had spent the past winter was less agreeable than the savor of fish. The name of this scattered settlement of huts, Godhaven, comes, clearly enough, from its offering fortunate refuge from storms; that the place is also known as Lively is not in the least to be wondered at, if one has watched a midnight dance of the little population and their visitors.

Before hauling in anchor in the harbor of Godhaven, we made some necessary repairs to the yacht and filled our tanks with water. With a free wind speeding onward to the west of Disco, we passed the narrow strait known as the Vaigat early the following morning. As I stood on deck and viewed the passing of icebergs, glittering in the limpid, silvery light of morning like monstrous diamonds, there began to grow within me a feeling—that throbbed in pulsation with the onward movement of the boat—that every minute, every mile, meant a nearing to that mysterious center, on the attaining of which I had set my heart, and which, even now, seemed unlikely, improbable.   Yet the thought gave me a thrill.

Before noon we reached the mouth of Umanak Fiord, into the delightful waters of which we were tempted to enter.   The lure of the farther North decided us against this, and soon the striking Svarten Huk (Black Hook), a great rock cliff, loomed upon the horizon. Beyond it, gradually appeared a long chain of those islands among which lies Upernavik, where the last traces of civilized or semi-civilized life are found. The wind increased in force but the horizon remained remarkably clear. Over a bounding sea we sped rapidly along to the west, into the labyrinth of islands that are sprinkled along the southern shore of Melville Bay.* Beyond, we were to come into the true boreal wilder-

---

* The killing of Astrup.—The head of Melville Bay was explored by Eivind Astrup while a member of the Peary expedition of 1894-1895. Astrup had been a member of the first expedition, serving without pay, during 1891 and 1892 and proving himself a loyal supporter and helper of Mr. Peary, when he crossed the inland ice in 1892. As a result of eating pemmican twenty years old, in 1895, Astrup was disabled by poisoning, due to Peary's carelessness in furnishing poisoned food. Recovering from this illness, he selected a trustworthy Eskimo companion, went south, and under almost inconceivable difficulties, explored and mapped the ice walls, with their glaciers and mountains, and the off-lying islands of Melville Bay. This proved a creditable piece of work of genuine discovery. Returning, he prepared his data and published it, thus bringing credit and honor on an expedition which was in other respects a failure.

Astrup's publication of this work aroused Peary's envy. Publicly,

ness of ice, where there were only a few savage aborigines, its sole inhabitants.

On the following day, with reduced sail and the help of the auxiliary engine, we pushed far up into Melville Bay, where we ran into fields of pack-ice. Here we decided to hunt for game. With this purpose it was necessary to keep close to land. Here also came our first realistic experience with the great forces of the North. The pack-ice floated close around us, young ice cemented the broken masses together, and for several days we were thus closely imprisoned in frozen seas.

These days of enforced delay were days of great pleasure, for the bears and seals on the ice afforded considerable sport. The constant danger of our position, however, required a close watch for the safety of the schooner. The Devil's Thumb, a high rock shaped like a dark thumb pointing at the sky, loomed darkly and beckoningly before us. A biting wind descended from the interior.

The ice groaned; the eiderducks, guillemots and gulls uttered shrill and disturbing cries, seemingly sensing the coming of a storm.

For three days we were held in the grip of the relentless pack; then the glimmer of the land ice changed

---

Peary denounced Astrup. Astrup, being young and sensitive, brooded over this injustice and ingratitude until he had almost lost his reason. The abuse was of the same nature as that heaped on others, the same as that finally hurled at me in the wireless "Gold Brick" slurs. For days and weeks, Astrup talked of nothing but the infamy of Peary's attack on himself and the contemptible charge of desertion which Peary made against Astrup's companions. Then he suddenly left my home, returned to Norway, and we next heard of his suicide. Here is one life directly chargeable to Peary's narrow and intolerant brutality. Directly this was not murder with a knife—but it was as heinous—for a young and noble life was cut short by the cowardly dictates of jealous egotism.

to an ugly gray, the pack around us began to crack threateningly, and the sky darkened to the southward.

The wind ominously died away. The air thickened rapidly. A general feeling of anxiety came over us, although my familiarity with storms in the North made it possible for me to explain that heavy seas are seldom felt within the zone of a large ice-pack, for the reason that the icebergs, the flat ice masses, and even the small floating fragments, ordinarily hold down the swells. Even when the pack begins to break, the lanes of water between the fragments thicken under the lower temperature like an oiled surface, and offer an easy sea. Furthermore, a really severe wind would be sure to release the schooner, and it would then be possible to trust it to its staunch qualities in free water.

Hardly had we finished dinner when we heard the sound of a brisk wind rushing through the rigging. Hurrying to the deck, we saw coils of what looked like smoky vapor rising in the south as if belched from some great volcano. The gloom on the horizon was rapidly growing deeper. The sound of the wind changed to a threatening, sinister hiss. In the piercing steel-gray light we saw the ice heave awesomely, like moving hills, above the blackening water. The bergs swayed and rocked, and the massed ice gave forth strange, troublous sounds.

Suddenly a channel began to open through the ice in front of us. The trisail was quickly set, the other sails being left tightly furled, and with the engine helping to push us in the desired direction, we drew deep breaths of relief as we moved out into the free water to the westward.

We felt a sense of safety now, although, clear of the ice, the sea rose about us with a sickening suddenness. Black as night, the water seemed far more dangerous because the waves were everywhere dashing angrily against walls of ice. Already strong, the wind veered slightly and increased to a fierce, persistent gale. Like rubber balls, the bergs bounded and rolled in the sea. The sound of the storm was now a thunder suggestive of constantly exploding cannons. But, fortunately, we were snug aboard, and, keeping the westerly course, soon escaped the dangers of ensnaring ice.

We were still in a heavy storm, and had we not had full confidence in the ship, built as she was to withstand the storms of the Grand Banks, we should still have felt anxiety, for the schooner rolled and pitched and the masts dipped from side to side until they almost touched the water.

Icy water swept the deck. A rain began to fall, and quickly sheathed the masts and ropes in ice. Snow followed, giving a surface as of sandpaper to the slippery, icy decks. The temperature was not low, but the cutting wind pierced one to the very marrow. Our men were drenched with spray and heavily coated with ice. Although suffering severely, the sailors maintained their courage and appeared even abnormally happy. Gradually we progressed into the open sea. In the course of four hours the storm began to abate, and, under a double-reefed foresail, at last we gleefully rode out the finish of the storm in safety.

THE DRIVING SPUR OF THE POLAR QUEST

ON THE FRIGID PATHWAY OF THREE CENTURIES OF
HEROIC MARTYRS—MEETING THE STRANGE PEOPLE
OF THE FARTHEST NORTH—THE LIFE OF THE STONE
AGE—ON THE CHASE WITH THE ESKIMOS—MANEE
AND SPARTAN ESKIMO COURAGE

III

STRANGE TRAITS OF NORTHERNMOST MAN

I have often wondered of late about the dazzling white, eerie glamor with which the Northland weaves its spell about the heart of a man. I know of nothing on earth so strange, so wonderful, withal so sad. Pursuing our course through Melville Bay, I felt the fatal magic of it enthralling my very soul. For hours I stood on deck alone, the midnight sun, like some monstrous perpetual light to some implacable frozen-hearted deity, burning blindingly upon the horizon and setting the sea aflame. The golden colors suffused my mind, and I swam in a sea of molten glitter.

I was consumed for hours by but one yearning—a yearning that filled and intoxicated me—to go on, and on, and ever onward, where no man had ever been. Perhaps it is the human desire to excel others, to prove, because of the innate egotism of the human unit, that one possesses qualities of brain and muscle which no other possesses, that has crazed men to perform this, the most difficult physical test in the world. The lure of the thing is unexplainable.

During those dizzy hours on deck I thought of those who had preceded me; of heroic men who for three centuries had braved suffering, cold and famine, who had sacrificed the comforts of civilization, their families and friends, who had given their own lives in the pursuit of this mysterious, yea, fruitless quest. I remembered reading the thrilling tales of those who returned—tales which had flushed me with excitement and inspired me with the same mad ambition. I thought of the noble, indefatigable efforts of these men, of the heart-sickening failures, in which I too had shared. And I felt the indomitable, swift surge of their awful, goading determination within me—to subdue the forces of nature, to cover as Icarus did the air those icy spaces, to reach the silver-shining vacantness which men called the North Pole.

As we cut the shimmering waters, I felt, as it were, the wierd, unseen presence of those who had died there —died horribly—men whose bodies had withered, with slow suffering, in frigid blasts and famine, who possibly had prolonged their suffering by feeding upon their own doomed companions—and of others who had perished swiftly in the sudden yawning of the leprous white mouth of the hungry frozen sea. It is said by some that souls live only after death by the energy of great emotions, great loves, or great ambitions generated throughout life. It seemed to me, in those hours of intoxication, that I could feel the implacable, unsatisfied desire of these disembodied things, who had vibrated with one aim and still yearned in the spirit for what now they were physically unable to attain. It seemed that my brain was fired with the intensity of all these dead men's ambition, that my heart in sympathy beat more turbulently with the throb of their dead hearts; I felt growing within me, irresistibly, what I did not dare, for fear it might not be possible, to confide to Bradley—a determination, even in the face of peril, to essay the Pole!

From this time onward, and until I turned my back upon the fruitless silver-shining place of desolation at the apex of the world, I felt the intoxication, the intangible lure of the thing exhilarating, buoying me gladsomely, beating in my heart with a singing rhythm. I recall it now with marveling, and am filled with the pathos of it. Yet, despite all that I have suffered since because of it, I regret not those enraptured hours of perpetual glitter of midnight suns.

One morning we reached the northern shore of Melville Bay, and the bold cliffs of Cape York were dimly outlined through a gray mist. Strong southern winds had carried such great masses of ice against the coast that it was impossible to make a near approach, and as a strong wind continued, there was such a heavy sea along the bobbing line of outer ice as to make it quite impossible to land and thence proceed toward the shore.

We were desirous of meeting the natives of Cape York, but these ice conditions forced us to proceed without touching here, and so we set our course for the next of the northernmost villages, at North Star Bay.

By noon the mist had vanished, and we saw clearly the steep slopes and warm color of crimson cliffs rising precipitously out of the water. The coast line is about two thousand feet high, evidently the remains of an old tableland which extends a considerable distance northward. Here and there were short glaciers which had worn the cliffs away in their ceaseless effort to reach the sea. The air was full of countless gulls, guillemots, little auks and eider-ducks.

As the eye followed the long and lofty line of crimson cliffs, there came into sight a towering, conical rock, a well-known guidepost for the navigator. Continuing, we caught sight of the long ice wall of Petowik Glacier, and behind this, extending far to the eastward, the scintillating, white expanse of the overland-ice which blankets the interior of all Greenland.

The small and widely scattered villages of the Eskimos of this region are hemmed in by the ice walls of Melville Bay on the southward, the stupendous cliffs of Humboldt Glacier on the north, an arm of the sea to the westward, and the hopelessly desolate Greenland interior toward the east.

There is really no reason why many Eskimos should not live here, for there is abundant food in both sea and air, and even considerable game on land. Blue and white foxes are everywhere to be seen. There is the seal, the walrus, the narwhal, and the white whale. There is the white bear, monarch of the Polar wilds, who roams in every direction over his kingdom. The principal reason why the population remains so small lies in the hazardous conditions of life. Children are highly prized, and a marriageable woman or girl who has one or more of them is much more valuable as a match than one who is childless.

The coast line here is paradoxically curious, for although the coast exceeds but barely more than two hundred miles of latitude it presents in reality a sea line of about four thousand miles when the great indentations of Wolstenholm Sound, Inglefield Gulf, and other bays, sounds and fiords are measured.

We sailed cautiously now about Cape Atholl, which we were to circle; a fog lay upon the waters, almost entirely hiding the innumerable icebergs, and making it difficult to pick our course among the dangerous rocks in this vicinity.

Rounding Cape Atholl, we sailed into Wolstenholm Sound and turned our prow toward the Eskimo village on North Star Bay.

North Star Bay is guarded by a promontory expressively named Table Mountain, "Oomanaq." As we neared this headland, many natives came out in kayaks to meet us. Inasmuch as I knew most of them personally, I felt a singular thrill of pleasure in seeing them. Years before, I learned their simple-hearted faithfulness. Knud Rasmussen, a Danish writer, living as a native among the Eskimos, apparently for the sake of getting local color, was in one of the canoes and came aboard the ship.

As it was necessary to make slight repairs to the schooner, we here had to follow the primitive method of docking by preliminary beaching her. This was done at high tide when the propeller, which had been bent—the principal damage to the ship—was straightened. At the same time we gave the yacht a general looking-over, and righted a universal joint whose loosening had disabled the engine.

Meanwhile the launch kept busy scurrying to and fro, our quest being occasionally rewarded with eiderducks or other game. Late at night, a visit was made to the village of Oomanooi. It could hardly be called a village, for it consisted merely of seven triangular sealskin tents, conveniently placed on picturesque rocks. Gathered about these in large numbers, were men, women and children, shivering in the midnight chill.

These were odd-looking specimens of humanity. In height, the men averaged but five feet, two inches, and the women four feet, ten. All had broad, fat faces, heavy bodies and well-rounded limbs. Their skin was slightly bronzed; both men and women had coal-black hair and brown eyes. Their noses were short, and their hands and feet short, but thick.

A genial woman was found at every tent opening, ready to receive visitors in due form. We entered and had a short chat with each family. Subjects of conversation were necessarily limited, but after all, they were about the same as they would have been in a civilized region. We conversed as to whether or not all of us had been well, of deaths, marriages and births. Then we talked of the luck of the chase, which meant prosperity or need of food. Even had it been a civilized community, there would have been little questioning regarding national or international affairs, because, in such case, everyone reads the papers. Here there was no comment on such subjects simply because nobody cares anything about them or has any papers to read.

That a prominent Eskimo named My-ah had disposed of a few surplus wives to gain the means whereby to acquire a few more dogs, was probably the most important single item of information conveyed. I was also informed that at the present time there happened to be only one other man with two wives.

Marriage, among these folk, is a rather free and easy institution. It is, indeed, not much more than a temporary tie of possession. Men exchange partners with each other much in the manner that men in other countries swap horses. And yet, the position of women is not so humble as this custom might seem to indicate, for they themselves are permitted, not infrequently, to choose new partners. These exceedingly primitive ideas work out surprisingly well in practice in these isolated regions, for such exchanges, when made, are seemingly to the advantage and satisfaction of all parties; no regrets are expressed, and the feuds of divorce courts, of alimony proceedings, of damages for alienation of affection, which prevail in so-called civilization, are unknown.

It is certainly a curious thing that these simple but intelligent people are able to control their own destinies with a comfortable degree of success, although they are without laws or literature and without any fixed custom to regulate the matrimonial bond.

It would seem as if there ought to be a large population, for there is an average of about three fat, clever children for each family, the youngest as a rule picturesquely resting in a pocket on the mother's back. But the hardships of life in this region are such that accidents and deaths keep down the population.

Each tent has a raised platform, upon which all sleep. The edge of this makes a seat, and on each side are placed stone lamps in which blubber is burned, with moss as a wick. Over this is a drying rack, also a few sticks, but there is no other furniture. Their dress of furs gives the Eskimos a look of savage fierceness which their kindly faces and easy temperament do not warrant.

On board the yacht were busy days of barter. Furs and ivory were gathered in heaps in exchange for guns, knives and needles. Every seaman, from cabin boy to captain, suddenly got rich in the gamble of trade for prized blue-fox skins and narwhal tusks.

The Eskimos were equally elated with their part of the bargain. For a beautiful fox skin, of less use to a native than a dog pelt, he could secure a pocket knife that would serve him half a lifetime!

A woman exchanged her fur pants, worth a hundred dollars, for a red pocket handkerchief with which she would decorate her head or her igloo for years to come.

Another gave her bearskin mits for a few needles, and she conveyed the idea that she had the long end of the trade! A fat youth with a fatuous smile displayed with glee two bright tin cups, one for himself and one for his prospective bride. He was positively happy in having obtained nine cents' worth of tin for only an ivory tusk worth ninety dollars!

With the coming of the midnight tide we lifted the schooner to an even keel from the makeshift drydock on the beach. She was then towed out into the bay by the launch and two dories, and anchored.

Our first walrus adventures began in Wolstenholm Sound during the beautiful nightless days of mid-August. The local environment was fascinating. The schooner was anchored in North Star Bay, a lake of glitter in which wild men in skin canoes darted after seals and eider-ducks. On grassy shores were sealskin tents, about which fur-clad women and children vied with wolf-dogs for favorite positions to see the queer doings of white men. A remarkable landmark made the place conspicuous. A great table-topped rock rose suddenly out of a low foreland to an altitude of about six hundred feet. About this giant cliff, gulls, guillemots and ravens talked and winged uproariously. The rock bore the native name of Oomanaq. With the unique Eskimo manner of name-coining, the village was called Oomanooi.

Wolstenholm Sound is a large land-locked body of water, with arms reaching to the narrow gorges of the overland sea of ice, from which icebergs tumble ceaselessly. The sparkling water reflected the surroundings in many shades of blue and brown, relieved by strong contrasts of white and black. On the western sky line were the chiseled walls of Acponie and other islands, and beyond a steel-gray mist in which was wrapped the frozen sea of the Polar gateway. Fleets of icebergs moved to and fro, dragging tails of drift bejeweled with blue crystal.

Far out—ten miles from our outlook—there was a meeting of the currents. Here, small pieces of sea-ice slowly circled in an eddy, and upon them were herds of walruses. We did not see them, but their shrill voices rang through the icy air like a wireless message. This was a call to action which Mr. Bradley could not resist, and preparations were begun for the combat.

The motor boat—the most important factor in the chase—had been especially built for just such an encounter. Covered with a folding whale-back top entirely painted white to resemble ice, we had hoped to hunt walrus under suitable Arctic cover.

Taking a white dory in tow, two Eskimo harpooners were invited to follow. The natives in kayaks soon discovered to their surprise that their best speed was not equal to ours—for the first time they were beaten in their own element. For ages the Eskimos had rested secure in the belief that the kayak was the fastest thing afloat. They had been beaten by big ships, of course, but these had spiritual wings and did not count in the race of man's craft. This little launch, however, with its rapid-fire gas explosions, made their eyes bulge to a wondering, wide-open, seal-like curiosity. They begged to be taken aboard to watch the loading of the engines; they thought we fed it with cartridges.

After a delightful run of an hour, a pan of ice was sighted with black hummocks on it. *"Ahwek! Ahwek!"* the Eskimos shouted. A similar sound floated over the oily waters from many walrus throats. The walruses were about three miles to the southwest. At a slower speed we advanced two miles more. In the meantime Mr. Bradley cleared the deck for action. The direction of the hunting tactics was now turned over to My-ah. The mate was at the wheel. I pushed the levers of the gasoline kicker. Our line of attack was ordered at right angles to the wind. As we neared the game, the engines were stopped.

Looking through glasses, the sight of the gregarious herd made our hearts quicken. They were all males of tremendous size, with glistening tusks with which they horned one another in efforts for favorable positions. Some were asleep, others basked in the sun with heads turning lazily from side to side. Now and then, they uttered sleepy, low grunts. They were quivering in a gluttonous slumber, while the organs piled up their bank account of fat to pay the costs of the gamble of the coming winter night.

With muffled paddles the launch was now silently propelled forward, while the kayaks stealthily advanced to deliver the harpoons. The Eskimo reason for this mode of procedure is based on a careful study of the walrus' habits. Its nose in sleep is always pointed windwards. Its ears are at all times sensitive to noises from every direction, while the eyes during wakeful moments sweep the horizon. But its horizon is very narrow. Only the nose and the ear sense the distant alarm. We advanced very slowly and cautiously, and that only when all heads were down. Our boat slowly got within three hundred yards of the herd. Preparing their implements to strike, the Eskimos had advanced to within fifty feet. The moment was tense. Of a sudden, a tumultuous floundering sound smote the air. The sleeping creatures awoke, and with a start leaped into the sea. Turning their kayaks, the Eskimos paddled a wild retreat and sought the security of the launch. The sport of that herd was lost to us. Although they darted about under water in a threatening manner, they only rose to the surface at a safe distance.

Scanning the surroundings with our glasses, about

two miles to the south another group was sighted. This time Bradley, as the chief nimrod, assumed direction. The kayaks and the Eskimos were placed in the dory. Tactics were reversed. Instead of creeping up slowly, a sudden rush was planned. No heed was taken of noise or wind. The carburetor was opened, the spark lever of the magneto was advanced to its limit, and we shot through the waters like a torpedo boat. As we neared the herd, the dory, with its Eskimos, was freed from the launch. The Eskimos were given no instructions, and they wisely chose to keep out of the battle.

As we got to within two hundred yards, the canvas top of the launch fell and a heavy gun bombardment began. The walruses had not had time to wake; the suddenness of the onslaught completely dazed them. One after another dropped his ponderous head with a sudden jerk as a prize to the marksmen, while the launch, at reduced speed, encircled the walrus-encumbered pan. Few escaped. There were heads and meat and skins enough to satisfy all wants for a long time to follow. But the game was too easy—the advantage of an up-to-date sportsman had been carried to its highest degree of perfection. It was otherwise, however, in the walrus battles that followed later—battles on the success of which depended the possibility of my being able to assail the northern ice desert, in an effort to reach the Polar goal.

Oomanooi was but one of six villages among which the tribe had divided its two hundred and fifty people for the current season. To study these interesting folk, to continue the traffic and barter, and to enjoy for a short time the rare sport of sailing and hunting in this wild region, we decided to visit as many of the villages as possible.

In the morning the anchor was raised and we set sail in a light wind headed for more northern villages. It was a gray day, with a quiet sea. The speed of the yacht was not fast enough to be exciting, so Mr. Bradley suggested lowering the launch for a crack at ducks, or a chase at walrus or a drive at anything that happened to cut the waters. His harpoon gun was taken, as it was hoped that a whale might come our way, but the gun proved unsatisfactory and did not contribute much to our sport. In the fleet launch we were able to run all around the schooner as she slowly sailed over Wolstenholm Sound.

Ducks were secured in abundance. Seals were given chase, but they were able to escape us. Nearing Saunders Island, a herd of walruses was seen on a pan of drift ice far ahead. The magneto was pushed, the carburetor opened, and out we rushed after the shouting beasts. Two, with splendid tusks, were obtained, and two tons of meat and blubber were turned over to our Eskimo allies.

The days of hunting proved quite strenuous, and in the evening we were glad to seek the comfort of our cosy cabin, after dining on eider-ducks and other game delicacies.

A few Eskimos had asked permission to accompany us to a point farther north. Among them was a widow, to whom, for herself and her children, we had offered a large bed, with straw in it, between decks, but which, savage as she was, she had refused, saying she preferred the open air on deck. There she arranged a den among the anchor chains, under a shelter of seal skins.

In tears, she told us the story of her life, a story which offered a peep into the tragedy and at the same time the essential comedy of Eskimo existence. It came in response to a question from me as to how the world had used her, for I had known her years before. At my simple question, she buried her face in her hands and for a time could only mutter rapidly and unintelligibly to her two little boys. Then, between sobs, she told me her story.

Ma-nee—such was her name—was a descendant of the Eskimos of the American side. A foreign belle, and, although thin, fair to look upon, as Eskimo beauty goes, her hand was sought early by the ardent youths of the tribe, who, truth to tell, look upon utility as more desirable than beauty in a wife. The heart of Ma-nee throbbed to the pleadings of one Ik-wa, a youth lithe and brave, with brawn and sinews as resilient as rubber and strong as steel, handsome, dark, with flashing eyes, yet with a heart as cruel as the relentless wind and cold sea of the North. Ma-nee married Ik-wa and bore to him several children. These, which meant wealth of the most valuable kind (children even exceeding in value dogs, tusks and skins), meant the attainment of Ik-wa's selfish purpose. Ma-nee was fair, but her hands were not adroit with the needle, nor was she fair in the plump fashion desirable in wives.

Ik-wa met Ah-tah, a good seamstress, capable of much toil, not beautiful, but round and plump. Whereupon, Ik-wa took Ah-tah to wife, and leading Ma-nee to the door of their igloo, ordered her to leave. Cruel as can be these natives, they also possess a persistence and a tenderness that manifest themselves in strange, dramatic ways. Ma-nee, disconsolate but brave, departed. There being at the time a scarcity of marriageable women in the village, Ma-nee was soon wooed by another, an aged Eskimo, whose muscles had begun to wither, whose eyes no longer flashed as did Ik-wa's, but whose heart was kind. To him Ma-nee bore two children, tnose which she had with her on deck. To them, unfortunately, descended the heritage of their father's frailities; one—now eight—being the only deaf and dumb Eskimo in all the land; the other, the younger, aged three, a weakling with a pinched and pallid face and thin, gaunt arms. Ma-nee's husband was not a good hunter, for age and cold had sapped his vigor. Their home was peaceful if not prosperous; the two loved one another, and, because of their defects, Ma-nee grew to love her little ones unwontedly.

Just before the beginning of the long winter night, the old father, anxious to provide food and deer skins for the coming months of continuous darkness, ventured alone in search of game among the mountains of the interior. Day after day, while the gloom descended, Ma-nee, dry eyed waited. The aged father never came back. Returning hunters finally brought news that he had perished alone, from a gun accident, in the icy wilderness, and they had found him, his frozen, mummied face peeping anxiously from the mantle of snow. Ma-nee wept broken-heartedly.

Ma-nee gazed into the faces of the two children with a wild, tragic wistfulness. By the stern and inviolable law of the Eskimos, Ma-nee knew her two beloved ones were condemned to die. In this land, where food is at a premium, and where every helpless and dependent life means a sensible drain upon the tribe's resources, they have evolved that Spartan law which results in the survival of only the fittest. The one child, because of its insufficient senses, the other because it was still on its mother's back and under three at the time its father died, and with no father to support them, were doomed. Kind-hearted as the Eskimos naturally are, they can at times, in the working out of that code which means continued existence, be terribly brutal. Their fierce struggle with the elements for very existence has developed in them an elemental fierceness. From probable experience in long-past losses of life from contagion, they instinctively destroy every igloo in which a native dies, or, at times, to save the igloo, they heartlessly seize the dying, and dragging him through the low door, cast him, ere breath has ceased, into the life-stilling outer world.

This inviolable custom of ages Ma-nee, with a Spartan courage, determined to break. During the long night which had just passed, friends had been kind to Ma-nee, but now that she was defying Eskimo usage, she could expect no assistance. Brutal as he had been to her, hopeless as seemed such prospects, Ma-nee thought of the cruel Ik-wa and determined to go to him, with the two defective children of her second husband, beg him to accept them as his own and to take her, as a secondary wife, a servant—a position of humiliation and hard labor. In this determination, which can be appreciated only by those who know how implacable and heartless the natives can be, Ma-nee was showing one of their marvellous traits, that indomitable courage, persistence and dogged hopefulness which, in my two later companions, E-tuk-i-shook and Ah-we-lah, enabled them, with me, to reach the Pole.

I admired the spirit of Ma-nee, and promised to help her, although the mission of reuniting the two seemed dubious.

Ma-nee was not going to Ik-wa entirely empty-handed, however, for she possessed some positive wealth in the shape of several dogs, and three bundles of skins and sticks which comprised her household furniture.

We soon reached the village where Ma-nee was to be put ashore. Very humbly, the heroic mother and her two frail children went to Ik-wa's tent. Ik-wa was absent hunting, and his wife, who had supplanted Ma-nee, a fat, unsociable creature, appeared. Weeping, Ma-nee told of her plight and begged for shelter. The woman stolidly listened; then, without a word, turned her back on the forlorn mother and entered her tent. For the unintentional part we had played she gave us exceedingly cold, frowning looks which were quite expressive.

Ma-nee now went to the other villagers. They listened to her plans, and their primitive faces lighted with sympathy. I soon saw them serving a pot of steaming oil meat in her honor—a feast in which we were urgently invited to partake, but which we, fortunately, found some good excuse for avoiding. Although she had violated a custom of the tribe, these people, both stern-hearted and tender, recognized the greatness of a mother-love which had braved an unwritten law of ages, and they took her in. Several months later, on a return to the village, I saw Ik-wa himself. Although he did not thank me for the unwitting part I had played in their reunion, he had taken Ma-nee back, and near his own house was a new igloo in which the mother lived with her children.

Resuming our journey, a snow squall soon frosted the deck of the yacht, and to escape the icy air we retired early to our berths. During the night the speed of the yacht increased, and when we appeared on deck again, at four o'clock in the morning, the rays of the August sun seemed actually warm.

We passed the ice-battered and storm-swept cliffs of Cape Parry and entered Whale Sound. On a sea of gold, strewn with ice islands of ultramarine and alabaster, whales spouted and walrus shouted. Large flocks of little auks rushed rapidly by.

The wind was light, but the engine took us along at a pace just fast enough to allow us to enjoy the superb surroundings. In the afternoon we were well into Inglefield Gulf, and near Itiblu. There was a strong head wind, and enough ice about to make us cautious in our prospect.

We aimed here to secure Eskimo guides and with them seek caribou in Olrik's Bay. While the schooner was tacking for a favorable berth in the drift off Kanga, the launch was lowered, and we sought to interview the Eskimos of Itiblu. The ride was a wet one, for a short, choppy sea poured icy spray over us and tumbled us about.

There were only one woman, a few children, and about a score of dogs at the place. The woman was a remarkably fast talker, long out of practice. She told

us that her husband and the other men were absent on a
caribou hunt, and then, with a remarkably rapid articu-
lation and without a single question from us, plunged
incessantly on through all the news of the tribe for a
year.   After gasping for breath like a smothered seal,
she then began with news of previous years and a history of forgotten ages.   We started back for the launch,
and she invited herself to the pleasure of our company
to the beach.

We had gone only a few steps before it occurred to
her that she was in need of something.   Would we not
get her a few boxes of matches in exchange for a narwhal
tusk?   We should be delighted, and a handful of sweets
went with the bargain.   Her boy brought down two
ivory tusks, each eight feet in length, the two being
worth one hundred and fifty dollars.   Had we a knife
to spare?   Yes; and a tin spoon was also given, just to
show that we were liberal.

The yacht was headed northward, across Inglefield
Gulf.   With a fair wind, we cut tumbling seas of ebony
with a racing dash.   Though the wind was strong, the
air was remarkably clear.

The great chiselled cliffs of Cape Auckland rose in
terraced grandeur under the midnight sun.   The distance was twelve miles, and it was twelve miles of submerged rocks and shallow water.

It was necessary to give Karnah a wide berth.
There were bergs enough about to hold the water down,
though an occasional sea rose with a sickening thump.
At Karnah we went ashore.   There was not a man in
town, all being absent on a distant hunting campaign.
But, though there were no men, the place was far from

being deserted, for five women, fifteen children and forty-five dogs came out to meet us.

Here we saw five sealskin tents pitched among the bowlders of a glacial stream.   An immense quantity of narwhal meat was lying on the rocks and stones to dry. Skins were stretched on the grass, and a general air of thrift was evidenced about the place.   Bundles of seal-skins, packages of pelts and much ivory were brought out to trade and establish friendly intercourse.   We gave the natives sugar, tobacco and ammunition in quantities to suit their own estimate of value.

Would we not place ourselves at ease and stay for a day or two, as their husbands would soon return?   We were forced to decline their hospitality, for without the harbor there was too much wind to keep the schooner waiting.   Eskimos have no salutation except a greeting smile or a parting look of regret.   We got both at the same time as we stepped into the launch and shouted good-bye.

The captain was told to proceed to Cape Robert-son.   The wind eased, and a descending fog soon blotted out part of the landscape, horizon and sky.   It hung like a gray pall a thousand feet above us, leaving the air below this bright and startlingly clear.

TO THE LIMITS OF NAVIGATION

EXCITING HUNTS FOR GAME WITH THE ESKIMOS—AR-
RIVAL AT ETAH—SPEEDY TRIP TO ANNOATOK, THE
WINDY PLACE, WHERE SUPPLIES ARE FOUND IN
ABUNDANCE—EVERYTHING AUSPICIOUS FOR DASH TO
THE POLE—DETERMINATION TO ESSAY THE EFFORT—
BRADLEY INFORMED—DEBARK FOR THE POLE—THE
YACHT RETURNS

IV

ALONE WITH OUR DESTINY, SEVEN HUNDRED MILES FROM THE POLE

We awoke off Cape Robertson early on August 13, and went ashore before breakfast. The picturesque coast here rises suddenly to an altitude of about two thousand feet, and is crowned with a gleaming, silver ice cap. Large bays, blue glacial walls and prominent headlands give a pleasing variety. It is much like the coast of all Greenland. On its southern exposure the eroded Huronian rocks provide shelter for millions of little auks. They dart incessantly from cliff to sea in a chattering cloud of wings. Rather rich and grassy verdure offers an oasis for the Arctic hare, while the blue fox finds life easy here, for he can fill his winter den with the fat feathered creatures which teem by millions.

The Eskimos profit by the combination, and pitch their camp at the foot of the cliffs, for the chase on sea is nearly as good here as in other places, while land creatures literally tumble into the larder.

As we approached the shore, ten men, nine women, thirty-one children and one hundred and six dogs came out to meet us. I count the children and dogs for they are equally important in Eskimo economy. The latter are by far the most important to the average Caucasian in the Arctic.

Only small game had fallen to the Eskimos' lot, and they were eager to venture out with us after big game. Mr. Bradley gathered a suitable retinue of native guides, and we were not long in arranging a compact.

Free passage, the good graces of the cook, and a knife each were to be their pay. A caribou hunt was not sufficiently novel to merit a return to Olrik's Bay, where intelligent hunting is always rewarded, but it was hoped we might get a hunt at Kookaan, near the head of Robertson Bay.*

Although hunting in the bay was not successful from a practical standpoint, it afforded exciting pleas-

---

*The Death of John M. Verhoeff.—As we passed Robertson Bay, there came up memories of the tragedy of Verhoeff. This young man was a member of Peary's first expedition, in 1891. He had paid $2,000 toward the fund of the expedition. Verhoeff was young and enthusiastic. He gave his time, his money, and he risked his life for Peary. He was treated with about the same consideration as that accorded the Eskimo dogs. When I last saw him in camp, he was in tears, telling of Peary's injustice. Mrs. Peary—I advert to this with all possible reluctance—had done much to make his life bitter, and over this he talked for days. Finally he said: "I will never go home in the same ship with that man and that woman." It was the last sentence he uttered in my hearing. He did not go home in that ship. Instead, he wandered off over the glacier, where he left his body in the blue depths of a crevasse.

ure in perilous waters. Even during these hours of sport, my mind was busy with tentative plans for a Polar journey. Whenever I aimed my gun at a snorting walrus, or at some white-winged Arctic bird, I felt a thrill in the thought that upon the skill of my arms, of my aim, and upon that of the natives we were later to join, would depend the getting of food sufficient to enable me to embark upon my dream. Everything I did now began to have some bearing upon this glorious, intoxicating prospect; it colored my life, day and night. I realized how easily I might fail even should conditions be favorable enough to warrant the journey; for this reason, because of the unwelcome doubt which at times chilled my enthusiasm, I did not yet confide to Bradley my growing ambition.

Returning to the settlement, we paid our hunting guides, made presents to the women and children, and set sail for Etah. An offshore breeze filled the big wings of the canvas. As borne on the back of some great white bird, we soared northward into a limpid molten sea. From below came the music of our phonograph, curiously shouting its tunes, classic and popular, in that grim, golden region of glory and death.

It is curious how ambition sets the brain on fire, and quickens the heart throbs. As we sped over the magical waters, the wild golden air electric about me, I believe I felt an ecstasy of desire such as mystics achieved from fasting and prayer. It was the surge of an ambition which began to grow mightily within me, which I felt no obstacle could withstand, and which, later, I believe carried me forward with its wings of faith when my body well nigh refused to move. We passed Cape Alexander and entered Smith Sound. We sped by storm-chiselled cliffs, whereupon the hand of nature had written a history, unintelligible to humans, as with a pen of iron. The sun was low. Great bergs loomed up in the radiant distance, and reflecting silver-shimmering halos, seemed to me as the silver-winged ghosts of those who died in this region and who were borne alone on the wind and air.

Nature seemed to sing with exultation. Approaching a highland of emerald green and seal brown, I heard the wild shouting of hawks from the summit, and from below the shrill chattering of millions of auks with baby families. And nearer, from the life enraptured waters, the minor note of softly cooing ducks and mating guillemots. From the interior land of ice, rising above the low booming of a sapphire glacier moving majestically to the sea, rang the bark of foxes, the shrill notes of the ptarmigan, and from an invisible farther distance the raucous wolf howl of Eskimo dogs.

Before us, at times, would come a burst of spouting spray, and a whale would rise to the surface of the sea. Nearby, on a floating island of ice, mother walrus would soothingly murmur to her babies. From invisible places came the paternal voices of the oogzook, and as we went forward, seals, white whales and unicorns appeared, speaking perhaps the sign language of the animal deaf and dumb in the blue submarine.

Occasionally, there was an explosion, when thunder as from a hundred cannons echoed from cliff to cliff. A berg was shattered to ruins. Following this would rise the frightened voices of every animal above water. Now and then, from ultramarine grottoes issued weird, echoing sounds, and almost continually rising to ringing peals and shuddering into silence, reiterant, incessant, came nature's bugle-calls—calls of the wind, of sundering glaciers, of sudden rushes of ice rivers, of exploding gases and of disintegrating bergs. With those sounds pealing in our ears clarion-like, we entered the "Gates of Hades," the Polar gateway, bound for the harbor where the last fringe of the world's humanity straggles finally up on the globe.

As we entered Foulke Fiord, half a gale came from the sea. We steered for the settlement of Etah. A tiny settlement it was, for it was composed of precisely four tents, which for this season, had been pitched beside a small stream, just inside of the first projecting point on the north shore. Inside this point there was sheltered water for the Eskimo's kayaks, and it also made a good harbor for the schooner. It is possible in favorable seasons to push through Smith Sound, over Kane Basin, into Kennedy Channel, but the experiment is always at the risk of the vessel.

So, as there was no special reasons for us to hazard life in making this attempt, we decided to prepare the schooner here for the return voyage.

These preparations would occupy several days. We determined to spend as much of this time as possible in sport, since much game abounded in this region. Before we landed we watched the Eskimos harpoon a white whale. There were no unexplored spots in this immediate vicinity, as both Doctor Kane and Doctor Hayes, in the middle of the last century, had been thoroughly over the ground. The little auks kept us busy for a day after our arrival, while hares, tumbling like snowballs over wind-polished, Archæan rocks, gave another day of gun recreation. Far beyond, along the inland ice, were caribou, but we preferred to confine our hunting to the seashore. The bay waters were alive with eider-ducks and guillemots, while, just outside, walruses dared us to venture in open contest on the wind-swept water.

After satisfying our desire for the hunt, we prepared to start for Annoatok, twenty-five miles to the northward. This is the northernmost settlement of the globe, a place beyond which even the hardy Eskimos attempt nothing but brief hunting excursions, and where, curiously, money is useless because it has no value.

We decided to go in the motor boat, so the tanks were filled with gasoline and suitable food and camp equipment were loaded. On the morning of August 24, we started for Annoatok.

It was a beautiful day. The sun glowed in a sky of Italian blue. A light air crossed the sea, which glowed dully, like ground glass. Passing inside of Littleton Island, we searched for relics along Life-boat Cove. There the *Polaris* was stranded in a sinking condition in 1872, with fourteen men on board. The desolate cliffs of Cape Hatherton were a midsummer blaze of color and light that contrasted strongly with the cold blue of the many towering bergs.

As we went swiftly past the series of wind-swept headlands, the sea and air became alive with seals, walruses and birds. We did little shooting as we were eagerly bent on reaching Annoatok.

As we passed the sharp rocks of Cairn Point, we saw a cluster of nine tents on a small bay under Cape Inglefield.

"Look, look! There is Annoatok!" cried Tung-we, our native guide. Looking farther, we saw that the entire channel beyond was blocked with a jam of ice. Fortunately we were able to take our boat as far as we desired. A perpendicular cliff served as a pier to which to fasten it. Here it could rise and fall with the tide, and in little danger from drifting ice.

Ordinarily, Annoatok is a town of only a single family or perhaps two, but we found it unusually large and populous, for the best hunters had gathered here for the winter bear hunt. Their summer game catch had been very lucky. Immense quantities of meat were strewn along the shore, under mounds of stone. More than a hundred dogs, the standard by which Eskimo prosperity is measured, yelped a greeting, and twelve long-haired, wild men came out to meet us as friends.

It came strongly to me that this was the spot to make the base for a Polar dash. Here were Eskimo helpers, strong, hefty natives from whom I could select the best to accompany me; here, by a fortunate chance, were the best dog teams; here were plenty of furs for clothing; and here was unlimited food. These supplies, combined with supplies on the schooner, would give all that was needed for the campaign. Nothing could have been more ideal.

For the past several days, having realized the abundance of game and the auspicious weather, I had thought more definitely of making a dash for the Pole. With all conditions in my favor, might I not, by one powerful effort, achieve the thing that had haunted me for years? My former failures dogged me. If I did not try now, it was a question if an opportunity should ever again come to me.

Now every condition was auspicious for the effort. I confess the task seemed audacious almost to the verge of impossibility. But, with all these advantages so fortunately placed in my hands, it took on a new and almost weird fascination. My many years of schooling in both Polar zones and in mountaineering would now be put to their highest test.

Yes, I would try, I told myself; I believed I should succeed. I informed Mr. Bradley of my determination. He was not over-optimistic about success, but he shook my hand and wished me luck. From his yacht he volunteered food, fuel, and other supplies, for local camp use and trading, for which I have been thankful.

"Annoatok" means "a windy place." There is really nothing there to be called a harbor; but we now planned to bring the schooner to this point and unload her on the rocky shore, a task not unattended with danger. However, the base had to be made somewhere hereabout, as Etah itself is still more windy than Annoatok. Moreover, at Etah the landing is more difficult, and it was not nearly so convenient for my purpose as a base.

Besides, there were gathered at Annoatok, as I have described, with needed food and furs in abundance, the best Eskimos* in all Greenland, from whom, by

---

*Before he sailed on his last Northern expedition Mr. Peary, learning that I had preceded him, took the initial step in his campaign to discredit me by issuing a statement to the effect that I was bent upon the unfair and dishonest purpose of enlisting in my aid Eskimos which he had the exclusive right to command. Mr. Peary's attitude that the Eskimos,

reason of the rewards from civilization which I could give them, such as knives, guns, ammunition, old iron, needles and matches, I could select a party more efficient, because of their persistence, tough fibre, courage and familiarity with Arctic traveling, than any party of white men could be.

The possible combination of liberal supplies and valiant natives left absolutely nothing to be desired to insure success, so far as preliminaries were concerned. It was only necessary that good health, endurable weather and workable ice should follow. The expenditure of a million dollars could not have placed an expedition at a better advantage. The opportunity was too good to be lost. We therefore returned to Etah to prepare for the quest.

At Etah, practically everything that was to be landed at Annoatok was placed on deck, so that the dangerous stop beside the rocks of Annoatok could be made a brief one. The ship was prepared for the contingency of a storm.

Late in the evening of August 26, the entire population of Etah was taken aboard, the anchor was

---

because he had given them guns, powder and needles, belong to him, is as absurd as his pretension to the sole ownership of the North Pole. Although Mr. Peary had spent about a quarter of a century essaying the task by means of luxurious expeditions, he had done little more than other explorers and did not, in my opinion, either secure an option on the Pole or upon the services of the natives. In giving guns, etc., to the natives he also did no more than other explorers, and the Danes for many years, have done. Nor was this with him a magnanimous matter of gracious bounty, for, in prodigal return for all he gave them, Mr. Peary on every expedition secured a fortune in furs and ivory. The Eskimos belong to no one. For ages they have worked out their rigorous existence without the aid of white men, and Mr. Peary's pretension becomes not only absurd but grotesque when one realizes that following the arrival of ships with white crews, the natives have fallen easy victims of loathsome epidemics, mostly of a specific nature, for which the trivial gifts of any explorer would ill repay them.

tripped, and soon the *Bradley's* bow put out on the waters of Smith Sound for Annoatok. The night was cold and clear, brightened by the charm of color. The sun had just begun to dip under the northern horizon, which marks the end of the summer double days of splendor and begins the period of storms leading into the long night. Early in the morning we were off Annoatok.

The launch and all the dories were lowered and filled. Eskimo boats were pressed into service and loaded. The boats were towed ashore. Only a few reached Annoatok itself, for the wind increased and a troublesome sea made haste a matter of great importance. Things were pitched ashore anywhere on the rocks where a landing could be found for the boats.

The splendid efficiency of the launch proved equal to the emergency, and in the course of about thirteen hours all was safely put on shore in spite of dangerous winds and forbidding seas. That the goods were spread along the shore for a distance of several miles did not much matter, for the Eskimos willingly and promptly carried them to the required points.

Now the time had come for the return of the schooner to the United States. Unsafe to remain longer at Annoatok at this advanced stage of the season, it was also imperative that it go right on with barely a halt at any other place. The departure meant a complete severance between the civilized world and myself. But I do not believe, looking back upon it, that the situation seemed as awesome as might be supposed. Other explorers had been left alone in the Northland, and I had been through the experience before.

The party, so far as civilized men were concerned, was to be an unusually small one. That, however, was not from lack of volunteers, for when I had announced my determination many of the crew had volunteered to accompany me. Captain Bartlett himself wished to go along, but generously said that if it seemed necessary for him to go back with the schooner, he would need only a cook and engineer, leaving the other men with me.

I wanted only one white companion, however, for I knew that no group of white men could possibly match the Eskimos in their own element. I had the willing help of all the natives, too, at my disposal. More than that was not required. I made an agreement with them for their assistance throughout the winter in getting ready, and then for as many as I wanted to start with me toward the uttermost North. For my white companion I selected Rudolph Francke, now one of the Arctic enthusiasts on the yacht. He had shipped for the experience of an Arctic trip. He was a cultivated young German with a good scientific schooling. He was strong, goodnatured, and his heart was in the prospective work. These were the qualities which made him a very useful man as my sole companion.

Early on the morning of September 3, I bade farewell to Mr. Bradley, and not long afterward the yacht moved slowly southward and faded gradually into the distant southern horizon. I was left alone with my destiny, seven hundred miles from the Pole.

BEGINNING PREPARATIONS FOR THE POLAR DASH

THE ARCTIC SOLITUDE—RETROSPECTION AND INTROSPEC-
TION—THE DETERMINATION TO ACHIEVE—PLAN-
NING OUT THE DETAILS OF THE CAMPAIGN—AN
ENTIRE TRIBE BUSILY AT WORK

V

THE POLE, THE ROUTE, AND THE INCENTIVE

When the yacht disappeared I felt a poignant pang at my heart. After it had faded, I stood gazing blankly at the sky, and I felt the lure of the old world. The yacht was going home—to the land of my family and friends. I was now alone, and, with the exception of Francke, there was no white man among this tribe of wild people with whom to converse during the long Arctic night that was approaching. I knew I should not be lonely, for there was a tremendous lot of work to do, although I had unstinted assistance. In every detail, the entire six months of labor including the catching of animals, the drying of meat, the making of such clothes and sledges as would be necessary, and the testing of them, would have to be managed by myself. Turning from the rocky highland where I stood, a wild thrill stirred my heart. The hour of my opportunity had come. After years of unavailing hopes and depressing defeats my final chance was presented! In the determination to succeed, every drop of blood in my body, every fibre of me responded.

Why did I desire so ardently to reach the North Pole? What did I hope to gain? What, if successful, did I expect to reap as the result of my dreams? These questions since have been asked by many. I have searched the chambers of my memory and have tried to resolve replies to myself. The attaining of the North Pole meant at the time simply the accomplishing of a splendid, unprecedented feat—a feat of brain and muscle in which I should, if successful, signally surpass other men. In this I was not any more inordinately vain or seekful of glory than one who seeks pre-eminence in baseball, running tournaments, or any other form of athletics or sport.

At the time, any applause which the world might give, should I succeed, did not concern me; I knew that this might come, but it did not enter into my speculations.

For years I had felt the lure of the silver glamor of the North, and I can explain this no more than the reason why a poet is driven to express himself in verse, or why one child preternaturally develops amazing proficiency in mathematics and another in music. Certain desires are born or unconsciously developed in us. I, with others before me, found my life ambition in the conquest of the Pole. To reach it would mean, I knew, an exultation which nothing else in life could give.

This imaginary spot held for me the revealing of no great scientific secrets. I never regarded the feat as of any great scientific value. The real victory would lie, not in reaching the goal itself, but in overcoming the obstacles which exist in the way of it. In the battle with these I knew there would be excitement, danger, necessary expedients to tax the brain and heroic feats to tax the muscles, the ever constant incentive which the subduing of one difficulty after another excites.

During the first day at Annoatok, after the yacht left, I thought of the world toward which it was going, of the continents to the south of me, of the cities with their teeming millions, and of the men with their multitudinous, conflicting ambitions. I could see, in my mind, the gigantic globe of my world swinging in cloud-swept emerald spaces, and far in the remote, vast, white regions in the north of it, far from the haunts of men, thousands of miles from its populous cities, beyond the raging of its blue-green seas, myself, alone, a wee, small atom on its vast surface, striving to reach its hitherto unattained goal. I felt, as I thought of my anticipation and lonely quest, a sense of the terrible overwhelming hugeness of the earth, and the poignant loneliness any soul must feel when it embarks upon some splendid solitary destiny.

Beyond and above me I visioned the unimaginable, blinding white regions of ice and cold, about which, like a golden-crowned sentinel, with face of flame, the circling midnight sun kept guard. Upon this desolate, awe-inspiring stage—unchanged since the days of its designing—I saw myself attempting to win in the most spectacular and difficult marathon for the testing of human strength, courage and perseverance, of body and brain, which God has offered to man. I could see myself, in my fancy pictures, invading those roaring regions, struggling over icy lands in the dismal twilight of the Arctic morning, and venturing, with a few companions, upon the lifeless, wind-swept Polar sea. A black mite, I saw myself slowly piercing those white and terrible spaces, braving terrific storms, assailing green, adamantine barriers of ice, crossing the swift-flowing, black rivers of those ice fields, and stoutly persisting until, successful, I stood alone, a victor, upon the world's pinnacle!

This thought gave me wild joy. That I, one white man, might alone succeed in this quest gave me an impetus which only single-handed effort and the prospect of single-handed success can give. There was pleasure in the thought that, in this effort, I was indebted to no one; no one had expended money for me or my trip; no white men were to risk their lives with me. Whether it resulted in success or defeat, I alone should exult or I alone should suffer. I was the mascot of no clique of friends, nor the pawn of scientists who might find a suppositious and mythical glory in the reflected light of another's achievement. The quest was personal; the pleasure of success must be personal.

Yet, I want you to understand this thing was no casual jaunt with me. All my life hinged about it, my hopes were bent upon it; the doing of it was part of me. My plans of action were not haphazard and hair-brained. Logically and clearly, I mapped out a campaign. It was based upon experience in known conditions, experience gathered after years of discouragement and failure.

At Annoatok we erected a house of packing

ON THE CHASE FOR BEAR
THE BOX-HOUSE AT ANNOATOK AND ITS WINTER ENVIRONMENT

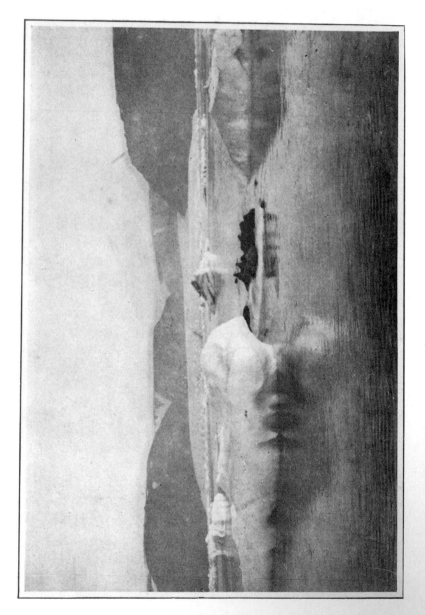

MAN'S PREY OF THE ARCTIC SEA—WALRUS ASLEEP

boxes.* The building of the house, which was to be both storehouse and workshop, was a simple matter. The walls were made of the packing boxes, especially selected of uniform size for this purpose.

Enclosing a space thirteen by sixteen feet, the cases were quickly piled up. The walls were held together by strips of wood, the joints sealed with pasted paper, with the addition of a few long boards. A really good roof was made by using the covers of the boxes as shingles. A blanket of turf over this confined the heat and permitted, at the same time, healthful circulation of air.

We slept under our own roof at the end of the first day. Our new house had the great advantage of containing within it all our possessions within easy

*One of the charges which Mr. Peary circulated before he returned North in 1908, was, that I violated a rule of Polar ethics by not applying for a license to seek the Pole, nor giving notice of my proposed trip. There is no such rule in Polar ethics. The following letter, however, to his press agent, Mr. Herbert Bridgman, dated Etah, August 26, 1907, answers the charge:

"My dear Bridgman: I have hit upon a new route to the North Pole and will stay to try it. By way of Buchanan Bay and Ellesmere Land and northward through Nansen Strait over the Polar sea seems to me to be a very good route. There will be game to the 82°, and here are natives and dogs for the task. So here ic for the Pole. Mr. Bradley will tell you the rest. Kind regards to all—F. A. Cook."

"It will be remembered," continued Mr. Bridgman, in his press reports, "that Dr. Cook, accompanied by John R. Bradley, Captain Moses Bartlett, and a number of Eskimos, left North Sidney, N. S., early last July on the American Auxiliary Schooner Yacht *John R. Bradley,* which landed the party at Smith Sound. Mr. Bradley returned to North Sydney on the yacht on October 1. *The expedition is provisioned for two years and fully equipped with dogs and sledges for the trip. The party is wintering thirty miles further north than Peary did two years ago.*"

And yet Bridgman, in line with the indefatigable pro-Peary boosters, later tried to lead the public to believe that I had nothing but gum drops with which to undertake a trip to the Pole. This same Bridgman also printed in what Brooklyn people call the "Standard Liar" the fake about my using, as my own, photographs said to belong to the newspaper cub, Herbert Berri.

For fifteen years Bridgman used my photographs and my material for his lectures on the Arctic and Antarctic, generally without giving credit. Evidently, my work and my results were good enough for him to borrow

reach at all times. When anything was needed in the way of supplies, all we had to do was to open a box in the wall.

The house completed, we immediately began the work of building sledges, and the equally important work, at which a large proportion of the Eskimos were at once set, of making up furs into clothing. According to my plans, each one of us embarking in the Polar journey would have to carry two suits of fur clothing. In the Arctic regions, especially when men are marching to the limit of their strength every day, the bodily heat puts the clothing into such condition that the only safe way, if health is to be preserved, is to change suits frequently, while the perspiration-soaked furs are laid out to dry.

The Eskimos had also to prepare for winter.

as Peary did. So long as my usefulness served the Bridgman-Peary interests, there was no question of my credibility, but when my success interfered with the monopoly of the fruits of Polar attainment, then I was to be striped with dark lines of dishonor.

The most amusing and also the most significant incident of the Bridgman-Peary humbug was the faked wireless message which Bridgman printed for Peary in his paper. Peary claims he reached the Pole on April 6, 1909. In the Standard Union, Brooklyn, of April 14, 1909 (eight days after the alleged discovery), Peary's friend H. L. Bridgman, one of the owners, printed the following:

"PEARY DUE NORTH POLE TWELVE M., THURSDAY" (APRIL 15, 1909).

Is Mr. Bridgman a psychic medium? How, with Peary thousands of miles away, hundreds of miles from the most northerly wireless station, did he sense the amazing feat? Were he and Peary in telepathic communication? Or, rather, does this not seem to point to an agreement entered into before the departure of Peary, about a year before the attempt was made, to announce on a certain day the "discovery" of the Pole?

From other sources we learn that the timing of the arrival of the ship at Cape Sheridan seems to have been made good, but in an apparent effort on the part of Peary to keep faith with Bridgman on April 15, we find him in trouble. If Peary arranged his "discovery" for this agreed date, he would have had to take nine days for his return trip from the Pole. This would increase his speed limit 50 per cent., and since he is regarded with suspicion on his speed limits, to make his "Pole Discovery" story fit in between the known time when he left Bartlett and the time when he got back to the ship, he was compelled to break faith with Bridgman and went back nine days on his calendar, placing the date of Pole reaching at April 6.

Tents of sealskin are inhabitable only in the summer time. For the coming period of darkness and bitter cold, they made igloos of stone and snow.

Meanwhile, they were not in the least averse to agreeable relaxation. I had with me a good supply of tea, and was in the habit of drinking a cup of it with Francke about four o'clock every afternoon. Observing this, the Eskimos at once began to present themselves at the tea hour. Fortunately, tea was one of the supplies of which I had brought a good deal for the sake of pleasing the natives, and it was not long before I had a very large and gossipy afternoon tea party every day, in this northernmost human settlement of the globe.

I planned to superintend every detail of progress, as far as it concerned our journey. I could watch the men, too, and see which ones promised to be the best to accompany me. And, what was a most important point, I could also perfect my final plans for the advance right at my final base.

I aimed to reach the top of the globe in the angle between Alaska and Greenland, a promising route through a new and lonesome region which had not been tried, abandoning what has come to be called the "American Route." I should strike westward and then northward, working new trails. With Annoatok as a base of operations, I planned to carry sufficient supplies over Schley Land and along the west coast of the game lands, trusting that the game along this region would furnish sufficient supplies en route to the shores of the Polar sea. This journey to land's end would also afford a test of every article of equipment needed in the field work, and would enable us to choose finally from a selected number of Eskimos those most able to endure the rigors of the unlimited journey which lay before us.

I sent out a few hunters along the intended line to seek for haunts of game, but I was not surprised that their searching in the dark was practically unsuccessful, and it merely meant that I must depend upon my previous knowledge of conditions. I knew from the general reports of the natives, and from the explorations of Sverdrup, that the beginning of the intended route offered abundant game, and the indications were that further food would likewise be found as we advanced. The readiness with which the Eskimos declared themselves ready to trust to the food supply of the unknown region was highly encouraging.

To start from my base with men and dogs in superb condition, with their bodies nourished with wholesome fresh meat instead of the nauseating laboratory stuff too often given to men in the North, was of vital importance; and if the men and dogs could afterwards be supported in great measure by the game of the region through which we were to pass, it would be of an importance more vital still. If my information was well founded and my general conjectures correct, I should have advantages which had not been possessed by any other leader of a Polar expedition. The new route seemed to promise, also, immunity from the highly disturbing effects of certain North Greenland currents. In all, the chances seemed not unfavorable.

With busy people hard at work about me, I knew that the months of the long night would pass rapidly by. There was much to do, and with the earliest dawn of the morning of the next year we must be ready to start for the Pole.

THE CURTAIN OF NIGHT DROPS

TRIBE OF TWO HUNDRED AND FIFTY NATIVES BUSILY
BEGIN PREPARATIONS FOR THE POLAR DASH—EXCIT-
ING HUNTS FOR THE UNICORN AND OTHER GAME
FROM ANNOATOK TO CAPE YORK—EVERY ANIMAL
CAUGHT BEARING UPON THE SUCCESS OF THE
VENTURE—THE GRAY-GREEN GLOOM OF TWILIGHT
IN WHICH THE ESKIMO WOMEN COMMUNICATE
WITH THE SOULS OF THE DEAD

VI

THE SUNSET OF 1907

Winter, long-lasting, dark and dismal, approached.
To me it was to be a season of feverish labor in which
every hand at work and every hour employed counted
in the problem of success. While the hands of the entire
tribe would be busy, and while I should direct and help
in the making of sleds, catching of game, preparing of
meat, I knew that my mind would find continual excitement in dreams of my quest, in anticipating and solving
its difficulties, in feeling the bounding pulse of the dash
over the ice of the Polar sea, with dogs joyously barking, whips cracking the air, and the reappearing sun
paving our pathway with liquid gold. In the labor of
the long winter which I began to map out I knew I
should find ceaseless zest, for the pursuit of every
narwhal, every walrus, every fox I should regard with

abated suspense, each one bearing upon my chances; in the employment of every pair of hands I should hang with an eager interest, the expediency and excellence of the work making for success or failure. From this time onward everything of my life, every native, every occurrence began to have some bearing upon the dominating task to which I had set myself.

With the advance of winter, storms of frightful ferocity began to arise. Inasmuch as we had stored meat and blubber in large quantities about our camp, it was not necessary at these times to venture out to dig up supplies from great depths of snow drift. During these periods hands were employed busily inside the igloos. Although a large quantity of animals and furs had been gathered by the hunters before our arrival, we now unexpectedly discovered that the supply was inadequate. According to my plans, a large party of picked natives would accompany me to land's end and somewhat beyond on the Polar sea when I started for my dash in the coming spring. As spring is the best hunting season, it was therefore imperative to secure sufficient advance provisions for the families of these men in addition to preparing requisites for my expedition. So the early days of the winter would have to be busily occupied by the men in a ceaseless hunt for game, and later, even when the darkness had fully fallen, the moonlight days and nights would thus have to be utilized also.

In the Polar cycle of the seasons there are peculiar conditions which apply to circumstances and movements. As the word, seasons, is ordinarily understood, there are but two, a winter season and a summer season—a winter season of nine months and a summer of three months.

But, for more convenient division of the yearly periods, it is best to retain the usual cycle of four seasons. Eskimos call the winter "ookiah," which also means year, and the summer "onsah." Days are "sleeps." The months are moons, and the periods are named in accord with the movements of various creatures of the chase.

In early September at Annoatok the sun dips considerably under the northern horizon. There is no night. At sunset and at sunrise storm clouds hide the bursts of color which are the glory of twilight, and the electric afterglow is generally lost in a dull gray.

The gloom of the coming winter night now thickens. The splendor of the summer day has gone. A day of six months and a night of six months is often ascribed to the Polar regions as a whole, but this is only true of a very small area about the Pole.

As we come south, the sun slips under the horizon for an ever-increasing part of each twenty-four hours. Preceding and following the night, as we come from the Pole, there is a period of day and night which lengthens with the descent of latitude.

It is this period which enables us to retain the names of the usual seasons—summer for the double days, fall for the period of the setting sun. This season begins when the sun first dips under the ice at midnight for a few moments. These moments increase rapidly, yet one hardly appreciates that the sun is departing until day and night are of equal length, for the night remains light, though not cheerful. Then the day rapidly shortens and darkens, and the sun sinks until at last there is but a mere glimmer of the glory of day. Winter is limited to the long night, and spring applies to the days of the rising sun, a period corresponding to the autumn days of the setting sun.

At Annoatok the midnight sun is first seen on April 23. It dips in the sea on August 19. It thus encircles the horizon, giving summer and continuous day for one hundred and eighteen days. It sets at midday on October 24, and is absent a period of prolonged night corresponding to the day, and it rises on February 19. The Arctic air, with its low temperature and its charge of frosted humidity, so distorts the sun's rays that when low it is frequently lifted one or two diameters; therefore, the exact day or hour for sunrise or sunset does not correspond to mathematical calculations. Then follow days of spring.

In the fall, when the harmonizing influence of the sun is withdrawn, there begins a battle of the elements which continues until stilled by the hopeless frost of early night.

At this time, although field work was painful, the needs of our venture forced us to persistent action in the chase of walrus, seal, narwhal and white whale. We thus harvested food and fuel.

Before winter ice spread over the sea, ptarmigan, hare and reindeer were sought on land to supply the table during the long night with delicacies, while bear and fox pleased the palates of the Eskimos, and their pelts clothed all.

Many long journeys were undertaken to secure an important supply of grass to pad boots and mittens and also to secure moss, which serves as wick for the Eskimo lamp. During the months of September and October, along the entire Greenland coast, the Eskimos were engaged in a feverish quest for reserve supplies. Shortly after my arrival, word had been carried from village to village that I was at Annoatok, and, intending to make a dash for the "Big Nail," desired the help of the entire tribe. Intense and spontaneous activity followed. Knowing the demands of the North, and of such work as I planned, the natives, without specific instructions from me and with only a brief outline of the planned Polar campaign which was sent from village to village, immediately got busy gathering the needed things. They knew better than I where to go for certain game, and where certain desirable things were obtainable. This relieved me of a great responsibility. Each local group of natives was to perform some important duty, suited to its available resources, in gathering the tremendous amount of material required for our trip. Each village had its peculiar game advantages.

In some places foxes and hares, the skins of which were necessary for coats and stockings, were abundant, and the Eskimos must not only gather the greatest number possible, but prepare the skins and make them into properly fitting garments. In other places reindeer were plentiful. The skin of these was needed for sleeping bags, while the sinew was required for thread. In still other places seal was the luck of the chase; its skin was one of our most important needs. Of it boots were made, and an immense amount of line and lashings prepared.

Thus, in one way or another, every man and woman and most of the children of this tribe of two hundred and fifty people were kept busy in the service of the expedition. The work was well done, and with much better knowledge of the fitness of things than could have been possessed by any possible gathering of alien white men.

The quest of the walrus and the narwhal came in our own immediate plan of adventure, although the narwhal, called by whale fishers the unicorn, does not often come under the eye of the white man. It afforded for a brief spell good results in sport and useful material. Its blubber is the pride of every housekeeper, for it gives a long, hot flame to the lamp, with no smoke to spot the igloo finery. The skin is regarded as quite a delicacy. Cut into squares, it looks and tastes like scallops, with only a slight aroma of train oil. The meat dries easily, and is thus prized as an appetizer or as a lunch to be eaten en route in sled or kayak. In this shape it was an extremely useful thing for us, for it took the place of pemmican on our less urgent journeys.

Narwhals played in schools, far off shore, and usually along the edges of some large ice field, their long ivory tusks rising under spouts of breath and spray. Whenever this glad sight was noted, every kayak about camp was manned, and the skin canoes went flittering like birds over the water. Some of the Eskimos climbed to the ice fields and delivered their harpoons from a secure footing. Others hid behind floating fragments of heavy ice and made a sudden rush as the animals passed. Still others came up in the rear, for the narwhal cannot easily see backward, and does not often turn to watch its enemies, its speed being so fast that it can easily keep ahead of them.

In these exciting hunts I participated with eager delight, and by proxy mentally engaged in every encounter. For, in this sea game, existed food supplies which, instead of entirely confining myself to pemmican, I planned also to use on my Polar journey. As the skin boats, like bugs, sped over the water, I felt the movement of them surge in my brain; with the upraising of each swift-darting native's arm I felt, as it were, my heart stop with bated suspense. With every failure I experienced a throb of dismay. With the hauling in of each slimy beast I felt, as it were, nearer my goal.

Narwhal hunting, in itself, and without the added spur of personal interest, which I had, is brimful of thrilling sport. The harpoon is always delivered at close range. Whenever the dragging float marks the end of the line in tow of the frightened creature, the line of skin canoes follows. Timid by nature and fearing to rise for breath, the narwhal plunges along until nearly strangled. When he does come up, there are likely to be several Eskimos near with drawn lances, which inflict deep gashes.

Again the narwhal plunges deep down, with but one breath, and hurries along as best it can. But its speed slackens and a line of crimson marks its hidden path. Loss of blood and want of air do not give it a chance to fight. Again it comes up with a spout. Again the lances are hurled.

The battle continues for several hours, with many exciting adventures, but in the end the narwhal always succumbs, offering a prize of several thousands of pounds of meat and blubber. Victory as a rule is not gained until the hunters are far from home, and also far from the shore line. But the Eskimo is a courageous hunter and an intelligent seaman.

To the huge carcass frail kayaks are hitched in a long line. Towing is slow, wind and sea combining to make the task difficult and dangerous. One sees nothing of the narwhal and very little of the kayak, for dashing seas wash over the little craft, but the double-bladed paddles see-saw with the regularity of a pendulum. Homecoming takes many hours and demands a prodigious amount of hard work, but there is energy to spare, for a wealth of meat and fat is the culmination of all Eskimo ambition.

Seven of these ponderous animals were brought in during five days, making a heap of more than forty thousand pounds of food and fuel. The sight of this tremulous, blubbering mass filled my heart with joy. Our success was not too soon, for now the narwhals suddenly disappeared, and we saw no more of them. About this time three white whales were also obtained at Etah by a similar method of hunting.

With the advent of actual winter, storms swept over the land and sea with such fury that it was no longer safe to venture out on the water in kayaks. After the catching of several walruses from boats, sea hunting now was confined to the quest of seal through young ice. As such hunting would soon be limited to only a few open spaces near prominent headlands, an industrious pursuit was feverishly engaged in at every village from Annoatok to Cape York, and hour by hour, day by day, until the hunt of necessity changed from sea to land, the husky natives engaged in seal catching. As yet we had no caribou meat, and the little auks, which had been gathered in nets during the summer, with the eider-duck bagged later, soon disappeared as a steady diet. We must now procure such available land game as hare, ptarmigan and reindeer, for we had not yet learned to eat with a relish the fishy, liver-like substance which is characteristic of all marine mammals.

Guns and ammunition were now distributed, and when the winds were easy enough to allow one to venture out, every Eskimo sought the neighboring hills. Francke also took his exercise with a gun on his shoulder.

The combined efforts resulted in a long line of ptarmigan, two reindeer and sixteen hares. As snow covered the upper slopes, the game was forced down near the sea, where we could still hope to hunt in the feeble light of the early part of the night.

With a larder fairly stocked and good prospects for other tasty meats, we were spared the anxiety of a winter without supplies. Francke was an ideal chef in the preparation of this game to good effect, for he had a delightful way of making our primitive provisions quite appetizing.

In the middle of October fox skins were prime, and then new steel traps were distributed and set near the many caches. By this time all the Eskimos had abandoned their sealskin tents and were snugly settled in their winter igloos. The ground was covered with snow, and the sea was almost entirely frozen.

Everybody was busy preparing for the coming cold and night. The temperature was about 20° below zero. Severe storms were becoming less frequent, and the air, though colder, was less humid and less disagreeable. An ice-foot was formed by the tides along shore, and over this the winter sledging was begun by short excursions to bait the fox traps and gather the foxes.

Our life now resolved itself into a systematic routine of work, which was practically followed throughout the succeeding long winter night. About the box-house in which Francke and I lived were igloos housing eight to twelve families. The tribe of two hundred and fifty was distributed in a range of villages along the coast, an average of four families constituting a community. Early each morning Koo-loo-ting-wah would bang at my door, enter, and I would drowsily awaken while he freshened the fire. Rising, we would prepare hot coffee and partake of breakfast with biscuits. By seven o'clock—according to our standard of time—five or six of the natives would arrive, and, after a liberal libation of coffee, begin work. I taught them to help me in the making of my hickory sleds. Some I taught to use modern carpentering instruments, which I had with me. Another group was schooled in bending the resilient but tough hickory. This was done by wrapping old cloths about the wood and steeping it in hot water. Others engaged, as the days went by, in making dog harness, articles of winter clothing, and drying meat. Not an hour was lost during the day. At noon we paused for a bite of frozen meat and hot tea. Then we fell to work again without respite until five or six o'clock.

Meanwhile, beginning in the early morning of our steadily darkening days, other male members of the tribe pursued game. Others again followed a routine of scouring of the villages and collecting all the furs and game which had been caught. The women of the tribe, in almost every dimly lighted igloo, were no less industrious. To them fell the task of assisting in drying the fur skins, preparing dried meat and making our clothing. Throughout the entire days they sat in their snow and stone houses, masses of ill-smelling furs before them, cutting the skins and sewing them into serviceable garments. This work I often watched, passing from igloo to igloo, with an interest that verged on anxiety; for upon the strength, thickness and durability of these depended my life, and that of the companions I should choose, on the frigid days which would inevitably come on my journey Poleward. But these broad-faced, patient women did their work well. Their skill is quite remarkable. They took my measurements, for instance, by roughly sizing up my old garments and by measuring me by sight. Garments were made to fit snugly after the preliminary making by cutting out or inserting patches of fur. Needles among the natives are indeed precious. So valuable are they that if a point or eye is broken, with infinite skill and patience the broken end is heated and flattened, and by means of a bow drill a new eye is bored. A new point is with equal skill shaped on local stones. With marvelous patience they make their own thread by drying and stripping caribou or narwhale sinews.

Were it not for their extraordinary eyesight, such work, under such conditions, would be impossible. But in the dark the natives can espy things invisible to white men. This owl-sight enables them to hunt, if necessary, in almost pitch darkness, and to perform tedious feats of hand skill which, in such dim light, an alien would bungle. I noticed, with much curiosity, that when the natives inspected any photograph or object which I gave them they always held it upside down. All objects, as is well known, are reflected in the retina thus, and it is our familiarity with the size and comparative relations of things which enables the brain to visualize an object or scene at its proper angle.   This strange, instinctive act of the natives might form an interesting chapter in optics.

Meanwhile, busy and interested in the beginning of our various pursuits, the great crust which was to hold down the sea for so many months, closed and thickened.

During the last days of brief sunshine the weather cleared, and at noon on October 24 everybody sought the open for a last glimpse of the dying day.   There was a charm of color and glitter, but no one seemed quite happy as the sun sank under the southern ice, for it was not to rise again for one hundred and eighteen days.

Just prior to the falling of darkness, with that instinctive and forced hilarity with which aboriginal beings seek to ward off an impending calamity, the Eskimos engaged in their annual sporting event.   It is a curious sight, indeed, to behold a number of excited, laughing Eskimos gathering about two champion dogs which are to fight.   Although the zest of betting is unknown, the natives regard dog fights with much the same eager excitement as a certain type of sporting man does a cock encounter.   Sometimes the dogs do not fight fairly, a number of the animals bunching together and attacking a single dog.   Dogs selected for the fight are, of course, the best of the teams.   A dog which maintains his fighting supremacy becomes a king dog, and when beaten becomes a first lieutenant to the king.

After the forced enthusiasm of this brief period of excitement, the Eskimos begin to succumb to the inevitable melancholia of nature, when the sun, the source of natural life, disappears and darkness descends. A gloom descends heavily upon their spirits. A subtle sadness tinctures their life, and they are possessed by an impulse to weep. At this season, hour by hour, the darkness thickens; the cold increases and chills their igloos; the wind, exultant while the sun shines, now whines and sobs dolorously—there is something gruesome, uncanny, supernatural, in its siren sorrow. Outside, the snow falls, the sea closes. Its clamant beat of waves is silenced. Sea animals mostly disappear; land animals are rare. Their source of physical supply vanished, the Eskimos unconsciously feel the grim hand of want, of starvation, which means death, upon them. The psychology of this period of depression partly lies, undoubtedly, in this instinctive dread of death from lack of food and the natural depression of unrelieved gloom. Moreover, there is a grief, born of the native superstition that, when the sea freezes, the souls of all who have perished in the waters are imprisoned during the long night. Too fierce is the struggle of these people with the elemental forces to permit them, like many other aboriginal peoples to be obsessed greatly with superstitions. Although their religion is a very primitive and native one, it is usually only at the inception of night that they feel the appalling nearness of a world that is supernatural. As the last rim of the sun sank over the southern ice, the natives entered upon a formal period of melancholy, during which the bereavements of each family, and the discomforts and disasters of the year, were memoralized.

I shall never forget that long, sad evening, which lasted many normal days. The sun had descended. A sepulchral, gray-green curtain of gloom hung over the chilled earth. In the dim semi-darkness could be vaguely seen the outlines of the igloos, of the heaving curvatures of snow-covered land, and the blacker, snake-like twistings of open lanes of water, where the sea had not yet frozen. Sitting in my box-house, I was startled suddenly by a sound that made my flesh for the instant creep. I walked to the door and threw it open. Over the bluish, snow-covered land, formed by the indentures and hollows, stretched dark-purplish shapes—Titan shadows, sepulchral and ominous, some with shrouded heads, others with spectral arms threateningly upraised. Nebulous and gruesome shreds of blue-fog like wraiths shifted over the sea. Out of the sombre, heavy air began to issue a sound as of many women sobbing. From the indistinct distance came moaning, crooning voices. Sometimes hysterical wails of anguish rent the air, and now and then frantic choruses shrieked some heart-aching despair. My impression was that I was in a land of the sorrowful dead, some mid-strata of the spirit world, where, in this gray-green twilight, formless things in the distance moved to and fro.

There is, I believe, in the heart of every man, an instinctive respect for sorrow. With muffled steps, I left the igloo and paced the dreariness of ice, treading slowly, lest, in the darkness, I slip into some unseen crevasse of the open sea. A strange and eerie sight confronted me. Along the seashore, bending over the lapping black water, or standing here and there by inky, open leads in the severed ice, many Eskimo women were gathered. Some stood in groups of two or three. Bowed and disconsolate, her arms about them, with almost every hundred steps, I saw a weeping mother and her children.   Standing rigid and stark, motionless graven images of despair, or frantically writhing to and fro, others stood far apart in desolate places, alone.

The dull, opaque air was tinged with a strange phosphorescent green, suggestive of a place of dead things; and now, like the flutterings of huge death-lamps, along the horizon, where the sun had sunk, gashes of crimson here and there fitfully glowed blood-red in the pall-like sky.

To the left, as I walked along, I recognized Tung-wingwah, with a child on her back and a bag of moss in her hand.   She stood behind a cheerless rock, with her face toward the faint red flushes of the sun. She stood motionless.   Big tears rolled from her eyes, but not a sound was uttered.   To my low queries she made no response.   I invited her to the camp to have a cup of tea, thinking to change her sad thoughts and loosen her tongue.   But still her eyes did not leave that last distant line of open water.   From another, I later learned that in the previous April her daughter of five, while playing on the ice-foot, slipped and was lost in the sea.   The mother now mourned because the ice would bury her little one's soul.

A little farther along was Al-leek-ah, a woman of middle age, with two young children by her side.   She was hysterical in her grief, now laughing with a weird giggle, now crying and groaning as if in great pain, and again dancing with emotions of madness.   .I learned her story from a chatter that ran through all her anguish. Towanah, her first husband, had been drawn under the ice, by the harpoon line, twenty years ago.   And though she had been married three times since, she was trying to keep alive the memory of her first love. I went on, marveling at a primitive fidelity so long enduring.

Still farther along towards the steep slopes of the main coast, I saw Ahwynet, all alone in the gloomy shadow of great cliffs. Her story was told in chants and moans. Her husband and all her children had been swept by an avalanche into the stormy seas. There was a kind of wild poetry in the song of her bereavement. Tears came to my eyes. The rush of the avalanche, the hiss of the wind, the pounding of the seas, were all indicated. And then, in heart-breaking tones, came "blood of her blood, flesh of her flesh, under the frozen waters," and other sentiments which I could not catch in the undertone of sobs.

Cold shivers began to run up my spine, and I turned to retreat to camp. Here was a scene that perhaps a Dante might adequately write about. I cannot. I felt that I, an alien, was intruding into the realm of some strange and mystic sorrow. I felt the sombre thrill of a borderland world not human. These women were communicating with the souls of their dead. To those who had perished in the sea they were telling, ere the gates of ice closed above them, all the news of the past year—things of interest and personal, and even of years before, as far back as they could remember. Almost every family each year loses someone in the sea; almost every family was represented by these weeping women, overburdened with their own naive sorrow, and who yet strangely sought to cheer the souls of the disconsolate and desolate dead.

Meanwhile, while the women were weeping and giving their parting messages to the dead, the male members of the tribe, in chants and dramatic dances, were celebrating, in the igloos, the important events of the past year.

Inside, the igloos were dimly lighted with stone blubber lamps. These, during the entire winter, furnish light and heat. The lamp consists of a crescent-shaped stone with a concavity, in which there is animal oil and a line of crushed moss as a wick. Lighted early in the season, for an entire winter, these lamps cast a faint, perpetual, flickering light. Shadows dance grotesquely about on the rounded walls. An oily stench pervades the unventilated enclosure. In this weird, yellow-blackish radiance the men engage in their fantastic dances. Moving the central parts of their bodies to and fro, they utter weird sing-song chants. They recite, in jerky, curious singing, the history of the big events of the year; of successful chases; of notable storms; of everything that means much in their simple lives. As they dance, their voices rise to a high pitch of excitement. Their eyes flash like smoldering coals. Their arms move frantically. Some begin to sob uncontrollably. A hysteria of laughter seizes others. Finally the dance ends; exhausted, they pass into a brief lethargy, from which they revive, their melancholia departed. The women return from the shores of the sea; they wipe their tears, and, with native spontaneity, forget their depression and smile again.

While I was interested in the curious spectacles presented, the sunset of 1907 to me was inspiration for the final work in directing the completion of the outfit with which to begin the conquest of the Pole at sunrise of

1908.   Fortunately, I was not handicapped by the company of the usual novices taken on Polar expeditions. There were only two of us white men, and white men, at the best, must be regarded as amateurs compared with the expert efficiency of Eskimos in their own environment.   Our food supply contained only the prime factors of primitive nourishment.   Special foods and laboratory concoctions and canned delicacies did not fill an important space in our larder.   Nor had we balloons, automobiles, motor sleds or other freak devices.   We did, however, I have said, have what was of utmost importance, an abundance of the best hickory and metal for the making of the sleds upon which our destinies were vitally to depend.

FIRST WEEK OF THE LONG NIGHT

HUNTING IN THE ARCTIC TWILIGHT—PURSUING BEAR, CARIBOU AND SMALLER GAME IN SEMI-GLOOM

VII

THE GLORY OF THE AURORA

The sun had dropped below the horizon. The gloom continued steadily to thicken. Each twenty-four hours, at the approximate approach of what was the noon hour when the sun had been above the horizon, the sky to the south of us glowed with marvelous, subdued sunset hues. By this time our work had gone ahead by progressive stages. Furs, to protect us from the cold of the uttermost North on my prospective trip, had been prepared and were being made into clothing; meat and fat, for food and fuel, were being dried and stored in numerous caches about Annoatok; several of the sledges and part of the equipment were ready.

We still had need of large quantities of supplies, and, while some of the natives were busy with their routine work, we planned that as many others as possible should use the twilight days pursuing bear, caribou, fox, hare and other game far beyond the usual Eskimo haunts. Before the dawn of the sun's afterglow, on the morning of October 26, seven sledges with sixty dogs were on the ice-foot near our camp, ready to start for hunting grounds near Humboldt Glacier, a distance of one hundred miles northward.*

While the teamsters waited for the final password the dogs chafed fiercely. I could barely see the outlines of my companions in the gloom, and it was difficult, in the irregular snow and tide-lifted ice descending to sea level, to find footing.

The word to start was given. My companions took up the cry.

"*Huk! Huk! Huk!*" (Go! Go!) they shouted.

The dogs responded in leaps and howls.

"*Howah! Howah!*" (Right! Right!) "*Egh! Egh!*" (Stop! Stop!) "*Aureti!*" (Behave!) came echoingly along the line of teams. Finally the wild dash slackened, the dogs regulated their paces to an easy trot, and we swept steadily along the frozen highway of the tide-made shelf of the ice-foot. The sledges dodged stones and ice-blocks, edged along dangerous precipices, in the depths of which I heard the swish of water, and glided miraculously over crevices and along deep gorges. Jumping about the sledges, guiding, pushing, or retarding their speed, cracking their whips in the air, the natives, with that art which only aborigines seem to have, picked the way and controlled the dogs, but a few generations removed from their wolf progenitors, with amazing dexterity.

A low wind blew down the slopes and froze our

_____

*Game List.—The following animals were captured from August 15, 1907, to May 15, 1909:

Two thousand four hundred and twenty-two birds, 311 Arctic hares, 320 blue and white foxes, 32 Greenland reindeer, 4 white reindeer, 22 polar bears, 52 seals, 73 walrus, 21 narwhals, 3 white whales, and 206 musk oxen.

breath in lines of frost about our heads. The temperature was 35° below zero. To the left of us was Kane
Basin, recalling its history of human strife northward.
It was filled with serried ranges of crushed ice, a berg
here and there, all in the light of the kindling sky, aglow
with purple and blue. To the far west I saw the
dim outline of Ellesmere, my promised land, over which
I hoped to force a new route to the Pole; upon its snowy
highlands was poured a soft creamy light from encouraging skies. To the right was the rugged coast of Greenland, its huge, ice-chiselled cliffs leaping portentously
forward in the gloom. Thrilling with the race, we made
a run of twenty miles and reached Rensselaer Harbor,
where Dr. Kane had spent his long nights of misfortune.

We pitched camp at the ice-foot at the head of the
bay. Although we found traces of hare and fox, it was
too dark to venture on the chase. The temperature had
fallen to —40°, the wind pierced with a sharp sting. For
my shelter I erected a new tent which I had invented,
and the efficiency of which I desired to test. Taking the
sledge frame work as a platform, a folding top of strong
canvas was fastened, and spread between two bars of
hickory from each end. The entrance was in front.
Inside was a space eight feet long and three and one-
half feet wide, with a round whaleback top. Inside this
a supplementary wall was constructed of light blankets,
offering an air space of an inch between the outer wall
as a non-conductor to confine the little heat generated
within. As there was ample room for only two persons,
Koo-loo-ting-wah, my leading man, was invited to share
the tent. The natives had not provided themselves with
shelter of any kind. They had counted on either build-

ing an igloo or seeking the shelter of the snows, as do the creatures of the wilds.

Inside my tent I prepared a meal on the little German stove, burning the vapor of alcohol. The meal consisted of a pail of hot corn meal, fried bacon and a liberal all-round supply of steaming tea. To accomplish this, which included melting the snow, heating the water, and cooking everything separately, required about two hours. As I considered eating outside with any degree of comfort impossible, my companions were invited to crowd inside the tent. The vapor of their breath and that of the cooking soon condensed into snow, and a miniature snowstorm covered everything within. After this was swept out, the Eskimos were invited to enter again. All partook of the meal ravenously, and then emerged to reconnoiter the surroundings. Tracks of ptarmigan, hare and foxes were found, and as we moved about with seeking, owl eyes, ravens shouted notes of welcome.

We then retired to rest. As there was no snow about that was sufficiently hard to cut blocks with which to erect snow houses, the natives placed themselves in semi-reclining positions on their sledges and slept in their traveling clothes. After a few hours they awoke and partook of chopped frozen meat and blubber; two hours later, they made a fire in a tin can, with moss and blubber as fuel, and over this prepared a pot of parboiled meat. A crescent-shaped wall of snow was built to break the wind; in the shelter of this they sat, grinning delightedly, and eating savagely, with much smacking of the lips, the steaming broth and walrus meat. All this I studied with intense interest. I desired on this trip not only to test

my tent, but to learn more of the native arts of the
Eskimo, knowing that I, on my Polar trip, must, if I
would be successful, adapt myself to just such methods
of living.

This was my first winter experience of camping out
in the night season for this year, and, with only a diet of
meal and bacon, I was miserably cold. I was now testing also for the first time the new winter clothing with
which I and all my companions were dressed. Our
shirts were made of bird skins. Over these were coats
of blue fox or caribou skins; our trousers were of bear,
our boots of seal, and our stockings of hare skins. This
was the usual native winter costume, but under it I had
added a suit of underwear.

Retiring again for rest, I left instructions to be
called for an early start. It seemed that I had hardly
settled comfortably in my sleeping bag when the call for
action came.

We hastily partook of tea and biscuits, harnessed
our teams and started through the dark. The Eskimos,
having eaten their fill of fat and frozen meat, to which I
must yet accustom myself, were thoroughly comfortable.
I was miserably cold.

By running behind my sledge I produced sufficient
bodily heat after awhile to feel comfortable. My face
suffered severely from the cutting slant of the winds.
We passed the perpendicular walls of Cape Seiper at
dawn. We ran along the long, straight coast into Ban-
croft Bay during the six hours of twilight. The journey
was continued to Dallas Bay by a forced march of fifty
miles before we halted.

The scene displayed the rare glory of twilight

charms as it had the day before, but the snow was deeper, the temperature lower. The wind steadily increased and veered northward. We made several efforts to cross the bay ice, but cracked ice, huge uplifted blocks and deep snows compelled a retreat to the ice-foot.

The ice-foot along Smith Sound is a superb highway, where otherwise sledge travel would be quite impossible along the coast.

Along Dallas Bay we found a great deal of grass-covered land in undulating valleys and on low hills, which offered grazing for caribou and hare. The preceding glimmer of the new moon, which was to rise a few days hence, offered sufficient light to search for game.

We now fed our dogs for the first time since leaving Annoatok. After a liberal drink of snow water, we started to seek our luck in the chase. In the course of an hour my companions returned with four hares which, when dressed, weighed about forty-eight pounds. Two of these were cached. The others were eaten later.

Before dawn of the day-long twilight the wind increased to a full gale. The sky to the north, smoky all night, now blackened as with soot. The wind came with a howl that brought to mind the despairing cries of the dying explorers whose bleached bones were strewn along the shore. The gloomy outline of the coast remained visible for awhile; but soon the air thickened and came weighted with snow that piled up in huge drifts.

The Eskimos took a few of their favorite dogs and sought shelter to the lee of the tent, where drift covered their blankets with snow. Breathing holes were kept open over their faces. Buried in snow drifts, they were imprisoned for twenty-eight hours. But this tent sled sheltered Koo-loo-ting-wah and myself. When the rush of the storm had abated we began digging our way out. In this effort we dug up men and dogs like potatoes from a patch. The northern sky had paled, the south was brightening. The pack was lined with long lines beyond each hummock; the snow was covered with a strong crust. But the ice-foot was a hopeless line of drifts which made travel over it quite impossible.

The work of pounding snow from the dogs and freeing the sledges brought to our faces beads of perspiration which rolled off and froze in lines of ice on our furs. We were none the worse as a result of the storm, and although hungry as wolves, time was too precious to stop for a full meal.

We now pushed out of the bay, on to the sea ice. At this point the dogs scented a bear and soon crossed its track. Rested and hungry, they were in condition for a desperate chase. Their sharp noses pointed keenly into the huge bear foot-prints, their little ears quivered, while, with howls, they started onward in a mad rush.

Neither our voices nor the whips made an impression on their wild speed. We crossed banks and ridges of snow and swirled about slopes of ice, gripping sledges violently. Now we were thrown to one side, again to the other, dragging resistlessly beside the sleds. Rising, we gripped the rear upstanders with fierce determination.

Just how we escaped broken limbs, and our sledges utter destruction, is a mystery to me. After a run of an hour we sighted the bear. The animal had evidently sighted us, for he was galloping for the open water toward the northwest. We cut the fleetest dogs loose from each team. Freed, they rushed over the snow like race-horses. But the bear had an advantage. As the first dog nipped his haunches he plunged into the black waters. We advanced and waited for him to rise. But this bruin had sense enough to emerge on the opposite shore, where he shook off the freezing waters vigorously, and then sat down as if to have a laugh at us.

I knew that to plunge into the waters would have been fatal to dog or man and equally fatal to a boat, as ice, in the intense cold, would form about it so rapidly that it could not be propelled.

The dogs sat down and howled a chorus of sad dis-appointment. For miles about, the men sought fruit-lessly for a way to cross. Outwitted, we returned to continue our journey Northward.

Advance Bay and its islands were in sight. Among these, we aimed to place our central camp. The light was fading fast, and a cold wind came from Humboldt Glacier, which at this time was located by a slight dark-ening of the sky. Many grounded icebergs were about, and the sea ice was much crossed. The hummocks and the snow were not as troublesome as farther south.

Two ravens followed us, their shrill cries echoing from berg to berg. The Eskimos inferred from their presence that bears were near, but we saw no tracks.

The cries of the ravens were nearly as provoking to the dogs as the bear tracks, and we moved along rapidly to Brook's Island. This was rather high, with a plateau and sharp cliffs. Bonsall Island near by was

rounded by glacial action. Between them we found a
place to camp somewhat sheltered from the wind.

While eating our ration of corn meal and bacon,
howls of the dogs rose to a fierce crescendo. I supposed
they were saluting the coming of the moon, as is their
custom, but the howls changed to tones of increasing
excitement. We went out to inquire, but saw nothing.
It was so dark that I could not see the dogs twenty feet
away, and the cold wind made breathing difficult.

"Nan nook" (Bear), the Eskimos said in an undertone. I looked around for some position of defense.
But the dense night-blackness rendered this hopeless, so
we took our position behind the tent, rifles in hand. The
bear, of an inquisitive turn of mind, deliberately advanced upon us. *"Taokoo! taokoo! igloo dia oo-ah-
tonie!"* (Look! look! beyond the iceberg!) said the
Eskimos. Neither the iceberg nor the bear was visible.
After a cold and exciting wait, the bear turned and hid
behind another iceberg. We separated a few of the
best bear dogs from each other. Bounding off, they
disappeared quietly in the darkness. The other dogs
were fastened to the sledges, and away we started.

I sat on To-ti-o's sledge, as he had the largest team.
We jumped crevasses, and occasionally dipped in open
water.

The track of the bear wound about huge bergs
which looked in the darkness like nebulous shadows.
The dogs, of themselves, followed the invisible line of
tracks.

Soon the wolfish dogs ahead began to shout the
chorus of their battle. We left the track in an air-line
course for the dark mystery out of which the noise came.

To-ti-o took the lead. As we neared the noise, all but two dogs of his sledge were cut loose. The sledge overturned, I under it. As Koo-loo-ting-wah came along, he freed all his dogs. I passed him my new take-down Winchester.

Hurrying after To-ti-o, he had advanced only a few steps when To-ti-o fired. Koo-loo-ting-wah, noting an effort of the bear to rise, fired the new rifle.

A flash of fire lit the darkness. Koo-loo-ting-wah rushed to me, asking for the folding lantern. The smokeless powder had broken the new gun. To-ti-o had no more cartridges. The bear, however, was quiet. We advanced, lances in hand.

The dogs danced wildly about the bear, but he managed to throw out his feet with sufficient force to keep the canine fangs disengaged. The other Eskimos now came, with rushing dogs in advance. To-ti-o dashed forward and delivered the lance under the bear's shoulder. The bear was his. He thereby not only gained the prize for the expedition, but, by the addition of the bear to his game list, completed his retinue of accomplishments whereby he could claim the full privileges of manhood.

Among other things, it gave him the right to marry. He had already secured a bride of twelve, but, without this bear conquest, the match would not have been permanent. He danced with the romantic joy of a young lover. We drove the dogs off from the victim with lashes, and fell to and skinned and dressed the carcass. A taste was given to each dog. The balance was placed on the sledges. Soon we were to camp, waiting for the sled loads of bear meat.

THE HELPERS—NORTHERNMOST MAN AND HIS WIFE

A MECCA OF MUSK OX ALONG EUREKA SOUND
A NATIVE HELPER
AH-WE-LAH'S PROSPECTIVE WIFE

On the day following we started to hunt caribou. The sky was beautifully clear; the glacial wind was lost as we left the ice. The party scattered among numerous old bergs of the glacier. Koo-loo-ting-wah accompanied me. We aimed to rise to a small tableland from which I might make a study of the surroundings.

We had not gone inland more than a mile when we saw numerous fresh caribou tracks. Following these, we moved along a steep slope to the tableland above at an altitude of about one thousand feet. We peeped over the crest. Below us were two reindeer digging under the snow for food. The light was good, and they were in gun range. An Eskimo, however, gets very near his game before he chances a shot, so, winding about under the crest of a cliff or a snow-covered shelf of rocks, we got to their range and fired.

The creatures fell. They were nearly white, young, and possessed long fur and thick skins, which we needed badly for sleeping bags. With pocket knives, the natives skinned the animals and divided the meat in three packs while I examined the surroundings.

Part of the face of Humboldt Glacier, which extends sixty miles north, was clearly visible in cliffs of a dark blue color. The interior ice ran in waves like the surface of stormy seas, perfectly free of snow, with many crevasses. An odd purplish-blue light upon it was reflected to the skies, resembling to some extent a water sky. The snow of the sea ice below was of a delicate lilac. Otherwise, sky and land were flooded with the usual dominant purple of the Arctic twilight.

This glacier, the largest in Arctic America, had at one time extended very much farther south. All the

islands, including Brook's, had at one time been under
its grinding influence. As a picture it was a charming
study in purple and blue, but the temperature was too
low and the light too nearly spent to venture a further
investigation.

The Eskimos fixed for me an extremely light pack.
This was comfortably placed on my back, with a bundle
of thongs over the forehead. The natives took their
huge bundles, and, together, we started for camp. At
every rest we cut off slices of caribou tallow. I was surprised to find that I had acquired a taste for a new
delicacy. At camp we found the natives, all in good
humor, awaiting us beside heaps of meat and skins. All
had been successful in securing from one to two animals
each in regions nearer by. In a further search they
had failed to find promising tracks, so we proposed to
return on the morrow, hoping to meet bears en route.

With the stupor of the gluttony of reindeer meat
and the fatigue of the long chase, we slept late. Awak-
ing, we partook each of a cup of tea, and packed and
loaded the meat. Drawing heavy loads, the dogs gladly
leaped forward. The twilight flush already suffused
the sky with incandescence. Against the southeastern
sky, glowing with rose, the great glaciers of Humboldt
loomed in walls of violet, while the sea displayed many
shades of rose and lilac, according to the direction of the
light on the slope of the drifts.

Knowing that their noses pointed to a land of walrus, the dogs kept up a lively pace. Not a breath of
air was stirring. The temperature was —42°. Aiming
to make Annoatok in two marches, we ran behind the
sledges to save dog energy as much as possible. The

cold enforced vigorous exercise. But, weighted down by furs, the comfort of the sledges was often sought to escape the tortures of perspiration. The source of light slowly shifted along shadowed mountains under the frozen sea. Our path glowed with electric, multi-colored splendor.

By degrees, the rose-colored sky assumed the hue of old gold, the violet embroideries of clouds changed to purple. The gold, in running bands, darkened; the purple thickened. Soon new celestial torches lighted the changing sheen of the snows. Into the dome of heaven swam stars of burning intensity, each of which rivalled the sun in a miniature way. In this new illumination the twilight fires lost flame and color. Cold white incandescence electrically suffused the frigid sky.

I strode onward, in that white, blazing air, the joy and beauty of it enthralling my soul. I felt as though I were walking in a world of heatless fire, a half super-natural realm such as that wherein reigned the gods of ancient peoples. I felt as an old Norseman must have felt when the glory of Valhalla burst upon him. For a long time I was unconscious of the fatigue which was growing upon me. Finally, overcome by the long forced march, I sank on my sled. The Eskimos, chant-ing songs, loomed ahead, their forms magnified in the unearthly light. Slowly a subtle change appeared along the horizon. Silent and impressed, I watched the chang-ing scenes and evolving lights as if all were some divine and awe-inspiring stage arranged by God for some heroic drama of man.

New and warm with shimmering veils of color, at-tended by four radiant satellites, the golden face of the moon rose majestically over the sparkling pinnacles of the Greenland glaciers. Below, the lovely planet-deflected images formed rainbow curves like rubied necklaces about her invisible neck. As the moon ascended in a spiral course the rose hues paled, the white light from the stars softened to a rich, creamy glow.

We continued our course, the Eskimos singing, the dogs occasionally barking. Hours passed. Then we all suddenly became silent. The last, the supreme, glory of the North flamed over earth and frozen sea. The divine fingers of the aurora,* that unseen and intangible thing of flame, who comes from her mysterious throne to smile upon a benighted world, began to touch the sky with glittering, quivering lines of glowing silver. With skeins of running, liquid fire she wove over the sky a shimmering panorama of blazing beauty. Forms of fire, indistinct and unhuman, took shape and vanished. From horizon to zenith, cascades of milk-colored fire ascended and fell, as must the magical fountains of heaven.

In the glory of this other-world light I felt the in-

_____

*Auroras in the Arctic are best seen in more southern latitudes. The display here described was the brightest observed on this trip. Not more than three or four others were noted during the following year, but in previous trips I have witnessed some very wonderful color and motion displays.

The best illustrations of this remarkable color of aurora and night come from the brush of Mr. Frank Wilbert Stokes. These were reproduced in the *Century Magazine* of February, 1903. After their appearance, Mr. Peary accorded to Mr. Stokes (a member of his expedition) the same sort of treatment as he had accorded Astrup—the same as that shown to others. In a letter to the late Richard Watson Gilder, editor of the *Century*, he denounced and did his utmost to discredit Mr. Stokes by insisting that no such remarkable colors are displayed by the aurora borealis. Mr. Gilder replied, in defense of Mr. Stokes, by quoting from Peary's own book, "Northward," Vol. II, pages 194, 195, 198 and 199, descriptions of even more remarkable color effects.

significance of self, a human unit; and, withal I became more intensely conscious than ever of the transfiguring influence of the sublime ideal to which I had set myself.   I exulted in the thrill of an indomitable determination, that determination of human beings to essay great things—that human purpose which, throughout history, has resulted in the great deeds, the great art, of the world, and which lifts men above themselves.   Spiritually intoxicated, I rode onward.   The aurora faded. But its glow remained in my soul.

We arrived at camp late on November 1.

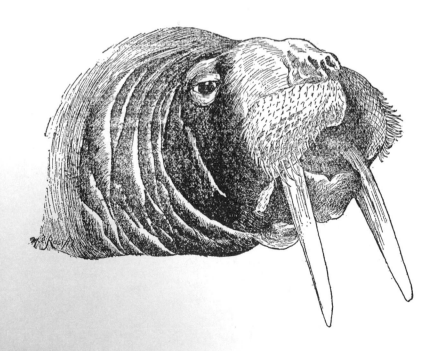

THE MOONLIGHT QUEST OF THE WALRUS

DESPERATE AND DANGEROUS HUNTING, IN ORDER TO
SECURE ADEQUATE SUPPLIES FOR THE POLAR DASH—
A THRILLING AND ADVENTUROUS RACE IS MADE OVER
FROZEN SEAS AND ICY MOUNTAINS TO THE WALRUS
GROUNDS—TERRIFIC EXPLOSION OF THE ICE ON
WHICH THE PARTY HUNTS—SUCCESS IN SECURING
OVER SEVEN SLED-LOADS OF BLUBBER MAKES THE
POLE SEEM NEARER—AN ARCTIC TRAGEDY

VIII

FIVE HUNDRED MILES THROUGH NIGHT AND STORM

The early days of November were devoted to routine work about Annoatok. Meat was gathered and dried in strips by Francke; a full force of men were put to the work of devising equipment; the women were making clothing and dressing skins; and then a traveling party was organized to go south to gather an additional harvest of meat and skins and furs. For this purpose we planned to take advantage of the November moon. Thus, in the first week of the month, we were ready for a five-hundred-mile run to the southern villages and to the night-hunting grounds for walrus.

A crack of whips explosively cut the taut, cold air. The raucous, weird and hungry howl of the wolf-dogs

replied: *"Ah-u-oo, Ah-u-oo, Ah-u-oo!"* rolled over
the ice; *"Huk-huk!"* the Eskimos shouted. There was a
sudden tightening of the traces of our seven sledges;
fifty lithe, strong bodies leaped forward; and, holding
the upstanders, the rear upright framework of the native
sledges, I and my six companions were off. In a few
moments the igloos of the village, with lights shining
through windows where animal membranes served as
glass, had sped by us. The cheering of the natives behind was soon lost in the grind of our sledges on the irregular ice and the joyous, unrestrained barking of the
leaping, tearing, restless dog-teams.

To the south of us, a misty orange flush suffused
the dun-colored sky. The sun, which we had not seen
for an entire month, now late in November far below
the horizon, sent to us the dim radiance of a far-away
smile. After its setting it had, about noon time of each
day, set the sky faintly aglow, this radiance decreasing
until it was lost in the brightness of the midday moon.
Rising above the horizon, a suspended lamp of frosty,
pearl-colored glass, the moon for ten days of twenty-
four hours, each month, encircled about us, now lost
behind ice-sheeted mountains, again subdued under
colored films of frost clouds, but always relieving the
night of its gloom, and permitting, when the wind was
not too turbulent, outside activity.

A wonderful animal is the sea-horse, or whale-
horse, as the Icelanders and Dutch (from whom we have
borrowed "walrus") call it. In the summer its life is
easy and its time is spent in almost perpetual sunny
dreams, but in winter it would be difficult to conceive
of a harder existence than its own. Finding food in

shallow Polar seas, it comes to permanent open water, or to the crevasses of an active pack for breath. With but a few minutes' rest on a storm-swept surface, it explores, without other relief for weeks, the double-night darkness of unknown depths under the frozen sea. At last, when no longer able to move its huge web feet, it rises on the ice or seeks ice-locked waters for a needed rest. In winter, the thump of its ponderous head keeps the young ice from closing its breathing place. If on ice, its thick skin, its blanket of blubber, and an automatic shiver, keep its blood from hardening. This is man's opportunity to secure meat and fuel, but the quest involves a task to which no unaided paleface is equal. The night hunt of the walrus is Eskimo sport, but it is nevertheless sport of a most engaging and exciting order.

So that I might not be compelled to start on my dash stintedly equipped, we now prepared for such an adventure by moonlight. Before this time there had not been sufficient atmospheric stability and ice continuity to promise comparative safety. My heart exulted as I heard the crack of the whips in the electric air and felt the earth rush giddily under my feet as I leaped behind the speeding teams. The fever of the quest was in my veins; its very danger lent an indescribable thrill, for success now meant more to me than perhaps hunting had ever meant to any man.

Not long after we started, darkness descended. The moon slowly passed behind an impenetrable curtain of inky clouds; the orange glow of the sun faded; and we were surrounded on every side by a blackness so thick that it was almost palpable.

As I now recall that mad race I marvel how we

escaped smashing sledges, breaking our limbs, crushing our heads. We tumbled and jumped in a frantic race over the broken, irregular pack-ice from Annoatok to Cape Alexander, a distance of thirty miles as the raven moves, but more than forty miles as we follow the sledge trail. Here the ice became thin; we felt cold mist rising from open water; and now and then, in an occasional breaking of the darkness, we could discern vast sheets or snaky leads of open sea ahead of us.

To reach the southern waters where the walrus were to be found, we now had to seek an overland route, which would take us over the frozen Greenland mountains and lead us through the murky clouds, a route of twisting detours, gashed glaciers, upturned barriers of rock and ice, swept by blinding winds, unmarked by any trail, and which writhed painfully beyond us for forty-seven miles.

Arriving at the limit of traversable sea-ice, we now paused before sloping cliffs of glacial land-ice which we had to climb. Picture to yourself a vast glacier rising precipitously, like a gigantic wall, thousands of feet above you, and creeping tortuously up its glassy, purple face, if such that surface could be called, formed by the piling of one glacial formation upon the other in the descent through the valleys, a twisting, retreating road of jagged ice strata, of earth and stone, blocked here and there by apparently impassable impediments, pausing at almost unscalable, frozen cliffs, and at times no wider than a few yards. Imagine yourself pausing, as we suddenly did, and viewing the perilous ascent, the only way open to us, revealed in the passing glimmer of the pale, circling moon, despair, fear and hope tugging at your heart. Whipped across the sky by the lashing winds, the torn clouds, passing the face of the moon, cast magnified and grotesquely gesticulating shadows on the glistening face of the icy Gibraltar before us. Some of these misty shapes seemed to threaten, others shook their rag-like arms, beckoning forward. Upon the face of the towering, perpendicular ice-wall, great hummocks like the gnarled black limbs of a huge tree twisted upwards.

I realized that the frightful ascent must be made. The goal of my single aim suddenly robbed the climb of its terrors. I dropped my whip. Six other whips cracked through the air. Koo-loo-ting-wah said, *"Kah-Kah!"* (Come, come!) But Sotia said, *"Iodaria-Iodaria!"* (Impossible, impossible!) The dogs emitted shrill howls. Holding the rear upstanders of the sledges, we helped to push them forward.

Before us, the fifty dogs climbed like cats through narrow apertures of the ice, or took long leaps over the serried battlements that barred our way. We stumbled after, sometimes we fell. Again we had to lift the sledges after the dogs.

From the top of the glacier a furious wind brushed us backwards. We felt the steaming breath of the laboring dogs in our faces. My heart thumped painfully. Now and then the moon disappeared; we followed the unfailing instinct of the animals. I realized that a misstep might plunge me to a horrible death in the ice abysm below. With a howl of joy from drivers, the dogs finally leaped to the naked surface of the wind-swept glacier. Panting in indescribable relief, we followed. But the worst part of the journey lay before us. The sable clouds, like the curtain of some cyclopean stage, seemed suddenly drawn aside as if by an invisible hand.

Upon the illimitable stretch of ice rising before us like the slopes of a glass mountain, the full rays of the moon poured liquid silver. Only in dreams had such a scene as this been revealed to me—in dreams of the enchanted North—which did not now equal reality. The spectacle filled me with both awed delight and a sense of terror.

Beyond the fan-shaped teams of dogs the eyes ran over fields of night-blackened blue, gashed and broken by bottomless canyons which twisted like purple serpents in every direction. Vast expanses of smooth surface, polished by the constant winds, reflected the glow of the moon and gleamed like isles of silver in a motionless, deep, sapphire sea; but all was covered with the air of night. In the moonlight, the jagged irregular contours of the broken ice became touched with a burning gilt. A constant effect like running quicksilver played about us as the moon sailed around the heavens.

Above us the ice pinnacles were lost in the clouds, huge billowy masses that were blown in the wind troublously, like the heavy black tresses of some Titan woman. I thrilled with the beauty of the magical spectacle, yet, when I viewed the perilous pathway, I felt the grip of terror again at my heart.

I was aroused from my brief reverie by the familiar "*Huk-huk! Ah-gah! Ah-gah!*" of the Eskimos, and placing our hands upon the sledges, we leaped forward into the purple-gashed sea, with its blinding sheets of silver. I seemed carried through a world such as the old Norsemen sang of in the sagas.

Of a sudden, as though extinguished, the moonlight faded, huge shadows leaped onto the ice before us, frenziedly waved their arms and melted into the pitch-black darkness which descended. I had read imaginative tales of wanderings in the nether region of the dead, but only now did I have a faint glimmering of the terror (with its certain, exultant intoxication) which lost souls must feel when they wander in a darkness beset with invisible horrors.

Over the ice, cut with innumerable chasms and neck-breaking irregularities, we rushed in the dark. The wind moaned down from the despairing cloud-enfolded heights above; it tore through the bottomless gullies on every side with a hungry roar. Beads of perspiration rolled down my face and froze into icicles on my chin and furs. The temperature was 48° below zero.

Occasionally we stopped a moment to gasp for breath. I could hear the panting of my companions, the labor of the dogs. A few seconds' inaction was followed by convulsive shivering; the pain of stopping was more excruciating than that of climbing. In the darkness, the calls of the invisible Eskimos to the dogs seemed like the weird appeals of disembodied things. I felt each moment the imminent danger of a frightful death; yet the dogs with their marvelous intuition, twisting this way and that, and sometimes retreating, sensed the open leads ahead and rushed forward safely.

At times I felt the yawning depth of ice canyons immediately by my side—that a step might plunge me into the depths. Desperately I held on to the sledges, and was dragged along. Such an experience might well turn the hair of the most expert Alpinist white in one night; yet I did not have time to dwell fully upon the dangers, and I was carried over a trip more perilous than, later, proved the actual journey on sea-ice to the Pole.

Occasionally the moon peered forth from its clouds and brightened the gloom. In its light the ice fields swam dizzily by us, as a landscape seen from the window of a train; the open gashed gullies writhed like snakes, pinnacles dancing like silver spears. By alternate running and riding we managed to keep from freezing and sweating. We finally reached an altitude of inland ice exceeding two thousand feet. Silver fog crept under our feet. We were traveling now in a world of clouds.

We paced twelve miles at a rapid speed. In the light of the moon-burned clouds which rolled about our heads, I could see the forms of my companions only indistinctly. The dogs ahead were veiled in the argent, tremulous mists; the ice sped under me; I was no longer conscious of an earthly footing; I might have been soaring in space.

We began to descend. Suddenly the dogs started in leaps to fly through the air. Our sleds were jerked into clouds of cutting snow. We jabbed our feet into the drift to check the mad speed. On each side we saw a huge mountain, seemingly thousands of feet above us, but ahead was nothing but the void of empty space. Soon the sledges shot beyond the dogs. We threw ourselves off to check the momentum. With dog intelligence and savage strength judiciously expended, we reached the sea level by flying flights over dangerous slopes, and, like cats, we landed on nimble feet in Sontag Bay.

A bivouac was arranged under a dome of snow-blocks, and exhausted by the mad journey, a sleep of twenty-four hours was indulged in.

Now, for a time, our task was easier. A course was set along the land, southward. Each of the native settlements was visited. The season's gossip was exchanged. Presents went into each household, and a return of furs and useful products filled our sledges. Thus the time was occupied in profitable visits during the feeble light of the November moon. With the December moon we returned northward to Ser-wah-ding-wah.

Then our struggle began anew for the walrus grounds. The Polar drift, forcing through Smith Sound, left an open space of water about ten miles south of Cape Alexander. This disturbed area was our destination. It was marked by a dark cloud, a "water-sky"—against the pearly glow of the southern heavens. The ice surface was smooth. We did not encounter the crushed heaps of ice of the northern route, but there were frequent crevasses which, though cemented with new ice, gave us considerable anxiety, for I realized that if a northwesterly storm should suddenly strike the pack we might be carried helplessly adrift.

The urgency of our mission to secure dog food, however, left no alternative. It was better to brave death now, I thought, than to perish from scant supplies on the Polar trip. We had not gone far before the ever-keen canine noses detected bear tracks on the ice. These we shot over the pack surface in true battle spirit. As the bears were evidently bound for the same hunting grounds, this course was accepted as good enough for us. Although the trail was laid in a circuitous route, it avoided the most difficult pressure angles. We traveled until late in the day. The moon was low, and the dark purple hue of the night blackened the snows.

Of a sudden we paused. From a distance came a low call of walrus bulls. The bass, nasal bellow was muffled by the low temperature, and did not thump the ear drums with the force of the cry in sunny summer. My six companions shouted with glee, and became almost hysterical with excitement. The dogs, hearing the call, howled and jumped to jerk the sledges. We dropped our whips, and they responded with all their brute force in one bound. It was difficult to hold to the sledges as we shot over the blackening snows.

The ice-fields became smaller as we advanced; dangerous thin ice intervened; but the owl-eyes of the Eskimos knew just where to find safe ice. The sounds increased as we approached. We descended from the snow-covered ice to thin, black ice and for a time I felt as if we were flying over the open surface of the deep. With a low call, the dogs were stopped. They were detached from the sledges and tied to holes drilled with a knife in ice boulders.

Pushing the sledges upon which rested the harpoon, the lance, the gun and knives, each one of us advanced at some distance from his neighbor. Soon, lines of mist told of dangerous breaks, and the ice was

carefully tested with the spiked shaft before venturing farther. I was behind Koo-loo-ting-wah's sledge.
While he was creeping up to the water's edge, there
came the rush of a spouting breath so near that we
seemed to feel the crystal spray. I took his place and
pushed the sledge along.

Taking the harpoon, with stealthy strides Koo-loo-
ting-wah moved to the water's edge and waited for the
next spout. We heard other spouts in various directions, and in the dark water, slightly lighted by the
declining moon, we saw other dark spots of spray.
Suddenly a burst of steam startled me. It was near
the ice where Koo-loo-ting-wah lay. I was about to
shout, but the Eskimo turned, held up his hand and
whispered *"Ouit-ou."* (Wait.)

Then, very slowly, he lowered his body, spread out
his form on the ice, and startlingly imitated the walrus call. His voice preternaturally bellowed through
the night. Out of the inky water, a walrus lifted its
head. I saw its long, white, spiral, ivory tusk and two
phosphorescent eyes. Koo-loo-ting-wah did not stir.
I shivered with cold and impatience. Why did he not
strike? Our prey seemed within our hands. I uttered
an exclamation of vexed disappointment when, with a
splash, the head disappeared, leaving on the water a
line of algae fire.

For several minutes I stood gazing seaward. Far
away on the black ocean, to my amazement, I saw
lights appearing like distant lighthouse signals, or the
mast lanterns on passing ships. They flashed and
suddenly faded, these strange will-o'-the wisps of the
Arctic sea. In a moment I realized that the lights were

caused by distant icebergs crashing against one another. On the bergs as on the surface of the sea, as it happened now, were coatings of a teeming germ life, the same which causes phosphorescence in the trail of an ocean ship. The effect was indescribably weird.

Suddenly I jumped backward, appalled by a noise that reverberated shudderingly under the ice on which I stood. The ice shook as if with an earthquake. I hastily retreated, but Koo-loo-ting-wah, lying by the water's edge, never stirred. A dead man could not have been less responsive. While I was wondering as to the cause of the upheaval, the ice, within a few feet of Koo-loo-ting-wah, was suddenly torn asunder as if by a submarine explosion. Koo-loo-ting-wah leaped into the air and descended apparently toward the distending space of turbulent open water. I saw him raise his arm and deliver a harpoon with amazing dexterity; at the same instant I had seen also the white tusk and phosphorescent eyes of a walrus appear for a moment in the black water and then sink.

The harpoon had gone home; the line was run out; a spiked lance shaft was driven into the ice through a loop in the end of the line, and the line was thus fastened. We knew the wounded beast would have to rise for air. With rifle and lance ready, we waited, intending, each time a spout of water arose, to drive holes into the tough armor of skin until the beast's vitals were tapped. By feeling the line, I could sense the struggles of the wild creature below in the depths of the sea. Then the line would slacken, a spout of steam would rise from the water, Koo-loo-ting-wah would drive a spear, I a shot from my gun. The air would become oppressive with the creature's frightful bellowing. Then would come an interval of silence.

For about two hours we kept up the battle. Then the line slackened, Koo-loo-ting-wah called the others, and together we drew the huge carcass, steaming with blood, to the surface of the ice. Smelling the odorous wet blood, the dogs exultantly howled.

Falling upon the animal, the natives, trained in the art, with sharp knives had soon dressed the thick meat and blubber from the bones and lashed the weltering mass on a sledge. This done, with quick despatch, they separated, dashed along the edge of the ice, casting harpoons whenever the small geysers appeared on the water. We were in excellent luck. One walrus after another was dragged lumberingly on the ice, and in the course of several hours the seven sledges were heavily loaded with the precious supplies which would now enable me, liberally equipped, to start Poleward. We gave our dogs a light meal, and started landward, leaving great piles of walrus meat behind us on the ice.

Although we were tired on reaching land, we began to build several snow-houses in which to sleep. Not far away was an Eskimo village. Summoning the natives to help us bring in the spoils of the hunt which had been left on the ice, we first indulged in a gluttonous feast of uncooked meat, in which the dogs ravenously joined. The meat tasted like train-oil. The work of bringing in the meat and blubber and caching it for subsequent gathering was hardly finished when, from the ominous, glacial-covered highlands, a winter blast suddenly began to come with terrific and increasing fury.

Blinding gusts of snow whipped the frozen earth.

The wind shrieked fiendishly. Above its roar, not three hours after our last trip on the ice, a resounding, crashing noise rose above the storm. Braving the blasts, I went outside the igloo. Through the darkness I could see white curvatures of piling sea-ice. I could hear the rush and crashing of huge floes and glaciers being carried seaward. Had we waited another day, had we been out on the ice seeking walrus just twenty-four hours after our successful hunt, we should have been carried away in the sudden roaring gale, and hopelessly perished in the wind-swept deep.

During the night, or hours usually allotted to rest, the noise continued unabated. I failed to sleep. Now and then, a crashing noise shivered through the storm. An igloo from the nearby settlement was swept into the sea. During the gale many of the natives who had retired with their clothes hung out to dry, awoke to find that the wind had robbed them of their valuable winter furs.

Some time along in the course of the night, I heard outside excited Eskimos shouting. There was terror in the voices. Arising and dressing hastily, I rushed into the teeth of the storm. Not far away were a number of natives rushing along the land some twenty feet beneath which the sea lapped the land-ice with furious tongues. They had cast lines into the sea and were shouting, it seemed, to someone who was struggling in the hopeless, frigid tumult of water.

I soon learned of the dreadful catastrophe. Ky-un-a, an old and cautious native, awakened by the storm a brief while before, after dressing himself, ventured outside his stone house to secure articles which he had

left there. As was learned later, he had just tied his
sledge to a rock when a gust of wind resistlessly rushed
seaward, lifted the aged man from his feet, and dropped
him into the sea. Through the storm, his dreadful
cries attracted his companions. Some who were now
tugging at the lines, were barely covered with fur rugs
which they had thrown about them, and their limbs
were partly bare. Now and then, a blinding gust of
wind, filled with freezing snow crystals, almost lifted
us from our feet. The sea lapped its tongues sicken-
ingly below us.

Finally a limp body, ice-sheeted, dripping with
water, yet clinging with its mummied frozen hands to
the line, was hauled up on the ice. Ky-un-a, unconscious, was carried to his house about five hundred feet
away. There, after wrapping him in furs, in a brave
effort to save his life, the natives cut open his fur garments. The fur, frozen solid by the frigid blasts in the
brief period which had elapsed since his being lifted from
the water, took with it, in parting from his body, long
patches of skin, leaving the quivering raw flesh exposed
as though by a burn. For three days the aged man lay
dying, suffering excruciating tortures, the victim of
merely a common accident, which at any time may happen to anyone of these Spartan people. I shall never
forget the harrowing moans of the suffering man piercing the storm. Perhaps it had been merciful to let him
perish in the sea.

Ky-un-a's old home was some forty miles distant.
To it, that he might die there, he desired to go. On the
fourth day after the accident, he was placed in a litter,
covered with warm furs, and borne over the smooth ice-

fields. I shall never forget that dismal and solemn
procession. A benign calm prevailed over land and sea.
The orange glow of a luxurious moon set the ice coldly
aflame. Long shadows, like spectral mourners, robed
in purple, loomed before the tiny procession. Now and
then, as they dwindled in the distance, I saw them, like
black dots, crossing areas of polished ice which glowed
like mirror lakes of silver. From the distance, softly
shuddered the decreasing moans of the dying man; then
there was silence. I marvelled again upon the lure of
this eerily, weirdly beautiful land, where, always imminent, death can be so terrible.

MIDNIGHT AND MID-WINTER

THE EQUIPMENT AND ITS PROBLEMS—NEW ART IN THE
MAKING OF SLEDGES COMBINING LIGHTNESS—PROG-
RESS OF THE PREPARATIONS—CHRISTMAS, WITH ITS
GLAD TIDINGS AND AUGURIES FOR SUCCESS IN QUEST
OF THE POLE

IX

THE COMING OF THE ESKIMO STORK

In planning for the Polar dash I appreciated fully
the vital importance of sledges. These, I realized,
must possess, to an ultimate degree, the combined
strength of steel with the lightness and elasticity of
the strongest wood. The sledge must neither be flimsy
nor bulky; nor should it be heavy or rigid. After a
careful study of the art of sledge-traveling from the
earliest time to the present day, after years of sledging
and sledge observation in Greenland, the Antarctic and
Alaska, I came to the conclusion that success was dependent, not upon any one type of sledge, but upon
local fitness.

All natives of the frigid wilds have devised sledges,
traveling and camp equipment to fit their local needs.
The collective lessons of ages are to be read in this development of primitive sledge traveling. If these wild
people had been provided with the best material from

which to work out their hard problems of life, then it is probable that their methods could not be improved. But neither the Indian nor the Eskimo was ever in possession of either the tools or the raw material to fit their inventive genius for making the best equipment. Therefore, I had studied first the accumulated results of the sledge of primitive man and from this tried to construct a sledge with its accessories in which were included the advantages of up-to-date mechanics with the use of the most durable material which a search of the entire globe had afforded me.*

The McClintock sledges, made of bent wood with wide runners, had been adopted by nearly all explorers, under different names and with considerable modifications, for fifty years. This sledge is still the best type for deep soft snow conditions, for which it was originally intended. But such snow is not often found on the ice of the Polar sea. The native sledge which Peary copied, although well adapted to local use along the ice-foot and the land-adhering pack, is not the best sledge for a trans-boreal run. This is because it is too heavy and too easily broken, and breakable in such a way that it cannot be quickly repaired.

---

*The so-called "Jesup" sled, which Mr. Peary used on his last Polar trip, is a copy of the Eskimo sledge, a lumbering, unwieldy thing weighing over one hundred pounds and which bears the same relation to a refined bent-hickory vehicle that a lumber cart does to an express wagon. In this "Jesup" sledge there is a dead weight of over fifty pounds of useless wood. The needless weight thus carried can, in a better sledge, be replaced by fifty pounds of food. This fifty pounds will feed one man over the entire route to the Pole. Mr. Peary claims that the Pole is not reachable without this sled, but Borup, in his book, reports that most of the sledges were broken at the first trial.

Since an explorer's success is dependent upon his ability to transport food it behooves him to eliminate useless weight. Therefore, the solid runner sled is as much out of place as a solid wood wheel would be in an automobile.

For the Arctic pack, a sledge must be of a moderate length, with considerable width. Narrow runners offer less friction and generally give sufficient bearing surface. The other qualities vital to quick movement and durability are lightness, elasticity and interchangeability of parts. All of these conditions I planned to meet in a new pattern of sledge which should combine the durability of the Eskimo sledges and the lightness of the Yukon sledge of Alaska.

The making of a suitable sledge caused me a good deal of concern. Before leaving New York I had taken the precaution of selecting an abundance of the best hickory wood in approximately correct sizes for sledge construction. Suitable tools had also been provided. Now, as the long winter with its months of darkness curtailed the time of outside movement, the box-house was refitted as a workshop. From eight to ten men were at the benches, eight hours each day, shaping and bending runners, fitting and lashing interchangeable cross bars and posts, and riveting the iron shoes. Thus the sledge parts were manufactured to possess the same facilities to fit not only all other sledges, but also other parts of the same sledge. If, therefore, part of a sledge should be broken, other parts of a discarded sledge could offer repair sections easily.

The general construction of this new sledge is easily understood from the various photographs presented. All joints were made elastic by seal-thong lashings. The sledges were twelve feet long and thirty inches wide; the runners had a width of an inch and an eighth. Each part and each completed sledge was thoroughly tested before it was finally loaded for the long run. For dog harness, the Greenland Eskimo pattern was adopted. But canine habits are such that when rations are reduced to minimum limits the leather strips disappear as food. To obviate this disaster, the shoulder straps were made of folds of strong canvas, while the traces were cut from cotton log line.

A boat is an important adjunct to every sledge expedition which hopes to venture far from its base of operations. It is a matter of necessity, even when following a coast line, as was shown by the mishap of Mylius Erickson, for if he had had a boat he would himself have returned to tell the story of the Danish Expedition to East Greenland.

Need for a boat comes with the changing conditions of the advancing season. Things must be carried for several months for a chance use in the last stages of the return. But since food supplies are necessarily limited, delay is fatal, and therefore, when open water prevents advance, a boat is so vitally necessary as to become a life preserver. Foolish indeed is the explorer who pays slight attention to this important problem.

The transportation of a boat, however, offers many serious difficulties. Nansen introduced the kayak, and most explorers since have followed his example. The Eskimo canoe serves the purpose very well, but to carry it for three months without hopeless destruction requires so tremendous an amount of energy as to make the task practically impossible.

Sectional boats, aluminum boats, skin floats and other devices had been tried, but to all there is the same fatal objection on a Polar trip, of impossible transportation. But it seems odd that the ordinary folding canvas boat has not been pressed into this service.

We found such a canoe boat to fit the situation exactly, and selected a twelve-foot Eureka-shaped boat with wooden frame. The slats, spreaders and floor-pieces were utilized as parts of sledges. The canvas cover served as a floor cloth for our sleeping bags. Thus the boat did useful service for a hundred days and never seemed needlessly cumbersome. When the craft was finally spread for use as a boat, in it we carried the sledge, in it we sought game for food, and in it or under it we camped. Without it we could never have returned.

Even more vital than the choice of sledges, more vital than anything else, I knew, in such a trip as I proposed, is the care of the stomach. From the published accounts of Arctic traveling it is impossible to learn a fitting ration, and I hasten to add that I well realized that our own experience may not solve the problem for future expeditions. The gastronomic need differs with every man. It differs with every expedition, and it is radically different with every nation. Thus, when De Gerlache, with good intentions, forced Norwegian food into French stomachs, he learned that there is a nationality in gastronomics. Nor is it safe to listen to scientific advice, for the stomach is arbitrary, and stands as autocrat over every human sense and passion and will not easily yield to dictates.

In this respect, as in others, I was helped very much by the natives. The Eskimo is ever hungry, but his taste is normal. Things of doubtful value in nutrition form no part in his dietary. Animal food, con-

sisting of meat and fat, is entirely satisfactory as a
steady diet without other adjuncts. His food requires
neither salt nor sugar, nor is cooking a matter of necessity.

Quantity is important, but quality applies only
to the relative proportion of fat. With this key to
gastronomics, pemmican was selected as the staple food,
and it would also serve equally well for the dogs.

We had an ample supply of pemmican, which was
made of pounded dried beef, sprinkled with a few
raisins and some currants, and slightly sweetened with
sugar. This mixture was cemented together with
heated beef tallow and run into tin cans containing six
pounds each.

This combination was invented by the American
Indian, and the supply for this expedition was made by
Armour of Chicago after a formula furnished by Captain Evelyn B. Baldwin. Pemmican had been used before as part of the long list of foodstuffs for Arctic expeditions, but with us there was the important difference
that it was to be almost entirely the whole bill of fare
when away from game haunts. The palate surprises
in our store were few.

By the time Christmas approached I had reason
indeed for rejoicing. Although this happy season
meant little to me as a holiday of gift-giving and feast
ing, it came with auguries for success in the thing my
heart most dearly desired, and compared to which earth
had nothing more alluring to give.

Our equipment was now about complete. In the
box house were tiers of new sledges, rows of boxes and
piles of bags filled with clothing, canned supplies,

dried meat, and sets of strong dog harness. The food, fuel and camp equipment for the Polar dash were ready. Everything had been thoroughly tested and put aside for a final examination. Elated by our success, and filled with gratitude to the faithful natives, I declared a week of holidays, with rejoicing and feasting. Feasting was at this time especially desirable, for we had now to fatten up for the anticipated race.

Christmas day in the Arctic does not dawn with the glow which children in waking early to seek their bedecked tree, view outside their windows in more southern lands. Both Christmas day and Christmas night are black. Only the stars keep their endless watch in the cold skies.

Standing outside my igloo on the happy night, I gazed at the Pole Star, the guardian of the goal I sought, and I remembered with a thrill the story of that mysterious star the Wise Men had followed, of the wonders to which it led them, and I felt an awed reverence for the Power that set these unfaltering beacons above the earth and had written in their golden traces, with a burning pen, veiled and unrevealed destinies which men for ages have tried to learn.

I retired to sleep with thoughts of home. I thought of my children, and the bated expectancy with which they were now going to bed, of their hopefulness of the morrow, and the unbounded joy they would have in gifts to which I could not contribute. I think tears that night wet my pillow of furs. But I would give them, if I did not fail, the gift of a father's achievement, of which, with a glow, I felt they should be proud.

The next morning the natives arrived at the box

house early. It had been cleared of seamstresses and workmen the day before, and put in comparatively spick and span order. I had told the natives they were to feed to repletion during the week of holiday, an injunction to the keeping of which they did not need much urging.

Early Christmas morning, men and women began working overtime on the two festive meals which were to begin that day and continue daily.

About this time, the most important duty of our working force had been to uncover caches and dig up piles of frozen meat and blubber. Of this, which possesses the flavor and odor of Limburger cheese, and also the advantage, if such it be, of intoxicating them, the natives are particularly fond. While a woman held a native torch of moss dipped in oils and pierced with a stick, the men, by means of iron bars and picks, dug up boulders of meat just as coal is forced from mines.

A weird spectacle was this, the soft light of the blubber lamp dancing on the spotless snows, the soot-covered faces of the natives grinning while they worked. The blubber was taken close to their igloos and placed on raised platforms of snow, so as to be out of reach of the dogs. Of this meat and blubber, which was served raw, partially thawed, cooked and also frozen, the natives partook during most of their waking hours. They enjoyed it, indeed, as much as turkey was being relished in my far-away home.

Moreover they had, what was an important delicacy, native ice cream. This would not, of course, please the palate of those accustomed to the American delicacy, but to the Eskimo maiden it possesses all the lure of creams, sherberts or ice cream sodas. With us, sugar in the process of digestion turns into fat, and fat into body fuel. The Eskimo, having no sugar, yearns for fat, and it comes with the taste of sweets.

The making of native ice cream is quite a task. I watched the process of making it Christmas day with amused interest. The native women must have a mixture of oils from the seal, walrus and narwhal. Walrus and seal blubber is frozen, cut into strips, and pounded with great force so as to break the fat cells. This mass is now placed in a stone pot and heated to the temperature of the igloo, when the oil slowly separates from the fibrous pork-like mass. Now, tallow from the suet of the reindeer or musk ox is secured, cut into blocks and given by the good housewife to her daughters, who sit in the igloo industriously chewing it until the fat cells are crushed. This masticated mass is placed in a long stone pot over the oil flame, and the tallow reduced from it is run into the fishy oil of the walrus or seal previously prepared.

This forms the body of native ice cream. For flavoring, the housewife has now a variety from which to select. This usually consists of bits of cooked meat, moss flowers and grass. Anticipating the absence of moss and grass in the winter, the natives, during the hunting season, take from the stomachs of reindeer and musk oxen which are shot, masses of partly digested grass which is preserved for winter use. This, which has been frozen, is now chipped in fragments, thawed, and, with bits of cooked meats, is added to the mixed fats. It all forms a paste the color of pistache, with occasional spots like crushed fruit.

The mixture is lowered to the floor of the igloo, which, in winter, is always below the freezing point, and into it is stirred snow water. The churned composite gradually brightens and freezes as it is beaten. When completed, it looks very much like ice cream, but it has the flavor of cod liver oil, with a similar odor. Nevertheless, it has nutritive qualities vastly superior to our ice cream, and stomach pains rarely follow an engorgement.

With much glee, the natives finished their Christmas repast with this so-called delicacy. For myself a tremendous feast was prepared, consisting of food left by the yacht and the choicest meat from the caches. My menu consisted of green turtle soup, dried vegetables, caviar on toast, olives, Alaskan salmon, crystallized potatoes, reindeer steak, buttered rice, French peas, apricots, raisins, corn bread, Huntley and Palmer biscuits, cheese and coffee.

As I sat eating, I thought with much humor of the curious combinations of caviar and reindeer steak, of the absurd contradiction in eating green turtle soup beyond the Arctic circle. I ate heartily, with more gusto than I ever partook of delicious food in the Waldorf Astoria in my far-away home city. After dinner I took a long stroll on snow shoes. As I looked at the star-lamps swung in heaven, I thought of Broadway, with its purple-pale strings of lights, and its laughing merry-makers on this festive evening.

I did not, I confess, feel lonely. I seemed to be getting something so much more wholesome, so much more genuine from the vast expanse of snow and the unhidden heavens which, in New York, are seldom seen.

Returning to the box-house, I ended Christmas evening with Edgar Allen Poe and Shakespeare as companions.

The box-house in which I lived was amply comfortable. It did not possess the luxury of a civilized house, but in the Arctic it was palatial. The interior fittings had changed somewhat from time to time, but now things were arranged in a permanent setting. The little stove was close to the door. The floor measured sixteen feet in length and twelve feet in width. On one side the empty boxes of the wall made a pantry, on the other side were cabinets of tools, and unfinished sledge and camp material.

With a step we rose to the next floor. On each side was a bunk resting on a bench. The bench was used as a bed, a work bench and seat. The long rear bench was utilized as a sewing table for the seamstresses and also for additional seating capacity. In the center was a table arranged around a post which supported the roof. Sliding shelves from the bunks formed table seats. A yacht lamp fixed to the post furnished ample light. There was no other furniture. All of our needs were conveniently placed in the open boxes of the wall.

The closet room therefore was unlimited. In the boxes near the floor, in which things froze hard, the perishable supplies were kept. In the next tier there was alternate freezing and thawing. Here we stored lashings and skins that had to be kept moist. The tiers above, usually warm and dry under the roof, were used for various purposes. There, fresh meat in strips, dried crisp in three days. Taking advantage of this, we had made twelve hundred pounds of dog pemmican from

THE CAPTURE OF A BEAR
ROUNDING UP A HERD OF MUSK OXEN

SVARTEVOEG—CAMPING FIVE HUNDRED MILES FROM THE POLE

walrus meat.   In the gable we placed furs and instruments.

The temperature changed remarkably as the thermometer was lifted.   On the floor in the lower boxes, it fell as low as —20°.   Under the bunks on the floor, it was usually —10°.   The middle floor space was above the freezing point.   At the level of the bunk the temperature was +48°.   At the head, standing, +70°, and under the roof, —105°.

We contrived to keep perfectly comfortable.   Our feet and legs were always dressed for low temperature, while the other portions of our body were lightly clad. There was not the usual accumulation of moisture except in the lower boxes, where it reinforced the foundation of the structure and did no harm.   From the hygienic standpoint, with the material at hand, we could not have improved the arrangement.   The ventilation was by small openings, mostly along the corners, which thus drew heat to remote angles.   The value of the long stove pipe was made evident by the interior accumulation of ice.   If we did not remove the ice every three or four days the draft was closed by atmospheric humidity condensed from the draft drawn through the fire.   From within, the pipe was also a splendid supplementary heater, as it led by a circuitous route about the vestibule before the open air was reached, thus keeping the workshop somewhat warm.   Two Eskimo lamps gave the added heat and light for the sledge builders.

From Christmas Day until New Year's there were daily feasts for the natives.   I luxuriated in a long rest, spending my time taking walks and reading.   I got a sort of pleasure by proxy in watching the delight of these primal people in real food, food which, although to us horribly unpalatable, never gives indigestion. This period was one of real Christmas rejoicing in many snow homes, and the spirit, although these people had never heard of the Christ child, was more truly in keeping with this holiday than it often is in lands where, in ostentatious celebration, the real meaning is lost.

Wandering from igloo to igloo, to extend greetings and thanks for their faithful work, I was often touched by the sounds of thin, plaintive voices in the darkness. Each time a pang touched my heart, and I remembered the time when I first heard my own baby girl's wee voice. The little ones had begun to arrive. The Eskimo stork, at igloo after igloo, was leaving its Christmas gift.

For some time before Christmas, Cla-you, easily our best seamstress, had not come for her assignment of sewing. To her had been given the delicate task of making hare skin stockings; but she had lost interest in needle-work and complained of not feeling well. E-ve-lue (Mrs. Sinue) was completing her task. Ac-po-di-soa (the big bird), Cla-you's husband, whom we called Bismark, had also deserted the bench where he had been making sledges. For his absence there was no explanation, for neither he nor his wife had ever shirked duties before. To solve the mystery I went to his igloo during Christmas week. There I first got news from the stork world. The boreal stork comes at a special season of the year, usually a few weeks after midnight when there is little else to interest the people. This season comes nine months after the days of budding passions in April, the first Arctic month of the year when all the world is happy. In the little underground home, the anticipated days of the stork visit were made interesting by a long line of preparations.

A prospective mother is busy as a bee in a charming effort to make everything new for the coming little one. All things about must be absolutely new if possible. Even a new house must be built. This places the work of preparation quite as much on the father as on the mother. There is in all this a splendid lesson in primitive hygiene.

To examine, first, the general home environment; there is a little girl four years old still taking nature's substitute for the bottle. She looks about for a meaning of all the changes about the home, but does not understand. You enter the new house on hands and knees through an entrance twelve or fifteen feet long, crowding upwards into an ever-open door just large enough to pass the shoulders. You rise into a dungeon oblong in shape. The rear two-thirds of this is raised about fifteen inches and paved with flat-rock. Upon this the furs are spread for a bed. The forward edge forms a seat. The space ahead of this is large enough for three people to stand at once. On each side there is a semi-circular bulge. In these are placed the crescent-shaped stone dishes, in which moss serves as a wick to burn blubber. Over this blubber flame, there is a long stone pot in which snow is melted for water and meats are occasionally cooked. Over this there is a drying rack for boots and furs. There is no other furniture. This house represents the home of the Eskimo family at its best. Do what she will, the best housewife cannot free it of oil and soot. It is not, indeed, a fit place for the immaculate stork to come.

For months, the finest furs have been gathered to prepare a new suit for the mother. Slowly one article of apparel after another has been completed and put aside. The boots, called *kamik,* are of sealskin, bleached to a spotless cream color. They reach halfway up the thigh. The inner boot, called *atesha,* of soft caribou fur, is of the same length; along its upper edge there is a decorative run of white bear fur. The silky fur pads protect the tender skin of limb and foot, for no stockings are used. Above these, there are dainty little pants of white and blue fox, to protect the body to a point under the hips, and for protection above that there is a shirt of birdskins or *aht-tee.* This is the most delicate of all garments. Hundreds of little auk skins are gathered, chewed and prepared, and as the night comes the garment is built blouse-shaped, with hood attached. It fits loosely. There are no buttons or openings. For the little one, the hood is enlarged and extended down the back, as the pocket for its future abode. The coat of fine blue fox skins, or *amoyt,* is of the same shape, but fits loosely over all.

The word *amoyt,* or *amoyt docsoa,* in its application, also covers the entire range of the art and function of pregnancy. This is regarded as an institution of the first order, second only to the art of the chase. All being ready for the mother, for the baby only a hood is provided, while bird-skins and grass are provided to take the place of absorbent cotton. For the first year, the child has absolutely no other wrap or cover but its little hood.

The Eskimo loves children. If the stork does not come in due time, he is likely to change his life partner. For this reason he looks forward to the Christmas season with eager anticipation. Seeking the wilds far and near for needed furs, in bitter winds and driving snows, he endures all kinds of hardships during the night of months for the sake of the expected child. Brave, good little man of iron, he fears nothing.

From a near-by bank of hard snow he cuts blocks for a new igloo. In darkness and wind he transports them to a point near the house. When enough have been gathered, he walls a dome like a bee-hive. The interior arrangement is like the winter underground home. The light is put into it. By this he can see the open cracks between snow blocks. These are filled in to keep wind and snow out. When all is completed, he cuts a door and enters. The bed of snow is flattened.

Then he seeks for miles about for suitable grass to cover the cheerless ice floor. To get this grass, he must dig under fields of hardened snow. Even then he is not always rewarded with success. The sledge, loaded with frozen grass, is brought to the little snow dome. The grass is carefully laid on the bed of leveled snow. Over it new reindeer skins are spread. Now the new house of snow blocks in which the stork is to come is ready.

As the stork's coming is announced the mother's tears give the signal. She goes to the new snowhouse alone. The father is frightened and looks serious. But she must tear herself away. With her new garments, she enters the dark chamber of the snowhouse, strikes a fire, lights the lamp. The spotless walls of snow are cheerful. The new things about give womanly pride. But life is hard for her. A soul-stirring battle follows in that den of ice.

There is a little cry. But there is no doctor, no nurse, no one, not a kindly hand to help. A piece of glass is used as a surgical knife. Then all is over. There is no soap, no water. The methods of a mother cat are this mother's. Then, in the cold, cheerless chamber of ice, she fondly examines the little one. Its eyes are blue, but they turn brown at once when opened. Its hair is coal black, its skin is golden. It is turned over and over in the search for marks or blemishes. The mother's eyes run down along the tiny spine. At its end there is a blue shield-shaped blot like a tattoo mark. This is the Eskimo guarantee of a well-bred child. If it is there, the mother is happy, if not, there are doubts of the child's future, and of the purity of the parents. Now the father and the grandmother come. All rejoice.

If misfortune at the time of birth befalls a mother, as is not infrequent, the snow mound becomes her grave; it is not opened for a long time.

After a long sleep, into which the mother falls after her first joy, she awakes, turns over, drinks some ice-water, eats a little half-cooked meat, and then, shaking the frozen breath from the covers, she wraps herself and her babe snugly in furs. Again she sleeps, perhaps twenty-four hours, seemingly in perfect comfort, while the life-stilling winter winds drive over the feeble wall of snow which shelters her from the chilly death outside.

One day during Christmas week there was a knock at our door. The proud Ac-po-di-soa walked in, followed by his smiling wife, with the sleeping stork gift on her back. The child had been born less than five days before. We walked over and admired the little one. It suddenly opened its brown eyes, screwed up its little blubber nose, and wrinkled its chin for a cry. The mother grabbed her, plunged out of the door, pulled the undressed infant out, and in the wind and cold served the little one's want.

New Year's Day came starlit and cold. The year had dawned in which I was to essay the task to which I had set myself, the year which would mean success or failure to me. The past year had been gracious and bountiful, so, in celebration, Francke prepared a feast of which we both ate to gluttonous repletion. This consisted of ox-tail soup, creamed boneless cod, pickles, scrambled duck eggs with chipped smoked beef, roast eider-duck, fresh biscuits, crystallized potatoes, creamed onions, Bayo beans and bacon, Malaga grapes, (canned), peach-pie, blanc-mange, raisin cake, Nabisco biscuits and steaming chocolate.

The day was spent in making calls among the Eskimos. In the evening several families were given a feast which was followed by songs and dances. This hilarity was protracted to the early hours of morning and ended in an epidemic of night hysteria. When thus afflicted the victims dance and sing and fall into a trance, the combination of symptoms resembling insanity.

In taking account of our stock we found that our baking powder was about exhausted. This was sad news, for a breakfast of fresh biscuits, butter and coffee was one of the few delights that remained for me in life. We had bicarbonate of soda, but no cream of tartar. I wondered whether we could not substitute for cream of tartar some other substance.

Curious experiments followed. The juice of sauerkraut was tried with good results. But the flavor, as a steady breakfast food, was not desirable. Francke had fermented raisins with which to make wine. As a wine it was a failure, but as a fruit acid it enabled us to make soda biscuits with a new and delicate flavor. Milk, we found, would also ferment. From the unsweetened condensed milk, biscuits were made that would please the palate of any epicure. My breakfast pleasure therefore was still assured for many days to come.

EN ROUTE FOR THE POLE

THE CAMPAIGN OPENS—LAST WEEKS OF THE POLAR
NIGHT—ADVANCE PARTIES SENT OUT—AWAITING
THE DAWN

X

THE START WITH SUNRISE OF 1908

Two weeks of final tests and re-examination of
clothing, sledges and general equipment followed the
New Year's festivities. On January 14 there was
almost an hour of feeble twilight at midday. The moon
offered light enough to travel. Now we were finally
ready to fire the first guns of the Polar battle. Scouts
were outside, waiting for the signal to proceed. They
were going, not only to examine the ice field for the
main advance, but to offer succor to a shipwrecked crew,
which the natives believed was at Cape Sabine.

The smoke of a ship had been seen late in the fall,
and much wood from a wrecked ship had been found.
The pack was, therefore, loaded with expedition supplies, with instructions to offer help to anyone in want
that might be found.

I had just finished a note to be left at Cape
Sabine, telling of our headquarters, our caches and
our willingness to give assistance. This was handed to
Koo-loo-ting-wah, standing before his restless dogs,

whip in hand, as were his three companions, who volunteered as scouts. They jumped on the sledges, and soon the dogs were rushing toward the Polar pack of Smith Sound.

It was a beautiful day. A fold of the curtain of night had been lifted for a brief spell. A strong mixed light, without shadows, rested on the snow. It changed in quality and color with the changing mystery of the aurora. One might call it blue, or purple, or violet, or no color at all, according to the color perception of the observer.

In the south the heavens glowed with the heralds of the advancing sun. The light was exaggerated by the blink of the ice over which the light was sent, for the brightness of the heavens was out of proportion to its illuminating effect upon the surface snows. In the north, the half-spent moon dispelled the usual blackness Poleward, while the zenith was lighted with stars of the first and second magnitude.

The temperature was —41° F. The weather was perfectly calm—all that could be expected for the important event of opening the campaign.

In the course of a few hours the cheerful light faded, the snows darkened to earthy fields, and out of the north came a smoky tempest. The snow soon piled up in tremendous drifts, making it difficult to leave the house without climbing new hills. The dogs tied about were buried in snow. Only the light passing through the membrane of intestines, which was spread over the ports to make windows for the native houses, relieved the fierce blackness.

The run to Cape Sabine, under fine conditions, was

about forty miles, and could be made in one day, but
Smith Sound seldom offers a fair chance. Insufficient
light, impossible winds or ice make the crossing hazardous at best. The Eskimos cross every year, but
they are out so much after bears that they have a good
knowledge of the ice before they start to reach the other
shores.

Coming from the north, with a low temperature
and blowing snow, the wind would not only stop our
scouts, but force the ice south, leaving open spaces of
water. A resulting disruption of the pack might greatly
delay our start with heavy sledges. Furthermore,
there was real danger at hand for the advance. If the
party had been composed of white men there surely
would have been a calamity. But the Eskimo
approaches the ventures of the wild with splendid endurance. Moreover, he has a weather intelligence which
seldom finds him unprepared.

At midnight of the second night the party returned.
They were none the worse for the storm. The main
intent of their mission had failed. The storm had forced
them into snow embankments, and before it was quite
spent a bear began to nose about their shelter places.
The dogs were so buried with drift that they were not on
watch until the bear had destroyed much of their food.
Then their mad voices aroused the Eskimos.

As they dug out of their shelter, the bear took a big
walrus leg and walked off, man-like, holding the meat in
his forepaws. In their haste to free the dogs, they cut
their harness to pieces, for snow and ice cemented the
creatures. Oo-tah ran out in the excitement to head
off the bear—not to make an attack, but simply to stop

his progress. The bear dropped the meat and grabbed Oo-tah by the seat of his trousers. The dogs, fortunately, came along in time to save Oo-tah's life, but he had received a severe leg wound, which required immediate surgical attention.

The bear was captured, and with loads of bear meat and the wounded scout the party returned as quickly as possible. In the retreat it was noticed that the ice was very much broken.

In the wreck of an Arctic storm there is always a subsequent profit for someone. The snow becomes crusted and hardened, making sledge travel easy. The breaking of the ice, which was a great hindrance to our advance, offered open water for walrus and bear hunting. At this time we went to Serwahdingwah for the last chase. Some of the Eskimos took their families, so Annoatok became depopulated for a while. But on our return, visitors came in numbers too numerous for our comfort.

Dogs and skins, bargained for earlier in the season, were now delivered. Each corps of excursionists required some attention, for they had done noble work for the expedition. We gave them dinners and allowed them to sit about our stove with picture-books in hand.

Another storm came, with still more violent force, a week later. This caused us much anxiety, for we counted on our people being scattered on the ice along the shores of Cape Alexander. In a storm this would probably be swept from the land and carried seaward. There was nothing that could be done except wait for news. Messengers of trouble were not long in reaching headquarters after the storm. None of the men were on the ice, but a hurricane from the land had wrecked the camps.

Our men suffered little, but many of the natives in neighboring villages were left without clothing or sleeping furs. In the rush of the storm the ice left the land, and the snowhouses were swept into the sea. Men and women, without clothing, barely escaped with their lives. Two of our new sledges, some dogs, and three suits of winter furs were lost. A rescue party with furs had to be sent to the destitute people. Fortunately, our people were well supplied with bed-furs, out of which new suits were made.

Sledge loads of our furs were also coming north, and instructions were sent to use these for the urgent needs of the sufferers. Other things were sent from Annoatok, with returning excursionists, and in the course of a week the damage was replaced. But the loss was all on the expedition, and deprived many of the men in their northern journey of suitable sleeping-furs. Walruses were obtained after the storm, and the natives now had no fear of a famine of meat or fat.

By the end of January most of the natives had returned, and new preparations were made for a second effort to cross the Sound. Francke asked to join the party, and prepared for his first camp outing. Four sledges were loaded with two hundred pounds each of expedition advance supplies. Four good drivers volunteered to move the sledges to the American side.

The light had gradually brightened, and the storms passed off and left a keen, cold air, which was as clear as crystal. But at best the light was still feeble, and could be used for only about four hours of each twenty-four.

If, however, the sky remained clear, the moon and stars would furnish enough illumination for a full day's travel. There was a little flush of color in the southern skies, and the snows were a pale purple as the sledges groaned in their rush over the frosty surface.

The second party started off as auspiciously as the first, and news of its luck was eagerly awaited.

They reached Cape Sabine after a long run of twenty hours, making a considerable detour to the north. The ice offered good traveling, but the cold was bitter, the temperature being —52° F., with light, extremely humid and piercing winds.

Along the land and within the bays the snow was found to be deep, and a bitter wind came from the west. Two of the party could not be persuaded to go farther, but Francke, with two companions, pushed on for another day along the shore to Cape Veile. Beyond, the snow was too deep to proceed. The supplies were cached in a snowhouse, while those at Cape Sabine were left in the old camp. The party returned at the end of four days with their object accomplished. Nothing was seen of the rumored shipwrecked crew.

The next party, of eight sledges, led by Es-se-you, Kud-la, and Me-tek, started on February 5. The object was to carry advance supplies to the head of Flagler Bay, and hunt musk ox to feed the sledge teams as they moved overland. We were to meet this party at an appointed place in the bay.

The light was still too uncertain to risk the fortunes of the entire force. With a hundred dogs, a delay of a day would be an expensive loss, for if fed upon the carefully guarded food of the advance stores, a rapid reduction in supplies would follow, which could not be replaced, even if abundant game were secured later. It was, therefore, desirable to await the rising sun.

We made our last arrangements, fastened our last packs, and waited impatiently for the sunrise, here at this northernmost outpost of human life, just seven hundred miles from the Pole. And this was the problem that now insistently and definitely confronted us after the months of planning and preparation: Seven hundred miles of advance, almost a thousand miles as our route was planned; one thousand miles of return; two thousand miles in all; allowing for detours (for the line to be followed could not be precisely straight), more than two thousand miles of struggling travel across icy and unknown and uninhabitable wastes of moving ice.

On the morning of February 19, 1908, I started on my trip to the North Pole.

Early, as the first real day of the year dawned, eleven sledges were brought to the door of our box-house and lashed with supplies for the boreal dash. There were four thousand pounds of supplies for use on the Polar sea, and two thousands pounds of walrus skin and fat for use before securing the fresh game we anticipated. The eleven sledges were to be driven by Francke, nine Eskimos, and myself. They were drawn by one hundred and three dogs, each in prime condition. The dogs had been abundantly fed with walrus skin and meat for several weeks, and would now be fed only every second day on fresh supplies.

My heart was high. I was about to start on the quest which had inspired me for many years! The natives were naturally excited. The dogs caught the contagious enthusiasm, and barked joyously. At eight o'clock in the morning our whips snapped, the spans of dog teams leaped forward, and we were off.

My Polar quest had begun!

Most of the tribe had seemed willing to go with me, and to take all their dogs, but the men and the dogs finally selected were the pick of the lot. All were in superb physical condition, this matter of condition being something that I had carefully looked out for during the winter months. I regard this as having been highly advantageous to me, that I have always been able to win the friendship and confidence of the Eskimos; for thus I found them extremely ready to follow my advice and instructions, and to do in general anything I desired. That I could speak Eskimo fairly well—well enough to hold ordinary conversations—was also a strong asset in my favor.

When we started, a few stars were seen between thin clouds, but the light was good. A soft wind came from the south; the temperature was —36° F. The Greenland ice-cap was outlined; a belt of orange in the south heralded the rising sun. The snow still retained the purple of twilight. The ice was covered with about three inches of soft snow over a hard crust, which made speed difficult. Before noon the sky was gray, but the light remained good enough for traveling until 4 P. M. A course was made about northwest, because a more direct line was still impractical.

A water sky to the west and south denoted open water. At 3 P. M. we ran into bear tracks, and the sledges bounced along as if empty. The tracks were making a good course for us, so the dogs were encouraged. By four o'clock the feeble light made it dangerous to proceed. Two hunters still followed the bear tracks, while the others built three snowhouses for camp. Nothing was seen of the bears.

The dogs were tied to holes cut in the ice, and we crept into our snow-mounds, tired, hungry and sleepy. The night was extremely uncomfortable—the first nights from camp always are.

The next day brought a still air with a temperature of —42° F., and brilliant light at eight o'clock. We had made twenty miles through the air-line distance from Annoatok, and Cape Sabine was but thirty miles away. We had been forced so far north that we still had thirty miles before us to the Cape. The dogs, however, were in better trim, and we had no doubt about reaching the off-shores for the next camp. We followed the edge of ice which had been made in a wide open space in December. Here the traveling was fairly level, but above was a hopeless jungle of mountains and ridges of ice. We made about three miles an hour, and were able to ride occasionally.

At noon of February 20th we stopped, and coffee was served from our ever-hot coffee box. A can had been placed in a box, and so protected by reindeer skins that the heat was retained for twelve hours during the worst weather. This proved a great luxury.

While we sat regaling ourselves, a great ball of fire rose along the icy horizon. Our hearts were glad. The weather was bitterly cold; the temperature was 51° F.: but the sun had risen; the long night was at end. There was little else to mark the glory of sunrise. The light was no brighter than it had been for two hours. The sky remained a purple blue, with a slight grayness in the south, darkening toward the horizon. The snows were purple, with just a few dashes of red in the road before us. This unpretentious burst of the sun opened our spirits to new delights. Even the dogs sat in graceful rows and sounded a chorus of welcome to the coming of the day.

Although Cape Sabine, on February 20, was in sight, we still headed for Bache Peninsula. Impossible ice and open water pushed us farther and farther north. It was three o'clock before the Cape was seen over the dogs' tails. Soon after four the light failed, the land colored to purple and gold toward the rim of the horizon, and we were left to guess the direction of our course. But Eskimos are somewhat better than Yankees at guessing, for we got into no troubles until 9 P. M., when we tried to scale the rafted ice against Cape Sabine. With only the camp equipment and dog food, the dogs crept up and down in the black hills of ice, while we followed like mountain-sheep.

Here had been the camp of the ill-fated Greely expedition. It recurred to me that it was a curious whim of fate that this ill-starred camp of famine and death, in earlier days, should have marked the very outset of our modern effort to reach the Pole. But later we were to learn that under similar conditions a modern expedition can meet the same fate as that of the Lady Franklin Bay Expedition.

We turned about, took the advance supplies, and picked a course through Rice Strait, to avoid the rough ice northward. Here the surface was good, but a light wind, with a temperature of —52° F., came with great bitterness. The dogs refused to face the wind, and required someone to lead the way. The men buried their faces in the fur mittens, leaned on the upstanders, and ran along.

Passing Cape Rutherford on February 22, we followed the coast. Here the wind came from the right, caught the tip of the nose, burning with a bleaching effect, which, in camp later, turned black. At Cape Veile the cache igloo was sighted, and there camp was pitched.

In the morning the minimum thermometer registered —58° F. We were evidently passing from the storms and open water of Smith Sound, from warm, moist air to a still, dry climate, with very low temperature. The day opened beautifully with a glow of rose to the south, which colored the snows in warm tones. At noon the sun showed half of its face over the cliffs as we crossed the bay and sought better ice along Bache Peninsula. That night we camped near the Weyprecht Islands. The day, although bright, proved severe, for most of the natives had frostbites about the face. Along Bache Peninsula we saw hares staring at us. Four were secured for our evening meal. In the very low temperature of —64° F. the hunters suffered from injuries like burns, due to the blistering cold metal of their guns.

Dog food had also to be prepared. In efforts to divide the walrus skin, two hatchets were broken. The Eskimo dog is a tough creature, but he cannot be expected to eat food which breaks an axe. Petroleum and alcohol were used liberally, and during the night the skin was sufficiently softened by the heat to be cut with the hatchets.   This skin seems to be good food for the dogs.   It is about one inch thick, and contains little water, the skin fibre being a kind of condensed nutriment, small quantities of which satisfy the dogs.   It digests slowly, and therefore has lasting qualities.

The lamps, burning at full force, made the igloos comfortable.   The temperature fell to —68° F.   It was the first satisfying sleep of the journey for me.   The economy of the blue fire stoves is beyond conception. Burning but three pounds of oil all night, the almost liquid air was reduced to a normal temperature of freezing point.

Francke used alcohol stoves, with a double consumption of fuel.   The natives, in their three igloos, used the copper lamp, shaped after the stone devices, but they did no cooking.

In the morning of the 23d we heard sounds to the south, which at first we thought to be walrus.   But after a time the noise was interpreted as that of the dogs of the advance party.   They were camped a few miles beyond, and came to our igloos at breakfast.   One musk ox and eleven hares had been secured.   The valley had been thoroughly hunted, but no other game was sighted.

The ground was nearly bare, and made sledge travel impossible.   They were bound for Annoatok at once.   This was sad news for us.   We had counted on game with which to feed the dog train en route to the Polar sea.   If animals were not secured, our project would fail at the very start, and this route would be impossible.   To push overland rapidly to the west coast was our only chance, but the report of insufficient snow seemed to forbid this.   Something, however, must be tried. We could not give up without a stronger fight. The strong probability of our failing to find musk ox, and extending the expedition for another year, over another route, made it necessary to send Francke back to headquarters to guard our supplies. There was no objection to the return of most of the other party, but we took their best dogs and sledges, with some exchange of drivers.

With this change in the arrangements, and the advance supplies from Cape Sabine and Cape Viele, each sledge now carried eight hundred pounds. Beyond, in Flagler Bay, the ice luckily became smooth and almost free of snow. An increased number of dogs, with good traveling, enabled us to make satisfactory progress, despite the steadily falling temperature.

The head of Flagler Bay was reached late at night, after an exhausting march of twenty-five miles. A hard wind, with a temperature of —60° F., had almost paralyzed the dogs, and the men were kept alive only by running with the dogs. Comfortable houses were built and preparations made for a day of rest. On the morrow we aimed to explore the land for an auspicious route. Many new frostbites were again noted in camp. One of the dogs died of the cold.

The party was by no means discouraged, however. We were as enthusiastic as soldiers on the eve of a longed-for battle. The reduced numbers of the return party gave us extra rations to use in times of need, and the land did not seem as hopeless as pictured by the returning natives. A cache was made here of needful things for use on the return. Other things, which we had found useless, were also left here.

EXPLORING A NEW PASS OVER ACPOHON

FROM THE ATLANTIC WATERS AT FLAGLER BAY TO THE
PACIFIC WATERS AT BAY FIORD—THE MECCA OF THE
MUSK OX—BATTLES WITH THE BOVINE MONSTERS OF
THE ARCTIC—SUNRISE AND THE GLORY OF SUNSET

XI

BREAKING A TRAIL BEYOND THE HAUNTS OF MAN

Early in the morning of February 25 the dogs were
spanned to sledges with heavy loads, and we pushed into
the valley of mystery ahead. Our purpose was to cross
the inland ice and descend into Cannon Bay. The
spread of the rush of glacial waters in summer had dug
out a wide central plain, now imperfectly covered with
ice and snow. Over this we lined a trail.

On each side of us were gradual slopes rising to
cliffs, above which I noted the blue wall of the overland sea of ice, at an altitude of about two thousand feet.
Nowhere did this offer a safe slope for an ascent. We
now explored the picturesque valley, for I knew that
our only hope was to push overland to Bay Fiord. The
easy slopes were enlivened with darting, downy hares.
Some sat motionless, with their long ears erect, while
they drank the first golden air of sunrise and watched
the coming of new life. Others danced about in frisky
play.

As we pushed along, the ascent of the slope was gradual. The necessity for crossing from side to side to find ice or snow lengthened our journey. Only the partially bare earth gave us trouble. The temperature was —62° F., but there was no wind. The upper slopes glittered with bright sunshine. Winding with a stream, we advanced twenty miles. Beyond there was the same general topography. The valley looked like a pass. Clouds of a different kind were seen through the gorges. At various places we noted old musk ox paths. I knew that where game trails are well marked on mountains one is certain to find a good crossing. This rule is equally good in the Arctic as elsewhere. At any rate, there was no alternative. The tortures of the top had to be risked. Pushing onward, we found no fresh signs of musk ox. A few bear tracks were seen, and a white fox followed us to camp. We shot sixteen hares, and for the evening meal unlimited quantities of savory hare meat made an appetizing broth.

On the day following, everything was advanced to this point. A prolonged search for musk ox was made, with negative results.

On the morning of the 27th, full loads were taken on our sledges. With slow progress we advanced on the rising bed of the stream, the valley moved, and the river ice was found in one channel, making better travel. Hare and fox tracks increased in number. The side slopes were grassy, and mostly swept bare of snow by strong winter winds. Sand dunes and gravel lines were also piled up, while huge drifts of pressed snow indicated a dangerous atmospheric agitation. Here, I knew, were excellent feeding grounds for musk ox and caribou. But a careful scrutiny gave no results for a long time.

To us the musk ox was now of vital importance. The shorter way, over Schley Land and northward through Nansen Sound, was possible only if game in abundance was secured en route. If the product of the chase gave us no reward, then our Polar venture was doomed at the outset.

One day, with a temperature of —100° below the freezing point, and with a light but sharp Arctic wind driving needles of frost to the very bone, we searched the rising slopes of ice-capped lands in the hope of spotting life.

For three days the dogs had not been fed. They sniffed the air, searched the horizon, and ranged the wilds with all the eagerness of their wolf progenitors. The hare and the fox were aroused from their winter's sleep, but such game was not what we now desired. Only meat and fat in heaps could satisfy the wants of over a hundred empty stomachs.

After a hard pull, ascending miniature, ice-covered hills, winding about big, polished boulders, we entered a wider section of the narrow gorge-like valley. Here the silurian rocks had broken down, and by the influence of glacier streams and glaciers, now receding, a good deal of rolling, grass-covered land spread from cliff to cliff. Strong winter gales had bared the ground. We sat down to rest. The dogs did likewise.

All searched the new lands with eager eyes. The dog noses pointed to a series of steep slopes to the north. They were scenting something, but were too tired to display the usual animation of the chase. Soon we detected three dark, moving objects on a snowy sun-flushed hill, under a huge cliff, about a thousand feet above us. *"Ah-ming-mah!"* shouted E-tuk-i-shook. The dogs jumped; the men grasped glasses; in a second the sledge train was in disorder.

Fifty dogs were hitched to three sledges. Rushing up three different gulches, the sledges, with tumbling human forms as freight, advanced to battle. The musk oxen, with heads pointed to the attacking forces, quietly awaited the onrush.

Within an hour three huge, fat carcasses were down in the river bed. A temporary camp was made, and before the meat froze most of it had passed palates tantalized by many days of gastronomic want.

Continuing our course, we crossed the divide in a storm. Beyond, in a canyon, the wind was more uncomfortable than in the open. Something must be done. We could not long breathe that maddening air, weighted by frost and thickened by snows. The snow-bank gave no shelter whatever, and a rush of snow came over, which quickly buried the investigators. But it was our only hope.

"Dig a hole," said Koo-loo-ting-wah.

Now, to try to dig a hole without a shovel, and with snow coming more rapidly than any power of man could remove, seemed a waste of needed vital force. But I had faith in the intelligence of my savage companions, and ordered all hands to work. They gathered at one corner of the bank, and began to talk and shout, while I allowed myself to be buried in a pocket of the cliffs to keep my tender skin from turning to ice. Every few minutes someone came along to see if I was safe.

The igloo was progressing. Two men were now inside. In the course of another hour they reported four men inside; in another hour seven men were inside, and the others were piling up the blocks, cut with knives from the interior. A kind of vestibule was made to allow the wind to shoot over the entrance. Inside, the men were sweating.

Soon afterward I was told that the igloo was completed. I lost no time in seeking its shelter. A square hole had been cut, large enough for the entire party if packed like sardines. Our fur clothing was removed, and beaten with sticks and stones.

The lamps sang cheerily of steaming musk ox steaks. The dogs were brought into the canyon. A more comfortable night was impossible. We were fifty feet under the snow. The noise of the driving storm was lost. The blinding drift about the entrance was effectually shut out by a block of snow as a door. Two holes afforded ventilation, and the tremendous difference between the exterior and the interior air assured a circulation.

When we emerged in the morning the sky was clear. A light wind came from the west, with a temperature of —78° F. Two dogs had frozen during the storm. All were buried in the edge of a drift that was piled fifteen feet. An exploration of the canyon showed other falls and boulders impossible for sledge travel.

A trail was picked over the hills to the side. The day was severe. How we escaped broken legs and smashed sleds was miraculous. But somehow, in our plunges down the avalanches, we always landed in a soft bed of snow. We advanced about ten miles, and made a descent of five hundred feet, first camping upon a glacial lake.

The temperature now was —79° F., and although there were about nine hours of good light, including twilight, we had continued our efforts too long, and were forced to build igloos by moonlight. Glad were we, indeed, when the candle was placed in the dome of snow, to show the last cracks to be stuffed.

In the searchlight of the frigid dawn I noticed that our advance was blocked by a large glacier, which tumbled barriers of ice boulders into the only available line for a path. A way would have to be cut into this barrier of icebergs for about a mile. This required the full energy of all the men for the day. I took advantage of the halt to explore the country through which we were forcing a pass. The valley was cut by ancient glaciers and more modern creeks along the meeting line of two distinct geological formations. To the north were silurian and cambro-silurian rocks; to the south were great archæan cliffs.

With the camera, the field-glass, and other instruments in the sack, I climbed into a gorge and rose to the level of the mountains of the northern slopes. The ground was here absolutely destitute of vegetation, and only old musk ox trails indicated living creatures. The snow had all been swept into the ditches of the lowlands. Climbing over frost-sharpened stones, I found footing difficult.

The average height of the mountains proved to be nineteen hundred feet. To the northeast there was land extending a few miles further, with a gradual rising slope. Beyond was the blue edge of the inland ice. To the northwest, the land continued in rolling hills, beyond which no land-ice was seen. The cliffs to the south were of about the same height, but they were fitted to the crest with an ice-cap. The overflow of perpetual snows descended into the gorges, making five overhanging glaciers.

The first was at the divide, furnishing in summer the waters which started the vigorous stream to the Atlantic slopes. It was a huge stream of ice, about a mile wide, and it is marked by giant cliffs, separated by wide gaps, indicating the roughness of the surface over which it pushes its frozen height. To the stream to which it gives birth, flowing eastward from the divide, I will give the name of Schley River, in honor of Rear-Admiral Schley.

The stream starting westward from the divide, through picturesque rocks, tumbles in icy falls into a huge canyon, down to the Pacific waters at Bay Fiord. To this I will give, in honor of General A. W. Greely, the name Greely River.

The second and third glaciers were overhanging masses about a half-mile wide, which gave volume in summer time to Greely River.

The fourth was a powerful glacier, with a discharging face of blue three miles long, closing up a valley and damming up a lake about four miles long and one mile wide. The lake was beyond the most precipitous of the descending slopes. The upper cliffs of the walled valley to Flagler Bay were still visible, while to the west was seen a line of mountains and cliffs which marked the head of Bay Fiord, under which was seen the ice covering the first water of the Pacific upon which our future fortunes would be told.   To this sea level there was an easy descent of four hundred feet on the river ice and snowdrifts, making, with good luck, a day's run of twenty miles.

Returning, at camp I was informed that not only had a trail been cut, but many of the sledges had been advanced to the good ice beyond.   Two of the sledges, however, had been badly broken, and must be mended at dawn before starting.

The day was beautiful.   For the first time I felt the heat of the sun.   It came through the thick fur of my shoulders with the tenderness of a warm human hand.   The mere thought of the genial sunbeams brought a glow of healthful warmth, but at the same time the thermometer was very low, —78½° F.   One's sense of cold, under normal conditions, is a correct instrument in its bearing upon animal functions, but as an instrument of physics it makes an unreliable thermometer.   If I had been asked to guess the temperature of the day I should have placed it at —25° F.

The night air had just a smart of bitterness.   The igloo failed to become warm, so we fed our internal fires liberally with warming courses, coming in easy stages. We partook of superheated coffee, thickened with sugar, and biscuits, and later took butter chopped in squares, which was eaten as cheese with musk ox meat chopped by our axes into splinters.   Delicious hare loins and hams, cooked in pea soup, served as dessert.

The amount of sugar and fat which we now consumed was quite remarkable.   Fortunately, during the journey to the edge of the Polar sea, there was no urgent limit to transportation, and we were well supplied with the luxury of sugar and civilized foods, most of which later were to be abandoned.

In this very low temperature I found considerable difficulty in jotting down the brief notes of our day's doings. The paper was so cold that the pencil barely left a mark. A few moments had to be spent warming each page and pencil before beginning to write. With the same operation, the fingers were also sufficiently warmed to hold the pencil. All had to be done by the light and heat of a candle.

To economize fuel, the fires later were extinguished before retiring to sleep. In the morning we were buried in the frost falling from our own breath.

It was difficult to work at dawn with fur-covered hands; but the Eskimo can do much with his glove-fitting mitten. The broken sledges were soon repaired. After tumbling over irregular ice along the face of the glacier, the river offered a splendid highway over which the dogs galloped with remarkable speed. We rode until cold compelled exercise. The stream descended among picturesque hills, but the most careful scrutiny found no sign of life except the ever-present musk ox trails of seasons gone by.

As we neared the sea line, near the mouth of the river, we began to see a few fresh tracks of hare and musk ox. Passing out on the south of Bay Fiord, we noted bear and wolf tracks. Then the eyes of the hunter and the dog rolled with eager anticipation.

The sun flushed the skies in flaming colors as it was about to sink behind a run of high peaks. The western sky burned with gold, the ice flashed with crimson inlets, but the heat was very feeble. The temperature was

—72° F. We had already gone twenty-five miles, and were looking forward to a point about ten miles beyond as the next camping place, when all my companions, seemingly at once, espied a herd of musk ox on the sky line of a whale-backed mountain to the north.

The distance was about three miles, but the eagle eyes of the natives detected the black spots.

We searched the gorge with our glasses. Suddenly one of the Eskimos cried out in a joyous tone: *"Ah-ming-ma! Ah-ming-ma!"*

I could detect only some dark specks on the snow, which looked like a hundred others that I knew to be rocks. I levelled my glasses on the whale-backed mountain at which the Eskimo was staring, and, sure enough, there were three musk oxen on a steep snow slope. They seemed to be digging up the winter snow fields to get "scrub" willows. They were not only three miles away, but at an altitude of perhaps a thousand feet above us.

The cumbersome loads were quickly pitched from three sledges. Rifles and knives were securely fastened. In a few moments the long lashes snapped, and away we rushed, with two men on each of the sledges and with double teams of twenty dogs.

The dogs galloped at a pace which made the sledges bound like rubber balls over irregularities of rocks, slippery ice, and hard-crusted snow, and our hold tightened on the hickory in the effort to keep our places. It disturbed the dogs not at all whether they were on rock or snow, or whether the sledge rested on runners or turned spirally; but it made considerable difference to us, and we lost much energy in the constant efforts to avoid somersaults. We did not dare release our grip for a moment, for to do so would have meant painful bumping and torn clothes, as well as being left behind in the chase.

It took but a brief time to cover the three miles. We made our final advance by three separate ravines, and for a time the musk oxen were out of sight. When we again saw them they had not taken the alarm, nor did they until we were ready to attack them from three separate points.

All but five dogs from each sledge were now freed from harness. They darted toward the oxen with fierce speed.

The oxen tried to escape through a ravine, but it was too late. The dogs were on every side of them, and all the oxen could do was to grunt fiercely and jump into a bunch, with tails together and heads directed at the enemy. There were seven musk oxen in all, and they tried to keep the dogs scattered at a safe distance.

The dogs would rush up to within a few feet, showing their teeth and uttering wolfish sounds, and every now and then an ox would rush out from its circle, with head down, in an effort to strike the dogs; but the dogs were always too quick to be caught by the savage thrust, and each time the ox, in its retreat, would feel canine fangs closing on its haunches.

After a few such efforts, the bulls, with lowered horns, merely held to the position, while the dogs, not daring actually to attack under such circumstances, sat in a circle and sent up blood-chilling howls. Meanwhile, the Eskimos and myself were hurrying up.

The strife was soon over. I snapped my camera at

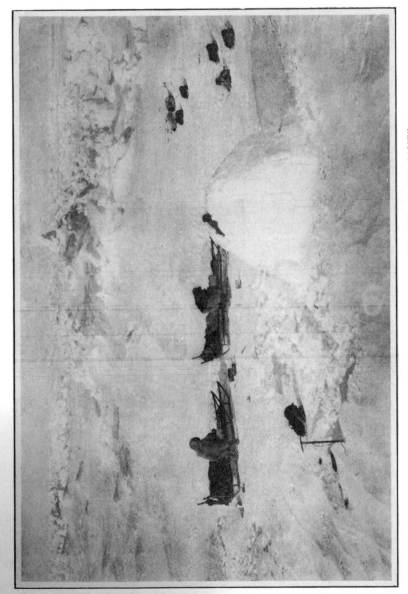

"THE IGLOO BUILT, WE PREPARE FOR OUR DAILY CAMP"

CAMPING TO EAT AND TAKE OBSERVATIONS
ON AGAIN!

an old bull which at that moment broke through the dogs and, followed by a group of them, was driven madly over a cliff in a plunge of five thousand feet. The other oxen were soon killed by the hunters.

The sun settled under mountains of ice, and the purple twilight rapidly thickened. It was very cold. The breath of each man came like jets of steam from a kettle. The temperature was now —81°F. No time could be lost in dressing the game. But the Eskimos were equal to the task, and showed such skill as only Indians possess.

While this was being done by my companions, I strolled about to note the ear-marks of the home of the musk ox. The mountain was in line of the sweep of the winds, and was bared of snows. Here were grass, mosses, and creeping willows in abundance, descending into the gullies. I found fossil-stumps of large trees and bits of lignite coal. The land in pre-glacial times had evidently supported a vigorous vegetation; but now the general aspect offered a scene of frosty hopelessness. Still, in this desolation of snowy wastes, nature had supplied creatures with food in their hard pressure of life.

Fox and wolf tracks were everywhere, while on every little eminence sat an Arctic hare, evincing ear-upraised surprise at our appearance. With the glasses I noted on neighboring hills three other herds of musk ox. This I did not tell the hunters, for they would not have rested until all were secured. Living in a land of cold and hunger, the Eskimo is insatiable for game. We had as much meat as we could possibly use for the next few days, and it was much easier to fill up, and secure more when we needed it, than now to carry almost impossible loads. In a remarkably short time the skins were removed and the meat was boned and cut in small strips in such a way that the axe would break it when frozen. Neatly wrapped in skins, the loads did not seem large.

Selecting a few choice bits for later use, the balance was separated and allowed to cool. I looked at the enormous quantity of meat, and wondered how it could be transported to camp, but no such thought troubled the Eskimos. Piece after piece went down the canine throats with a gulp. No energy was wasted in mastication. With a drop of the jaws and a twist of the neck, the task of eating was finished and the stomach began to spread. The dogs had not yet reached their limit when the snow was cleared of its weight of dressed meat and a canine wrangle began for the possession of the cleaned bones.

With but little meat on the sledges, we began the descent, but the spirit of the upward rush was lost. The dogs, too full to run, simply rolled down the slopes, and we pushed the sledges ourselves. The ox that had made the death plunge was picked up and taken as reserve meat. It was midnight before camp was pitched. The moon burned with a cheerful glow. The air was filled with liquid frost, but there was no wind and consequently no suffering from cold.

Two comfortable snowhouses were built, and in them our feasts rivalled the canine indulgence. Thus was experienced the greatest joy of savage life in boreal wilds—the hunt of the musk ox, with the advantage of the complex cunning gathered by forgotten ages. The balance of the meat left after our feast was buried, with the protecting skins, in the snow. On opening the meat on the following morning, it was still warm, although the minimum thermometer registered —80° F. for the night.

A few minutes before midday, on our next march, the sledge train halted. We sat on the packs, and, with eyes turned southward, waited. Even an Eskimo has an eye for color and a soul for beauty. To us there appeared a play of suppressed light and bleached color tints, as though in harmony with bars of music, which inspired my companions to shouts of joy.

Slowly and majestically the golden orb lifted. The dogs responded in low, far-reaching calls. The Eskimos greeted the day god with savage chants. The sun, a flushed crimson ball, edged along the wintry outline of the mountains' purplish snowy glitter. The pack was suddenly screened by a moving sheet of ever-changing color, wherein every possible continuation of purple and gold merged with rainbow hues.

Soon the dyes changed to blue, and eventually the sky was fired by flames of red. Then, slowly, the great blazing globe sank into seas of fire-flushed ice. The snowy mountains about glowed with warm cheer. The ice cooled again to purple, and again to blue, and then a winter blackness closed the eye to color and the soul to joy.

IN GAME TRAILS TO LAND'S END

XII

SHORES OF THE CIRCUMPOLAR SEA

March 2 was bright and clear and still. The ice
was smooth, with just snow enough to prevent the dogs
cutting their feet. The heavy sledges bounded along
easily, but the dogs were too full of meat to step a lively
pace. The temperature was —79° F. We found it
comfortable to walk along behind the upstanders of the
sledges. Some fresh bear tracks were crossed. These
denoted that bears had advanced along the coast on an
exploring tour, much as we aimed to do. Scenting
these tracks, the dogs forgot their distended stomachs,
and braced into the harness with full pulling force. We
were still able to keep pace by running. Hard exercise brought no perspiration.

After passing the last land point, we noted four
herds of musk oxen. The natives were eager to embark
for the chase. I tried to dissuade them, but, had we not
crossed the bear trail, no word of mine would have kept
them from another chase of the musk ox.

Long after sunset, as we were about to camp, a bear was sighted advancing on us behind a line of hummocks. The light was already feeble. It was the work of but a minute to throw our things on the ice and start the teams on the scent of the bear.   But this bear was thin and hungry. He gave us a lively chase. His advance was checked, however, as our rush began, and he spread his huge paws into a step which outdistanced our dogs. The chase was continued on the ice for about three miles. Then bruin, with sublime intelligence, took to the land and the steep slopes, leading us over hilly, bare ground, rocks, and soft snows. He gained the top of the tall cliffs while we were still groping in the darkness among the rocks at the base, a thousand feet below.

The sledges were now left, and the dogs freed. They flew up a gully in which the bear tracks guided an easy path. In a short time their satisfying howls told of the bear's captivity. He had taken a position on a table-rock, which was difficult for the dogs to climb. At an easy distance from this rock were steep slopes of snow. One after another, the dogs came tumbling down these slopes. With but a slight cuff of his paw, the bear could toss the attacking dogs over dizzy heights. His position was impregnable to the dogs, but, thus perched, he was a splendid mark for E-tuk-i-shook. That doughty huntsman raised his gun, and, following a shot, the bear rolled down the same slopes on which he had hurled the dogs. To his carcass a span of strong dogs were soon hitched, and it was hauled down to the sea level. Quickly dressed and distributed, the bear was only a teasing mouthful to the ever-hungry dogs.

It was nearly midnight before we returned to our

sledge packs. The work of building the houses was rendered difficult by the failing moon and the very low temperature. The lowest temperature of the season, —83°, was reached this night.

The sun rose in the morning of March 3 with warm colors, painting the crystal world surrounding us with gorgeous tints of rose and old gold. It was odd that in the glare of this enrapturing glory we should note the coldest day of the year.

With the returning sun in the Arctic comes the most frigid season. The light is strongly purple, and one is tempted to ascribe to the genial rays a heating influence which is as yet absent, owing to their slant. The night-darkened surfaces prevent the new sun-beams from disseminating any considerable heat, and the steadily falling temperature indicates that the crust of the earth, as a result of its long desertion by the sun in winter, is still unchecked in its cooling. Because of the persistence of terrestrial radiation, we have the coldest weather of the year with the ascending sun.

It is a fortunate provision of nature that these icy days of the ascending sun are usually accompanied by a breathless stillness. When wind and storms come, the temperature quickly rises. It is doubtful if any form of life could withstand a storm at —80° F. A quiet charm comes with this eye-opening period. The spirits rise with indescribable gladness, and, although the mercury is frozen, the body, when properly dressed, is perfectly comfortable. The soft light of purple and gold, or of lilac and rose, on the snowy slopes, dispels the chronic gloom of the long night, while the tonic of a brightening air of frost returns the flush to the pale cheeks. The stillness adds a charm, with which the imagination plays. It is not the music of silence, nor the gold solitude of summer, nor the deathlike stillness of the winter blackness. It is the stillness of zero's lowest, which has a beauty of its own.

The ice pinnacles are lined with hoar frost, on which there is a play of rainbow colors. The tread of one's feet is muffled by feathery beds of snow. The mountains, raised by the new glow of light or outlined by colored shadows, stand against the brightened heavens in sculptured magnificence.

The bear admires his shadow, the fox peeps from behind his bushy tail, devising a new cult, for his art of night will soon be a thing of the past. The hare sits, with forelegs bent reverently, as if offering prayers of gratitude. The musk ox stands in the brightest sun, with his beautiful coat of black and blue, and absorbs the first heaven-given sun bath, and man soars high in dreams of happiness.

Shadows always attract the eye of primitive people and children. In a world such as the one we were invading, with little to rest the eye from perpetual glitter, they were to become doubly interesting. When we first began observing our shadows, on March 3, I did not dream that a thing so simple could rise to the dignity of a proof of the Polar conquest. But, since then, I have come to the conclusion that, if a proof of this much-discussed problem is at all possible, it is in the corroborative evidence of just such little things as shadows.

Accordingly, I have examined every note and impression bearing on natural phenomena en route.

To us, in our daily marches from Bay Fiord, the

shadow became a thing of considerable interest and importance. The Eskimo soul is something apart from the body. The native believes it follows in the shadow. For this reason, stormy, sunless days are gloomy times to the natives, for the presence of the soul is then not in evidence. The night has the same effect, although the moon often throws a clear-cut shadow. The native believes the soul at times wanders from the body. When it does this, the many rival spirits, which in their system of beliefs tenant the body, get into all sorts of trouble.

Every person, and every animal, has not only a soul which guards its destiny, but every part of the body has an individual spirit—the arm, the leg, the nose, the eye, the ear, and every other conceivable part of the anatomy, with a peculiar individuality, throbs with a separate life. The separate, wandering soul in the shadow is the guiding influence.

Furthermore, there is no such conception as an absolutely inanimate thing. The land, the sea, the air, ice, and snow, have great individual spirits that ever engage in battle with each other. Even mountains, valleys, rocks, icebergs, wood, iron, fire—all have spirits. All of this gives them a keen interest in shadows in an otherwise desert of gloom and death.

Their entire religious creed would require a long time to work out. Even that part of it which is represented by the shadow is quite beyond me. As I observed in our following marches toward Svartevoeg, their keen eyes detect in shadows incidents and messages of life, histories that would fill volumes. The shadow is long or short, clear-cut or vague, dark or light, blue or purple, violet or black. Each phase of it has a special significance. It presages luck or ill-luck on the chase, sickness and death in the future, the presence or unrest of the souls of parted friends. Even the souls of the living sometimes get mixed. Then there is love or intrigue. All the passions of wild life can be read from the shadows. The most pathetic shadows had been the vague, ghastly streaks of black that followed the body about a week before sunset in October. At that time all the Arctic world is sad, and tears come easily.

The shadow does not quickly come back with the returning sun. Continuous storms so screen the sunbeams that only a vague, diffused light reaches the long night-blackened snows. When the joy of seeing the first shadows exploded among my companions I did not know just what intoxication infected the camp. With full stomachs of newly acquired musk ox loins, we had slept. Suddenly the sun burst through a maze of burning clouds and made our snow palace glow with electric darts. The temperature was very low. Only half-dressed, the men rushed out, dancing with joy.

Their shadows were long, sharp-cut, and of a deep, purple blue. They danced with them. This brought them back to the normal life of Eskimo hilarity. Then followed the pleasures of the thrill of the sunny days of crystal air and blinding sparkle during never-to-be forgotten days of the enervating chill of zero's lowest at —83° F.

In the northward progress, for a long time the shadows did not perceptibly shorten or brighten to my eyes. The natives, however, on our subsequent marches, got from these shadows a never-ending variety of topics to talk about. They foretold storms, located game, and read the story of respective home entanglements of the Adamless Eden which we had left far away on the Greenland shore.

Our bear adventures took us on an advance trail over which progress was easy. Beyond, the snow increased rapidly in depth with every mile. Snowshoes were lashed to our feet for the first mile. We halted in our march at noon, attacked suddenly by five wolves. The rifles were prepared for defense. No shots were to be fired, however, unless active battle was commenced. The creatures at close range were slightly cream-colored, with a little gray along their backs, but at a greater distance they seemed white. They came from the mountains, with a chilling, hungry howl that brought shivers. The dogs were interested, but made no offer to give chase.

The wolves passed the advancing sledges at a distance, and gathered about the rear sledge, which was separated from the train. The driver turned his team to help in the fight. As the sledges neared, the teams were stopped, the wolves sat down and delivered a maddening chorus of chagrin. The dogs were restless, but only wiggled their tails. The men stood still, with rifles pointed. The chorus ended. The battle was declared off. Seeing that they were outnumbered, the howling creatures turned and dashed up the snowy slopes, from which they had come, with a storming rush. The train was lined up, and through the deep snow we plowed westward.

In two difficult marches we reached Eureka Sound.

Wolves continued on our trail nearly every day

along the west coast of Acpohon, and also along North
Devon.

In the extreme North, the wolf, like the fox, is pure
white, with black points to the ears, and spots over the
eyes.   In the regions farther south his fur is slightly
gray.   In size, he is slightly larger than the Eskimo
dog, his body longer and thinner, and he travels with his
tail down.   Like the bear, he is a ceaseless wanderer
during all seasons of the year.

In winter, wolves gather in groups of six or eight,
and attack musk ox, or anything in their line of march.
But in summer they travel in pairs, and become scaven-
gers.   The wolf is alert in estimating the number of his
combatants and their fighting qualities.   Men and dogs
in numbers he never approaches within gunshot, con-
tenting himself by howling piercingly from mountains
at a long distance.   When a single sledge was separated
from the others, he would approach to an uncomfortable
range.

Bear tracks were also numerous.   We were, however, too tired to give chase.   Close to a cape where we
paused, on Eureka Sound, to cut snow-blocks for igloos
attached to the sledges, E-tuk-i-shook noted two bears
wandering over the lands not far away.   Watching for
a few moments with the glasses, we noted that they were
stalking a sleeping musk ox.   Now we did not care particularly for the bears, but the musk ox was regarded as
our own game, and we were not willing to divide it
knowingly.   The packs were pitched into the snow, and
the dogs rushed through deep snow, over hummocks
and rocks, to the creeping bears.

As the bears turned, the rear attack seemed to offer

sport, and they rose to meet us. But as one team after the other bounced over the nearest hills, their heads turned and they rushed up the steep slopes. We now saw twenty musk oxen asleep in scattered groups. These interested us more than the bears. The dogs were seemingly of the same mind, for they required no urging to change the noses from the bears to the musk oxen.

As we wound around the hill upon which they rested, all at once arose, shook off the snow, rubbed their horns on their knees, and then formed a huge star. In a short time the entire herd was ours. The meat was dressed, wrapped in skins, the dogs lightly fed, and the carcasses hauled to camp. Then we completed our igloos. Bears and wolves wandered about camp all night, but with one hundred dogs, whose eyes were on the swelled larder, there was no danger from wild brutes.

Early in the morning of March 4 we were awakened by a furious noise from the dogs. Koo-loo-ting-wah peeked out and saw a bear in the act of taking a choice strip of tenderloin from the meat. With a deft cut of the knife, a falling block of snow made a window, and through it the rifle was leveled at the animal. He was big, fat, and gave us just the blubber required for our lamps.

A holiday was declared. It would take time to stuff the dogs with twenty musk oxen and a bear. Furthermore, our clothing needed attention. Boots, mittens, and stockings had to be dried and mended. Some of our garments were torn in places, permitting winds to enter. Much of the dog harness required fixing.

The Eskimos' sledges had been slightly broken. Later, the same day, another herd of twenty musk oxen were seen. Now even the Eskimo's savage thirst for blood was satisfied. The pot was kept boiling, and the igloos rang with chants of primitive joys.

On March 7 we began a straight run to the Polar sea, a distance of one hundred and seventy miles. The weather was superb and the ice again free of heavy snow.

In six marches we reached Schei Island, which we found to be a peninsula. We halted here and a feast day was declared. Twenty-seven musk oxen and twenty-four hares were secured in one after-dinner hunt. This meat guaranteed a food supply to the shores of the Poar sea. A weight was lifted from my load of cares, for I had doubted the existence of game far enough north to count on fresh meat to the sea. The temperature was still low (—50° F.), but the nights were brightening, and the days offered twelve hours of good light. Our outlook was hopeful indeed.

In the Polar campaign, the bear was unconsciously our best friend, and also consciously our worst enemy. There were times when we admired him, although he was never exactly friendly to us. There were other times when we regarded him with a savage wrath. Only beyond the range of life in the utmost North were we free from his attacks. In other places he nosed our trail with curious persistence. He had attacked the first party that was sent out to explore a route, under cover of night and storms. One man was wounded, another lost the tail of his coat and a part of his anatomy.

In our march of glory through the musk ox land,

the bear came as a rival, and disputed not only our right
to the chase, but also our right to the product from our
own catch.   But we had guns and dogs, and the bears
fell easily.   We were jealous of the quest of the musk
ox.   It seemed properly to belong to the domain of
man's game.   We were equal at the time to the task,
and did not require the bear's help.

The bears were good at figures, and quickly realized ours was a superior fighting force.   So they joined
the ranks in order that they might share in the division
of the spoils.   The bear's goodly mission was always
regarded with suspicion.   We could easily spare the
bones of our game, which he delighted to pick.   We were
perfectly able to protect our booty with one hundred
dogs, whose dinners depended on open eyes.   But the
bear did not always understand our tactics.   We afterwards learned that we did not always understand his,
for he drove many prizes into our arms.   But man is a
short-sighted critic—he sees only his side of the game.'

In the northern march a much more friendly spirit
was developed.   We differed on many points of ethics
with bruin, and our fights, successful or otherwise, were
too numerous and disagreeable to relate fully.   Only
one of these battles will be recorded here, to save the
reputation of man as a superior fighting animal.

We had made a long march of about forty miles.
Already the dull purple of twilight was resting heavily
on darkening snows.   The temperature was —81°.
There was no wind.   The air was semi-liquid with suspended crystals.   When standing still we were perfectly
comfortable, although jets of steam from our nostrils
arranged frost crescents about our faces.

We had been advancing towards a group of musk oxen for more than an hour.   We were now in the habit of living from catch to catch, filling up on meat at the end of each successful hunt, and waiting for pot-luck for the next meal.   The sledges were too heavily loaded to carry additional weight.   Furthermore, the temperature was too low to split up frozen meat.   Indeed, most of our axes had been broken in trying to divide meat as dog food.   It was plainly an economy of axes and fuel to fill up on warm meat as the skin was removed, and wait for the next plunder.

We had been two days without setting eyes on an appetizing meal of steaming meat.   Not a living speck had crossed our horizon; and, therefore, when we noted the little cloud of steam rise from a side hill, and guessed that under it were herds of musk ox, our palates moistened with anticipatory joys.   A camping place was sought.   Two domes of snow were erected as a shelter.

Through the glasses we counted twenty-one musk oxen.   Some were digging up snow to find willows; others were sleeping.   All were unsuspecting.   After the experience we had in this kind of hunting, we confidently counted the game as ours.   A holiday was declared for the morrow, to dispose of the surplus.   Nourishment in prospect, one hundred dogs started with a jump, under the lashes of ten Eskimos.   Our sledges began shooting the boreal shoots.   After rushing over minor hills, the dog noses sank into bear tracks.   A little farther along, we realized we had rivals.   Two bears were far ahead, approaching the musk oxen.

The dogs scented their rivals.   The increased

bounding of the sledges made looping-the-loop seem
tame.   But we were too late; the bears ran into the
bunch of animals, and spoiled our game with no advantage to themselves.   Giving a half-hearted chase, they
rose to a bank of snow, deliberately sat down, and turned
to a position to give us the laugh.

The absence of musk ox did not slacken the pace
of the dogs.   The bears were quick to see the force of
our intent.   They scattered and climbed.   A bear is an
expert Alpinist; he requires no ice axe and no lantern.
The moon came out, and the snow slopes began to glare
with an electric incandescence.

In this pearly light, the white bear seemed black,
and was easily located.   One bear slipped into a ravine
and was lost.   All attention was now given to the other,
which was ascending an icy ridge to a commanding
precipice.   We cut the dogs from the sledges.   They
soared up the white slope as if they had wings.   The
bear gained the crest in time to cuff away each rising
antagonist.   The dogs tumbled over each other, down
several hundred feet into a soft snow-padded gully.
Other dogs continued to rise on the ridge to keep the
bear guessing.   The dogs in the pit discovered a new
route, and made a combined rear attack.   Bruin was
surprised, and turned to face his enemies.   Backing from
a sudden assault, he stepped over a precipice, and tumbled in a heap into the dog-strewn pit.   The battle was
now on in full force.   Finding four feet more useful
than one mouth, the bear turned on his back and sent his
paws out with telling effect.   The dogs, although not
giving up the battle, scattered, for the swing of the
creature's feet did not suit their battle methods.   Sit-

ting on curled tails, they filled the air with murderous howls and raised clouds of frozen breath in the flying snow.

We were on the scene at a safe distance, each with a tight grip on his gun, expecting the bear to make a sudden plunge.   But he was not given a choice of movement, and we could not shoot into the darting pit of dogs without injuring them.   At this moment Ah-we-lah, youngest of the party, advanced.   Leaving his gun, he descended through the dog ranks into the pit, with the spiked harpoon shaft.   The bear threw back its head to meet him.   A score of dogs grabbed the bear's feet.   Ah-we-lah raised his arm.   A sudden savage thrust sank the blunt steel into the bear's chest.   Cracking whips, we scattered the guarding dogs   The prize was quickly divided.

On our advance to the Polar sea, I found that there is considerable art in building snowhouses.   The casual observer is likely to conclude that it is an easy problem to pile up snow-blocks, dome-shaped, but to do this properly, so that the igloo will withstand wind, requires adept work.   From the lessons of my companions in this art I now became more alert to learn, knowing the necessity of protection on our Polar dash.

The first problem is to find proper snow.   One has often to seek for banks where the snow is just hard enough.   If it is too hard, it cannot be easily cut with knives.   If it is too soft, the blocks will crush, and cause the house to cave in.   Long knives are the best instruments—one of fifteen inches and another about ten. From sixty to seventy-five blocks, fifteen by twenty-four inches, are required to make a house ten feet by ten.

The blocks are cut according to the snow, but fifteen by twenty-four by eight inches is the best size.

The lower tiers of blocks are set in slight notches in the snow, to prevent the blocks from slipping out. A slight tilt begins from the first tiers; the next tier tilts still more, and so the next. The blocks are set so that the upper blocks cover the breaks in the lower tier. The fitting is done mostly with the blocks in position, the knife being passed between the blocks to and fro, with a pressure on the blocks with the other hand. The hardest task is to make the blocks stick without holding in the upper tiers. This is done by deft cuts with the knife and a slight thump of the blocks.

The dome is the most difficult part to build. In doing this all blocks are leveled and carefully set to arch the roof.

When the structure is completed, a candle is lit and the cracks are stuffed by cutting the edges off the nearest blocks, and pressing the broken snow into the cracks with the mittens. After this process, the interior arrangement is worked out. The foot space is first cut out in blocks. If the snow is on a slope, as it often happens, these blocks are raised and the upper slopes are cut down to a level plane.

The foot space is a very important matter, first for the comfort of sitting, and also to let off the carbonic acid gas, which quickly settles in these temperatures and extinguishes the fires. It, of course, has also an important bearing on human breathing.

Inhalation of very cold air at this time forced an unconscious expenditure of very much energy. The extent of this tax can be gauged only by the enormous difference between the temperature of the body and that of the air.   One day it was —72° F.   The difference was, therefore, 170°.   It is hard to conceive of normal breathing under such difficulties; but when properly clothed and fed, no great discomfort or ill-effects are noted.   The membranes of the air passages are, however, overflushed with blood.   The chest circulation is forced to its limits, and the heart beats are increased and strengthened.   The organs of circulation and respiration, which do ninety per cent. of the work of the body, are taxed with a new burden that must be counted in estimating one's day's task.   This loss of power in breathing extreme frost is certain to reduce working time and bodily force.

The land whose coast we were following to the shores of the Polar sea is part of the American hemisphere, and one of the largest islands of the world, spreading 30° longitude and rising 7° of latitude.   What is its name?   The question must remained unanswered, for it not only has no general name, but numerous sections are written with names and outlines that differ to a large extent with the caprice of the explorers who have been there.

The south is called Lincoln Land; above it, Ellesmere Land.   Then comes Schley Land, Grinnell Land, Arthur Land, and Grant Land, with other lands of later christening by Sverdrup and others.

No human beings inhabit the island.   No nation assumes the responsibility of claiming or protecting it. The Eskimo calls the entire country Acpohon, or "the Land of Guillemots," which are found in great abundance along the southeast point.   I have, therefore, to avoid conflictions, affixed the name of Acpohon as the general designation.

We had now advanced beyond the range of all primitive life. No human voice broke the frigid silence. The Eskimos had wandered into the opening of the musk ox pass. Sverdrup had mapped the channels of the west coast. But here was no trace of modern or aboriginal residence. There is no good reason why men should not have followed the musk oxen here, but the nearest Eskimos on the American side are those on Lancaster Sound.

I found an inspiration in being thus alone at the world's end. The barren rocks, the wastes of snow-fields, the mountains stripped of earlier ice-sheets, and every phase of the landscape, assured a new interest. There was a note of absolute abandon on the part of nature. If our own resources failed, or if a calamity overtook us, there would be no trace to mark icy graves forever hidden from surviving loved ones.

My Eskimo comrades were enthusiastic explorers. The game trails gave a touch of animation to their steps, which meant much to the progress of the expedition. We not only saw musk oxen in large herds, but tracks of bears and wolves were everywhere in line with our course. On the sea-ice we noted many seal blow-holes. Already the natives talked of coming here on the following year to cast their lot in the new wilds.

The picturesque headland of Schie we found to be a huge triassic rock of the same general formation as that indicated along Eureka Sound. Its west offered a series of grassy slopes bared by persistent winds, upon which animal life found easy access to the winter-cured

grass.   A narrow neck of land connected what seemed
like an island with the main land.   Here caches of fur
and fuel were left for the return.   In passing Snag's
Fiord the formation changed.   Here, for several
marches, game was scarce.   The temperature rose as we
neared the Polar sea.   The snow became much deeper
but it was hardened by stronger winds and increased
humidity.   High glacier-abandoned valleys with gradual slopes to the water's edge, gave the Heiberg shores
on Nansen Sound a different type of landscape from
that of the opposite shores.   Here and there we found
pieces of lignite coal, and as we neared Svartevoeg the
carboniferous formation became more evident.

Camping in the lowlands just south of Svartevoeg
Cliffs we secured seven musk oxen and eighty-five hares.
Here were immense fields of grass and moss bared by
persistent winter gales.   By a huge indentation here,
through which we saw the sea-level ice of the west, the
shores seemed to indicate that the point of Heiberg is an
island, but of this we were not absolutely sure.   To us
it was a great surprise that here, on the shores of the
Polar sea, we found a garden spot of plant luxuriance
and animal delight.   For this assured, in addition to the
caches left en route, a sure food supply for the return
from our mission to the North.

THE TRANS-BOREAL DASH BEGINS

BY FORCED EFFORTS AND THE USE OF AXES SPEED IS MADE OVER THE LAND-ADHERING PACK ICE OF POLAR SEA— THE MOST DIFFICULT TRAVEL OF THE PROPOSED JOURNEY SUCCESSFULLY ACCOMPLISHED—REGRET- FUL PARTING WITH THE ESKIMOS

XIII

FIVE HUNDRED MILES FROM THE POLE

Svartevoeg is a great cliff, the northernmost point of Heiberg Land, which leaps precipitously into the Polar sea. Its negroid face of black scarred rocks frowns like the carven stone countenance of some hide- ously mutilated and enraged Titan savage. It ex- presses, more than a human face could, the unendurable sufferings of this region of frigid horrors. It is five hundred and twenty miles from the North Pole.

From this point I planned to make my dash in as straight a route as might be possible. Starting from our camp at Annoatok late in February, when the cur- tain of night was just beginning to lift, when the chill of the long winter was felt at its worst, we had forced progress through deep snows, over land and frozen seas, braving the most furious storms of the season and trav- eling despite baffling darkness, and had covered in less than a month about four hundred miles—nearly half the distance between our winter camp and the Pole.

Arriving at land's end my heart had cause for gratification. We had weathered the worst storms of the year. The long bitter night had now been lost. The days lengthened and invaded with glitter the decreasing nights. The sun glowed more radiantly daily, rose higher and higher to a continued afterglow in cheery blues, and sank for periods briefer and briefer in seas of running color. Our hopes, like those of all mankind, had risen with the soul-lifting sun. We had made our progress mainly at the expense of the land which we explored, for the game en route had furnished food and clothing.

The supplies we had brought with us from Annoatok were practically untouched. We had stepped in overfed skins, were fired by a resolution which was recharged by a strength bred of feeding upon abundant raw and wholesome meat. Eating to repletion on unlimited game, our bodies were kept in excellent trim by the exigencies of constant and difficult traveling.

As a man's mental force is the result of yesteryears' upbuilding, so his strength of to-day is the result of last week's eating. With the surge of ambition which had been formulating for twenty years, and my body in best physical shape for the supreme test, the Pole now seemed almost near.

As the great cliffs of Svartevoeg rose before us my heart leaped. I felt that the first rung in the ladder of success had been climbed, and as I stood under the black cliffs of this earth's northernmost land I felt that I looked through the eyes of long experience. Having reached the end of Nansen Sound, with Svartevoeg on my left, and the tall, scowling cliffs of Lands-Lokk on my right, I viewed for the first time the rough and heavy ice of the untracked Polar sea, over which, knowing the conditions of the sea ice, I anticipated the most difficult part of our journey lay. Imagine before you fields of crushed ice, glimmering in the rising sunlight with shooting fires of sapphire and green; fields which have been slowly forced downward by strong currents from the north, and pounded and piled in jagged mountainous heaps for miles about the land. Beyond this difficult ice, as I knew, lay more even fields, over which traveling, saving the delays of storms and open leads, would be comparatively easy. To encompass this rough prospect was the next step in reaching my goal. I felt that no time must be lost. At this point I was now to embark upon the Polar sea; the race for my life's ambition was to begin here; but first I had finally to resolve on the details of my campaign.

I decided to reduce my party to the smallest possible number consistent with the execution of the problem in hand. In addition, for greater certainty of action over the unknown regions beyond, I now definitely resolved to simplify the entire equipment. An extra sled was left at the cache at this point to insure a good vehicle for our return in case the two sleds which we were to take should be badly broken en route. I decided to take only two men on the last dash. I had carefully watched and studied every one of my party, and had already selected E-tuk-i-shook and Ah-we-lah, two young Eskimos, each about twenty years old, as best fitted to be my sole companions in the long run of destiny.

Twenty-six of the best dogs were picked, and upon

two sleds were to be loaded all our needs for a trip estimated to last eighty days.

To have increased this party would not have enabled
us to carry supplies for a greater number of days.

The sleds might have been loaded more heavily, but
I knew this would reduce the important progress of the
first days.

With the character of ice which we had before us,
advance stations were impossible. A large expedition
and a heavy equipment would have been imprudent.
We must win or lose in a prolonged effort at high pressure. Therefore, absolute control and ease of adaptability to a changing environment was imperative.

From past experience I knew it was impossible to
control adequately the complex human temperament of
white men in the Polar wilderness. But I felt certain
the two Eskimo boys could be trusted to follow to the
limit of my own endurance. So our sleds were bur-
dened only with absolute necessaries.

Because of the importance of a light and efficient
equipment, much care had to be taken to reduce every
ounce of weight. The sleds were made of hickory, the
lightest wood consistent with great endurance, and
every needless fibre was gouged out. The iron shoes
were ground thin, and up to the present had stood the
test of half the Polar battle.

Eliminating everything not actually needed, but
selecting adequate food, I made the final preparations.

The camp equipment selected included the following articles: One blow fire lamp (jeuel), three aluminum pails, three aluminum cups, three aluminum tea-
spoons, one tablespoon, three tin plates, six pocket

knives, two butcher knives (ten inches), one saw knife (thirteen inches), one long knife (fifteen inches), one rifle (Sharp's), one rifle (Winchester .22), one hundred and ten cartridges, one hatchet, one Alpine axe, extra line and lashings, and three personal bags.

The sled equipment consisted of two sleds weighing fifty-two pounds each; one twelve-foot folding canvas boat, the wood of which formed part of a sled; one silk tent, two canvas sled covers, two reindeer skin sleeping bags, floor furs, extra wood for sled repairs, screws, nails and rivets.

My instruments were as follows: One field glass; one pocket compass; one liquid compass; one aluminum surveying compass, with azimuth attachment; one French surveyor's sextant, with radius $7\frac{1}{2}$, divided on silver to 10', reading by Vernier to 10" (among the extra attachments were a terrestrial and an astronomical telescope, and an extra night telescope mounted in aluminum, and also double refracting prisms, thermometers, etc.—the instrument was made by Hurleman of France and bought of Keuffel & Esser); one glass artificial horizon; three Howard pocket chronometers; one Tiffany watch; one pedometer; map-making material and instruments; three thermometers; one aneroid barometer; one camera and films; notebook and pencils.

The personal bags contained four extra pairs of kamiks, with fur stockings, a woolen shirt, three pairs of sealskin mittens, two pairs of fur mittens, a piece of blanket, a sealskin coat (netsha), extra fox tails and dog harness, a repair kit for mending clothing, and much other necessary material.

On the march we wore snow goggles, blue fox coats

(kapitahs) and birdskin shirts (Ah-tea), bearskin pants
(Nan-nooka), sealskin boots (Kam-ik), hare-skin stockings (Ah-tee-shah), and a band of fox tails under the
knee and about the waist.

The food supply, as will be seen by the following
list, was mostly pemmican:

Eight hundred and five pounds of beef pemmican,
one hundred and thirty pounds of walrus pemmican,
fifty pounds of musk ox tenderloin, twenty-five pounds
of musk ox tallow, two pounds of tea, one pound of
coffee, twenty-five pounds of sugar, forty pounds of
condensed milk, sixty pounds of milk biscuit, ten pounds
of pea soup powdered and compressed, fifty pounds of
surprises, forty pounds petroleum, two pounds of wood
alcohol, three pounds of candles and one pound of
matches.

We planned our future food supply with pemmican
as practically the sole food; the other things were to be
mere palate satisfiers. For the eighty days the supply
was to be distributed as follows:

For three men: Pemmican, one pound per day for
eighty days, two hundred and forty pounds.   For six
dogs: Pemmican, one pound per day for eighty days,
four hundred and eighty pounds.   This necessitated a
total of seven hundred and twenty pounds of pemmican.

Of the twenty-six dogs, we had at first figured on
taking sixteen over the entire trip to the Pole and back
to our caches on land, but in this last calculation only six
were to be taken.   Twenty, the least useful, were to
be used one after the other, as food on the march, as
soon as reduced loads and better ice permitted.   This,
we counted, would give one thousand pounds of fresh

meat over and above our pemmican supply. We carried about two hundred pounds of pemmican above the expected consumption, and in the final working out the dogs were used for traction purposes longer than we anticipated. But, with a cautious saving, the problem was solved somewhat more economically than any figuring before the start indicated.

Every possible article of equipment was made to do double service; not an ounce of dead weight was carried which could be dispensed with.

After making several trips about Svartevoeg, arranging caches for the return, studying the ice and land, I decided to make the final start on the Polar sea on March 18, 1908.

The time had come to part with most of our faithful Eskimo companions. Taking their hands in my manner of parting, I thanked them as well as I could for their faithful service to me. *"Tigishi ah yaung-uluk!"* (The big nail!), they replied, wishing me luck.

Then, in a half gale blowing from the northwest and charged with snow, they turned their backs upon me and started upon the return track. They carried little but ammunition, because we had learned that plenty of game was to be provided along the return courses.

Even after they were out of sight in the drifting snowstorm their voices came cheerily back to me. The faithful savages had followed me until told that I could use them no longer; and it was not only for their simple pay of knives and guns, but because of a real desire to be helpful. Their parting enforced a pang of loneliness.*

---

*A great deal of careful search and study was prosecuted about Svartevoeg, for here Peary claims to have left a cache, the alleged placing

With a snow-charged blast in our faces it was impossible for us to start immediately after the Eskimos returned. Withdrawing to the snow igloo, we entered our bags and slept a few hours longer. At noon the horizon cleared. The wind veered to the southwest and came with an endurable force. Doubly rationed the night before, the dogs were not to be fed again for two days. The time had come to start. We quickly loaded our sleds. Hitching the dogs, we let the whips fall, and with bounds they leaped around deep ice grooves in the great paleocrystic floes.

Our journey was begun. Swept of snow by the force of the preceding storm, the rough ice crisply cracked under the swift speed of our sleds. Even on this uneven surface the dogs made such speed that I kept ahead of them only with difficulty. Their barking pealed about us and re-echoed from the black cliffs behind. Dashing about transparent ultramarine gorges, and about the base of miniature mountains of ice, we soon came into a region of undulating icy hills. The hard irregularity of the ice at times endangered our sleds. We climbed over ridges like walls. We jumped dangerous crevasses, keeping slightly west by north; the land soon sank in the rear of us. Drifting clouds and wind-driven snows soon screened the tops of black mountains. Looking behind, I saw only a swirling, moving scene of dull white and nebulous gray. On every side ice hummocks heaved their backs and writhed by. Be-

of which he has used as a pretext for attempting to take from the map the name of Svartevoeg, given by Sverdrup, when he discovered it, to the northern part of Heiberg Land. Peary, coming later, put on his map the name Cape Thomas Hubbard, for one who had put easy money in his hands. But no such cache was found, and I doubt very much if Peary ever reached this point, except through a field-glass at very long range.

hind me followed four snugly loaded sleds, drawn by
forty-four selected dogs, under the lash of four expert
Eskimo drivers.   The dogs pranced; the joyous cries of
the natives rose and fell.   My heart leaped; my soul
sang. I felt my blood throb with each gallop of the leaping dog teams. The sound of their feet pattering on the
snow, the sight of their shaggy bodies tossing forward,
gave me joy.   For every foot of ice covered, every minute of constant action, drew me nearer, ever nearer, to
my goal.

Our first run was auspicious; it seemed to augur
success.   By the time we paused to rest we had covered
twenty-six miles.

We pitched camp on a floeberg of unusual height;
about us were many big hummocks, and to the lee of
these banks of hardened snow.   Away from land it is
always more difficult to find snow suitable for cutting
building blocks.   There, however, was an abundance.
We busily built, in the course of an hour, a comfortable
snow igloo.   Into it we crept, grateful for shelter from
the piercing wind.

The dogs curled up and went to sleep without a call,
as if they knew that there would be no food until tomorrow.   My wild companions covered their faces with their
long hair and sank quietly into slumber.   For me sleep
was impossible.   The whole problem of our campaign
had again to be carefully studied, and final plans made,
not only to reach our ultimate destination, but for the
two returning Eskimos and for the security of the things
left at Annoatok, and also to re-examine the caches left
en route for our return.   These must be protected as
well as possible against the bears and wolves.

Already I had begun to think of our return to land. It was difficult at this time even to approximate any probable course. Much would depend upon conditions to be encountered in the northward route. Although we had left caches of supplies with the object of returning along Nansen Sound, into Cannon Fiord and over Arthur Land, I entertained grave doubts of our ability to return this way. I knew that if the ice should drift strongly to the east we might not be given the choice of working out our own return. For, in such an event, we should perhaps be carried helplessly to Greenland, and should have to seek a return either along the east or the west coast.

This drift, in my opinion, would not necessarily mean dangerous hardships, for the musk oxen would keep us alive to the west, and to the east it seemed possible to reach Shannon Island, where the Baldwin-Zeigler expeditions had abandoned a large cache of supplies. It appeared not improbable, also, that a large land extension might offer a safe return much further west. I fell asleep while pondering over these things. By morning the air was clear of frost crystals. It was intensely cold, not only because of a temperature of 56° below zero, Fahrenheit, but a humid chill which pierced to the very bones. A light breeze came from the west. The sun glowed in a freezing field of blue.

Hitching our dogs, we started. For several hours we seemed to soar over the white spaces. Then the ice changed in character, the expansive, thick fields of glacier-like ice giving way to floes of moderate size and thickness. These were separated by zones of troublesome crushed ice thrown into high-pressure lines, which offered serious barriers. Chopping the pathway with an ice axe, we managed to make fair progress. We covered twenty-one miles of our second run on the Polar sea. I expected, at the beginning of this final effort, to send back by this time the two extra men, Koo-loo-ting-wah and In-u-gi-to, who had remained to help us over the rough pack-ice. But progress had not been as good as I had expected; so, although we could hardly spare any food to feed their dogs, the two volunteered to push along for another day without dog food.

Taking advantage of big, strong teams and the fire of early enthusiasm, we aimed to force long distances through the extremely difficult ice jammed here against the distant land. The great weight of the supplies intended for the final two sleds were now distributed over four sleds. With axe and compass in hand, I led the way. With prodigious effort I chopped openings through barriers after barriers of ice. Sled after sled was passed over the tumbling series of obstacles by my companions while I advanced to open a way through the next. With increasing difficulties in some troublesome ice, we camped after making only sixteen miles. Although weary, we built a small snowhouse. I prepared over my stove a pot of steaming musk ox loins and broth and a double brew of tea. After partaking of this our two helpers prepared to return. To have taken them farther would have necessitated a serious drain on our supplies and an increased danger for their lives in a longer return to land.

By these men I sent back instructions to Rudolph Francke to remain in charge of my supplies at Annoatok until June 5th, 1908, and then, if we should not have re-

DASHING FORWARD EN ROUTE TO THE POLE

DEPARTURE OF SUPPORTING PARTY
A BREATHING SPELL
POLEWARD!

turned by that date, to place Koo-loo-ting-wah in charge
and go home either by a whaler or some Danish ship. I
knew that, should we get in trouble, he could offer no
relief to help us, and that his waiting an indefinite time
alone would be a needless hardship.

The way before Koo-loo-ting-wah and In-u-gi-to,
who had so cheerfully remained to the last possible moment that they could be of help, was not an entirely
pleasant one. Their friends were by now well on their
journey toward Annoatok, and they had to start after
them with sleds empty of provisions and dogs hungry for
food.

They hoped to get back to land and off the ice of
the Polar sea in one long day's travel of twenty-four
hours. Even this would leave their fourth day without
food for their dogs. In case of storms or moving of
the ice, other days of famine might easily fall to their lot.
However, they faced possible dangers cheerfully rather
than ask me to give them anything from the stores that
were to support their two companions, myself and our
dogs on our way onward to the Pole and back. I was
deeply touched by this superlative devotion. They assured me too (in which they were right) that they had
an abundance of possible food in the eighteen dogs they
took with them. If necessary, they could sacrifice a few
at any time for the benefit of the others, as must often
be done in the Northland.

There were no formalities in our parting on the
desolate ice. Yet, as the three of us who were left
alone gazed after our departing companions, we felt a
poignant pang in our hearts. About us was a cheerless
waste of crushed wind-and-water-driven ice. A sharp

wind stung our faces. The sun was obscured by clouds which piled heavily and darkly about the horizon. The ' cold and brilliant jeweled effects of the frozen sea were lost in a dismal hue of dull white and sombre gray. On the horizon, Svartevoeg, toward which the returning Eskimos were bound, was but a black speck. To the north, where our goal lay, our way was untrodden, unknown. The thought came to me that perhaps we should never see our departing friends. With it came a pang of tenderness for the loved ones I had left behind me. Although our progress so far had been successful, and half the distance was made, dangers unknown and undreamed of existed in the way before us. My Eskimos already showed anxiety—an anxiety which every aboriginal involuntarily feels when land disappears on the horizon. Never venturing themselves far onto the Polar sea, when they lose sight of land a panic overcomes them. Before leaving us one of the departing Eskimos had pointed out a low-lying cloud to the north of us. "Noona" (land), he said, nodding to the others. The thought occurred to me that, on our trip, I could take advantage of the mirages and low clouds on the horizon and encourage a belief in a constant nearness to land, thus maintaining their courage and cheer.*

Regrets and fears were not long-lasting, however,

---

*On their return to Etah, and after I had left for Upernavik, my Eskimos, questioned by Mr. Peary, who was anxious to secure anything that might serve towards discrediting me, answered innocently that they had been only a few sleeps from land. This unwilling and naive admission was published in a pretentious statement, the purpose of which was to cast doubt on my claim. Other answers of my Eskimos, to the effect that I had instruments and had made constant observations, it is curious to note, were suppressed by Mr. Peary and his party on their return. Every insinuation was made to the effect that I had had no instruments, had consequently taken no observations, and had, therefore, no means of ascertaining the Pole even had I wished to do so.

for the exigencies of our problem were sufficiently imperative and absorbing.   To the overcoming of these we had now to devote our entire attention and strain every fibre.

We had now advanced, by persistent high-pressure efforts, over the worst possible ice conditions, somewhat more than sixty miles.   Of the 9° between land's end and the Pole, we had covered one; and we had done this without using the pound of food per day allotted each of us out of the eighty days' supply transported.

POLAR BEAR

OVER THE POLAR SEA TO THE BIG LEAD

WITH TWO ESKIMO COMPANIONS, THE RACE POLEWARD
CONTINUES OVER ROUGH AND DIFFICULT ICE—THE
LAST LAND FADES BEHIND—MIRAGES LEAP INTO
BEING AND WEAVE A MYSTIC SPELL—A SWIRLING
SCENE OF MOVING ICE AND FANTASTIC EFFECTS—
STANDING ON A HILL OF ICE, A BLACK, WRITHING,
SNAKY CUT APPEARS IN THE ICE BEYOND—THE BIG
LEAD—A NIGHT OF ANXIETY—FIVE HUNDRED MILES
ALREADY COVERED—FOUR HUNDRED TO THE POLE

XIV

To Eighty-Third Parallel

Our party, thus reduced to three, went onward.
Although the isolation was more oppressive, there were
the advantages of the greater comfort, safety, speed and
convenience that came from having only a small band.
The large number of men in a big expedition always
increases responsibilities and difficulties. In the early
part of a Polar venture this disadvantage is eliminated
by the facilities to augment supplies by the game en
route and by ultimate advantages of the law of the survival of the fittest. But after the last supporting sleds
return, the men are bound to each other for protection
and can no longer separate. A disabled or unfitted

dog can be fed to his companions, but an injured or
weak man cannot be eaten nor left alone to die.   An
exploring venture is only as strong as its weakest member, and increased numbers, like increased links in a
chain, reduce efficiency.

Moreover, personal idiosyncrasies and inconven-
iences always shorten a day's march.   And, above all, a
numerous party quickly divides into cliques, which are
always opposed to each other, to the leader, and invariably to the best interests of the problem in hand.
With but two savage companions, to whom this arduous
task was but a part of an accustomed life of frost, I did
not face many of the natural personal barriers which contributed to the failure of former Arctic expeditions.

In my judgment, when you double a Polar party
its chances for success are reduced one-half; when you
divide it, strength and security are multiplied.

We had been traveling about two and one-half miles
per hour.   By making due allowances for detours and
halts at pressure lines, the number of hours traveled
gave us a fair estimate of the day's distance.   Against
this the pedometer offered a check, and the compass
gave the course.   Thus, over blank charts, our course
was marked.

By this kind of dead reckoning our position on
March 20 was: Latitude, 82° 23'; Longitude, 95° 14'.
A study of our location seemed to indicate that we had
passed beyond the zone of ice crushed by the influence
of land pressure.   Behind were great hummocks and
small ice; ahead was a cheerful expanse of larger, clearer
fields, offering a promising highway.

Our destination was now about four hundred and

sixty miles beyond. Our life, with its pack environment, assumed another aspect. Previously we permitted ourselves some luxuries. A pound of coal oil and a good deal of musk ox tallow were burned each day to heat the igloo and to cook abundant food. Extra meals were served when occasion called for them, and for each man there had been all the food and drink he desired. If the stockings or the mittens were wet there was fire enough to dry them out. All of this had now to be changed.

Hereafter there was to be a short daily allowance of food and fuel—one pound of pemmican a day for the dogs, about the same for the men, with just a taste of other things. Fortunately, we were well provided with fresh meat for the early part of the race by the lucky run through game lands. Because of the need of fuel economy we now cut our pemmican with an axe. Later it split the axe.

At first no great hardship followed our changed routine. We filled up sufficiently on two cold meals daily and also depended on superfluous bodily tissue. It was no longer possible to jump on the sled for an occasional breathing spell, as we had done along the land.

Such a journey as now confronted us is a long-continued, hard, difficult, sordid, body-exhausting thing. Each day some problem presents some peculiar condition of the ice or state of the weather. The effort, for instance, to form some shield from intense cold gives added interest to the game. That one thing after another is being met, with always the anticipation of next day's struggle, adds a thrill to the conquest, spurs one to greater and ever greater feats, and really constitues the actual victory of such a quest. With overloaded sleds the drivers must now push and pull at them to aid the dogs. My task was to search the troubled ice for easy routes, cutting away here and there with the ice-axe to permit the passing of the sleds.

Finally stripping for the race, man and dog must walk along together through storms and frost for the elusive goal. Success or failure must depend mostly upon our ability to transport nourishment and to keep up the muscular strength for a prolonged period.

As we awoke on the morning of March 21 and peered out of the eye-port of the igloo, the sun edged along the northeast. A warm orange glow suffused the ice and gladdened our hearts. The temperature was 63° below zero, Fahrenheit; the barometer was steady and high. There was almost no wind. Not a cloud lined the dome of pale purple blue, but a smoky streak along the west shortened our horizon in that direction and marked a lead of open water.

Our breakfast consisted of two cups of tea, a watch-sized biscuit, a chip of frozen meat and a boulder of pemmican. Creeping out of our bags, our shivering legs were pushed through bearskin cylinders which served as trousers. We worked our feet into frozen boots and then climbed into fur coats. Next we kicked the front out of the snowhouse and danced about to stimulate heart action.

Quickly the camp furnishings were tossed on the sleds and securely lashed. We gathered the dog traces into the drag lines, vigorously snapped the long whips, and the willing creatures bent to the shoulder straps.

The sleds groaned.   The unyielding snows gave a metallic ring.   The train moved with a cheerful pace.

"*Am-my noona terronga dosangwah*" (Perhaps land will be out of sight today), we said to one another.* But the words did not come with serious intent.   In truth, each in his own way felt keenly that we were leaving a world of life and possible comfort for one of torment and suffering.   Axel Heiberg Land, to the south, was already only a dull blue haze, while Grant Land, on the eastward, was making fantastic figures of its peaks and ice walls.   The ice ran in waves of undulating blue, shimmering with streams of gold, before us.   Behind, the last vestiges of jagged land rose and fell like marionettes dancing a wild farewell.   Our heart-pulls were backward, our mental kicks were forward.

Until now this strange white world had been one of grim reality.   As though some unseen magician had waved his wand, it was suddenly transformed into a land of magic.   Leaping into existence, as though from realms beyond the horizon, huge mirages wove a web of marvelous delusional pictures about the horizon. Peaks of snow were transformed into volcanoes, belching smoke; out of the pearly mist rose marvelous cities with

---

*My enemies credit me with a journey of two thousand miles, which is double Peary's greatest distance; but then, to deny my Polar attainment, they keep me sitting here, on a sterile waste of ice, for three months. Would any man sit down there and shiver in idleness, when the reachable glory of Polar victory was on one side and the get-at-able gastronomic joy of game land on the other? Only a crazy man would do that, and we were too busy to lose our mental balance at that time. When leg-force controls human destiny, and a half-filled stomach clears the brain for action, for a long time, at least, insanity is very remote. Furthermore, the Eskimo boys said we traveled on the ice-pack for seven moons, and that we reached a place where the sun does not dip at night; where the day and night shadows were of equal length. Has Mr. Peary reached that point? If so, neither he nor his Eskimos have noted it.

fairy-like castles; in the color-shot clouds waved golden and rose and crimson pennants from pinnacles and domes of mosaic-colored splendor. Huge creatures, misshapen and grotesque, writhed along the horizon and performed amusing antics.

Beginning now, and rarely absent, these spectral denizens of the North accompanied us during the entire journey; and later, when, fagged of brain and sapped of bodily strength, I felt my mind swimming in a sea of half-consciousness, they filled me almost with horror, impressing me as the monsters one sees in a nightmare.

At every breathing spell in the mad pace our heads now turned to land. Every look was rewarded by a new prospect. From belching volcanoes to smoking cities of modern bustle, the mirages gave a succession of striking scenes which filled me with awed and marveling delight. A more desolate line of coast could not be imagined. Along its edge ran low wind-swept and wind-polished mountains. These were separated by valleys filled with great depths of snow and glacial ice.

Looking northward, the sky line was clear of the familiar pinnacles of icebergs. In the immediate vicinity many small bergs were seen; some of these were grounded, and the pack thus anchored was thrown in huge uplifts of pressure lines and hummocks. The sea, as is thereby determined, is very shallow for a long distance from land.

This interior accumulation of snow moves slowly to the sea, where it forms a low ice wall, a glacier of the Malaspina type. Its appearance is more like that of heavy sea ice; hence the name of the paleocrystic ice, fragments from this glacier, floebergs, which, seen in

Lincoln Sea and resembling old floes, were supposed to be the product of the ancient upbuilding of the ice of the North Polar Sea.

Snapping our whips and urging the dogs, we traveled until late in the afternoon, mirages constantly appearing and melting about us. Now the land suddenly settled downward as if by an earthquake. The pearly glitter, which had raised and magnified it, darkened. A purple fabric fell over the horizon and merged imperceptibly into the lighter purple blue of the upper skies. We saw the land, however, at successive periods for several days. This happened whenever the atmosphere was in the right condition to elevate the terrestrial contour lines by refracting sun rays.

Every condition favored us on this march. The wind was not strong and struck us at an angle, permitting us to guard our noses by pushing a mitten under our hoods or by raising a fur-clad hand.

We had not been long in the field, however, when the wind, that ever-present dragon guardian of the unseen northern monarch's demesne, began to suck strength from our bodies. Shortly before Grant Land entirely faded the monster fawned on us with gentle breathing.

The snow was hard, and the ice, in fairly large fields separated by pressure lines, offered little resistance. On March 21, at the end of a forced effort of fourteen hours, the register indicated a progress of twenty-nine miles.

Too weary to build an igloo, we threw ourselves thoughtlessly upon the sleds for a short rest, and fell asleep. I was awakened from my fitful slumber by a feeling of compression, as if stifling arms hideously gripped me. It was the wind. I breathed with difficulty. I struggled to my feet, and about me hissed and wailed the dismal sound. It was a sharp warning to us that to sleep without the shelter of an igloo would probably mean death.

On the heavy floe upon which we rested were several large hummocks. To the lee of one of these we found suitable snow for a shelter.

Lines of snowy vapor were rushing over the pack. The wind came with rapidly increasing force. We erected the house, however, before we suffered severely from the blast. We crept into it out of the storm and nested in warm furs.

The wind blew fiercely throughout the night. By the next morning, March 22, the storm had eased to a steady, light breeze. The temperature was 59° below zero. We emerged from our igloo at noon. Although the cheerless gray veil had been swept from the frigid dome of the sky, to the north appeared a low black line over a pearly cloud which gave us much uneasiness. This was a narrow belt of "water-sky," which indicated open water or very thin ice at no great distance.

The upper surface of Grant Land was now a mere thin pen line on the edge of the horizon. But a play of land clouds above it attracted the eyes to the last known rocks of solid earth. We now felt keenly the piercing cold of the Polar sea. The temperature gradually rose to 46° F. below zero, in the afternoon, but there was a deadly chill in the long shadows which increased with the swing of the lowering sun.

A life-sapping draught, which sealed the eyes and

bleached the nose, still hissed over the frozen sea. We had hoped that this would soften with the midday sun. Instead, it came with a more cutting sharpness. In the teeth of the wind we persistently pursued a course slightly west of north. The wind was slightly north of west. It struck us at a painful angle and brought tears. Our moistened lashes quickly froze together as we winked, and when we rubbed them and drew apart the lids the icicles broke the tender skin. Our breath froze on our faces. Often we had to pause, uncover our hands and apply the warm palms to the face before it was possible to see.

Every minute thus lost filled me with impatience and dismay. Minutes of traveling were as precious as bits of gold to a hoarding miser.

In the course of a brief time our noses became tipped with a white skin and also required nursing. My entire face was now surrounded with ice, but there was no help for it. If we were to succeed the face must be bared to the cut of the elements. So we must suffer. We continued, urging the dogs and struggling with the wind just as a drowning man fights for life in a storm at sea.

About six o'clock, as the sun crossed the west, we reached a line of high-pressure ridges. Beyond these the ice was cut into smaller floes and thrown together into ugly irregularities. According to my surmises, an active pack and troubled seas could not be far away. The water-sky widened, but became less sharply defined.

We laboriously picked a way among hummocks and pressure lines which seemed impossible from a distance. Our dogs panted with the strain; my limbs ached. In a few hours we arrived at the summit of an unusual uplift of ice blocks.. Looking ahead, my heart pained as if in the grip of an iron hand. My hopes sank within me. Twisting snake-like between the white field, and separating the packs, was a tremendous cut several miles wide, which seemed at the time to bar all further progress. It was the Big Lead, that great river separating the land-adhering ice from the vast grinding fields of the central pack beyond, at which many heroic men before me had stopped. I felt the dismay and heartsickness of all of them within me now. The wind, blowing with a vengeful wickedness, laughed sardonically in my ears.

Of course we had our folding canvas boat on the sleds. But in this temperature of 48° below zero I knew no craft could be lowered into water without fatal results. All of the ice about was firmly cemented together, and over it we made our way toward the edge of the water line.

Passing through pressure lines, over smaller and more troublesome fields, we reached the shores of the Big Lead. We had, by two encouraging marches, covered fifty miles. The first hundred miles of our journey on the Polar pack had been covered. The Pole was four hundred miles beyond!

Camp was pitched on a secure old ice field. Cutting through huge ice cliffs, the dark crack seemed like a long river winding between palisades of blue crystal. A thin sheet of ice had already spread over the mysterious deep. On its ebony mirrored surface a profusion of fantastic frost crystals arranged themselves in bunches resembling white and saffron-colored flowers.

Through the apertures of this young ice dark vapors rose like steam through a screen of porous fabrics and fell in feathers of snow along the sparkling shores. After partaking of a boulder of pemmican, E-tuk-i-shook went east and I west to examine the lead of water for a safe crossing. There were several narrow places, while here and there floes which had been adrift in the lead were now fixed by young ice. Ah-we-lah remained behind to make our snowhouse comfortable.

For a long time this huge separation in the pack had been a mystery to me. At first sight there seemed to be no good reason for its existence. Peary had found a similar break north of Robeson Channel. It was likely that what we saw was an extension of the same, following at a distance the general trend of the north-ernmost land extension.

This is precisely what one finds on a smaller scale when two ice packs come together. Here the pack of the central polar sea meets the land-adhering ice. The movement of the land pack is intermittent and usually along the coast. The shallows, grounded ice and projecting points interfere with a steady drift. The movement of the central pack is quite constant, in almost every direction, the tides, currents and winds each giving momentum to the floating mass. The lead is thus the breaking line between the two bodies of ice. It widens as the pack separates, and narrows or widens with an easterly or westerly drift, according to the pressure of the central pack. Early in the season, when the pack is crevassed and not elastic, it is probably wide; later, as the entire sea of ice becomes active, it may dis-appear or shift to a line nearer the land.

In low temperature new ice forms rapidly. This
offers an obstruction to the drift of the old ice. As the
heavy central pack is pressed against the unyielding
land pack the small ice is ground to splinters, and even
heavy floes are crushed. This reduced mass of small
ice is pasted and cemented along the shores of the Big
Lead, leaving a broad band of troublesome surface as
a serious barrier to sled travel. It seems quite probable
that this lead, or a condition similar to it, extends entirely around the Polar sea as a buffer between the land
and the middle pack.

In exploring the shore line, a partially bridged
place was found about a mile from camp, but the young
ice was too elastic for a safe track. The temperature,
however, fell rapidly with the setting sun, and the wind
was just strong enough to sweep off the heated vapors.
I knew better atmospheric condition could not be
afforded quickly to thicken the young ice.

Returning to camp that night, we surprised our
stomachs by a little frozen musk ox tenderloin and
tallow, the greatest delicacy in our possession. Then
we retired. Ice was our pillow. Ice was our bed. A
dome of snow above us held off the descending liquid air
of frost. Outside the wind moaned. Shudderingly,
the deep howl of the dogs rolled over the ice. Lying on
the sheeted deep, beneath my ears I heard the noise of
the moving, grinding, crashing pack. It sounded terri-
fyingly like a distant thunder of guns. I could not
sleep. Sick anxiety filled me. Could we cross the
dreadful river on the morrow? Would the ice freeze?
Or might the black space not hopelessly widen during
the night? I lay awake, shivering with cold. I felt

within me the blank loneliness of the thousands of desolate miles about me.

One hundred miles of the unknown had been covered; five hundred miles of the journey from our winter camp were behind us. Beyond, to the goal, lay four hundred unknown miles. Nothing dearly desired of man ever seemed so far away.

ESKIMO TORCH

CROSSING MOVING SEAS OF ICE

CROSSING THE LEAD—THE THIN ICE HEAVES LIKE A SHEET OF RUBBER—CREEPING FORWARD CAUTIOUSLY, THE TWO DANGEROUS MILES ARE COVERED —BOUNDING PROGRESS MADE OVER IMPROVING ICE— THE FIRST HURRICANE—DOGS BURIED AND FROZEN INTO MASSES IN DRIFTS OF SNOW—THE ICE PARTS THROUGH THE IGLOO—WAKING TO FIND ONE'S SELF FALLING INTO THE COLD SEA.

XV

The First Steps Over the Grinding Central Pack

Ill at ease and shivering, we rose from our crystal berths on March 23 and peeped out of a pole-punched porthole. A feeble glow of mystic color came from everywhere at once. Outside, toward a sky of dull purple, columns of steam-like vapor rose from open ice water, resembling vapors from huge boiling cauldrons. We sank with chattering teeth to our cheerless beds and quivered with the ghostly unreality of this great vibrating unknown.

Long before the suppressed incandescent night changed to the prism sparkle of day we were out seeking a way over the miles of insecure young ice separating us from the central pack. On our snowshoes, with an easy tread, spread feet and with long life lines tied to each other, we ventured to the opposite shores of that dangerous spread of young ice. Beyond, the central pack glittered in moving lines and color, like quick-silver shot with rainbow hues.

The Big Lead was mottled and tawny colored, like the skin of a great constrictor. As we stood and looked over its broad expanse to the solid floes, two miles off, there came premonitions to me of impending danger. Would the ice bear us? If it broke, and the life line was not quickly jerked, our fate would almost certainly be sure death. Sontag, the astronomer of Dr. Hay's Expedition, thus lost his life. Many others have in like manner gone to the bottomless deep. On two occasions during the previous winter I had thus gone through, but the life line had saved me. What would be our fate here? But, whatever the luck, we must cross. I knew delay was fatal, for at any time a very light wind or a change in the drift might break the new ice and delay us long enough to set the doom of failure upon our entire venture.

Every precaution was taken to safeguard our lives. The most important problem was to distribute the weight so that all of it would not be brought to bear on a small area. We separated our dog teams from the sleds, holding to long lines which were fastened about our bodies and also to the sleds. The sleds were hitched to each other by another long line.

With bated breath and my heart thumping, I advanced at the end of a long line which was attached to the first sled, and picked my way through the crushed and difficult ice along shore. With the life-saving line fastened to each one of us, we were insured against possible dangers as well as forethought could provide. Running from sled to sled, from dog to dog, and man to man, it would afford a pulling chance for life should anyone break through the ice. It seemed unlikely that the ice along the entire chain would break at once, but its cracking under the step of one of us seemed probable.

I knew, as I gently placed my foot upon the thin yellowish surface, that at any moment I might sink into an icy grave. Yet a spirit of bravado thrilled my heart. I felt the grip of danger, and also that thrill of exultation which accompanies its terror.

Gently testing the ice before me with the end of my axe, with spread legs, on snowshoes, with long, sliding steps, I slowly advanced.

A dangerous cracking sound pealed in every direction under my feet. The Eskimos followed. With every tread the thin sheet ice perceptibly sank under me, and waved, in small billows, like a sheet of rubber.

Stealthily, as though we were trying to filch some victory, we crept forward. We rocked on the heaving ice as a boat on waves of water. Now and then we stepped upon sheets of thicker ice, and hastily went forward with secure footing. None of us spoke during the dangerous crossing. I heard distinctly the panting of the dogs and the patter of their feet. We covered the two miles safely, yet our snail-like progress seemed to cover many anxious years.

I cannot describe the exultation which filled me when the crossing was accomplished. It seemed as though my goal itself were stretching toward me. I experienced a sense of unbounded victory. I could have cheered with joy. Intoxicated with it, I and my companions leaped forward, new cheer quickening our steps. The dangers to come seemed less formidable now, and as we journeyed onward it was the mastering of these, as did our accomplishment in crossing the Big Lead, which gave us a daily incentive to continue our way and ever to apply brain and muscle to the subduing of even greater difficulties with zest.

It was in doing this that the real thrill, the real victory—the only thrill and victory, indeed—of reaching the North Pole lay. The attaining of this mythical spot did not then, and does not now, seem in itself to mean anything; I did not then, and do not now, consider it the treasure-house of any great scientific secrets. The only thing to be gained from reaching the Pole, the triumph of it, the lesson in the accomplishment, is that man, by brain power and muscle energy, can subdue the most terrific forces of a blind nature if he is determined enough, courageous enough, and undauntedly persistent despite failure.

On my journey northward I felt the ever constant presence of those who had died in trying to reach the goal before me. There were times when I felt a startling nearness to them—a sense like that one has of the proximity of living beings in an adjoining room. I felt the goad of their hopes within me; I felt the steps of their dead feet whenever my feet touched the ice. I felt their unfailing determination revive me when I was tempted to turn back in the days of inhuman suffering that were to come. I felt that I, the last man to essay this goal, must for them justify humanity; that I must crown three centuries of human effort with success.

With the perilous Big Lead behind us, a bounding

course was set to reach the eighty-fifth parallel on the ninety-seventh meridian. What little movement was noted on the ice had been easterly. To allow for this drift we aimed to keep a line slightly west of the Pole.

We bounded northward joyously. Under our speeding feet the ice reverberated and rumbled with the echo of far-away splitting and crashing.

The sun sank into a haze like mother-of-pearl. Our pathway glowed with purple and orange. We paused only when the pale purple blue of night darkened the pack.

Starting forward in the afternoon of March 24, we crossed many small floes with low-pressure lines separated by narrow belts of new ice. Our speed increased. At times we could hardly keep pace with our dogs. The temperature rose to forty-one below zero. The western sky cleared slightly. Along the horizon remained misty appearances resembling land. This low-lying fog continued during our entire second hundred miles over the Polar basin. Under it we daily expected to see new land.

But Nature did not satisfy our curiosity for a long time. Both Ah-we-lah and E-tuk-i-shook were sure of a constant nearness to land. Because of the native panic out of its reassuring sight, I encouraged this belief, as I did concerning every other possible sign of land further northward. I knew that only by encouraging a delusion of nearness to land could I urge them ever farther in the face of the hardships that must inevitably come.

An altitude of the sun at noon on March 24 gave our position as latitude 83° 31'. The longitude was estimated at 96° 27′. The land clouds of Grant Land were still visible. The low bank of mist in the west occasionally brightened. For a while I believed this to be an indication of Crocker Land.

Until midday I took observations and endeavored to study the appearances of land. Our dogs sniffed the air as if scenting game. After a diligent search, one seal blow-hole was located, and later we saw an old bear track. No algæ or other small life was detected in the water between the ice crevices. At the Big Lead a few algæ had been gathered. But here the sea seemed sterile. Signs of seal and bear, however, were encouraging to us as possible future food supply. In returning, I calculated the season would be more advanced, and it was possible that life might move northward, thus permitting an extension of the time allowance of our rations.

Although the heat of the sun was barely felt, its rays began to pierce our eyes with painful effects. Reflected from the spotless surface of the storm-driven snows, the bright light could not long be endured without some protection, even by the Eskimos. Now came the time to test a simple expedient that had occurred to me at Annoatok. Amber-colored goggles, darkened or smoked glasses and ordinary automobile goggles had all been tried with indifferent results. They failed for one reason or another, mostly because of an insufficient range of vision or because of a faulty construction that made it impossible to proceed more than a few minutes without removing the accumulated condensation within them. At Annoatok I had made amber-colored goggles from the glass of my photographic supplies. By adjusting them I soon found they were a priceless discovery.   They entirely eliminated one of the greatest torments of Arctic travel.

While effectually screening the active rays that would have injured the eye, these amber glasses at the same time possessed the inestimable advantage of not interfering with the range of vision.

Relieved of the snow glare, the eye was better enabled to see distant objects than through field glasses. It is frequently extremely difficult to detect icy surface irregularities on cloudy days.   The amber glass dispelled this trouble perfectly, enabling the eye to search carefully every nook and crevice through the vague incandescence which blinds the observer in hazy weather. The glasses did not reduce the *quantity* of light, as do smoked glasses, but the *quality;* the actinic rays, which do the greatest harm, were eliminated.   We were not only relieved of the pain and fatigue of eye strain, but the color imparted a touch of cheer and warmth to our chilled blue horizon.   The usual snow goggles add to the ugly gray-blue of the frozen seas, which alone sends frosty waves through the nervous fibers.

So thoroughly delighted were we with these goggles that later we wore them even in igloos while asleep, with the double object of screening the strong light which passes through the eyelids and of keeping the forehead warm.

On our march in the early part of the afternoon of the 24th the weather proved good.   The ice, though newly crevassed, improved as we advanced.   The late start spread our day's work close to the chill of midnight.   When we started the wind blew kindly.   With glad hearts we forged forward without delays.   On the ice I heard the soft patter of swift dog feet and the dashing, cutting progress of the sleds.   As a scene viewed from a carousel, the field of ice swept around me in our dizzy, twisting progress.   We swept resistlessly onward for twenty-three miles.   As we had taken a zigzag course to follow smooth ice, I therefore recorded only eighteen miles to our credit.

The night was beautiful.   The sun sank into a purple haze.   Soon, in the magic of the atmosphere, appeared three suns of prismatic colors.   These settled slowly into the frozen sea and disappeared behind that persistent haze of obscuring mist which always rests over the pack when the sun is low.   During the night a narrow band of orange was flung like a ribbon across the northern skies.   The pack surface glowed with varying shades of violet, lilac and pale purplish blue.   Many such splendid sights are to be constantly seen in the Arctic.   Although I reveled in it now, the time was soon to come when weariness and hunger numbed my faculties into a dreary torpor in which the splendor was not seen.

Signs appeared of a gale from the west before we were quite ready to camp.   Little sooty clouds with ragged edges suddenly began to cover the sky, scurrying at an alarming pace.   Beyond us a huge smoky volume of cloud blackened the pearly glitter.

Suitable camping ice was sought.   In the course of an hour we built an igloo.   We made the structure stronger than usual on account of the threatening storm. We constructed double tiers of snow blocks to the windward.   A little water was thrown over the top to cement the blocks. We fastened the dogs to the lee of hummocks. The sleds were securely lashed and fastened to the ice.

We expected a hurricane, and had not to wait to taste its fury. Before we were at rest in our bags the wind lashed the snows with a force inconceivable. With rushing drift, the air thickened. Dogs and sleds in a few minutes were buried under banks of snow and great drifts encircled the igloo. The cemented blocks of our dome withstood the sweep of the blast well. Yet, now and then, small holes were burrowed through the snow wall by the sharp wind. Drift entered and covered us. I lay awake for hours. I felt the terrible oppression of that raging, life-sucking vampire force sweeping over the desolate world. Disembodied things—the souls of those, perhaps, who had perished here—seemed frenziedly calling me in the wind. I felt under me the surge of the sweeping, awful sea. I felt the desolation of this stormy world within my shuddering soul; but, withal, I throbbed with a determination to assert the supremacy of living man over these blind, insensate forces; to prove that the living brain and palpitating muscle of a finite though conscious creature could vanquish a hostile Nature which creates to kill. I burned to justify those who had died here; to fulfill by proxy their hopes; to set their calling souls at rest. The storm waked in me an angry, challenging determination.

Early in the morning of the 25th the storm ceased as suddenly as it had come. A stillness followed which was appalling. It seemed as if the storm had heard my thoughts and paused to contemplate some more dreadful onslaught. The dogs began to howl desperately, as if attacked by a bear. We rushed out of our igloo, seeking guns. There was no approaching creature. It was, however, a signal of serious distress that we had heard. The dogs were in acute misery. The storm-driven snows had buried and bound them in unyielding ice. They had partly uncovered themselves. United by trace and harness, they were imprisoned in frozen masses. Few of them could even rise and stretch. They were in severe torment.

We hurriedly freed their traces and beat the cemented snows from their furs with sticks. Released, they leaped about gladly, their cries, curling tails and pointed noses telling of gratitude. While we danced about, stretching our limbs and rubbing our hands to get up circulation, the sun rose over the northern blue, flushing the newly driven snows with warm tones. The temperature during the storm had risen to only 26° below, but soon the thermometer sank rapidly below 40°. The west was still smoky and the weather did not seem quite settled. As it was still too early to start, we again slipped into the bags and sought quiet slumber.

As yet the dreadful insomnia which was to rob me of rest on my journey had not come, and I slept with the blissful soundness of a child. I must have been asleep several hours, when, of a sudden, I opened my eyes.

Terror gripped my heart. Loud explosive noises reverberated under my head. It seemed as though bombs were torn asunder in the depths of the cold sea beneath me. I lay still, wondering if I were dreaming. The sounds echoingly died away. Looking about the igloo, I detected nothing unusual. I saw Ah-we-lah and E-tuk-i-shook staring at me with wide-open frightened eyes. I arose and peeped through the eye port. The fields of ice without reflected the warm light of the rising sun in running waves of tawny color. The ice was undisturbed. An unearthly quiet prevailed. Concluding that the ice was merely cracking under the sudden change of temperature, in quite the usual harmless manner, I turned over again, reassuring my companions, and promptly fell asleep.

Out of the blankness of sleep I suddenly wakened again. Half-dazed, I heard beneath me a series of echoing, thundering noises. I felt the ice floor on which I lay quivering. I experienced the sudden giddiness one feels on a tossing ship at sea. In the flash of a second I saw Ah-we-lah leap to his feet. In the same dizzy instant I saw the dome of the snowhouse open above me; I caught a vision of the gold-streaked sky. My instinct at the moment was to leap. I think I tried to rise, when suddenly everything seemed lifted from under me; I experienced the suffocating sense of falling, and next, with a spasm of indescribable horror, felt about my body a terrific tightening pressure like that of a chilled and closing shell of steel, driving the life and breath from me.

In an instant it was clear what had happened. A crevasse had suddenly opened through our igloo, directly under the spot whereon I slept; and I, a helpless creature in a sleeping bag, with tumbling snow blocks and ice and snow crashing about and crushing me, with the temperature 48° below zero, was floundering in the opening sea!

LAND DISCOVERED

FIGHTING PROGRESS THROUGH CUTTING COLD AND TER-
RIFIC STORMS—LIFE BECOMES A MONOTONOUS ROU-
TINE OF HARDSHIP—THE POLE INSPIRES WITH ITS
REISISTLESS LURE—NEW LAND DISCOVERED BEYOND
THE EIGHTY-FOURTH PARALLEL—MORE THAN TWO
HUNDRED MILES FROM SVARTEVOEG—THE FIRST SIX
HUNDRED MILES COVERED

XVI

THREE HUNDRED MILES TO THE APEX OF THE WORLD

I think I was about to swoon when I felt hands
beneath my armpits and heard laughter in my ears.
With an adroitness such as only these natives possess,
my two companions were dragging me from the water.
And while I lay panting on the ice, recovering
from my fright, I saw them expeditiously rescue our
possessions.

It seemed that all this happened so quickly that
I had really been in the water only a few moments. My
two companions saw the humor of the episode and
laughed heartily. Although I had been in the water
only a brief time, a sheet of ice surrounded my sleeping
bag. Fortunately, however, the reindeer skin was
found to be quite dry when the ice was beaten off. The
experience, while momentarily terrifying, was instruc-

tive, for it taught us the danger of spreading ice, especially in calms following storms.

Gratitude filled my heart. I fully realized how narrow had been the escape of all of us. Had we slept a few seconds longer we should all have disappeared in the opening crevasse. The hungry Northland would again have claimed its human sacrifice.

The ice about was much disturbed. Numerous black lines of water opened on every side; from these oozed jets of frosty, smoke-colored vapor. The difference between the temperature of the sea and that of the air was 76°. With this contrast, the open spots of ice-water appeared to be boiling.

Anxious to move along, away from the troubled angle of ice, our usual breakfast was simplified. Melting some snow, we drank the icy liquid as an eye-opener, and began our ration of a half-pound boulder of pemmican. But with cold fingers, blue lips and no possible shelter, the stuff was unusually hard. To warm up, we prepared the sleds. Under our lashes the dogs jumped into harness with a bound. The pemmican, which we really found too hard to eat, had to be first broken into pieces with an axe. We ground it slowly with our molars as we trudged along. Our teeth chattered while the stomach was thus being fired with durable fuel.

As we advanced the ice improved to some extent. With a little search safe crossings were found over new crevices. A strong westerly wind blew piercingly cold.

Good progress was made, but we did not forget at any time that we were invading the forbidden domains of a new polar environment.

Henceforth, one day was to be much like another.

Beyond the eighty-third parallel life is devoid of any pleasure. The intense objective impressions of cold and hunger assailing the body rob even the mind of inspiration and exhilaration. Even the best day of sun and gentle wind offers no balm.

One awakes realizing the wind has abated and sees the cheerless sun veering about the side of the ice shelter. One kicks the victim upon whom, that morning, duty has fixed the misfortune to be up first—for we tried to be equals in sharing the burdens of life. And upon him to whose lot falls this hardship there is a loss of two hours' repose. He chops ice, fills the kettles, lights the fire, and probably freezes his fingers in doing so. Then he wiggles back into his bag, warms his icy hands on the bare skin of his own stomach; or, if he is in a two-man bag, and the other fellow is awake, Arctic courtesy permits the icy hands on the stomach of his bedfellow.

In due time the blood runs to the hand and he sets about tidying up the camp. First, the hood of his own bag. It is loaded with icicles and frost, the result of the freezing of his breath while asleep. He brushes off the ice and snow. The ice has settled in the kettles in the meantime. More ice must be chopped and put into the kettle. The chances are that he now breaks a commandment and steals what to us is a great luxury— a long drink of water to ease his parched throat. Because of the need of fuel economy, limit is placed on drinks.

Then the fire needs attention; the flame is imperfect and the gas hole needs cleaning. He thoughtlessly grips the little bit of metal to the end of which the priming needle is attached. That metal is so cold that it

burns, and he leaves a piece of his skin on it. Then
the breakfast ration of pemmican must be divided. It
is not frozen, for it contains no water. But it is hard.
The stuff looks like granite. Heat would melt it
—but there is no fuel to spare. The two slumberers
are given a thump, and their eyes open to the stone-like
pemmican. Between yawns the teeth are set to grind
the pemmican. The water boils, the tea is tossed in it
and the kettle is removed.

We rise on elbows, still in the bags, to enjoy the
one heavenly treat of our lives, the cup of tea which
warms the hand and the stomach at once.

Then we dress. It is remarkable how cold compels
speed in dressing.

The door of the snowhouse is now kicked out—all
tumble about to warm up and stop chattering teeth.
Breaking camp is a matter of but a minute, for things
fall almost automatically into convenient packs. The
sledges are loaded and lashed in a few minutes. Then
the teams are gathered to the pulling lines, and off we
go with a run. The pace for dog and man is two and a
half miles an hour, over good ice or bad ice, hard snow
or soft snow, or tumbling over neckbreaking irregularities. There is no stop for lunch, no riding, or rest, or
anything else. It is drive—drive.

At times it was impossible to perspire, and the toxin
of fatigue, generating unearthly weariness, filled the
brain with fag. When perspiration oozed from our
pores, as we forced forward, step by step, it froze in the
garments and the warmer portions of our bodies were
ringed with snow. Daily, unremittingly, this was our
agony.

In starting before the end of the winter night, and camping on the open ice fields in the long northward march, we had first accustomed our eyes to frigid darkness and then to a perpetual glitter. This proved to be the coldest season of the year, and we ought to have been hardened to all kinds of Arctic torment. But man gains that advantage only when his pulse ceases to beat.

Continuing the steady stride of forward marches, far from land, far from life, there was nothing to arouse a warming spirit. Along the land there had been calms and gales and an inspiring contrast, even in the dark days and nights, but here the frigid world was felt at its worst. The wind, which came persistently from the west—now strong, now feeble, but always sharp—inflicted a pain to which we never became accustomed.

The worst torture inflicted by the wind and humid air of an Arctic pack came from a mask of ice about the face. It was absurdly picturesque but painful. Every bit of exhaled moisture condensed and froze either to the facial hair or to the line of fox tails about the hood. It made comical caricatures of us.

Frequent turns in our course exposed both sides of the face to the wind and covered with icicles every hair offering a convenient nucleus. These lines of crystal made an amazing dash of light and color as we looked at each other. But they did not afford much amusement to the individual exhibiting them. Such hairs as had not been pulled from the lips and chin were first weighted, and then the wind carried the breath to the long hair with which we protected our heads, and left a mass of dangling frost. Accumulated moisture from the eyes coated the eyelashes and brows. The humidity

BRADLEY LAND DISCOVERED
SUBMERGED ISLAND OF POLAR SEA
GOING BEYOND THE BOUNDS OF LIFE

SWIFT PROGRESS OVER SMOOTH ICE
BUILDING AN IGLOO
A LIFELESS WORLD OF COLD AND ICE

escaping about the forehead left a crescent of snow above, while that escaping under the chin, combined with falling breath, formed there a semi-circle of ice. The most uncomfortable icicles, however, were those that formed on the coarse hair within the nostrils. To keep the face free, the Eskimos pull the facial hair out by the roots, the result of which is a rarity of mustaches and beards. Thus, with low temperature and persistent winds, life was one of constant torture on the march; but cooped in snowhouses, eating dried beef and tallow, and drinking hot tea, some animal comforts were occasionally to be gained in the icy camps.

We forced the dogs onward during two days of cheery bluster, with encouraging results. At times we ran before the teams, calling and urging the brutes to leaping progress. On the evening of March 26, with a pedometer and other methods of dead reckoning for position, we found ourselves at latitude 84° 24', longitude 96° 53'.

The western horizon remained persistently dark. A storm was gathering, and slowly moving eastward. Late in the evening we prepared for the anticipated blast. We built an igloo stronger than usual, hoping that the horizon would be cleared with a brisk wind by the morrow and afford us a day of rest. The long, steady marches, without time for recuperation, necessarily dampened our enthusiasm for a brief period of physical depression, which, however, was of short duration.

Daily we had learned to appreciate more and more the joy of the sleeping bag. It was the only animal comfort which afforded a relief to our life of frigid hardship, and often with the thought of it we tried to force upon the weary body in the long marches a pleasing anticipation.

In the evening, after blocks of snow walled a dome in which we could breathe quiet air, the blue-flame lamp sang notes of gastronomic delights. We first indulged in a heaven-given drink of ice-water to quench the intense thirst which comes after hours of exertion and perspiration. Then the process of undressing began, one at a time, for there was not room enough in the igloo for all to undress at once.

The fur-stuffed boots were pulled off and the bear-skin pants were stripped. Then half of the body was quickly pushed into the bag. A brick of pemmican was next taken out and the teeth were set to grind on this bone-like substance. Our appetites were always keen, but a half pound of cold withered beef and tallow changes a hungry man's thoughts effectually.

The tea, an hour in making, was always welcome, and we rose on elbows to take it. Under the influence of the warm drink, the fur coat with its mask of ice was removed. Next the shirt, with its ring of ice about the waist, would come off, giving the last sense of shivering. Pushing the body farther into the bag, the hood was pulled over the face, and we were lost to the world of ice.

The warm sense of mental and physical pleasure which follows is an interesting study. The movement of others, the sting of the air, the noise of torturing winds, the blinding rays of a heatless sun, the pains of driving snows and all the bitter elements are absent. One's mind, freed of anxiety and suffering, wanders to home and better times under these peculiar circumstances;

there comes a pleasurable sensation in the touch of one's own warm skin, while the companionship of the arms and legs, freed from their cumbersome furs, makes a new discovery in the art of getting next to one's self.

Early on March 27, a half gale was blowing, but at noon the wind ceased. The bright sun and rising temperature were too tempting to let us remain quiescent. Although the west was still dark with threatening clouds we hitched the dogs to the sleds. We braced ourselves. "Huk! Huk!" we called, and bounded away among the wind-swept hummocks. The crevices of the ice wound like writhing snakes as we raced on. We had not gone many miles before the first rush of the storm struck us. Throwing ourselves over the sleds, we waited the passing of the icy blast. No suitable snow with which to begin the erection of a shelter was near. A few miles northward, as we saw, was a promising area for a camp. This we hoped to reach after a few moments' rest. The squall soon spent its force. In the wind which followed good progress was made without suffering severely. The temperature was 41° below zero, Fahrenheit, and the barometer 29.05.

Once in moving order, the drivers required very little encouragement to prolong the effort to a fair day's march despite the weather. As the sun settled in the western gloom the wind increased in fury and forced us to camp. Before the igloo was finished a steady, rasping wind brushed the hummocks and piled the snow in large dunes about us, like the sand of home shores.

The snowhouse was not cemented as usual with water, as was our custom when weather permitted. The tone of the wind did not seem to indicate danger, and furthermore, there was no open sea water near. Because of the need of fuel economy we did not deem it prudent to use oil for fire to melt snow, excepting for water to quench thirst.

Not particularly anxious about the outcome of the storm, and with senses blunted by overwork and benumbed with cold, we sought the comfort of the bags. Awakened in the course of a few hours by drifts of snow about our feet, I noted that the wind had burrowed holes at weak spots through the snow wall. We were bound, however, not to be cheated of a few hours' sleep, and with one eye open we turned over. I was awakened by falling snow blocks soon after.

Forcing my head out of my ice-encased fur hood, I saw the sky, cloud-swept and grey. The dome of the igloo had been swept away. We were being quickly buried under a dangerous weight of snow. In some way I had tossed about sufficiently during sleep to keep on top of the accumulating drift, but my companions were nowhere to be seen. About me for miles the white spaces were vacant. With dread in my heart I uttered a loud call, but there came no response.

A short frenzied search revealed a blowhole in the snow. In response to another call, as from some subterranean place came muffled Eskimo shouts. Tearing and burrowing at the fallen snow blocks I made violent efforts to free them, buried as they were in their bags. But to my dismay the soft snow settled on them tighter with each tussle.

I was surprised, a few moments later, as I was working to keep their breathing place open, to feel them burrowing through the snow. They had entered their bags without undressing. Half clothed in shirt and pants, but with bare feet, they writhed and wriggled through the bags and up through the breathing hole.

After a little digging their boots were uncovered, and then, with protected feet, the bag was freed and placed at the side of the igloo.

Into it the boys crept, fully dressed, with the exception of coats. I rolled out beside them in my bag. We lay in the open sweep of furious wind, impotent to move, for twenty-nine hours. Only then the frigid blast eased enough to enable us to creep out into the open. The air came in hissing spouts, like jets of steam from an engine.

Soon after noon of March 29 the air brightened. It became possible to breathe without being choked with floating crystals, and as the ice about our facial furs was broken, a little blue patch was detected in the west. We now freed the dogs of their snow entanglement and fed them. A shelter was made in which to melt snow and brew tea. We ate a double ration.

Hitching the dogs we raced off. The monotonous fields of snow swept under us. Soon the sun burst through separating clouds and upraised icy spires before us. The wind died away. A crystal glory transfigured the storm-swept fields. We seemed traveling over fields of diamonds, scintillant as white fire, which shimmered dazzlingly about us. It is curious to observe an intense fiery glitter and glow, as in the North, which gives absolutely no impression of warmth. Fire here seems cold. With full stomachs, fair weather and a much needed rest, we moved with renewed inspiration. The dogs ran with tails erect, ears pricked. I and my companions ran behind with the joy of contestants in a race. Indeed, we felt refreshed as one does after a cold bath.

Considerable time and distance, however, were lost in seeking a workable line of travel about obstructions and making detours. Camping at midnight, we had made only nine miles by a day's effort. The conditions under which this second hundred miles were forced, proved to be in every respect the most exciting of the run of five hundred miles over the Polar sea. The mere human satisfaction of overcoming difficulties was a daily incentive to surmount obstacles and meet baffling problems. The weather was unsettled. Sudden storms broke with spasmodic force, the barometer was unsteady and the temperature ranged from 20° below zero to 60° below zero. The ice showed signs of recent agitation.

New leads and recent sheets of new ice combined with deep snow made travel difficult. Persistently onward, pausing at times, we would urge the dogs to the limit. One dog after another went into the stomachs of the hungry survivors. Camps were now swept by storms. The ice opened out under our bodies, shelter was often a mere hole in the snow bank. Each of us carried painful wounds, frost bites; and the ever chronic emptiness of half filled stomachs brought a gastric call for food, impossible to supply. Hard work and strong winds sent unquenched thirst tortures to burning throats, and the gloom of ever clouded skies sent despair to its lowest reaches.

But there was no monotony; our tortures came from different angles, and from so many sources, that we were ever aroused to a fighting spirit. With a push at the sled or a pull at the line we helped the wind-teased dogs to face the nose cutting drift that swept the pack mile after mile. Day after day we plunged farther and farther along into the icy despair and stormy bluster.

Throughout the entire advance northward I found there was some advantage in my Eskimo companions having some slight comprehension of the meaning of my aim. Doubtless through information and ideas that had sifted from explorers to Eskimos for many generations past, the aborigines had come to understand that there is a point at the top of the globe, which is somehow the very top of the world, and that at this summit there is something which white men have long been anxious to find—a something which the Eskimo describe as the "big nail." The feeling that they were setting out with me in the hope of being the first to find this "big nail"—for, of course, I had told them of the possibility—helped to keep up the interest and courage of my two companions during long days of hardship.

Naturally enough, I could not expect their interest in the Pole itself to be great. Their promised reward for accompanying me, a gun and knife for each, maintained a lively interest in them. After a ceaseless warfare lasting seven days, on March 30 the eastern sky broke in lines of cheering blue. Whipped by low winds the clouds broke and scurried.

Soon the western heavens, ever a blank mystery, cleared. Under it, to my surprise, lay a new land. I think I felt a thrill such as Columbus must have felt when the first green vision of America loomed before his eye.

My promise to the good, trusty boys of nearness to land was unwittingly on my part made good, and the

delight of eyes opened to the earth's northernmost rocks
dispelled all the physical torture of the long run of
storms. As well as I could see, the land seemed an interrupted coast extending parallel to the line of march
for about fifty miles, far to the west. It was snow
covered, ice-sheeted and desolate. But it was real land
with all the sense of security solid earth can offer. To
us that meant much, for we had been adrift in a moving
sea of ice, at the mercy of tormenting winds. Now came,
of course, the immediate impelling desire to set foot
upon it, but to do so I knew would have side-tracked
us from our direct journey to the Polar goal. In any
case, delay was jeopardous, and, moreover, our food
supply did not permit our taking time to inspect the
new land.*

---

* After my return to Copenhagen I was widely quoted as declaring that
I had discovered and traversed 30,000 square miles of new land. What I
did report was that in my journey I had passed through an area wherein
it was possible to declare 30,000 square miles—a terrestrial unknown of
water and ice—cleared from the blank of our charts. I have been quoted
as describing this land as "a paradise for hunters" and criticised on the
ground that animal life does not exist so far north. Whether animal life
existed there, I do not know, for the impetus of my quest left no time to
investigate. I passed the last game at Heiberg Land.

In my diary of the day's doings, only the results of observations were
written down. The detail calculations were made on loose sheets of paper
and in other note books—wherein was recorded all instrumental data. Later
all my observations were reduced in the form in which they were to be
finally presented. Therefore, these field papers with their miscellaneous
notes had served their purpose, as had the instruments; and for this reason
most of the material was left with Harry Whitney. A few of the important calculations were kept more as a curiosity. These will be presented as we go along. Those left I thought might later be useful for a
re-examination of the results; but it never occurred to me that Whitney
would be forced to bury the material, as he was by Peary. I do not regard
those buried notes as being proof or as being particularly valuable, except
as proving Peary to be one of the most ungracious and selfish characters
in history.

In the subsequent excitement, because Peary cried fraud on the very
papers which he had buried for me, an agitated group of American armchair explorers came to the conclusion against the dictates of history that
the proof of the Polar quest was to be found in the re-examination of the
figures of the observations for position.

This new land was never clearly seen. A low mist, seemingly from open water, hid the shore line. We saw the upper slopes only occasionally from our point of observation. There were two distinct land masses. The most southern cape of the southern mass bore west by south, but still further to the south there were vague indications of land. The most northern cape of the same mass bore west by north. Above it there was a

---

Part of mine were buried. Peary had his. Thus handicapped, because blocks of my field calculations were absent, with the instruments and chronometer corrections, I rested my case at Copenhagen on a report, the original notes giving the brief tabulations of the day's doings, and the complete set of reduced observations.

My friends have criticised me for not sending the data given below and similar observations to Copenhagen to prove my claim, but I did not deem it worth while to present more, taking the ground that if in this there was not sufficient material to explain the movement step by step of the Polar quest, then no academic examination could be of any value. This viewpoint, as I see it at present, was a mistake. I am now presenting every scrap of paper and every isolated fact, not as proof but as part of the record of the expedition, with due after-thought, and the better perspective afforded by time. Every explorer does this. Upon such a record history has always given its verdict of the value of an explorer's work. It will do the same in estimating the relative merits of the Polar quest.

Observation as figured out in original field paper for March 30, 1908: Longitude 95.36. Bar. 30.10 had risen from 29.50 in 2 hours. Temp. —34°. Wind 2. Mag. N. E. Clouds Mist W.-Water bands E.

95½	Noon, $\overline{0}$	18—46—10
4	0	18—48—20
60 ⌐382	2 ⌐37—34—30	
6—22	18—47—15	
	I. E.	+2
	2 ⌐18—49—15	
58	9—24—38	
6½ h.	—16— 2	
29	9— 8—36	
348	R. & P.	— 9
60 ⌐377	8—59—36	
6—17	90	
3—43—15	81—00—24	
3—49—32	3—49—32	
	84—49—56	

Shadows 39 ft. (of tent pole 6 ft. above snow).
(Directions Magnetic.)

distinct break for 15 or 20 miles, and beyond the northern mass extended above the eighty-fifth parallel to the northwest. The entire coast was at this time placed on our charts as having a shore line along the one hundred and second meridian, approximately parallel to our line of travel. At the time the indications suggested two distinct islands. Nevertheless, we saw so little of the land that we could not determine whether it consisted of islands or of a larger mainland. The lower coast resembled Heiberg Island, with mountains and high valleys. The upper coast I estimated as being about one thousand feet high, flat, and covered with a thin sheet ice. Over the land I write "Bradley Land" in honor of John R. Bradley, whose generous help had made possible the important first stage of the expedition. The discovery of this land gave an electric impetus of driving vigor at just the right moment to counterbalance the effect of the preceding week of storm and trouble.

Although I gazed longingly and curiously at the land, to me the Pole was the pivot of ambition. My boys had not the same northward craze, but I told them to reach the land on our return might be possible. We

---

Because of the impossibility of making correct allowances for refraction, I have made a rough allowance of —9' for refraction and parallax in all my observations.

The tent pole was a hickory floor slat of one of the sledges. It was 6 ft. 6 ins. high, 2 ins. wide, and ½ in. thick. This stick was marked in feet and inches, to be used as a measuring stick. It also served as a paddle and steering oar for the boat.

By pressing this tent pole 6 ins. into the snow, it served as a 6 ft. pole to measure the shadows. These measurements were recorded on the observation blanks. Absolute accuracy for the measurements is not claimed, because of the difficulty of determining the line of demarcation in long, indistinct shadows; but future efforts will show that my shadow measurements are an important check on all sun observations by which latitude and longitude are determined.

never saw it again. This new land made a convenient mile-post, for from this time on the days were counted to and from it. A good noon sight fixed the point of observation to 84° 50', longitude 95° 36". We had forced beyond the second hundred miles from Svartevoeg. Before us remained about three hundred more miles, to my alluring, mysterious goal.

ARCTIC FOX

BEYOND THE RANGE OF LIFE

WITH A NEW SPRING TO WEARY LEGS BRADLEY LAND IS
LEFT BEHIND—FEELING THE ACHING VASTNESS OF
THE WORLD BEFORE MAN WAS MADE—CURIOUS
GRIMACES OF THE MIDNIGHT SUN—SUFFERINGS IN-
CREASE—BY PERSISTENT AND LABORIOUS PROGRESS
ANOTHER HUNDRED MILES IS COVERED

XVII

Two Hundred Miles From The Pole

A curtain of mist was drawn over the new land in
the afternoon of March 31, and, although we gazed
westward longingly, we saw no more of it. Day after
day we now pushed onward in desperate northward
efforts. Strong winds and fractured, irregular ice, increased our difficulties. Although progress was slow
for several days we managed to gain a fair march between storms during each twenty-four hours. During
occasional spells of icy stillness mirages spread screens
of fantasy out for our entertainment. Curious cliffs,
odd-shaped mountains and inverted ice walls were displayed in attractive colors.

Discoveries of new land seemed often made. But
with a clearing horizon the deception was detected.

The boys believed most of these signs to be indications of real land—a belief I persistently encouraged,

because it relieved them of the panic of the terror of the unknown.

On April 3, the barometer remained steady and the thermometer sank. The weather became settled and fairly clear, the horizon was freed of its smoky vapors, the pack assumed a more permanent aspect of glittering color. At noon there was now a dazzling light, while at night the sun kissed the frozen seas behind screens of mouse-colored cloud and haze. At the same moment the upper skies flushed with the glow of color of the coming double-days of joy.

As we advanced north of Bradley Land the pack disturbance of land-divided and land-jammed ice disappeared. The fields became larger and less troublesome, the weather improved, the temperature ranged from 20° to 50° below zero, the barometer rose and remained steady, the day sky cleared with increasing color, but a low haze blotted out much of the night glory which attended the dip of the nocturnal sun. With dogs barking and rushing before speeding sleds, we made swift progress. But the steady drag and monotony of the never changing work and scene reduced interest in life.

The blankness of the mental desert which moved about us as we ran along was appalling. Nothing changed materially. The horizon moved. Our footing was seemingly a solid stable ice crust, which was, however, constantly shifting eastward. All the world on which we traveled was in motion. We moved, but we took our landscape with us.

At the end of the day's march we were often too tired to build snow houses, and in sheer exhaustion we bivouacked in the lee of hummocks. Here the over-worked body called for sleep, but my mind refused to close the eyes. My boys had the advantage of sleep. I envied them. Anyone who has suffered from in-somnia may be able in a small degree to gauge my condition when sleep became impossible. To reach the end of my journey became the haunting, ever-present goading thought of my wakeful existence.

As I lay painfully trying to coax slumber, my mind worked like the wheels of a machine. Dizzily the jour-ney behind repeated itself; I again crossed the Big Lead, again floundered in an ice-cold open sea. Dangers of all sorts took form to harass me. Instead of sleep, a delirium of anxiety and longing possessed me.

Beyond the eighty-fourth parallel we had passed the bounds of visible life. Lying wakeful in that barren world, with my companions asleep, I felt what few men of cities, perhaps, ever feel—the tragic isolation of the human soul—a thing which, dwelt upon, must mean madness. I think I realized the aching vastness of the world after creation, before man was made.

For many days we had not seen a suggestion of animated nature. There were no longer animal trails to indicate life; no breath spouts of seal escaped from the frosted bosom of the sea. Not even the microscopic life of the deep was longer detected under us. We were alone—alone in a lifeless world. We had come to this blank space of the earth by slow but progressive stages. Sailing from the bleak land of the fisher folk along the out-posts of civilization, the complex luxury of met-ropolitan life was lost. Beyond, in the half savage wil-derness of Danish Greenland, we partook of a new life of primitive simplicity. Still farther along, in the Ultima Thule of the aborigines, we reverted to a pre-historic plane of living. Advancing beyond the haunts of men, we reached the noonday deadliness of a world without life.

As we pushed beyond into the sterile wastes, with eager eyes we constantly searched the dusky plains of frost, but there was no speck of life to grace the purple run of death.*

During these desolate marches, my legs working mechanically, my mind with anguish sought some object upon which to fasten itself. My eyes scrutinized the horizon. I saw, every day, every sleeping hour, hills of ice, vast plains of ice, now a deadly white, now a dull gray, now a misty purple, sometimes shot with gold or gleaming with lakes of ultramarine, moving towards and by me, an ever-changing yet ever-monotonous pano-rama which wearied me as does the shifting of unchang-ing scenery seen from a train window. As I paced the weary marches, I fortunately became unconscious of the painful movement of my legs. Although I walked I had a sensation of being lifted involuntarily onward.

The sense of covering distance gave me a dull, pleasurable satisfaction. Only some catastrophe, some sudden and overwhelming obstacle would have aroused me to an intense mental emotion, to a passionate despair, to the anguish of possible defeat.

I was now becoming the unconscious instrument of

---

* Peary claims to have seen life east of this position. This is perfectly possible, for Arctic explorers have often noted when game trails were abundant one year, none were seen the next. In these tracks of foxes and bears, as noted by Baldwin, are positive proofs of the position of Bradley Land—for such animals work only from a land base.

my ambition; almost without volition my body was being carried forward by a subconscious force which had fastened itself upon a distant goal. Sometimes the wagging of a dog's tail held my attention for long minutes; it afforded a curious play for my morbidly obsessed imagination. In an hour I would forget what I had been thinking. To-day I cannot remember thé vague, fanciful illusions about curiously insignificant things which occupied my faculties in this dead world. The sun, however, did relieve the monotony, and created in the death-chilled world skies filled with elysian flowers and mirages of beauty undreamed of by Aladdin.

My senses at the time, as I have said, were vaguely benumbed. While we traveled I heard the sound of the moving sledges. Their sharp steel runners cut the ice and divided the snow like a cleaving knife. I became used to the first shudder of the rasping sound. In the dead lulls between wind storms I would listen with curious attention to the soft patter of our dogs' feet. At times I could hear their tiny toe nails grasping at forward ice ridges in order to draw themselves forward, and, strangely—so were all my thoughts interwoven with my ambition—this clenching, crunching, gritty sound gave me a delighted sense of progress, a sense of ever covering distance and nearing, ever nearing the Pole.

In this mid-Polar basin the ice does not readily separate. It is probably in motion at all times of the year. In this readjustment of fields following motion and expansion, open spaces of water appear. These, during most months, are quickly sheeted with new ice.

In these troubled areas I had frequent opportunities to measure ice-thickness. From my observation I had come to the conclusion that ice does not freeze to a depth of more than twelve or fifteen feet during a single year. Occasionally we crossed fields fifty feet thick. These invariably showed signs of many years of surface upbuilding.

It is very difficult to estimate the amount of submerged freezing after the first year's ice, but the very uniform thickness of Antarctic sea ice suggests that a limit is reached the second year, when the ice, with its cover of snow, is so thick that very little is added afterward from below.

Increase in size after that is probably the result mostly of addition to the superstructure. Frequent falls of snow, combined with alternate melting and freezing in summer, and a process similar to the upbuilding of glacial ice, are mainly responsible for the growth in thickness of the ice on the Polar sea.

The very heavy, undulating fields, which give character to the mid-Polar ice and escape along the east and west coasts of Greenland, are, therefore, mostly augmented from the surface.

Continuing north, at no time was the horizon perfectly clear. But the weather was good enough to permit frequent nautical observations. Our course was lined on uninteresting blank sheets. There were elusive signs of land frequent enough to maintain an exploring enthusiasm, which helped me also in satisfying my companions. For thus they were encouraged to believe in a nearness to terrestrial solidity. At every breathing spell, when we got together for a little chat, Ah-we-lah's hand, with pointed finger, was directed to some spot on the horizon or some low-lying cloud, with the shout of *"Noona?"* (land), to which I always replied in the affirmative; but, for me, the field-glasses and later positions dispelled the illusion.

Man, under pressure of circumstances, will adapt himself to most conditions of life. To me the other-world environment of the Polar-pack, far from continental fastness, was beginning to seem quite natural.

We forced marches day after day. We traveled until dogs languished or legs failed. Ice hills rose and fell before us. Mirages grimaced at our dashing teams with wondering faces. Daily the incidents and our position were recorded, but our adventures were promptly forgotten in the mental bleach of the next day's effort.

Night was now as bright as day. By habit, we emerged from our igloos later and later. On the 5th and 6th we waited until noon before starting, to get observations; but, as was so often the case, when the sun was watched, it slipped under clouds. This late start brought our stopping time close to midnight, and infused an interest in the midnight sun; but the persistent haze which clouded the horizon at night when the sun was low denied us a glimpse of the midnight luminary.

The night of April 7 was made notable by the swing of the sun at midnight, above the usual obscuring mist, behind which it had, during previous days, sunk with its night dip of splendor. For a number of nights it made grim faces at us in its setting. A tantalizing mist, drawn as a curtain over the northern sea at midnight, had afforded curious advantages for celestial staging. We were unable to determine sharply the advent of the midnight sun, but the colored cloud and haze into which it nightly sank produced a spectacular play which interested us immensely.

Sometimes the great luminary was drawn out into an egg-shaped elongation with horizontal lines of color drawn through it. I pictured it as some splendid fire-colored lantern flung from the window of Heaven. Again, it was pressed into a basin flaming with magical fires, burning behind a mystic curtain of opalescent frosts. Blue at other times, it appeared like a huge vase of luminous crystal, such as might be evoked by the weird genii of the Orient, from which it required very little imagination to see purple, violet, crimson and multi-colored flowers springing beauteously into the sky.

These changes took place quickly, as by magic. Usually the last display was of distorted faces, some animal, some semi-human—huge, grotesque, and curiously twitching countenances of clouds and fire. At times they appallingly resembled the hideous teeth-gnashing deities of China, that, with gnarled arms upraised, holding daggers of flame and surrounded by smoke, were rising toward us from beyond the horizon.

Sometimes in our northward progress these faces laughed, again they scowled ominously. What the actual configurations were I do not know; I suppose two men see nothing exactly alike in this topsy-turvy world.

Rushing northward with forced haste, unreal beauties took form as if to lure us to pause. Clouds of steam rising from frozen seas like geysers assumed the aspects of huge fountains of iridescent fire. As the sun rose, lines of light like quicksilver quivered and writhed about the horizon, and in swirling, swimming circles closed and narrowed about us on the increasingly color-burned but death-chilled areas of ice over which we worked. Setting amid a dance of purple radiance, the sun, however, instead of inspiring us, filled us with a sick feeling of giddiness. What beauty there was in these spectacles was often lost upon our benumbed senses.

Nowhere in the world, perhaps, are seen such spectacles of celestial glory. The play of light on clouds and ice produces the illusion of some supernatural realm.

We had now followed the sun's northward advance—from its first peep, at midday, above the southern ice of the Polar gateway, to its sweep over the northern ice at midnight. From the end of the Polar night, late in February, to the first of the double days and the midnight suns, we had forced a trail through darkness and blood-hardening temperature, and over leg-breaking irregularities of an unknown world of ice, to a spot almost exactly two hundred miles from the Pole! To this point our destiny had been auspiciously protected. Ultimate success seemed within grasp. But we were not blind to the long line of desperate effort still required to push over the last distance.

Now that we had the sun unmistakably at midnight, its new glory before us was an incentive to onward efforts. Previous to this the sun had been undoubtedly above the horizon, but, as is well known, when the sun is low and the atmospheric humidity is high, as it always is over the pack, a dense cloud of frost crystals rests on the ice and obscures the horizon. During the previous days the sun sank into this frosty haze and was lost for several hours.

Observations on April 8* placed camp at latitude 86° 36', longitude 94° 2'. Although we had made long marches and really great speed, we had advanced only ninety-six miles in the nine days. Much of our hard work had been lost in circuitous twists around troublesome pressure lines and high, irregular fields of very old ice. The drift ice was throwing us to the east with sufficient force to give us some anxiety, but with eyes closed to danger and hardships, double days of fatigue and double days of glitter quickly followed one another.

*Observation on April 8, from original field-papers. April 8, 1908, Longitude 94°-2'. Bar. 29.80, rising. Temp. —31°. Wind 2, Mag. N. E. Clouds St. 3.

```
              94°                0........21°—59'—30"
               4'                0........21 —08 —20
        60 | 876'                ──
           ─────                 2 | 43 — 7 —50
           6-16        I. E.     ─────────
            56"                  21 —33 —55
            x6¼                  +2
           ────                  ─────
            14                   2 | 21 —35 —50
           336                   ─────────
        60 | 350                 10 —47 —55
           ─────                 —9
           5—50                  ─────
        7— 9—33                  10 —38 —55
        ─────────                90—
        7—15—23                  ─────
                                 79 —21 — 5
                                 7 —15—23
                                 ─────
                                 86 —36 —28
```

Shadows 32 ft. (of pole 6 ft. above snow).

Everything was now in our favor, but here we felt most of the accumulating effect of long torture, in a world where every element of Nature is hostile. Human endurance has distinct limits. Bodily abuse will long be counterbalanced by man's superb recuperative power, but sooner or later there comes a time when out-worn cells call a halt.

We had lived for weeks on a steady diet of withered beef and tallow. There was no change, we had no hot meat, and never more to eat than was absolutely necessary to keep life within the body. We became indifferent to the aching vacant pain of the stomach. Every organ had been whipped to serve energy to the all important movement of our legs. The depletion of energy, the lassitude of overstrained limbs, manifested themselves. The Eskimos were lax in the swing of the whip and indifferent in urging on the dogs. The dogs displayed the same spirit by lowered tails, limp ears, and drooping noses, as their shoulders dragged the sleds farther, ever farther from the land of life.

A light life-sapping wind came from the west. We battled against it. We swung our arms to fight it and maintain circulation, as a swimmer in water. Veering a little at times, it always struck the face at a piercing angle. It froze the tip of my nose so often that that feature felt like a foreign bump on my face. Our cheeks had in like manner been so often bleached in spots that the skin was covered with ugly scars. Our eyes were often sealed by frozen eyelashes. The tear sack made icicles. Every particle of breath froze as it left the nostrils, and coated the face in a mask of ice.

The sun at times flamed the clouds, while the snow glowed in burning tones. In the presence of all this we suffered the chill of death. All Nature exulted in a wave of hysteria. Delusions took form about us— in mirages, in the clouds. We moved in a world of delusions. The heat of the sun· was a sham, its light a torment. A very curious world this, I thought dumbly, as we pushed our sleds and lashed our lagging dogs. Our footing was solid; there was no motion. Our horizon was lined with all the topographic features of a solid land scene, with mountains, valleys and plains, rivers of open water; but under it all there was the heaving of a restless sea. Although nothing visibly moved, it was all in motion. Seemingly a solid crust of earth, it imperceptibly drifts in response to every wind. We moved with it, but ever took our landscape with us.

Of the danger of this movement, of the possibility of its hopelessly carrying us away from our goal, and the possibility of ultimate starvation, I never lost consciousness. Although the distance may seem slight, now that we had gone so far, the last two hundred miles seemed hopelessly impossible. With aching, stiffened legs we started our continuing marches without enthusiasm, with little ambition. But marches we made— distance leaped at times under our swift running feet.

It sometimes now seems that unknown and subtle forces of which we are not cognizant supported me. I could almost believe that there were unseen beings there, whose voices urged me in the wailing wind; who, in my success, themselves sought soul peace, and who, that I might obtain it, in some strange, mysterious way succored and buoyed me.

OVER POLAR SEAS OF MYSTERY

THE MADDENING TORTURES OF A WORLD WHERE ICE
WATER SEEMS HOT, AND COLD KNIVES BURN ONE'S
HANDS—ANGUISHED PROGRESS ON THE LAST STRETCH
OF TWO HUNDRED MILES OVER ANCHORED LAND ICE—
DAYS OF SUFFERING AND GLOOM—THE TIME OF
DESPAIR—"IT IS WELL TO DIE," SAYS AH-WE-LAH;
"BEYOND IS IMPOSSIBLE."

XVIII

One Hundred Miles From the Pole

We pushed onward. We cracked our whips to urge
the tiring dogs. We forced to quick steps weary leg
after weary leg. Mile after mile of ice rolled under our
feet. The maddening influence of the shifting desert of
frost became almost unendurable in the daily routine.
Under the lash of duty interest was forced, while the
merciless drive of extreme cold urged physical action.
Our despair was mental and physical—the result of
chronic overwork.

Externally there was reason for rejoicing. The
sky had cleared, the weather improved, a liquid charm
of color poured over the strange other-world into which
we advanced. Progress was good, but the soul refused
to open its eyes to beauty or color. All was a lifeless

waste. The mind, heretofore busy in directing arm and foot, to force a way through miniature mountains of uplifted floes, was now, because of better ice, relieved of that strain, but it refused to seek diversion.

The normal run of hardship, although eased, now piled up the accumulated poison of overwork, and when I now think of the terrible strain I fail to see how a workable balance was maintained.

As we passed the eighty-sixth parallel, the ice increased in breadth and thickness. Great hummocks and pressure lines became less frequent. A steady progress was gained with the most economical human drain possible. The temperature ranged between 36° and 40° below zero, Fahrenheit, with higher and lower midday and midnight extremes. Only spirit thermometers were useful, for the mercury was at this degree of frost either frozen or sluggish.

Although the perpetual sun gave light and color to the cheerless waste we were not impressed with any appreciable sense of warmth. Indeed, the sunbeams by their contrast seemed to cause the frost of the air to pierce with a more painful sting. In marching over the golden glitter, snow scalded our faces, while our noses were bleached with frost. The sun rose into zones of fire and set in burning fields of ice, but, in pain, we breathed the chill of death.

In camp a grip of the knife left painful burns from cold metal. To the frozen fingers ice cold water was hot. With wine-spirits the fire was lighted, while oil delighted the stomach. In our dreams Heaven was hot, the other place was cold. All Nature was false; we seemed to be nearing the chilled flame of a new Hades.

We now changed our working hours from day to night, beginning usually at ten o'clock and ending at seven. The big marches and prolonged hours of travel with which fortune favored us earlier were no longer possible. Weather conditions were more important in determining a day's run than the hands of the chronometers.

That I must steadily keep up my notes and the records of observations was a serious addition to my daily task. I never permitted myself to be careless in regard to this, for I never let myself forget the importance of such data in plotting an accurate course.

I kept my records in small notebooks, writing very fine with a hard pencil on both sides of the paper. At the beginning of the journey I had usually set down the day's record by candle light, but later, when the sun was shining both day and night, I needed no light even inside the walls of the igloo, for the sunlight shone strongly enough through the walls of snow. Shining brilliantly at times, I utilized the opportunity it afforded, every few marches, to measure our shadows. The daily change marked our advance Poleward.

When storms threatened, our start was delayed. In strong gales the march was shortened. But in one way or another we usually found a few hours in each turn of the dial during which a march could be forced between winds. It mattered little whether we traveled night or day—all hours and all days were alike to us— for we had no accustomed time to rest, no Sundays, no holidays, no landmarks, or mile-posts to pass.

To advance and expend the energy accumulated during one sleep at the cost of one pound of pemmican

was our sole aim in life.   Day after day our legs were
driven onward.   Constantly new but similar panoramas
rolled by us.

Our observations on April 11, gave latitude 87°
20′, longitude 95° 19′.   The pack disturbance of the
new land was less and less noted as we progressed in the
northward movement.   The fields became heavier,
larger and less crevassed.   Fewer troublesome old floes
and less crushed new ice were encountered.   With the
improved conditions, the fire of a racing spirit surged
up for a brief spell.

We had now passed the highest reaches of all our
predecessors.   The inspiration of the Farthest North
for a brief time thrilled me.   The time was at hand,
however, to consider seriously the possible necessity of
an early return.

Nearly half of the food allowance had been used.
In the long marches supplies had been more liberally
consumed than anticipated.   Now our dog teams were
much reduced in numbers.   Because of the cruel law of
the survival of the fittest, the less useful dogs had gone
into the stomachs of their stronger companions.   With
the lessening of the number of dogs had come at the
same time a reduction of the weight of the sledge loads,
through the eating of the food.   Now, owing to food
limitations and the advancing season, we could not pru-
dently continue the onward march a fortnight longer.

We had dragged ourselves three hundred miles
over the Polar sea in twenty-four days.   Including delays and detours, this gave an average of nearly thirteen
miles daily on an airline in our course.   There remained
an unknown line of one hundred and sixty miles to the

Pole. The same average advance would take us to the Pole in thirteen days. There were food and fuel enough to risk this adventure. With good luck the prize seemed within our grasp. But a prolonged storm, a deep snowfall, or an active ice-pack would mean failure.

In new cracks I measured the thickness of the ice. I examined the water for life. The technical details for the making and breaking of ice were studied, and some attention was given to the altitude of uplifted and submerged irregularities. Atmospheric, surface water and ice temperatures were taken, the barometer was noted, the cloud formations, weather conditions and ice drifts were tabulated. There was a continuous routine of work, but like the effort of the foot in the daily drive, it became more or less automatic.

Running along over seemingly endless fields of ice, the physical appearances now came under more careful scrutiny. I watched daily for possible signs of failing in the strength of any of us, because a serious disability would now mean a fatal termination. A disabled man could neither continue nor return. Each new examination gave me renewed confidence and was another reason to push human endurance to the limit of straining every fibre and cell.

As a matter of long experience I find life in this extreme North is healthful so long as there is sufficient good food, so long as exertion is not overdone. A weakling would easily be killed, but a strong man is splendidly hardened and kept in perfect physical trim by sledging and tramping in this germless air. But, as I have said, sufficient food and not too much exertion are requisites to full safety, and in our case we were working to the limit, with rations running low.   Still, the men responded superbly.

Our tremendous exertion in forcing daily rushing marches, under occasional bursts of burning sunbeams, provoked intense thirst.   Following the habit of the camel, we managed to take enough water before starting to keep sufficient liquid in the stomach and veins for the ensuing day's march.   Yet it was painful to await the melting of ice at camping time.

In two sittings, evening and morning, each of us took an average of three quarts of water daily.   This included tea and also the luxury of occasional soup. Water was about us everywhere in heaps, but before the thirst could be quenched, several ounces of precious fuel, which had been sledged for hundreds of miles, must be used.   And yet, this water, so expensive and so necessary to us, became the cause of our greatest discomfort.   It escaped through pores of the skin, saturated the boots, formed a band of ice under the knee and a belt of frost about the waist, while the face was nearly always encased in a mask of icicles from the moist breath.   We learned to take this torture philosophically.

With our dogs bounding and tearing onward, from the eighty-seventh to the eighty-eighth parallel we passed for two days over old ice without pressure lines or hummocks.   There was no discernible line of demarcation to indicate separate fields, and it was quite impossible to determine whether we were on land or sea ice.   The barometer indicated no perceptible elevation, but the ice had the hard, wavering surface of glacial ice, with only superficial crevasses.   The water obtained from this was not salty. All of the upper surface of old hummock and high ice of the Polar sea resolves into unsalted water. My nautical observations did not seem to indicate a drift, but nevertheless my combined tabulations do not warrant a positive assertion of either land or sea; I am inclined, however, to put this down as ice on low or submerged land.

The ice presented an increasingly cheering prospect. A plain of purple and blue ran in easy undulations to the limits of vision without the usual barriers of uplifted blocks. Over it a direct air-line course was possible. Progress, however, was quite as difficult as over the irregular pack. The snow was crusted with large crystals. An increased friction reduced the sled speed, while the snow surface, too hard for snowshoes, was also too weak to give a secure footing to the unprotected boot. The loneliness, the monotony, the hardship of steady, unrelieved travel were keenly felt.

Day after day we pushed along at a steady pace over plains of frost and through a mental desert. As the eye opened at the end of a period of shivering slumber, the fire was lighted little by little, the stomach was filled with liquids and solids, mostly cold—enough to last for the day, for there could be no halt or waste of fuel for midday feeding. We next got into harness, and, under the lash of duty, paced off the day's pull; we worked until standing became impossible.

As a man in a dream I marched, set camp, ate and tried to rest. I took observations now without interest; under those conditions no man could take an interest in mathematics. Eating became a hardship, for the pemmican, tasteless and hard as metal, was cold. Our feet were numb—it seemed fortunate they no longer even ached.

The arduous task of building a snowhouse meant physical hardship. In this the eyes, no longer able to wink, quickly closed. Soon the empty stomach complained. Then the gastric wants were half served. With teeth dropping to the spasm of cold and skins in an electric wave of shivers to force animal heat, the boys fell to unconscious slumbers, but my lids did not easily close. The anxiety to succeed, the eagerness to draw out our food supply and the task of infusing courage into my savage helpers kept the mind active while the underfed blood filled the legs with new power.

There was no pleasurable mental recreation to relieve us; there was nothing to arouse the soul from its icy inclosure. To eat, to sleep, endlessly to press one foot ahead of the other—that was all we could do. We were like horses driven wearily in carts, but we had not their advantages of an agreeable climate and a comfortable stable at night. Daily our marches were much the same. Finishing our frigid meal, we hitched the dogs and lashed the sleds.

In the daily routine of our onward struggle, there was an inhuman strain which neither words nor pictures could adequately describe. The maddening influence of the sameness of Polar glitter, combined as it was with bitter winds and extreme cold and overworked bodies, burned our eyes and set our teeth to a chronic chattering. To me there was always the inspiration of ultimate success. But for my young savage companions, it was a torment almost beyond endurance. They were, however, brave and faithful to the bitter end, seldom allowing hunger or weariness or selfish ambition or fierce passions seriously to interfere with the effort of the expedition. We suffered, but we covered distance.

On the morning of April 13, the strain of agitating torment reached the breaking point. For days there had been a steady cutting wind from the west, which drove despair to its lowest reaches. The west again blackened, to renew its soul-despairing blast. The frost-burn of sky color changed to a depressing gray, streaked with black. The snow was screened with ugly vapors. The path was absolutely cheerless. All this was a dire premonition of storm and greater torture.

No torment could be worse than that never-ceasing rush of icy air. It gripped us and sapped the life from us. Ah-we-lah bent over his sled and refused to move. I walked over and stood by his side. His dogs turned and looked inquiringly at us. E-tuk-i-shook came near and stood motionless, like a man in a trance, staring blankly at the southern skies. Large tears fell from Ah-we-lah's eyes and froze in the blue of his own shadow. Not a word was uttered. I knew that the dreaded time of utter despair had come. The dogs looked at us, patient and silent in their misery. Silently in the descending gloom we all looked over the tremendous dead-white waste to the southward. With a tear-streaked and withered face, Ah-we-lah slowly said, with a strangely shrilling wail, *"Unne-sinig-po—Oo-ah-tonie i-o-doria—Ooh-ah-tonie i-o-doria!"* ("It is well to die—Beyond is impossible—Beyond is impossible!")

"TOO WEARY TO BUILD IGLOOS WE USED THE SILK TENT"
"ACROSS SEAS OF CRYSTAL GLORY TO THE BOREAL CENTRE"

MENDING NEAR THE POLE

TO THE POLE—THE LAST HUNDRED MILES

OVER PLAINS OF GOLD AND SEAS OF PALPITATING COLOR
THE DOG TEAMS, WITH NOSES DOWN, TAILS ERECT,
DASH SPIRITEDLY LIKE CHARIOT HORSES—CHANTING
LOVE SONGS THE ESKIMOS FOLLOW WITH SWINGING
STEP—TIRED EYES OPEN TO NEW GLORY—STEP BY
STEP, WITH THUMPING HEARTS THE EARTH'S APEX
IS NEARED—AT LAST! THE GOAL IS REACHED! THE
STARS AND STRIPES ARE FLUNG TO THE FRIGID
BREEZES OF THE NORTH POLE!

XIX

BOREAL CENTER IS PIERCED

I shall never forget that dismal hour. I shall never forget that desolate drab scene about us—those endless stretches of gray and dead-white ice, that drab dull sky, that thickening blackness in the west which entered into and made gray and black our souls, that ominous, eerie and dreadful wind, betokening a terrorizing Arctic storm. I shall never forget the mournful group before me, in itself an awful picture of despair, of man's ambition failing just as victory is within his grasp. Ah-we-lah, a thin, half-starved figure in worn furs, lay over his sled, limp, dispirited, broken. In my ears I can now hear his low sobbing words, I can see the tears on his yellow fissured face. I can see E-tuk-i-shook standing gaunt and grim, and as he gazed yearningly onward to the south, sighing pitifully, shudderingly for the home, the loved one, An-na-do-a, left behind, whom, I could tell, he did not expect to see again.

It was a critical moment. Up to this time, during the second week of April, we had, by intense mental force, goaded our wearied legs onward to the limit of endurance. With a cutting wind in our faces, feeling with each step the cold more severely to the marrow of our bones, with our bodily energy and our bodily heat decreasing, we had traveled persistently, suffering intolerable pains with every breath. Despite increasing despair, I had cheered my companions as best I could; I had impressed upon them the constant nearing of my goal. I had encouraged in them the belief of nearness of land; each day I had gone on, fearing what had now come, the utter breaking of their spirits.

"*Unne-sinikpo-ashuka.*" (Yes, it is well to die.)

"*Awonga-up-dow-epuksha!*" (Yesterday I, too, felt that way), I said to myself. The sudden extinction of consciousness, I thought, might be indeed a blessed relief. But as long as life persisted, as long as human endurance could be strained, I determined to continue. Desperate as was my condition, and suffering hellish tortures, the sight of the despair of my companions re-aroused me. Should we fail now, after our long endurance, now, when the goal was so near?

The Pole was only one hundred miles beyond. The attainment seemed almost certain.

"*Accou-ou-o-toni-ah-younguluk*" (Beyond to-morrow it will be better), I urged, trying to essay a smile. *"Igluctoo!"* (Cheer up!)

Holding up one hand, with a reach Poleward, bending five fingers, one after the other, I tried to convey the idea that in five sleeps the "Big Nail" would be reached, and that then we would turn (pointing with my fingers) homeward.

"Noona-me-neulia-capa—ahmisua" (For home, sweethearts and food in abundance), I said.

"Noona-terronga, neuliarongita, ootah—peterongito" (Land is gone; loved ones are lost; signs of life have vanished).

"Tig-i-lay-waongacedla—nellu ikah-amisua" (Return will I, the sky and weather I do not understand. It is very cold), said Ah-we-lah.

"Attuda-emongwah-ka" (A little farther come) I pleaded. *Attudu-mikisungwah"* (Only a little further).

"Sukinut-nellu" (The sun I do not understand), said E-tuk-i-shook.

This had been a daily complaint for some days— the approaching equality of the length of shadows for night and day puzzled them. The failing night dip of the sun left them without a guiding line to give direction. They were lost in a landless, spiritless world, in which the sky, the weather, the sun and all was a mystery.

I knew my companions were brave. I was certain of their fidelity. Could their mental despair be alleviated, I felt convinced they could brace themselves for another effort. I spoke kindly to them; I told them what we had accomplished, that they were good and brave, that their parents and their sweethearts would be proud of them, and that as a matter of honor we must not now fail.

"*Tigishu-conitu,*" I said. (The Pole is near.)

"*Sinipa tedliman dossa-ooahtonie tomongma ah youngulok tigilay toy hoy.*" (At the end of five sleeps it is finished, beyond all is well, we return thereafter quickly.)

"*Seko shudi iokpok. Sounah ha-ah!*" they replied. (On ice always is not good. The bones ache.)

Then I said, "The ice is flat, the snow is good, the sky is clear, the Great Spirit is with us, the Pole is near!"

Ah-we-lah dully nodded his head. I noticed, however, he wiped his eyes.

"*Ka-bishuckto-emongwah*" (Come walk a little further), I went on. "*Accou ooahtoni-ahningahna-matluk-tigilay-Inut-noona.*" (Beyond to-morrow within two moons we return to Eskimo lands.)

"*Kisah iglucto-tima-attahta-annona-neuliasing-wah,*" said Ah-we-lah. (At last, then it is to laugh! There we will meet father and mother and little wives!)

"*Ashuka-alningahna-matluk,*" I returned. (Yes, in two moons there will be water and meat and all in plenty.)

E-tuk-i-shook gazed at me intently. His eyes brightened.

As I spoke my own spirits rose to the final effort, my lassitude gave way to a new enthusiasm. I felt the fire kindling for many years aglow within me. The goal was near; there remained but one step to the apex of my ambition. I spoke hurriedly. The two sat up and listened. Slowly they became inspired with my intoxication. Never did I speak so vehemently.

E-tuk-i-shook gripped his whip. *"Ka, aga"* (Come, go!) he said.

Ah-we-lah, determined but grim, braced his body and shouted to the dogs—*"Huk, Huk, Huk,"* and then to us he said, *"Aga-Ka!"* (Go-come).

With snapping whip we were off for that last hundred miles.

The animals pricked their ears, re-curled their tails, and pulled at the traces. Shouting to keep up the forced enthusiasm, we bounded forward on the last lap. A sort of wild gratification filled my heart. I knew that only mental enthusiasm would now prevent the defeat which might yet come from our own bodies refusing to go farther. Brain must now drive muscle. Fortunately the sense of final victory imparted a supernormal mental stimulus.

Gray ice hummocks sped by us. My feet were so tired that I seemed to walk on air. My body was so light from weakness that I suppose I should hardly have been surprised had I floated upward from the ice in a gust of wind. I felt the blood moving in my veins and stinging like needles in my joints as one does when suffering with neurasthenia. I swung my axe. The whip of my companions cut the air. The dogs leaped over the ice, with crunching progress they pulled themselves over hummocks much as cats climb trees. Distance continued to fade behind us.

On April 14, my observations gave latitude, 88° 21'; longitude, 95° 52'. The wind came with a satanic cut from the west. There had been little drift. But with a feeling of chagrin I saw that the ice before us displayed signs of recent activity. It was more irregular, with open cracks here and there. These we had to avoid, but the sleds glided with less friction, and the weary dogs maintained a better speed.

With set teeth and newly sharpened resolutions, we continued mile after mile of that last one hundred. More dogs had gone into the stomachs of their hungry companions, but there still remained a sufficient pull of well-tried brute force for each sled. Although their noisy vigor had been gradually lost in the long drag, they still broke the frigid silence with an occasional outburst of howls. Any fresh enthusiasm from the drivers was quickly responded to by canine activity.

We were in good trim to cover distance economically. Our sledges were light, our bodies were thin. We had lost, since leaving winter camp, judging from appearances, from twenty-five to forty pounds each. All our muscles had shriveled. The dogs retained strength that was amazing. Stripped for the last lap, one horizon after another was lifted.

From original field papers.—Observations of April 14, 1908. Long 95-52. Bar. 29.90 Falling. Temp. —44°. Clouds Cu. St. & Alt. St. 4. Wind 1-3. Mag. E.

```
                          Noon 0......=22—02—05
        96                      ==
         4                   0......=22—56—20
    60 | 384               2 | 44—58—25
       6—24                   22—29—12
                                  +2
        54                2 | 22—31—12
        6½                    11—15—36
        27                       —9
       324                    11— 6—36
    60 | 351               90
       5—51                 78—53—24
    9—21—50                  9—27—41
    9—27—41                 88—21— 5
```

Shadow 30½ ft. (of tent pole 6 ft. above snow.)

In the forced effort which followed we frequently became overheated. The temperature was steady at 44° below zero, Fahrenheit. Perspiration came with ease, and with a certain amount of pleasure. Later followed a train of suffering for many days. The delight of the birdskin shirt gave place to the chill of a wet blanket. Our coats and trousers hardened to icy suits of armor. It became quite impossible to dress after a sleep without softening the stiffened furs with the heat of our bare skin. Mittens, boots and fur stockings became quite useless until dried out.

Fortunately, at this time the rays of the sun were warm enough to dry the furs in about three days, if lashed to the sunny side of a sled as we marched along, and strangely enough, the furs dried out without apparent thawing. In these last days we felt more keenly the pangs of perspiration than in all our earlier adventures. We persistently used the amber-colored goggles. They afforded protection to the eyes, but in spite of every precaution, our distorted, frozen, burned and withered faces lined a map in relief, of the hardships endured en route.

We were curious looking savages. The perpetual glitter of the snows induced a squint of our eyes which distorted our faces in a remarkable manner. The strong light reflected from the crystal surface threw the muscles about the eyes into a state of chronic contraction. The iris was reduced to a mere pin-hole.

The strong winds and drifting snows necessitated the habit of peeping out of the corners of the eyes. Nature, in attempting to keep the ball from hardening, flushed it at all times with blood. To keep the seeing windows of the mind open required a constant exertion of will power. The effect was a set of expressions of hardship and wrinkles which might be called the boreal squint.

This boreal squint is a part of the russet-bronze physiognomy which falls to the lot of every Arctic explorer. The early winds, with a piercing temperature, start a flush of scarlet, while frequent frostbites leave figures in black. Later the burning sun browns the skin; subsequently, strong winds sap the moisture, harden the skin and leave open fissures on the face. The human face takes upon itself the texture and configuration of the desolate, wind-driven world upon which it looks.

Hard work and reduced nourishment contract the muscles, dispel the fat and leave the skin to shrivel in folds. The imprint of the goggles, the set expression of hard times, and the mental blank of the environment remove all spiritual animation. Our faces assumed the color and lines of old, withering, russet apples, and would easily pass for the mummied countenances of the prehistoric progenitors of man.

In enforced efforts to spread out our stiffened legs over the last reaches, there was left no longer sufficient energy at camping times to erect snow shelters. Our silk tent was pressed into use. Although the temperature was still very low, the congenial rays pierced the silk fabric and rested softly on our eye lids closed in heavy slumber. In strong winds it was still necessary to erect a sheltering wall, whereby to shield the tent.

As we progressed over the last one hundred mile-step, my mind was divested of its lethargy. Unconsciously I braced myself. My senses became more keen. With a careful scrutiny I now observed the phenomena of the strange world into which fortune had pressed us—first of all men.

Step by step, I invaded a world untrodden and unknown. Dulled as I was by hardship, I thrilled with the sense of the explorer in new lands, with the thrill of discovery and conquest. "Then," as Keats says, "felt I like some watcher of the skies, when a new planet swims into his ken." In this land of ice I was master, I was sole invader. I strode forward with an undaunted glory in my soul.

Signs of land, which I encouraged my companions to believe were real, were still seen every day, but I knew, of course, they were deceptive. It now seemed to me that something unusual must happen, that some line must cross our horizon to mark the important area into which we were passing.

Through vapor-charged air of crystal, my eyes ran over plains moving in brilliant waves of running colors toward dancing horizons. Mirages turned things topsy-turvy. Inverted lands and queer objects ever rose and fell, shrouded in mystery. All of this was due to the atmospheric magic of the continued glory of midnight suns in throwing piercing beams of light through superimposed strata of air of varying temperature and density.

Daily, by careful measurements, I found that our night shadows shortened and became more uniform during the passing hours of the day, as the shadow dial was marked.

With a lucky series of astronomical observations

our position was fixed for each stage of progress.

Nearing the Pole, my imagination quickened. A restless, almost hysterical excitement came over all of us. My boys fancied they saw bears and seals. I had new lands under observation frequently, but with a change in the direction of light the horizon cleared. We became more and more eager to push further into the mystery. Climbing the long ladder of latitudes, there was always the feeling that each hour's work was bringing us nearer the Pole—the Pole which men had sought for three centuries, and which, fortune favoring, should be mine!

Yet, I was often so physically tired that my mind was, when the momentary intoxications passed, in a sense, dulled. But the habit of seeing and of noting what I had seen, had been acquired. The habit, yes, of putting one foot in front of the other, mile after mile, through the wild dreariness of ice, the habit of observing, even though with aching, blurred eyes, and noting, methodically, however wearily, what the tired eyes had seen.

From the eighty-eighth to the eighty-ninth parallel the ice lay in large fields, the surface was less irregular than formerly. In other respects it was about the same as below the eighty-seventh. I observed here also, an increasing extension of the range of vision. I seemed to scan longer distances, and the ice along the horizon had a less angular outline. The color of the sky and the ice changed to deeper purple-blues. I had no way of checking these impressions by other observations; the eagerness to find something unusual may have fired my imagination, but since the earth is flattened at the Pole, perhaps a widened horizon would naturally be detected there.

At eight o'clock on the morning of April 19, we camped on a picturesque old field, with convenient hummocks, to the top of which we could easily rise for the frequent outlook which we now maintained. We pitched our tent, and silenced the dogs by blocks of pemmican. New enthusiasm was aroused by a liberal pot of pea-soup and a few chips of frozen meat. Then we bathed in life-giving sunbeams, screened from the piercing air by the strands of the silk-walled tent.

The day was beautiful. Had our sense of appreciation not been blunted by accumulated fatigue we should have greatly enjoyed the play of light and color in the ever-changing scene of sparkle. But in our condition it was but an inducement to keep the eyes open and to prolong interest long enough to dispel the growing complaint of aching muscles.

Ah-we-lah and E-tuk-i-shook were soon lost in profound sleep, the only comfort in their hard lives. I remained awake, as had been my habit for many preceding days, to get nautical observations. My longitude calculations lined us at 94° 3'. At noon the sun's altitude was carefully set on the sextant, and the latitude, quickly reduced, gave 89° 31'. The drift had carried us too far east, but our advance was encouraging.

I put down the instrument, wrote the reckonings in my book. Then I gazed, with a sort of fascination, at the figures. My heart began to thump wildly. Slowly my brain whirled with exultation. I arose jubilant. We were only 29 miles from the North Pole!

I suppose I created quite a commotion about the

little camp. E-tuk-i-shook, aroused by the noise, awoke and rubbed his eyes. I told him that in two average marches we should reach the *"tigi-shu"*—the big nail. He sprang to his feet and shouted with joy. He kicked Ah-we-lah, none too gently, and told him the glad news.

Together they went out to a hummock, and through glasses, sought for a mark to locate so important a place as the terrestrial axis! If but one sleep ahead, it must be visible! So they told me, and I laughed. The sensation of laughing was novel. At first I was quite startled. I had not laughed for many days. Their idea was amusing, but it was eminently sensible from their standpoint and knowledge.

I tried to explain to them that the Pole is not visible to the eye, and that its position is located only by a repeated use of the various instruments. Although this was quite beyond their comprehension the explanation entirely satisfied their curiosity. They burst out in hurrahs of joy. For two hours they chanted, danced and shouted the passions of wild life. Their joy, however, was in the thought of a speedy turning back homeward, I surmised.

This, however, was the first real sign of pleasure or rational emotion which they had shown for several weeks. For some time I had entertained the fear that we no longer possessed strength to return to land. This unbridled flow of vigor dispelled that idea. My heart throbbed with gladness. A font of new strength seemed to gush forth within me. Considering through what we had gone, I now marvel at the reserve forces latent in us, and I sometimes feel that I should write, not of human weakness, but a new gospel of human strength.

With the Pole only twenty-nine miles distant, more sleep was quite impossible. We brewed an extra pot of tea, prepared a favorite broth of pemmican, dug up a surprise of fancy biscuits and filled up on good things to the limit of the allowance for our final feast days. The dogs, which had joined the chorus of gladness, were given an extra lump of pemmican. A few hours more were agreeably spent in the tent. Then we started out with new spirit for the uttermost goal of our world.

Bounding joyously forward, with a stimulated mind, I reviewed the journey. Obstacle after obstacle had been overcome. Each battle won gave a spiritual thrill, and courage to scale the next barrier. Thus had been ever, and was still, in the unequal struggles between human and inanimate nature, an incentive to go onward, ever onward, up the stepping-stones to ultimate success. And now, after a life-denying struggle in a world where every element of Nature is against the life and progress of man, triumph came with steadily measured reaches of fifteen miles a day!

We were excited to fever heat. Our feet were light on the run. Even the dogs caught the infectious enthusiasm. They rushed along at a pace which made it difficult for me to keep a sufficient advance to set a good course. The horizon was still eagerly searched for something to mark the approaching boreal center. But nothing unusual was seen. The same expanse of moving seas of ice, on which we had gazed for five hundred miles, swam about us as we drove onward.

Looking through gladdened eyes, the scene assumed a new glory. Dull blue and purple expanses were transfigured into plains of gold, in which were

lakes of sapphire and rivulets of ruby fire. Engirdling
this world were purple mountains with gilded crests.
It was one of the few days on the stormy pack when all
Nature smiled with cheering lights.

As the day advanced beyond midnight and the
splendor of the summer night ran into a clearer continued day, the beams of gold on the surface snows
assumed a more burning intensity. Shadows of hummocks and ice ridges became dyed with a deeper purple,
and in the burning orange world loomed before us Titan
shapes, regal and regally robed.

From my position, a few hundred yards ahead of
the sleds, with compass and axe in hand, as usual, I
could not resist the temptation to turn frequently to see
the movement of the dog train with its new fire. In
this backward direction the color scheme was reversed.
About the horizon the icy walls gleamed like beaten
gold set with gem-spots of burning colors; the plains
represented every shade of purple and blue, and over
them, like vast angel wings outspread, shifted golden
pinions. Through the sea of palpitating color, the dogs
came, with spirited tread, noses down, tails erect and
shoulders braced to the straps, like chariot horses. In
the magnifying light they seemed many times their normal size. The young Eskimos, chanting songs of love,
followed with easy, swinging steps. The long whip
was swung with a brisk crack. Over all arose a cloud
of frosted breath, which, like incense smoke, became sil-
vered in the light, a certain signal of efficient motive
power.

With our destination reachable over smooth ice, in
these brighter days of easier travel our long chilled blood

was stirred to double action, our eyes opened to beauty and color, and a normal appreciation of the wonders of this new strange and wonderful world.

As we lifted the midnight's sun to the plane of the midday sun, the shifting Polar desert became floored with a sparkling sheen of millions of diamonds, through which we fought a way to ulterior and greater glory.

Our leg cramps eased and our languid feet lifted buoyantly from the steady drag as the soul arose to effervescence. Fields of rich purple, lined with running liquid gold, burning with flashes of iridescent colors, gave a sense of gladness long absent from our weary life. The ice was much better. We still forced a way over large fields, small pressure areas and narrow leads. But, when success is in sight, most troubles seem lighter. We were thin, with faces burned, withered, frozen and torn in fissures, with clothes ugly from overwear. Yet men never felt more proud than we did, as we militantly strode off the last steps to the world's very top!

Camp was pitched early in the morning of April 20. The sun was northeast, the pack glowed in tones of lilac, the normal westerly air brushed our frosty faces. Our surprising burst on enthusiasm had been nursed to its limits. Under it a long march had been made over average ice, with the usual result of overpowering fatigue. Too tired and sleepy to wait for a cup of tea, we poured melted snow into our stomach and pounded the pemmican with an axe to ease the task of the jaws. Our eyes closed before the meal was finished, and the world was lost to us for eight hours. Waking, I took observations which gave latitude 89° 46′.

Late at night, after another long rest, we hitched the dogs and loaded the sleds. When action began, the feeling came that no time must be lost. Feverish impatience seized me.

Cracking our whips, we bounded ahead. The boys sang. The dogs howled. Midnight of April 21 had just passed.

Over the sparkling snows the post-midnight sun glowed like at noon. I seemed to be walking in some splendid golden realms of dreamland. As we bounded onward the ice swam about me in circling rivers of gold.

E-tuk-i-shook and Ah-we-lah, though thin and ragged, had the dignity of the heroes of a battle which had been fought through to success.

We all were lifted to the paradise of winners as we stepped over the snows of a destiny for which we had risked life and willingly suffered the tortures of an icy hell. The ice under us, the goal for centuries of brave, heroic men, to reach which many had suffered terribly and terribly died, seemed almost sacred. Constantly and carefully I watched my instruments in recording this final reach. Nearer and nearer they recorded our approach. Step by step, my heart filled with a strange rapture of conquest.

At last we step over colored fields of sparkle, climbing walls of purple and gold—finally, under skies of crystal blue, with flaming clouds of glory, we touch the mark! The soul awakens to a definite triumph; there is sunrise within us, and all the world of night-darkened trouble fades. We are at the top of the world! The flag is flung to the frigid breezes of the North Pole!

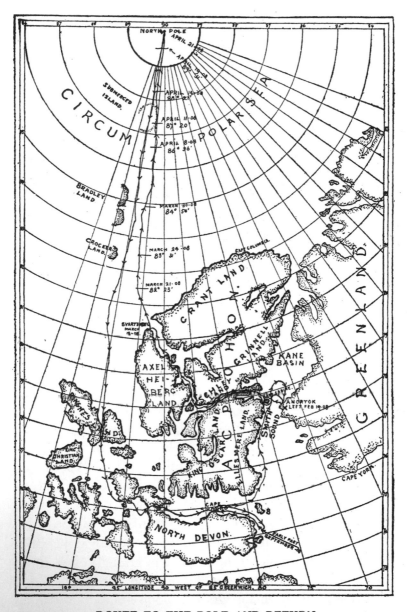

ROUTE TO THE POLE AND RETURN
A triangle of 30,000 square miles cut out of the mysterious unknown

AT THE NORTH POLE

OBSERVATIONS AT THE POLE—METEOROLOGICAL AND AS-
TRONOMICAL PHENOMENA—SINGULAR STABILITY
AND UNIFORMITY OF THE THERMOMETER AND
BAROMETER—A SPOT WHERE ONE'S SHADOW IS THE
SAME LENGTH EACH HOUR OF THE TWENTY-FOUR—
EIGHT POLAR ALTITUDES OF THE SUN

XX

FULL AND FINAL PROOFS OF THE ATTAINMENT

Looking about me, after the first satisfactory observation, I viewed the vacant expanse. The first realization of actual victory, of reaching my lifetime's goal,
set my heart throbbing violently and my brain aglow.
I felt the glory which the prophet feels in his vision,
with which the poet thrills in his dream. About the
frozen plains my imagination evoked aspects of grandeur. I saw silver and crystal palaces, such as were
never built by man, with turrets flaunting "pinions glorious, golden." The shifting mirages seemed like the
ghosts of dead armies, magnified and transfigured, huge
and spectral, moving along the horizon and bearing the
wind-tossed phantoms of golden blood-stained banners.
The low beating of the wind assumed the throb of
martial music. Bewildered, I realized all that I had

suffered, all the pain of fasting, all the anguish of long weariness, and I felt that this was my reward. I had scaled the world, and I stood at the Pole!

By a long and consecutive series of observations and mental tabulations of various sorts on our journey northward, continuing here, I knew, beyond peradventure of doubt, that I was at a spot which was as near as possible, by usual methods of determination, five hundred and twenty miles from Svartevoeg, a spot toward which men had striven for more than three centuries—a spot known as the North Pole, and where I stood first of white men. In my own achievement I felt, that dizzy moment, that all the heroic souls who had braved the rigors of the Arctic region found their own hopes' fulfilment. I had realized their dream. I had culminated with success the efforts of all the brave men who had failed before me. I had finally justified their sacrifices, their very death; I had proven to humanity humanity's supreme triumph over a hostile, death-dealing Nature. It seemed that the souls of these dead exulted with me, and that in some sub-strata of the air, in notes more subtle than the softest notes of music, they sang a pæan in the spirit with me.

We had reached our destination. My relief was indescribable. The prize of an international marathon was ours. Pinning the Stars and Stripes to a tent-pole, I asserted the achievement in the name of the ninety millions of countrymen who swear fealty to that flag. And I felt a pride as I gazed at the white-and-crimson barred pinion, a pride which the claim of no second victor has ever taken from me.

My mental intoxication did not interfere with the

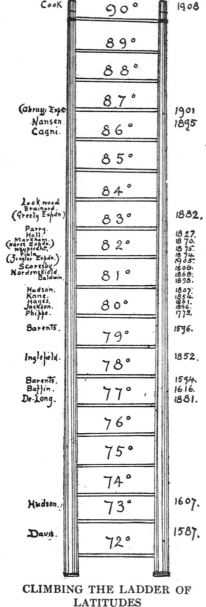

CLIMBING THE LADDER OF
LATITUDES

routine work which was now necessary. Having reached the goal, it was imperative that all scientific observations be made as carefully as possible, as quickly as possible. To the taking of these I set myself at once, while my companions began the routine work of unloading the sledges and building an igloo.

Our course when arriving at the Pole, as near as it was possible to determine, was on the ninety-seventh meridian. The day was April 21, 1908. It was local noon. The sun was 11° 55″ above the magnetic northern horizon. My shadow, a dark purple-blue streak with ill-defined edges, measured twenty-six feet in length. The tent pole, marked as a measuring stick, was pushed into the snow, leaving six feet above the surface. This gave a shadow twenty-eight feet long.

Several sextant observations gave a latitude a few seconds below 90°, which, because of unknown refraction and uncertain accuracy of time, was placed at 90°. (Other observations on the next day gave similar results, although we shifted camp four miles toward magnetic south.) A broken hand-axe was tied to the end of a life-line; this was lowered through a fresh break in the ice, and the angle which it made with the surface indicated a drift toward Greenland. The temperature, gauged by a spirit thermometer, was 37.7°, F. The mercury thermometer indicated —36°. The atmospheric pressure by the aneroid barometer was at 29.83. It was falling, and indicated a coming change in the weather. The wind was very light, and had veered from northeast to south, according to the compass card.

The sky was almost clear, of a dark purple blue, with a pearly ice-blink or silver reflection extending east, and a smoky water-sky west, in darkened, ill-defined streaks, indicating continuous ice or land toward Bering Sea, and an active pack, with some open water, toward Spitzbergen. To the north and south were wine-colored gold-shot clouds, flung in long banners, with ragged-pointed ends along the horizon. The ice about was nearly the same as it had been continuously since leaving the eighty-eighth parallel. It was slightly more active, and showed, by news cracks and oversliding, young ice signs of recent disturbance.

The field upon which we camped was about three miles long and two miles wide. Measured at a new crevasse, the ice was sixteen feet thick. The tallest hummock measured twenty-eight feet above water. The snow lay in fine feathery crystals, with no surface crust.

About three inches below the soft snow was a sub-surface crust strong enough to carry the bodily weight. Below this were other successive crusts, and a porous snow in coarse crystals, with a total depth of about fifteen inches.

Our igloo was built near one edge in the lee of an old hummock about fifteen feet high. Here a recent bank of drift snow offered just the right kind of material from which to cut building blocks. While a shelter was thus being walled, I moved about constantly to read my instruments and to study carefully the local environment.

In a geographic sense we had now arrived at a point where all meridians meet. The longitude, therefore, was zero. Time was a negative problem. There being no longitude, there can be no time. The hour lines of Greenwich, of New York, of Peking, and of all the world here run together. Figuratively, if this position is the pin-point of the earth's axis, it is possible to have all meridians under one foot, and therefore it should be possible to step from midnight to midday, from the time of San Francisco to that of Paris, from one side of the globe to the other, as time is measured.

Here there is but one day and but one night in each year, but the night of six monhs is relieved by about one hundred days of continuous twilight. Geographically, there was here but one direction. It was south on every line of the dial of longitude—north, east and west had vanished. We had reached a point where true direction became a paradox and a puzzle. It was south before us, south behind us, and south on every side. But the compass, pointing to the magnetic Pole along the ninety-

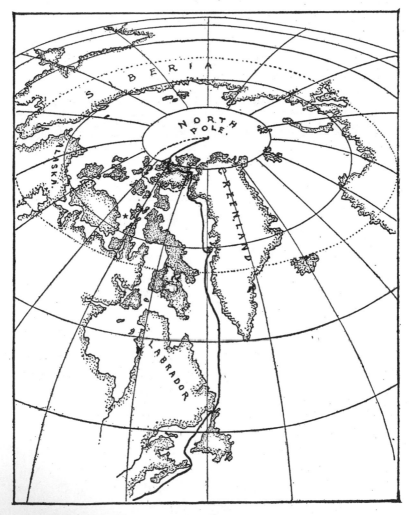

**WHERE ALL MERIDIANS MEET AND EVERY DIRECTION
IS SOUTH**

The Pivotal Point on which the earth turns.
*Magnetic Pole

seventh meridian, was as useful as ever. (To avoid statements easily misunderstood, all our directions about the Pole will be given as taken from the compass, and without reference to the geographer's anomaly of its being south in every direction.)

My first noon observations gave the following result, which is copied from the original paper, as it was written at the Pole and reproduced photographically on another page. April 21, 1908: Long., 97-W.; Bar., 29-83; Temp.,—37.7; Clouds Alt., St., 1; Wind, 1; Mag., S.; Iceblink E.; Water Sky W.

```
Noon Alt.  0            23—33—25
                            +2
                      2 | 23—35—25
                        11—47—42   5
                          +15—56
        50              12— 3—38
        6½                  —9
        25              11—54—38
       300              90
  60 | 325              78— 5—22
       5—25             11—54—23
  11—48—58              89—59—45
  11—54—23
```

Shadows 28 ft. (of 6 ft. pole).

Taking advantage of our brief stay, the boys set up the ice-axe and drying sticks, and hung upon them their perspiration-wetted and frosted furs to dry. Hanging out wet clothes and an American flag at the North Pole seemed an amusing incongruity.

The puzzled standpoint of my Eskimos was amusing. They tried hard to appreciate the advantages of finding this supposititious *"tigi shu"* (big nail), but actually here, they could not, even from a sense of deference to me and my judgment, entirely hide their feeling of disappointment.

On the advance I had told them that an actual "big nail" would not be found—only the point where it ought to be. But I think they really hoped that if it had actually disappeared they should find that it had come back into place after all!

In building our igloo the boys frequently looked about expectantly. Often they ceased cutting snow-blocks and rose to a hummock to search the horizon for something which, to their idea, must mark this important spot, for which we had struggled against hope and all the dictates of personal comforts. At each breathing spell their eager eyes picked some sky sign which to them meant land or water, or the play of some god of land or sea. The naive and sincere interest which the Eskimos on occasions feel in the mystery of the spirit-world gives them an imaginative appreciation of nature often in excess of that of the more material and skeptical Caucasian.

Arriving at the mysterious place where, they felt, something should happen, their imagination now forced an expression of disappointment. In a high-keyed condition, all their superstitions recurred to them with startling reality.

In one place the rising vapor proved to be the breath of the great submarine god—the *"Ko-Koyah."* In another place, a motionless little cloud marked the land in which dwelt the *"Turnah-huch-suak,"* the great Land God, and the air spirits were represented by the different winds, with sex relations.

Ah-we-lah and E-tuk-i-shook, with the astuteness of the aborigine, who reads Nature as a book, were sharp enough to note that the high air currents did not correspond to surface currents; for, although the wind was blowing homeward, and changed its force and direction, a few high clouds moved persistently in a different direction.

This, to them, indicated a warfare among the air spirits. The ice and snow were also animated. To them the whole world presented a rivalry of conflicting spirits which offered never-ending topics of conversation.

As the foot pressed the snow, its softness, its rebound, or its metallic ring indicated sentiments of friendliness or hostility. The ice, by its color, movement or noise, spoke the humor of its animation, or that of the supposed life of the restless sea beneath it. In interpreting these spirit signs, the two expressed considerable difference of opinion. Ah-we-lah saw dramatic situations and became almost hysterical with excitement; E-tuk-i-shook saw only a monotone of the normal play of life. Such was the trend of interest and conversation as the building of the igloos was completed.

Contrary to our usual custom, the dogs had been allowed to rest in their traces attached to the sleds. Their usual malicious inquisitiveness exhausted, they were too tired to examine the sleds to steal food. But now, as the house was completed, holes were chipped with a knife in ice-shoulders, through which part of a trace was passed, and each team was thus securely fastened to a ring cut in ice-blocks. Then each dog was given a double ration of pemmican. Their pleasure was expressed by an extra twist of the friendly tails and an extra note of gladness from long-contracted stomachs. Finishing their meal, they curled up and warmed the snow, from which they took an occasional bite to furnish liquid for their gastric economy. Almost two days of rest followed, and this was the canine celebration of the Polar attainment.

We withdrew to the inside of the dome of snow-blocks, pulled in a block to close the doors, spread out our bags as beds on the platform of leveled snow, pulled off boots and trousers, and slipped half-length into the bristling reindeer furs. We then discussed, with chummy congratulations, the success of our long drive to the world's end.

While thus engaged, the little Juel stove piped the cheer of the pleasure of ice-water, soon to quench our chronic thirst. In the meantime, Ah-we-lah and E-tuk-i-shook pressed farther and farther into their bags, pulled over the hoods, and closed their eyes to an overpowering fatigue. But my lids did not easily close. I watched the fire. More ice went into the kettle. With the satisfaction of an ambition fulfilled, I peeped out occasionally through the pole-punched port, and noted the horizon glittering with gold and purple.

Quivers of self-satisfying joy ran up my spine and relieved the frosty mental bleach of the long-delayed Polar anticipation.

In due time we drank, with grateful satisfaction, large quantities of ice-water, which was more delicious than any wine. A pemmican soup, flavored with musk ox tenderloins, steaming with heat—a luxury seldom enjoyed in our camps—next went down with warming, satisfying gulps. This was followed by a few strips of frozen fresh meat, then by a block of pemmican. Later, a few squares of musk ox suet gave the taste of sweets to round up our meal. Last of all, three cups of tea spread the chronic stomach-folds, after which we reveled in the sense of fulness of the best meal of many weeks.

With full stomachs and the satisfaction of a worthy task well performed, we rested.

We had reached the zenith of man's Ultima Thule, which had been sought for more than three centuries. In comfortable berths of snow we tried to sleep, turning with the earth on its northern axis.

But sleep for me was impossible. At six o'clock, or six hours after our arrival at local noon, I arose, went out of the igloo, and took a double set of observations. Returning, I did some figuring, lay down on my bag, and at ten o'clock, or four hours later, leaving Ah-we-lah to guard the camp and dogs, E-tuk-i-shook joined me to make a tent camp about four miles to the magnetic south. My object was to have a slightly different position for subsequent observations.

Placing our tent, bags and camp equipment on a sled, we pushed it over the ice field, crossed a narrow lead sheeted with young ice, and moved on to another field which seemed to have much greater dimensions. We erected the tent not quite two hours later, in time for a midnight observation. These sextant readings of the sun's altitude were continued for the next twenty-four hours.

In the idle times between observations, I went over to a new break between the field on which we were camped and that on which Ah-we-lah guarded the dogs. Here the newly-formed sheets of ice slid over each other as the great, ponderous fields stirred to and fro. A peculiar noise, like that of a crying child, arose. It came seemingly from everywhere, intermittently, in successive crying spells. Lying down, and putting my fur-cushioned ear to the edge of the old ice, I heard a distant thundering noise, the reverberations of the moving, grinding pack, which, by its wind-driven sweep, was drifting over the unseen seas of mystery. In an effort to locate the cry, I searched diligently along the lead. I came to a spot where two tiny pieces of ice served as a mouthpiece. About every fifteen seconds there were two or three sharp, successive cries. With the ice-axe I detached one. The cries stopped; but other cries were heard further along the line.

The time for observations was at hand, and I returned to take up the sextant. Returning later to the lead, to watch the seas breathe, the cry seemed stilled. The thin ice-sheets were cemented together, and in an open space nearby I had an opportunity to study the making and breaking of the polar ice.

That tiny film of ice which voiced the baby cries spreads the world's most irresistible power. In its making we have the nucleus for the origin of the polar pack, that great moving crust of the earth which crunches ships, grinds rocks, and sweeps mountains into the sea. Beginning as a mere microscopic crystal, successive crystals, by their affinity for each other, unite to make a disc. These discs, by the same law of cohesion, assemble and unite. Now the thin sheet, the first sea ice, is complete, and either rests to make the great field of ice, or spreads from floe to floe and from field to field, thus spreading, bridging and mending the great moving masses which cover the mid-polar basin.

Another law of nature was solved by a similar insignificant incident. In spreading our things out to air and dry (for things will dry in wind and sun, even at a very low temperature), two pieces of canvas were thrown on a hummock. It was a white canvas sled-cover and a black strip of canvas, in which the boat fittings were wrapped. When these strips of canvas were lifted it was found that under the part of the black canvas, resting on a slope at right angles to the sun, the snow had melted and recongealed. Under the white canvas the snow had not changed. The temperature was —41°; we had felt no heat, but this black canvas had absorbed enough heat from a feeble sun to melt the snow beneath it. This little lesson in physics began to interest me, and on the return many similar experiments were made. As the long, tedious marches were made, I asked myself the questions: Why is snow white? Why is the sky blue? And why does black burn snow when white does not?

Little by little, in the long drive of monotony, satisfactory answers came to these questions. Thus, in seeking abstract knowledge, the law of radiation was thoroughly examined. In doing this, there came to me slowly the solution of various problems of animal life, and eventually there was uncovered what to me proved a startling revelation in the incidents that led up to animal coloring in the Arctic. For here I found that the creatures' fur and feathers were colored in accord with their needs of absorbing external heat or of conserving internal heat. The facts here indicated will be presented later, when we deal with the snow-fitted creatures at close range.

One of the impressions which I carried with me of this night march was that the sun seemed low—lower, indeed, than that of midday, which, in reality, was not true, for the observations placed it nine minutes higher. This was an indication of the force of habit. In the northward march we had noted a considerable relative difference in the height of the night sun and that of the day. Although this difference had vanished now, the mind at times refused to grasp the remarkable change.*

At the Pole I was impressed by a peculiar uniformity in the temperature of the atmosphere throughout the twenty-four hours, and also by a strange monotone in color and light of sea and sky. I had begun to observe this as I approached the boreal center. The strange equability of light and color, of humidity and of air temperatures extended an area one hundred miles about the Pole. This was noted both on my coming and going over this district.

Approaching the Pole, and as the night sun gradually lifted, an increasing equalization of the temperature of night and day followed. Three hundred miles from the Pole the thermometer at night had been from 10° to 20° lower than during the day. There the shivering chill of midnight made a strong contrast to the burning, heatless glitter of midday. At the Pole the thermometer did not rise or fall appreciably for certain fixed hours of the day or night, but remained almost uniform during the entire twenty-four hours.

---

* After trying to explain this impression fifteen months later to a Swiss professor, who spoke little English, he quoted me as saying that the sun at night about the Pole was much lower than at noon. No such ridiculous remark was ever made. In reality the eye did not detect any difference in the distance between the sun and the horizon through the next twenty-four hours. There was no visible rise or set, the night dip of the nocturnal swing of the sun was entirely eliminated. We had, however, several ways of checking this important phenomena, which will be introduced later.

This, to a less notable extent, was true also of the barometer. Farther south there had been a difference in the day and night range of the barometer. Here, although the night winds continued more actively than those of the day, the barometer was less variable than at any time on my journey.

At the Pole the tendency of change in force and direction of air currents, observed farther south, for morning and evening periods, was no longer noted. But when strong winds brushed the pack, a good deal of the Polar equalization gave place to a radical difference, giving a period for high and low temperatures; which period, however, did not correspond to the usual hours of day or night. The winds, therefore, seemed to carry to us the sub-Polar inequality of atmospheric variation in temperature and pressure. Many of the facts bearing upon this problem were not learned until later. Subsequently, I learned, also, that strong winds often disturb the Polar atmospheric sameness; but all is given here because of the striking impression which it made upon me at this time.

In the region about the Pole I observed that, although there were remarkable and beauteous color blendings in the sky, the intense contrasts and the spectacular display of cloud effects, seen in more southern regions, were absent.

A color suffusion is common throughout the entire Arctic zone. Light, pouring from the low-lying sun, is reflected from the ice in an indescribable blaze. From millions of ice slopes, with millions and millions of tiny reflecting surfaces, each one a mirror, some large, some smaller than specks of diamond dust, this light is sent

FIRST CAMP AT THE POLE, APRIL 21, 1908

AT THE POLE—"WE WERE THE ONLY PULSATING CREATURES IN A
DEAD WORLD OF ICE"

back in different directions in burning waves to the sky. A liquid light seems forced back from the sky into every tiny crevice of this bejeweled wonderland. One color invariably predominates at a time. Sometimes the ice and air and sky are suffused with a hue of rose, again of orange, again of a light alloyed yellow, again blue; and, as we get farther north, more dominantly purple. Farther south, in our journey northward, we had viewed color effects in reality incomparably more beautiful than those in the regions about the Pole. The sun, farther south, in rising and setting, and with limitless changes of polarized and refracted light, passing through strata of atmosphere of varying depths of different density, produces kaleidoscopic changes of burning color.

At the Pole there were sunbursts, but because of the slight change in the sun's dip to the horizon, the prevailing light was invariably in shades running to purple. At first my imagination evoked a more glowing wonder than in reality existed; as the hours wore on, and as the wants of my body asserted themselves, I began to see the vacant spaces with a disillusionizing eye.

The set of observations given here, taken every six hours, from noon on April 21 to midnight on April 22, 1908, fixed our position with reasonable certainty.

These figures do not give the exact position for the normal spiral ascent of the sun, which is about fifty seconds for each hour, or five minutes for each six hours; but the uncertainties of error by refraction and ice-drift do not permit such accuracy of observations. These figures are submitted, therefore, not to establish the pinpoint accuracy of our position, but to show that we had approximately reached a spot where the sun, throughout the twenty-four hours, circled the heavens in a line nearly parallel to the horizon.

THE SUN'S TRUE CENTRAL ALTITUDE AT THE POLE.

April 21 and 22, 1908.

Seven successive observations, taken every six hours.
Each observation is reduced for an instrumental error of $+2'$.
For semi-diameter and also for refraction and parallax, $-9'$.
The seven reductions are each calculated from two sextant readings, generally of an upper and lower limb.

(TAKEN FROM MY FIELD NOTES.)

April 21, 1908, 97th meridian local time—12 o'clock noon—11°—54'—40"
6 P. M. (same camp).   12—00—10
Moved camp 4 miles magnetic South
12 o'clock (midnight)   12— 3—50
April 22nd, 6 A. M.   12— 9—30
12 o'clock noon   12—14—20
6 P. M.   12—18—40
12 o'clock (midnight)   12—25—10
Temperature, —41. Barometer, 30.05.
Shadow 27½ feet (of 6-foot pole).

With the use of the sextant, the artificial horizon, pocket chronometers, and the usual instruments and methods of explorers, our observations were continued and our positions were fixed with the most painstakingly careful safeguards possible against inaccuracy. The value of all such observations as proof of a Polar success, however, is open to such interpretation as the future may determine. This applies, not only to me, but to anyone who bases any claim upon them.

To me there were many seemingly insignificant facts noted in our northward progress which left the imprint of milestones. Our footprints marked a road ever onward into the unknown. Many of these almost unconscious reckonings took the form of playful impressions, and were not even at the time written down.

In the first press reports of my achievement there was not space to go into minute details, nor did the presentation of the subject permit an elaboration on all the data gathered. But now, in the light of a better perspective, it seems important that every possible phase of the minutest detail be presented. For only by a careful consideration of every phase of every phenomena en route can a true verdict be obtained upon this widely discussed subject of Polar attainment.

And now, right here, I want you to consider carefully with me one thing which made me feel sure that we had reached the Pole. This is the subject of shadows—our own shadows on the snow-covered ice. A seemingly unimportant phenomenon which had often been a topic of discussion, and so commonplace that I only rarely referred to it in my notebooks, our own shadows on the snow-cushioned ice had told of northward movement, and ultimately proved to my satisfaction that the Pole had been reached.

In our northward progress—to explain my shadow observations from the beginning—for a long time after our start from Svortevoeg, our shadows did not perceptibly shorten or brighten, to my eyes. The natives, however, got from these shadows a never-ending variety of topics of conversation. They foretold storms, located game and read the story of home entanglements. Far from land, far from every sign of a cheering, solid earth, wandering with our shadows over the hopeless desolation of the moving seas of glitter, I, too, took a keen interest in the blue blots that represented our bodies. At noon, by comparison with later hours, they were sharp, short, of a dark, restful blue. At this time a thick atmosphere of crystals rested upon the ice pack, and when the sun sank the strongest purple rays could

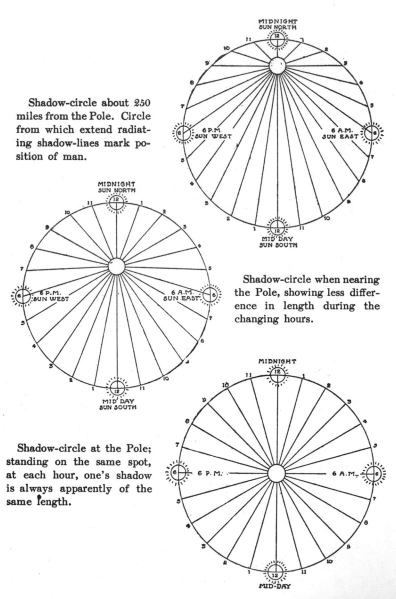

Shadow-circle about 250 miles from the Pole. Circle from which extend radiating shadow-lines mark position of man.

Shadow-circle when nearing the Pole, showing less difference in length during the changing hours.

Shadow-circle at the Pole; standing on the same spot, at each hour, one's shadow is always apparently of the same length.

SHADOW-CIRCLES INDICATING THE APPROACH TO THE POLE

Showing approximately the relative length of a man's shadow for each hour of the twenty-four-hour day.

not penetrate the frosty haze. Long before the time for sunset, even on clear days, the sun was lost in low clouds of drifting needles.

After passing the eighty-eighth parallel there was a notable change in our shadows. The night shadow lengthened; the day shadow, by comparison, shortened. The boys saw in this something which they could not understand. The positive blue grew to a permanent purple, and the sharp outlines ran to vague, indeterminate edges.

Now at the Pole there was no longer any difference in length, color or sharpness of outline between the shadow of the day or night.

"What does it all mean?" they asked. The Eskimos looked with eager eyes at me to explain, but my vocabulary was not comprehensive enough to give them a really scientific explanation, and also my brain was too weary from the muscular poison of fatigue to frame words.

The shadows of midnight and those of midday were the same. The sun made a circle about the heavens in which the eye detected no difference in its height above the ice, either night or day. Throughout the twenty-four hours there was no perceptible rise or set in the sun's seeming movement. Now, at noon, the shadow represented in its length the altitude of the sun—about twelve degrees. At six o'clock it was the same. At midnight it was the same. At six o'clock in the morning it was the same.

A picture of the snowhouse and ourselves, taken at the same time and developed a year later, gives the same length of shadow. The compass pointed south. The

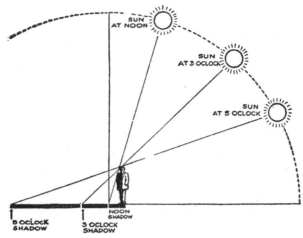

At a latitude about New York, a man's shadow lengthens hour by hour as the sun descends toward the horizon at nightfall.

night drop of the thermometer had vanished. Let us, for the sake of argument, grant that all our instrumental observations are wrong. Here is a condition of things in which I believed, and still believe, the eye, without instrumental assistance, places the sun at about the

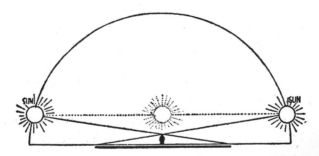

At the North Pole, a man's shadow is of equal length during the entire twenty-four hours, since the sun moves spirally around the heavens at about the same apparent height above the horizon throughout the twenty-four-hour day.

same height for every hour of the day and night. It is only on the earth's axis that such an observation is possible.

There was about us no land. No fixed point. Absolutely nothing upon which to rest the eye to give the sense of location or to judge distance.

Here everything moves. The sea breathes, and lifts the crust of ice which the wind stirs. The pack ever drifts in response to the pull of the air and the drive of the water. Even the sun, the only fixed dot in this stirring, restless world, where all you see is, without your seeing it, moving like a ship at sea, seems to have a rapid movement in a gold-flushed circle not far above endless fields of purple crystal; but that movement is never higher, never lower—always in the same fixed path. The instruments detect a slight spiral ascent, day after day, but the eye detects no change.

Although I had measured our shadows at times on the northward march, at the Pole these shadow notations were observed with the same care as the measured altitude of the sun by the sextant. A series was made on April 22, after E-tuk-i-shook and I had left Ah-we-lah in charge of our first camp at the Pole. We made a little circle for our feet in the snow. E-tuk-i-shook stood in the foot circle. At midnight the first line was cut in the snow to the end of his shadow, and then I struck a deep hole with the ice-axe. Every hour a similar line was drawn out from his foot. At the end of twenty-four hours, with the help of Ah-we-lah, a circle was circumscribed along the points, which marked the end of the shadow for each hour. The result is represented in the snow diagram on the next page.

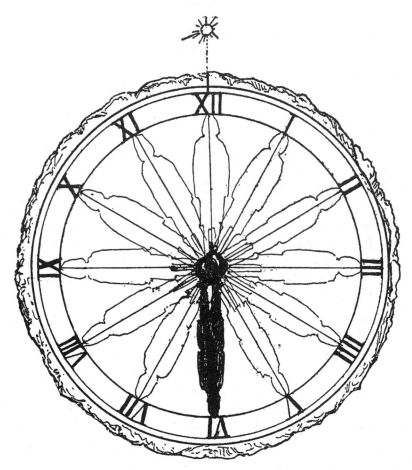

SHADOW DIAL AT THE POLE

At the Pole, a man's shadow is about the same length for every hour of the double day. When a shadow line is drawn in the snow from a man's foot in a marked dial, the human shadows take the place of the hands of a clock and mark the time by compass bearing. The relative length of these shadows also give the latitude or a man's position north or south of the equator. When during two turns around the clock dial, the shadows are all of about equal length, the position of the earth's axis is positively reached—even if all other observations fail. This simple demonstration is an indisputable proof of being on the North Pole.

In the northward march we did not stay up all of bedtime to play with shadow circles. But, at this time, to E-tuk-i-shook the thing had a spiritual interest. To me it was a part of the act of proving that the Pole had been attained. For only about the Pole, I argued, could all shadows be of equal length. Because of this combination of keen interests, we managed to find an •excuse, even during sleep hours, to draw a line on our shadow circle.

Here, then, I felt, was an important observation placing me with fair accuracy at the Pole, and, unlike all other observations, it was not based on the impossible dreams of absolutely accurate time or sure corrections for refraction.

HOW THE ALTITUDE OF THE SUN ABOVE THE HORIZON FIXES THE POSITION OF THE NORTH POLE

OBSERVED ALTITUDES, APRIL 22, 1908

6 A.M.	NOON	6 P.M.
12° 9' 30"	12° 14' 20"	12° 18' 40"

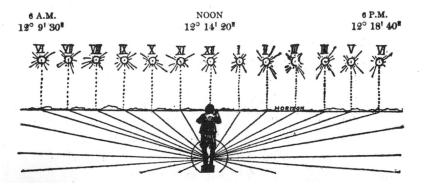

The exact altitude of the sun at noon of April 22, 1908, on the pole, was 12° 9' 16", but owing to ice-drift—the impossibility of accurate time—and unknown error by refraction, no such pin-point accuracy can be recorded. At each hour the sun, circling about the horizon, cast a shadow of uniform length.

At the place where E-tuk-i-shook and I camped, four miles south of where I had left Ah-we-lah with the dogs, only two big ice hummocks were in sight. There were more spaces of open water than at our first camp. After a midnight observation—of April 22—we returned to camp. When the dogs saw us approaching in the distance they rose, and a chorus of howls rang over the regions of the Pole—regions where dogs had never howled before. All the scientific work being finished, we began hastily to make final preparations for departure.

We had spent two days about the North Pole. After the first thrills of victory, the glamor wore away as we rested and worked. Although I tried to do so, I could get no sensation of novelty as we pitched our last belongings on the sleds. The intoxication of success had gone. I suppose intense emotions are invariably followed by reactions. Hungry, mentally and physically exhausted, a sense of the utter uselessness of this thing, of the empty reward of my endurance, followed my exhilaration. I had grasped my *ignus fatuus*. It is a misfortune for any man when his *ignus fatuus* fails to elude him.

During those last hours I asked myself why this place had so aroused an enthusiasm long-lasting through self-sacrificing years; why, for so many centuries, men had sought this elusive spot? What a futile thing, I thought, to die for! How tragically useless all those heroic efforts—efforts, in themselves, a travesty, an ironic satire, on much vainglorious human aspiration and endeavor! I thought of the enthusiasm of the people who read of the spectacular efforts of men to reach this

vacant silver-shining goal of death. I thought, too, in
that hour, of the many men of science who were devoting
their lives to the study of germs, the making of toxins;
to the saving of men from the grip of disease—men who
often lost their own lives in their experiments; whose
world and work existed in unpicturesque laboratories,
and for whom the laudations of people never rise. It
occurred to me—and I felt the bitterness of tears in my
soul—that it is often the showy and futile deeds of men
which men praise; and that, after all, the only work
worth while, the only value of a human being's efforts,
lie in deeds whereby humanity benefits. Such work as
noble bands of women accomplish who go into the slums
of great cities, who nurse the sick, who teach the ignorant, who engage in social service humbly, patiently, un-
expectant of any reward! Such work as does the scientist who studies the depredations of malignant germs,
who straightens the body of the crippled child, who pre-
cipitates a toxin which cleanses the blood of a frightful
and loathsome disease!

As my eye sought the silver and purple desert about
me for some stable object upon which to fasten itself, I
experienced an abject abandon, an intolerable loneliness.
With my two companions I could not converse; in my
thoughts and emotions they could not share. I was
alone. I was victorious. But how desolate, how dreadful was this victory! About us was no life, no spot to
relieve the monotony of frost. We were the only pulsating creatures in a dead world of ice.

A wild eagerness to get back to land seized me. It
seemed as though some new terror had arisen from the
icy waters. Something huge, something baneful . . .

invisible . . . yet whose terror-inspiring, burning eyes I felt . . . the master genii of the goal, perhaps . . . some vague, terrible, disembodied spirit force, condemned for some unimaginable sin to solitary prisonment here at the top of the world, and who wove its malignant, awful spell, and had lured men on for centuries to their destruction. . . . The desolation of the place was such that it was almost palpable; it was a thing I felt I must touch and see. My companions felt the heavy load of it upon them, and from the few words I overheard I knew they were eagerly picturing to themselves the simple joys of existence at Etah and Annoatok. I remember that to me came pictures of my Long Island home. All this arose, naturally enough, from the reaction following the strain of striving so long and so fiercely after the goal, combined with the sense of the great and actual peril of our situation. But what a cheerless spot this was, to have aroused the ambition of man for so many ages!

There came forcibly, too, the thought that although the Pole was discovered, it was not essentially discovered, that it could be discovered, in the eyes of the world, unless we could return to civilization and tell what we had done. Should we be lost in these wastes or should we be frozen to death, or buried in the snow, or drowned in a crevasse, it would never be known that we had been here. It was, therefore, as vitally necessary to get back in touch with human life, with our report, as it had been to get to the Pole.

Before leaving, I enclosed a note, written on the previous day, in a metallic tube. This I buried in the surface of the Polar snows. I knew, of course, that this

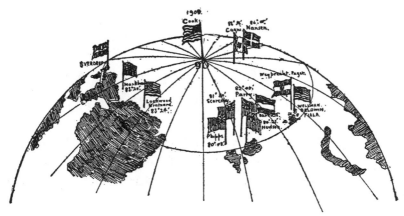

POLAR ADVANCE OF THE NATIONAL STANDARDS
Climax of four centuries of Arctic exploration—Stars and Stripes at the Pole.

would not remain long at the spot, as the ice was in the grip of a slow-drifting movement. I felt the possibility of this slow movement was more important than if it remained stationary; for, if ever found in the south, the destination of the tube would indicate the ice drift from the Pole. The following is an exact copy of the original note, which is reproduced photographically on another page:

COPY OF NOTE IN TUBE.
April 21—at the North Pole.

Accompanied by the Eskimo boys Ah-we-lah and E-tuk-i-shuk I reached at noon to-day 90° N. a spot on the polar sea 520 miles north of Svartevoeg. We were 35 days en route. Hope to return to-morrow on a line slightly west of the northward track.

New land was discovered along the 102 M. between 84 and 85. The ice proved fairly good, with few open leads, hard snow and little pressure trouble. We are in good health, and have food for forty days. This, with the meat of the dogs to be sacrificed, will keep us alive for fifty or sixty days.

This note is deposited with a small American flag in a metallic tube on the drifting ice.

Its return will be appreciated, to the International Bureau of Polar Research at the Royal Observatory, Uccle, Belgium.

(Signed)   FREDERICK A. COOK.

THE RETURN—A BATTLE FOR LIFE
AGAINST FAMINE AND FROST

TURNED BACKS TO THE POLE AND TO THE SUN—THE DOGS,
SEEMINGLY GLAD AND SEEMINGLY SENSIBLE THAT
THEIR NOSES WERE POINTED HOMEWARD, BARKED
SHRILLY—SUFFERING FROM INTENSE DEPRESSION—
THE DANGERS OF MOVING ICE, OF STORMS AND SLOW
STARVATION—THE THOUGHT OF FIVE HUNDRED AND
TWENTY MILES TO LAND CAUSES DESPAIR

XXI

SOUTHWARD OVER THE MID-POLAR SEA

With few glances backward, we continued the homeward run in haste, crossing many new crevasses and bound on a course along the one hundredth meridian.

The eagerness to solve the mystery had served its purpose. The memory of the adventure for a time remained as a reminder of reckless daring. As we now moved along, there came more and more strongly the realization of the prospective difficulties of the return. Although the mercury was still frozen and the sun's perpetual flush was lost in a frigid blue, the time was at hand in lower latitudes for the ice to break and drift southward.

With correct reasoning, all former expeditions had planned to return to land and a secure line of retreat by May 1. We could not hope to do this until early in June. It seemed probable, therefore, that the ice along the outskirts of the Polar sea would be much disrupted and that open water, small ice and rapid drifts would seriously interfere with our return to a sure footing on the shores of Fridtjof Nansen Sound. This and many other possible dangers had been carefully considered before, but the conquest of the Pole was not possible without such risks.

We had started earlier than all other Polar expeditions and no time had been lost en route. If misfortune came to us, it could not be because of wasted energies or unnecessary delay. In the last days of the onward rush to success there had been neither time nor opportunity to ponder over future dangers, but now, facing the southern skies, under which lay home and all for which we lived, the back trail seemed indescribably long. In cold, sober thought, freed of the intoxication of Polar enthusiasm, the difficulties increasingly darkened in color. We clearly saw that the crucial stage of the campaign was not the taking of the Pole. The test of our fitness as boreal conquerors was to be measured by the outcome of a final battle for life against famine and frost.

Figuring out the difficulties and possibilities of our return, I came to the conclusion that to endeavor to get back by our upward trail would not afford great advantage. Much time would be lost seeking the trail. The almost continuous low drift of snow during some part of nearly every day would obliterate our tracks and render the trail useless as a beaten track in making travel easier. The advantage of previously constructed snow houses as camps did not appeal to us.

After one is accustomed to a new, clean, bright dome of snow every night, as we were, the return to such a camp is gloomy and depressing. The house is almost invariably left in such a shape that, for hygienic reasons alone, it should not be occupied. Furthermore, the influence of sun and storm absolutely destroys in a few days two out of three of all such shelter places. Moreover, we were now camping in our silk tent and did not require other shelter. At the season of the year in which we were traveling, the activity of the pack farther south made back-tracking impossible, because of irregular lateral drift of individual fields. And to me the most important reason was an eager desire to ascertain what might be discovered on a new trail farther west. It was this eagerness which led to our being carried adrift and held prisoners for a year.

The first days, however, passed rapidly. The ice fields became smoother. On April 24 we crossed five crevasses. With fair weather and favorable ice, long marches were made. On the 24th we made sixteen miles, on the 25th fifteen miles, on the 26th, 27th and 28th, fourteen miles a day. The fire of the homing sentiment began to dispel our overbearing fatigue. The dogs sniffed the air. The Eskimos sang songs of the chase. To me also there came cheering thoughts of friends and loved ones to be greeted. I thought of delightful dinners, of soul-stirring music. For all of us, the good speed of the return chase brought a mental atmosphere of dreams of the pleasures of another world.

For a time we were blinded to ultimate dangers, just as we had been in the northward dash.

In our return along the one hundredth meridian, there were three important objects to be gained by a route somewhat west of the northward march. The increasing easterly drift would thus be counterbalanced. We hoped to get near enough to the new lands to explore a part of the coast. And a wider belt would be swept out of the unknown area. On April 30 the pedometer registered one hundred and twenty-one miles, and by our system of dead reckoning, which was usually correct, we should have been at latitude 87°, 59′, longitude 100°. The nautical observations gave latitude 88°, 1′, longitude 97°, 42′. We were drifting eastward, therefore, with increasing speed. To counterbalance our being moved by this drift, we turned and bounded southward in a more westerly course.

The never-changing sameness of the daily routine was again felt. The novelty of success and the passion of the run for the goal were no longer operative. The scenes of shivering blue wearied the eye, and there was no inspiration in the moving sea of ice to gladden the heart. The thermometer rose and fell between 30 and 40° below zero, Fahrenheit, with a ceaseless wind. The first of May was at hand, bringing to mind the blossoms and smiles of a kindly world. But here all nature was narrowed to lines of ice.

May 1 came with increasing color in the sunbursts, but without cheer. The splendor of terrestrial fire was a cheat. Over the horizon, mirages displayed celestial hysterics. The sun circled the skies in lines of glory, but its heat was a sham, its light a torment. The ice was heavy and smooth. On May 2, clouds obscured the sky, fog fell heavily over the ice, we struck our course with difficulty but made nineteen miles. On May 3 snow fell, but the end of the march brought clear skies, and, with them, the longing for my land of blossoming cherry and apple trees.

With weary nerves, and with compass in hand, my lonely march ahead of the sledges continued day by day. Progress was satisfactory. We had passed the eighty-ninth and eighty-eighth parallels. The eighty-seventh and the eighty-sixth would soon be under foot, and the sight of the new lands should give encouragement. These hard-fought times were days long to be remembered. The lack of cerebral stimulation and nutrition left no cellular resource to aid the memory of those fateful hours of chill.

The long strain of the march had established a brotherly sympathy amongst the trio of human strugglers. The dogs, though still possessing the savage ferocity of the wolf, had taken us into their community. We now moved among them without hearing a grunt of discord, and their sympathetic eyes followed until we were made comfortable on the cheerless snows. If they happened to be placed near enough, they edged up and encircled us, giving the benefit of their animal heat. To remind us of their presence, frost-covered noses were frequently pushed under the sleeping bag, and occasionally a cold snout touched our warm skin with a rude awakening.

We loved the creatures, and admired their superb brute strength. Their superhuman adaptability was a frequent topic of conversation. With a pelt that was

a guarantee against all weather condition, they threw
themselves down to the sweep of winds, in open defiance
of death-dealing storms.   Eating but a pound of pemmican a day, and demanding neither water nor shelter,
they willingly did a prodigious amount of work and
then, as bed-fellows, daily offered their fur as shelter and
their bones as head-rests to their two-footed companions.
We had learned to appreciate the advantage of their
beating breasts.   The bond of animal fellowship had
drawn tighter and tighter in a long run of successive
adventures.   And now there was a stronger reason than
ever to appreciate power, for together we were seeking
an escape from a world which was never intended for
creatures with pulsating hearts.

Much very heavy ice was crossed near the eighty-
eighth parallel, but the endless unbroken fields of the
northward trails were not again seen.   Now the weather
changed considerably.   The light, cutting winds from
the west increased in force, and the spasmodic squalls
came at shorter intervals.   The clear purples and blues
of the skies gradually gave place to an ugly hue of gray.
A rush of frosty needles came over the pack for several
hours each day.

The inducement to seek shelter in cemented walls
of snow and to wait for better weather was very great.
But such delay would mean certain starvation.   Under
fair conditions, there was barely food enough to reach
land, and even short delays might seriously jeopardize
our return.   We could not, therefore, do otherwise than
force ourselves against the wind and drift with all possible speed, paying no heed to unavoidable suffering.
As there was no alternative, we tried to persuade our-

selves that existing conditions might be worse than they were.

The hard work of igloo building was now a thing of the past—only one had been built since leaving the Pole, and in this a precious day was lost, while the atmospheric fury changed the face of the endless expanse of desolation. The little silk tent protected us sufficiently from the icy airs. There were still 50° of frost, but, with hardened skins and insensible nerve filaments, the torture was not so keenly felt. Our steady diet of pemmican, tea and biscuits was not entirely satisfactory. We longed for enough to give a real filling sense, but the daily ration had to be slightly reduced rather than increased. The change in life from winter to summer, which should take place at about this time of the year, was, in our case, marked only by a change in shelter, from the snow house to the tent, and our beds were moved from the soft snow shelf of the igloo to the hard, wind-swept crust.

In my watches to get a peep of the sun at just the right moment, I was kept awake during much of the resting period. For pastime, my eyes wandered from snorting dogs to snoring men. During one of these idle moments there came a solution of the utility of the dog's tail, a topic with which I had been at play for several days. It is quoted here at the risk of censure, because it is a typical phase of our lives which cannot be illustrated otherwise. Seeming trivialities were seized upon as food for thought. Why, I asked, has the dog a tail at all? The bear, the musk ox, the caribou and the hare, each in its own way, succeeds very well with but a dwarfed stub. Why does nature, in the dog, expend its best effort in growing the finest fur over a seemingly useless line of tail bones? The thing is distinctive, and one could hardly conceive of the creature without the accessory, but nature in the Arctic does not often waste energy to display beauties and temperament. This tail must have an important use; otherwise it would soon fall under the knife of frost and time. Yes! It was imported into the Arctic by the wolf progenitor of the dog from warmer lands, where its swing served a useful purpose in fly time. A nose made to breathe warm air requires some protection in the far north and the dog supplied the need with his tail. At the time when I made this discovery a cold wind, charged with cutting crystal, was brushing the pack. Each dog had his back arched to the wind and his face veiled with an effective curl of his tail. Thus each was comfortably shielded from icy torment by an appendage adapted to that very purpose.

In the long tread over snowy wastes new lessons in human mechanism aroused attention. At first the effort to find a workable way over the troublesome pack surface had kept mind and body keyed to an exciting pitch, but slowly this had changed. By a kind of unconscious intuition, the eye now found easy routes, the lower leg mechanically traveled over yards and miles and degrees without even consulting the brain, while the leg trunk, in the effort to conserve energy, was left in repose at periods during miles of travel, thus saving much of the exertion of walking.

The muscles, thus schooled to work automatically, left the mind free to work and play. The maddening monotone of our routine, together with the expenditure of every available strain of force, had left the head dizzy with emptiness. Something must be done to lift the soul out of the boreal bleach.

The power of the mind over the horse-power of the body was here shown at its best. The flesh proved loyal to the gray matter only while mental entertainment was encouraged. Thus aching muscles were persuaded to do double duty without sending up a cry of tired feeling. The play of the mind with topics of its own choosing is an advantage worth seeking at all times. But, to us, it multiplied vital force and increased greatly the daily advance. Science, art and poetry were the heights to which the wings of thought soared. Beginning with the diversion of making curious speculations on subjects such as that of the use of the dog's tail and the Arctic law of animal coloring, the first period of this mental exercise closed with my staging a drama of the comedies and tragedies of the Eskimos.

In the effort to frame sentiment in measured lines, a weird list of topics occupied my strained fancy. In more agreeable moods I always found pleasure in imagining a picture of the Polar sunrise, that budding period of life when all Nature awakens after its winter sleep. It was not difficult to start E-tuk-i-shook and Ah-we-lah on similar flights of fancy. A mere suggestion would keep up a flow of agreeable thought for several days.

By such forced mental stimuli the centers of fatigue were deluded into insensibility. The eighty-seventh parallel was crossed, the eighty-sixth was neared, but there came a time when both mind and body wearied of the whole problem of forced resolution.

On May 6 we were stopped at six in the morning by the approach of an unusual gale. The wind had been steady and strong all night, but we did not heed its threatening increase of force until too late. It came from the west, as usual, driving coarse snow with needle points. The ice about was old and hummocky, offering a difficult line of march, but some shelter. In the strongest blasts we threw ourselves over the sled behind hummocks and gathered new breath to force a few miles more.

Finally, when no longer able to force the dogs through the blinding drift we sought the lee of an unlifted block of ice. Here suitable snow was found for a snow house. A few blocks were cut and set, but the wind swept them away as if they were chips. The tent was tried, but it could not be made to stand in the rush of the roaring tumult. In sheer despair we crept into the tent without erecting the pole. Creeping into bags, we then allowed the flapping silk to be buried by the drifting snow. Soon the noise and discomfort of the storm were lost and we enjoyed the comfort of an icy grave. An efficient breathing hole was kept open, and the wind was strong enough to sweep off the weight of a dangerous drift. A new lesson was thus learned in fighting the battle of life, and it was afterwards useful.

Several days of icy despair now followed one another in rapid succession. The wind did not rise to the full force of a storm, but it was too strong and too cold to travel. The food supply was noticeably decreasing. The daily advance was less. With such weather, starvation seemed inevitable. Camp was moved nearly every day, but ambition sank to the lowest ebb. To the atmospheric unrest was added the instability of broken ice and the depressing mystery of an unknown position. For many days no observations had been possible. Our location could only be guessed at.

Through driving storms, with the wind wailing in our ears and deafening us to the dismal howling of the hungry dogs, we pushed forward in a daily maddening struggle. The route before us was unknown. We were in the fateful clutch of a drifting sea of ice. I could not guess whither we were bound. At times I even lost hope of reaching land. Our bodies were tired. Our legs were numb. We were almost insensible to the mad craving hunger of our stomachs. We were living on a half ration of food, and daily becoming weaker.*

Sometimes I paused, overcome by an almost overwhelming impulse to lie down and drift through sleep into death. At these times, fortunately, thoughts of home came thronging, with memories as tender as are the memories of singing spring-time birds in winter

---

*The Fall of Body Temperature—The temperature of the body was frequently taken. Owing to the breathing of very cold air, the thermometer placed in the mouth gave unreliable results, but by placing the bulb in the armpits, when in the sleeping bag, fairly accurate records were kept. These proved that extreme cold had little influence on bodily heat; but when long-continued overwork was combined with insufficient food, the temperature gradually came down. On the route to the Pole the bodily temperature ranged from 97° 5' to 98° 4'. In returning, the subnormal temperature fell still lower. When the worry of being carried adrift and the danger of never being able to return became evident, then the mental anguish, combined as it was with prolonged overwork, continued thirst and food insufficiency, was strikingly noted by our clinical thermometer. During the last few weeks, before reaching land at Greenland in 1909, the subnormal temperature sank to the remarkable minimum of 96° 2' F. The Eskimos usually remained about half a degree warmer. The respiration and heart action was at this time fast and irregular.

In the summer period of famine about Jones Sound the temperature was normal. At that time we had an abundance of water and an interesting occupation in quest of game, but we often felt the cold more severely than in the coldest season of winter.

time.   And, although the stimulating incentive of reaching the Pole on going north was gone, now, having accomplished the feat, there was always the thought that unless I got home no one should ever learn of that superhuman struggle, that final victory.

Empty though it was, I had, as I had hoped, proved myself to myself; I had justified the three centuries of human effort: I had proven that finite human brain and palpitating muscle can be victorious over a cruel and death-dealing Nature.   It was a testimony that it was my duty to give the world of struggling, striving men, and which, as a father, I hoped with pride to give to my little children.

PTARMIGAN

BACK TO LIFE AND BACK TO LAND

THE RETURN—DELUDED BY DRIFT AND FOG—CARRIED
ASTRAY OVER AN UNSEEN DEEP—TRAVEL FOR
TWENTY DAYS IN A WORLD OF MISTS, WITH THE
TERROR OF DEATH—AWAKENED FROM SLEEP BY
A HEAVENLY SONG—THE FIRST BIRD—FOLLOWING
THE WINGED HARBINGER—WE REACH LAND—A
BLEAK, BARREN ISLAND POSSESSING THE CHARM OF
PARADISE—AFTER DAYS VERGING ON STARVATION, WE
ENJOY A FEAST OF UNCOOKED GAME.

XXII

SOUTHWARD INTO THE AMERICAN ARCHIPELAGO

On May 24 the sky cleared long enough to permit
me to take a set of observations. I found we were on
the eighty-fourth parallel, near the ninety-seventh
meridian. The new land I had noted on my northward
journey was hidden by a low mist. The ice was much
crevassed, and drifted eastward. Many open spaces
of water were denoted in the west by patches of water
sky. The pack was sufficiently active to give us considerable anxiety, although pressure lines and open
water did not at the time seriously impede our progress.

Scarcely enough food remained on the sledges to

reach our caches unless we should average fifteen miles
a day. On the return from the Pole to this point we had
been able to make only twelve miles daily. Now our
strength, even under fair conditions, did not seem to be
equal to more than ten miles. The outlook was threatening, and even dangerous, but the sight of the cleared
sky gave new courage to E-tuk-i-shook and Ah-we-lah.

Our best course was to get to Fridtjof Nansen
Sound as soon as possible. The new land westward was
invisible, and offered no food prospects. An attempted
exploration might cause a fatal delay.

Still depending upon a steady easterly drift of the
pack, a course was set somewhat west of Svartevoeg, the
northern point of Axel Heiberg Land. In pressing onward, light variable winds and thick fogs prevailed.
The ice changed rapidly to smaller fields as we advanced.
The temperature rose to zero, and the air really began
to be warm. Our chronic shivering disappeared. With
light sledges and endurable weather, we made fair progress over the increasing pack irregularities.

As we crossed the eighty-third parallel we found
ourselves to the west of a large lead, extending slightly
west of south. Immense quantities of broken and pul-
verized ice lined the shores to a width of several miles.
The irregularities of this surface and the uncemented
break offered difficulties over which no force of man or
beast could move a sledge or boat. Compelled to follow the line of least resistance, a southerly course was set
along the ice division. The wind now changed and came
from the east, but there was no relief from the heavy
banks of fog that surrounded us.

The following days were days of desperation. The

food for man and dog was reduced, and the difficulties
of ice travel increased dishearteningly. We traveled
twenty days, not knowing our position. A gray mystery
enshrouded us. Terror followed in our wake. Beneath
us the sea moved—whither it was carrying us I did not
know. That we were ourselves journeying toward an
illimitable, hopeless sea, where we should die of slow,
lingering starvation, I knew was a dreadful probability.
Every minute drew its pangs of despair and fear.

The gray world of mist was silent. My companions gazed at me with faces shriveled, thinned and hardened as those of mummies. Their anguish was unspeak-
able. My own vocal powers seemed to have left me.
Our dogs were still; with bowed heads, tails drooping,
they pulled the sledges dispiritedly. We seemed like
souls in torment, traveling in a world of the dead, condemned to some Dantesque torture that should never
cease.

After the mental torment of threatened starvation,
which prevented, despite the awful languor of my tor-
tured limbs, any sleep; after heart-breaking marches
and bitter hunger and unquenched thirst, the baffling
mist that had shut us from all knowledge at last cleared
away one morning. Our hearts bounded. I felt such
relief as a man buried alive must feel when, after struggling in the stifling darkness, his grave is suddenly
opened. Land loomed to the west and south of us.

Yet we found we had been hardly dealt with by
fate. Since leaving the eighty-fourth parallel, without
noticeable movement, we had been carried astray by the
ocean drift. We had moved with the entire mass that
covered the Polar waters. I took observations. They

gave latitude 79° 32', and longitude 101° 22'. At last
I had discovered our whereabouts, and found that we
were far from where we ought to be. But our situation
was indeed nearly hopeless. The mere gaining a knowledge of where we actually were, however, fanned again
the inextinguishable embers of hope.

We were in Crown Prince Gustav Sea. To the
east were the low mountains and high valleys of Axel
Heiberg Land, along the farther side of which was our
prearranged line of retreat, with liberal caches of good
things and with big game everywhere. But we were
effectually barred from all this.

Between us and the land lay fifty miles of small
crushed ice and impassable lines of open water. In hard-
fought efforts to cross these we were repulsed many
times. I knew that if by chance we should succeed in
crossing, there would still remain an unknown course of
eighty miles to the nearest cache, on the eastern coast of
Axel Heiberg Land.

We had no good reason to expect any kind of subsistence along the west coast of Axel Heiberg Land.
We had been on three-fourths rations for three weeks,
and there remained only half rations for another ten
days. Entirely aside from the natural barriers in the
way of returning eastward and northward, we were now
utterly unequal to the task, for we had not the food to
support us.

The land to the south was nearer. Due south there
was a wide gap which we took to be Hassel Sound. On
each side there was a low ice-sheeted island, beyond the
larger islands which Sverdrup had named Ellef Ringnes
Land and Amund Ringnes Land. The ice southward

was tolerably good and the drift was south-south-east.

In the hope that some young seals might be seen we moved into Hassel Sound toward the eastern island. To satisfy our immediate pangs of hunger was our most important mission.

The march on June 14 was easy, with a bright warm sun and a temperature but little under the freezing point. In a known position, on good ice, and with land rising before us, we were for a brief period happy and strong, even with empty stomachs. The horizon was eagerly sought for some color or form or movement to indicate life. We were far enough south to expect bears and seals, and expecting the usual luck of the hungry savage, we sought diligently. Our souls reached forth through our far-searching eyes. Our eyes pained with the intense fixity of gazing, yet no animate thing appeared. The world was vacant and dead. Our beating hearts, indeed, seemed to be the only palpitating things there.

In the piercing rays of a high sun the tent was erected, and in it, after eating only four ounces of pemmican and drinking two cups of icy water, we sought rest. The dogs, after a similar ration, but without water, fell into an easy sleep. I regarded the poor creatures with tenderness and pity. For more than a fortnight they had not uttered a sound to disturb the frigid silence. When a sled dog is silent and refuses to fight with his neighbor, his spirit is very low. Finally I fell asleep.

At about six o'clock we were awakened by a strange sound. Our surprised eyes turned from side to side. Not a word was uttered. Another sound came—a series of soft, silvery notes—the song of a creature that might have come from heaven. I listened with rapture. I believed I was dreaming. The enchanting song continued—I lay entranced. I could not believe this divine thing was of our real world until the pole of our tent gently quivered. Then, above us, I heard the flutter of wings. It was a bird—a snow bunting trilling its ethereal song—the first sound of life heard for many months.

We were back to life! Tears of joy rolled down our emaciated faces. If I could tell you of the resurrection of the soul which came with that first bird note, and the new interest which it gave in our subsequent life, I should feel myself capable of something superhuman in powers of expression.

With the song of that marvelous bird a choking sense of homesickness came to all of us. We spoke no word. The longing for home gripped our hearts.

We were hungry, but no thought of killing this little feathered creature came to us. It seemed as divine as the bird that came of old to Noah in the ark. Taking a few of our last bread crumbs, we went out to give it food. The little chirping thing danced joyously on the crisp snows, evidently as glad to see us as we were to behold it. I watched it with fascination. At last we were back to life! We felt renewed vigor. And when the little bird finally rose into the air and flew homeward, our spirits rose, our eyes followed it, and, as though it were a token sent to us, we followed its winged course landward with eager, bounding hearts.

We were now on immovable ice attached to the land. We directed our course uninterruptedly landward, for there was no thought of further rest or sleep after the visit of the bird had so uplifted our hearts. Our chances of getting meat would have been bettered by following close to the open water, but the ice there was such that no progress could be made. Furthermore, the temptation quickly to set foot on land was too great to resist. At the end of a hard march—the last few hours of which were through deep snows—we mounted the ice edge, and finally reached a little island—a bare spot of real land. When my foot touched it, my heart sank. We sat down, and the joy of the child in digging the sand of the seashore was ours.

I wonder if ever such a bleak spot, in a desert of death, had so impressed men before as a perfect paradise. In this barren heap of sand and clay, we were at last free of the danger, the desolation, the sterility of that soul-withering environment of a monotonously moving world of ice and eternal frost.

We fastened the dogs to a rock, and pitched the tent on earth-soiled snows. In my joy I did not forget that the Pole was ours, but, at that time, I was ready to offer freely to others the future pleasures of its crystal environment and all its glory. Our cup had been filled too often with its bitters and too seldom with its sweets for us to entertain further thirst for boreal conquest.

And we also resolved to keep henceforth from the wastes of the terrible Polar sea. In the future the position of lands must govern our movements. For, along a line of rocks, although we might suffer from hunger, we should no longer be helpless chips on the ocean drift, and if no other life should be seen, at least occasional shrimps would gladden the heart.

"WITH EAGER EYES WE SEARCHED THE DUSKY PLAINS OF CRYSTAL, BUT THERE WAS NO LAND, NO LIFE, TO RELIEVE THE PURPLE RUN OF DEATH"

Copy of note in Tube

Apr. 21, 1908 at the North Pole

Accompanied by the eskimos boys
Ahwelah and Etukishook I reached at
noon to-day 90°, a spot on the pole
star 520 miles N. of Svartevoeg.
We were 35 days enroute. hope to
return to message on a line slightly
west of three arrow around through
Nero land was discerned along
the 102-m. between 84 & 85°. The
ice proved fairly good with few
open leads, hard snow and little
pressing trouble.

We are in good health and have
food for 40 days This with the meat
of the dogs to be successful with
Kassun alone for 50 or 60 days

The winter is deposited with
a small am. flag in a metalic
tube on the drifting ice.

Its return will be appreciated
to the International Bureau of
Polar research at the
Royal observatory Uccle Belgium

Frederick A. Cook

RECORD LEFT IN BRASS TUBE AT NORTH POLE

We stepped about on the solid ground with a new sense of security. But the land about was low, barren, and shapeless. Its formation was triassic, similar to that of most of Heiberg land, but in our immediate surroundings, erosion by frost, the grind of ice sheets, and the power of winds, had leveled projecting rocks and cliffs.   Part of its interior was blanketed with ice. Its shore line had neither the relief of a colored cliff nor a picturesque headland; there was not even a wall of ice; there were only dull, uninteresting slopes of sand and snow separating the frozen sea from the land-ice. The most careful scrutiny gave no indication of a living creature. The rocks were uncovered even with black lichens. A less inviting spot of earth could not be conceived, yet it aroused in us a deep sense of enthusiasm. A strip of tropical splendor could not have done more. The spring of man's passion is sprung by contrast, not by degrees of glory.

In camp, the joy of coming back to earth was chilled by the agonizing call of the stomach. The effervescent happiness could not dispel the pangs of hunger. A disabled dog which had been unsuccessfully nursed for several days was sacrificed on the altar of hard luck, and the other dogs were thereupon given a liberal feed, in which we shared. To our palates the flesh of the dog was not distasteful, yet the dog had been our companion for many months, and at the same time that our conscienceless stomachs were calling for more hot, blood-wet meat, a shivering sense of guilt came over me. We had killed and were eating a living creature which had been faithful to us.

We were hard-looking men at this time. Our fur

garments were worn through at the elbows and at the knees. Ragged edges dangled in the winds. All the boot soles were mere films, like paper with many holes. Our stockings were in tatters. The bird-skin shirts had been fed to the dogs, and strips of our sleeping bags had day by day been added to the canine mess. It took all our spare time now to mend clothing. Dressed in rags, with ugly brown faces, seamed with many deep wind-fissures, we had reached, in our appearance, the extreme limit of degradation.

At the Pole I had been thin, but now my skin was contracted over bones offering only angular eminences as a bodily outline. The Eskimos were as thin as myself. My face was as black as theirs. They had risen to higher mental levels, and I had descended to lower animal depths. The long strain, the hard experiences, had made us equals. We were, however, still in good health and were capable of considerable hard work. It was not alone the want of food which had shriveled our bodies, for greater pangs of hunger were reserved for a later run of misfortune. Up to this point persistent overwork had been the most potent factor.

As we passed out of Hassel Sound, the ice drifted southward. Many new fractures were noted, and open spaces of water appeared. Here was seen the track of a rat—the first sign of a four-footed creature—and we stopped to examine the tiny marks with great interest. Next, some old bear tracks were detected. These simple things had an intense fascination for us, coming as we did out of a lifeless world; and, too, these signs showed that the possibilities of food were at hand, and the thought sharpened our senses into savage fierceness.

We continued our course southward, as we followed, wolf-like, in the bear footprints. The sledges bounded over the icy irregularities as they had not done for months. Every crack in the ice was searched for seals, and with the glasses we mounted hummock after hummock to search the horizon for bears.

We were not more than ten miles beyond land when Ah-we-lah located an auspicious spot to leeward. After a peep through the glasses he shouted. The dogs understood. They raised their ears, and jumped to the full length of their traces. We hurried eastward to deprive the bear of our scent, but we soon learned that he was as hungry as we were, for he made an air line for our changed position. We were hunting the bear—the bear was also hunting us.

Getting behind a hummock, we awaited developments. Bruin persistently neared, rising on his haunches frequently so as the better to see E-tuk-i-shook, who had arranged himself like a seal as a decoy. When within a few hundred yards the dogs were freed. They had been waiting like entrenched soldiers for a chance to advance. In a few moments the gaunt creatures encircled the puzzled bear. Almost without a sound, they leaped at the great animal and sank their fangs into his hind legs. Ah-we-lah fired. The bear fell.

Camp technique and the advantages of a fire were not considered—the meat was swallowed raw, with wolfish haste, and no cut of carefully roasted bullock ever tasted better. It was to such grim hunger that we had come.

Then we slept, and after a long time our eyes reopened upon a world colored with new hope. The immediate threat of famine was removed, and a day was given over to filling up with food. Even after that, a liberal supply of fresh meat rested on the sledge for successive days of feasting. In the days which followed, other bears, intent on examining our larder, came near enough at times to enable us to keep up a liberal supply of fresh meat.

With the assurance of a food supply, a course was set to enter Wellington Channel and push along to Lancaster Sound, where I hoped a Scottish whaler could be reached in July or August. In this way it seemed possible to reach home shores during the current year. If we should try to reach Annoatok I realized we should in all probability be compelled to winter at Cape Sabine. The ice to the eastward in Norwegian Bay offered difficulties like those of Crown Prince Gustav Sea, and altogether the easterly return to our base did not at this time seem encouraging. The air-line distance to Smith Sound and that to Lancaster Sound were about the same, with the tremendous advantage of a straight course—a direct drift—and fairly smooth ice to the southward.

This conclusion to push forward for Lancaster Sound was reached on June 19. We were to the west of North Cornwall Island, but a persistent local fog gave only an occasional view of its icy upper slopes. The west was clear, and King Christian Land appeared as a low line of blue. About us the ice was small but free of pressure troubles. Bear tracks were frequently seen as we went along. The sea was bright. The air was delightfully warm, with the thermometer at 10° above zero.

At every stop, the panting dogs tumbled and rolled playfully on the snows, and pushed their heated muzzles deep into the white chill. If given time they would quickly arrange a comfortable bed and stretch out, seemingly lifeless, for a refreshing slumber. At the awakening call of the lash, all were ready with a quick jump and a daring snarl, but the need of a tight trace removed their newly-acquired fighting propensity. They had gained strength and spirit with remarkable rapidity. Only two days before, they stumbled along with irregular step, slack traces, and lowered tails, but the fill of juicy bear's meat raised their bushy appendages to a coil of pride—an advantage which counted for several miles in a day's travel.

The drift carried us into Penny Strait, midway between Bathurst Land and Grinnell Peninsula. The small islands along both shores tore up the ice and piled it in huge uplifts. There was a tremendous pressure as the floes were forced through narrow gorges. Only a middle course was possible for us, with but a few miles' travel to our credit for each day. But the southerly movement of the groaning ice was rapid. A persistent fog veiled the main coast on both sides, but off-lying islands were seen and recognized often enough to note the positions. At Dundas Island the drift was stopped, and we sought the shores of Grinnell Peninsula. Advancing eastward, close to land, the ice proved extremely difficult. The weather, however, was delightful. Between snowdrifts, purple and violet flowers rose over warm beds of newly invigorated mosses—the first flowers that we had seen for a long and weary time, and the sight of them, with their blossoms and color, deeply thrilled me. From misty heights came the howl of the white wolf. Everywhere were seen the traces of the fox and the lemming. The eider-duck and the ivory gull had entered our horizon.

All nature smiled with the cheer of midsummer. Here was an inspiring fairyland for which our hearts had long yearned. In it there was music which the long stiffened tympanums were slow in catching. The land was an oasis of hardy verdure. The sea was a shifting scene of frost and blue glitter. With the soul freed from its icy fetters, the soft, sunny airs came in bounds of gladness. In dreamy stillness we sought the bosom of the frozen sea, and there heard the groan of the pack which told of home shores. Drops of water from melting snows put an end to thrist tortures. The blow of the whales and the seals promised a luxury of fire and fuel, while the low notes of the ducks prepared the palate for dessert.

As we neared a little moss-covered island in drift-ing southward, we saw the interesting chick footprints of ptarmigan in the snow. The dogs pointed their ears and raised their noses, and we searched the clearing skies with eye and ear for the sudden swoop of the boreal chicken. I had developed a taste for this delicate fowl as desperate as that of the darky for chicken, and my conscience was sufficiently deadened by cold and hunger to break into a roost by night or day to steal anything that offered feathery delights for the palate.

I was courting gastric desire, but the ptarmigan was engaged in another kind of courtship. Two singing capons were cooing notes of love to a shy chick, and they suddenly decided that there was not room for two, whereupon a battle ensued with a storm of wings and much darting of bills.   In this excitement they got into an ice crevasse, where they might have become easy victims without the use•of ammunition.   But, with empty stomachs, there is also at times a heart-hunger, which pleases a higher sense and closes the eye to gastric wants.

Later in the same day, we saw at a great distance what seemed like two men in motion.   We hastened to meet them with social anticipations.   Now they seemed tall—now mere dots on the horizon.   I thought this due to their movement over ice irregularities.   But boreal optics play havoc with the eye and the sense of perspective.   As we rose suddenly on a hummock, where we had a clearer view, the objects rose on wings!   They were ravens which had been enlarged and reduced by reflecting and refracting surfaces and a changing atmosphere, in much the same manner as a curved mirror makes a caricature of one's self.   I laughed—bitterly.   Dazed, bewildered, there was nevertheless for me a joy in seeing these living creatures, denizens of the land toward which we were directed.

The bears no longer sought our camp, but the seals were conveniently scattered along our track.   A kindly world had spread our waistbands to fairly normal dimensions.   The palate began to exercise its discriminating force.   Ducks and land animals were sought with greater eagerness.   While in this mood, three white caribou were secured.   They were beautiful creatures, and as pleasing to the palate as to the eye, but owing to the very rough ice it was quite impossible to carry more than a few days' supply.   Usually we took only the choice parts of the game, but every eatable morsel of caribou that we could carry was packed on the sledges.

With this wealth of food and fuel we moved along the shores of Wellington Channel to Pioneer Bay. We felt that we were steadily on our way homeward. There was no premonition of the keen disappointment that awaited us, of the inevitable imprisonment for the long Arctic winter and the days of starvation that were to come.

PTARMIGAN CHICKS

OVERLAND TO JONES SOUND

HOURS OF ICY·TORTURE—A FRIGID SUMMER STORM IN
THE BERG-DRIVEN ARCTIC SEA—A PERILOUS DASH
THROUGH TWISTING LANES OF OPENING WATER IN A
CANVAS CANOE—THE DRIVE OF HUNGER.

XXIII

ADRIFT ON AN ICEBERG

As we neared Pioneer Bay, along the coast of
North Devon, it became quite evident that farther advance by sledge was quite impossible. A persistent
southerly wind had packed the channel with a jam of
small ice, over which the effort of sledging was a hopeless task. The season was too far advanced to offer the
advantage of an ice-foot on the shore line. There was
no open water, nor any game to supply our larder. The
caribou was mostly used. We began to feel the craving pain of short rations.

Although the distance to Lancaster Sound was
short, land travel was impossible, and, with no food, we
could not await the drift of the ice. The uncertainty
of game was serious, with nothing as a reserve to await
the dubious coming of a ship. If game should appear,
we might remain on the ice, accumulating in the meantime a supply of meat for travel by canvas boat later.

This boat had been our hope in moving south, but thus far had not been of service. Forced to subsist mainly on birds, the ammunition rapidly diminished, and something had to be done at once to prevent famine.

We might have returned to the game haunts of Grinnell Peninsula, but it seemed more prudent to cross the land to Jones Sound. Here, from Sverdrup's experience, we had reason to expect abundant game. By moving eastward there would be afforded the alternative of pushing northward if we failed to get to the whalers. The temperature now remained steadily near the freezing point, and with the first days of July the barometer became unsteady.

On the 4th of July we began the climb of the highlands of North Devon, winding about Devonian cliffs toward the land of promise beyond. The morning was gray, as it had been for several days, but before noon black clouds swept the snowy heights and poured icy waters over us. We were saturated to the skin, and shivered in the chill of the high altitude. Soon afterwards a light breath-taking wind from the northwest froze our pasty furs into sheets of ice. Still later, a heavy fall of snow compelled us to camp. The snowstorm continued for two days, and held us in a snow-buried tent, with little food and no fuel.

Although the storm occasioned a good deal of suffering, it also brought some advantages. The land had been imperfectly covered with snow, and we had been forced to drive from bank to bank, over bared ground, to find a workable course. But now all was well sheeted with crusted snow. Soon the gaunt, dun-colored cliffs of North Devon ended the monotony of interior snows, and beyond was seen the cheering blue of Jones Sound.

Much open water extended along the north shore to beyond Musk Ox Fiord. The southern shores were walled with pack-ice for a hundred miles or more. In bright, cold weather we made a descent to Eidsbotn on July 7th. Here a diligent search for food failed. Daily the howl of wolves and the cry of birds came as a response to our calling stomachs. A scant supply of ducks was secured for the men with an expenditure of some of the last rifle ammunition, but no walruses, no seals, and no other big game were seen. To secure dog food seemed quite hopeless.

We now had the saddest incident of a long run of trouble. Open water ran the range of vision, sledges were no longer possible, game was scarce, our ammunition was nearly exhausted. Our future fate had to be worked out in a canvas boat. What were we to do with the faithful dog survivors? In the little boat they could not go with us. We could not stay with them and live. We must part. Two had already left us to join their wolf progenitors. We gave the others the same liberty. One sledge was cut off and put into the canvas boat which we had carried to the Pole and back. Our sleeping-bags and old winter clothing were given as food to the dogs. All else was snugly packed in waterproof packages as well as possible, and placed in the boat. With sad eyes, we left the shore. The dogs howled like crying children; we still heard them when five miles off shore.

Off Cape Vera there was open water, and beyond, as far eastward as we could see, its quivering surface offered a restful prospect. As we advanced, however, the weather proved treacherous, and the seas rose with sudden and disagreeable thumps.

At times we camped on ice islands in the pack, but the pack-ice soon became too insecure, being composed of small pieces, and weakened in spots by the sun. Even a moderate gale would tear a pack apart, to be broken into smaller fragments by the water. Sometimes we made camp in the boat, with a box for a pillow and a piece of bear skin for a cover.

With great anxiety we pulled to reach the land at Cape Sparbo before a storm entrapped us. To the north, the water was free of ice as far as the shores of Ellesmere Land, forty miles away. To avoid the glare of the midday sun, we chose to travel by night, but we were nearing the end of the season of Arctic double-days and midnight suns, when the winds come suddenly and often.

Soon after midnight the wind from the Pacific came in short puffs, with periods of calm so sudden that we looked about each time for something to happen. At about the same time there came long swells from the northwest. We scented a storm, although at that time there were no other signs. The ice was examined for a possible line of retreat to the land, but, with pressure ridges, hummocks and breaks, I knew this was impossible. It was equally hopeless to camp on such treacherous ice. Berg ice had been passed the day before, but this was about as far behind as the land was ahead.

So we pulled along desperately, while the swells shortened and rose. The atmosphere became thick and steel gray. The cliffs of Ellesmere Land faded, while lively clouds tumbled from the highlands to the sea.

We were left no alternative but to seek the shelter of the disrupted pack, and press landward as best we could. We had hardly landed on the ice, and drawn our boat after us, when the wind struck us with such force that we could hardly stand against it. The ice immediately started in a westward direction, veering off from the land a little and leaving open leads. These leads, we now saw, were the only possible places of safety. For, in them, the waters were easy, and the wind was slightly shut off by the walls of pressure lines and hummocks. Furthermore, they offered slants now and then by which we could approach the land.

The sledge was set under the boat and lashed. All our things were lashed to the wooden frame of the canoe to prevent the wind and the sea from carrying them away. We crossed several small floes and jumped the lines of water separating them, pulling sledge and canoe after us. The pressure lines offered severe barriers. To cross them we were compelled to separate the canoe from its sledge and remove the baggage. All of this required considerable time. A sense of hopelessness filled my heart. In the meantime, the wind veered to the east and came with a rush that left us helpless. We sought the lee of a hummock, and hoped the violence of the storm would soon spend itself, but there were no easy spells in this storm, nor did it show signs of early cessation. The ice about us moved rapidly westward and slowly seaward.

It was no longer possible to press toward the land, for the leads of water were too wide and were lined with small whitecaps, while the tossing seas hurled mountains of ice and foaming water over the pack edge.

The entire pack was rising and falling under faint swells, and gradually wearing to little fragments. The floe on which we stood was strong. I knew it would hold out longer than most of the ice about, but it was not high enough above water to give us a dry footing as the seas advanced.

From a distance to the windward we noted a low iceberg slowly gaining on our floe. It was a welcome sight, for it alone could raise us high enough above the soul-despairing rush of the icy water.

Its rich ultramarine blue promised ice of a sufficient strength to withstand the battling of the storm. Never were men on a sinking ship more anxious to reach a rock than we were to reach this blue stage of ice. It offered several little shelves, upon which we could rise out of the water upon the ice. We watched with anxious eyes as the berg revolved and forced the other ice aside.

It aimed almost directly for us, and would probably cut our floe. We prepared for a quick leap upon the deck of our prospective craft.

Bearing down upon us it touched a neighboring piece and pushed us away. We quickly pulled to the other pan, and then found, to our dismay, a wide band of mushy slush, as impossible to us for a footing as quicksand would have been. As the berg passed, however, it left a line of water behind it. We quickly threw boat and sledge into this, paddled after the berg, and, reaching it, leaped to its security. What a relief to be raised above the crumbling pack-ice and to watch from safety the thundering of the elements!

The berg which we had boarded was square, with

rounded corners. Its highest points were about twenty feet above water; the general level was about ten feet. The ice was about eighty feet thick, and its width was about a hundred feet. These dimensions assured stability, for if the thing had turned over, as bergs frequently do, we should be left to seek breath among the whales.

It was an old remnant of a much larger berg which had stood the Arctic tempest for many years. This we figured out from the hard blue of the ice and its many caverns and pinnacles. We were, therefore, on a secure mass of crystal which was not likely to suffer severely from a single storm. Its upper configuration, however, though beautiful in its countless shades of blue, did not offer a comfortable berth. There were three pinnacles too slippery and too steep to climb, with a slope leading by a gradual incline on each side. Along these the seas had worn grooves leading to a central concavity filled with water. The only space which we could occupy was the crater-like rim around this lake. At this time we had to endure only the seething pitch of the sea and the cutting blast of the storm.

The small ice about kept the seas from boarding. To prevent our being thrown about on the slippery surface, we cut holes into the pinnacles and spread lines about them, to which we clung. The boat was securely fastened in a similar way by cutting a makeshift for a ringbolt in the floor of ice. Then we pushed from side to side along the lines, to encourage our hearts and to force our circulation. Although the temperature was only at the freezing point, it was bitterly cold, and we were in a bad way to weather a storm.

The sea had drenched us from head to foot. Only our shirts were dry. With hands tightly gripped to the line and to crevasses, we received the spray of the breaking icy seas while the berg ploughed the scattered pack and plunged seaward. The cold, though only at the freezing point, pierced our snow-pasted furs and brought shivers worse than that of zero's lowest. Thus the hours of physical torture and mental anguish passed, while the berg moved towards the gloomy black cliff of Hell Gate. Here the eastern sky bleached and the south blued, but the falling temperature froze our garments to coats of mail. We were still dressed in part of our winter garments.

The coat was of sealskin, with hood attached; the shirt of camel's hair blanket, also with a hood; the trousers of bear fur; boots of seal, with hair removed, and stockings of hare fur. The mittens were of seal, and there were pads of grass for the palms and soles. Our garments, though not waterproof, shed water and excluded the winds, but there is a cold that comes with wet garments and strong winds that sets the teeth to chattering and the skin to quivering.

As all was snug and secure on the berg, we began to take a greater interest in our wind and sea-propelled craft. Its exposed surface was swept by the winds, while its submarine surface was pushed by tides and undercurrents, giving it a complex movement at variance with the pack-ice. It ploughed up miles of sea-ice, crushing and throwing it aside.

After several hours of this kind of navigation—which was easy for us, because the movement of the swell and the breaking of the sea did not inflict a hardship—the berg suddenly, without any apparent reason, took a course at right angles to the wind, and deliberately pushed out of the pack into the seething seas. This rapid shift from comfort to the wild agitation of the black waters made us gasp. The seas, with boulders of ice, rolled up over our crest and into the concavity of the berg, leaving no part safe. Seizing our axes, we cut many other anchor holes in the ice, doubly secured our life lines, and shifted with our boat to the edge of the berg turned to the wind. The hours of suspense and torment thus spent seemed as long as the winters of the Eskimo. The pack soon became a mere pearly glow against a dirty sky. We were rushing through a seething blackness, made more impressive by the pearl and blue of the berg and the white, ice-lined crests.

What could we do to keep the springs of life from snapping in such a world of despair? Fortunately, we were kept too busy dodging the storm-driven missiles of water and ice to ponder much over our fate. Otherwise the mind could not have stood the infernal strain.

Our bronze skins were adapted to cold and winds, but the torture of the cold, drenching water was new. For five months we had been battered by winds and cut by frosts, but water was secured only by melting ice with precious fuel which we had carried thousands of miles. If we could get enough of the costly liquid to wash our cold meals down, we had been satisfied. The luxury of a face wash or a bath, except by the wind-driven snows, was never indulged in. Now, in stress of danger, we were getting it from every direction. The torments of frost about the Pole were nothing compared to this boiling blackness.

Twenty-four hours elapsed before there was any change. Such calls of nature as hunger or thirst or sleep were left unanswered. We maintained a terrific struggle to keep from being washed into the sea. At last the east paled, the south became blue, and the land on both sides rose in sight. The wind came steadily, but reduced in force, with a frosty edge that hardened our garments to sheets of ice.

We were not far from the twin channels, Cardigan Strait and Hell Gate, where the waters of the Pacific and Atlantic meet. We were driving for Cardigan Strait, past the fiords into which we had descended from the western seas two weeks before. We had, therefore, lost an advance of two weeks in one day, and we had probably lost our race with time to reach the life-saving haunts of the Eskimo.

Still, this line of thought was foreign to us. Not far away were bold cliffs from which birds descended to the rushing waters. At the sight my heart rose. Here we saw the satisfying prospect of an easy breakfast if only the waves would cease to fold in white crests. Long trains of heavy ice were rushing with railroad speed out of the straits. As we watched, the temperature continued to fall. Soon the north blackened with swirling curls of smoke. The wind came with the sound of exploding guns from Hell Gate. What, I asked myself, was to be our fate now?

We took a southwest course. Freezing seas washed over the berg and froze our numbed feet to the ice, upon which a footing otherwise would have been very difficult. Adrift in a vast, ice-driven, storm-thundering ocean, I stood silent, paralyzed with terror. After a few hours, sentinel floes of the pack slowly shoved toward us, and unresistingly, we were ushered into the harboring influence of the heavy Polar ice.

The berg lost its erratic movement, and soon settled in a fixed position. The wind continued to tear along in a mad rage, but we found shelter in our canoe, dozing away for a few moments while one paced the ice as a sentinel. Slowly a lane of quiet water appeared among the floes. We heard a strangely familiar sound which set our hearts throbbing. The walrus and the seal, one by one, came up to the surface to blow. Here, right before us, was big game, with plenty of meat and fat. We were starving, but we gazed almost helplessly on plenty, for its capture was difficult for us.

We had only a few cartridges and four cans of pemmican in our baggage. These were reserved for use to satisfy the last pangs of famine. That time had not yet arrived. Made desperate by hunger, after a brief rest we began to seek food. Birds flying from the land became our game at this time. We could secure these with the slingshot made by the Eskimos, and later, by entangling loops in lines, and in various other ways which hunger taught us.

A gull lighted on a pinnacle of our berg. Quietly but quickly we placed a bait and set a looped line. We watched with bated breath. The bird peered about, espied the luring bait, descended with a flutter of wings, pecked the pemmican. There was a snapping sound—the bird was ours. Leaping upon it, we rapidly cut it in bits and ravenously devoured it raw. Few things I have ever eaten tasted so delicious as this meat, which had the flavor of cod-liver oil.

The ice soon jammed in a grinding pack against the land, and the wind spent its force in vain. We held our position, and two of us, after eating the bird, slept until the sentinel called us. At midnight the wind eased and the ice started its usual rebound, seaward and eastward, with the tide.

This was our moment for escape. We were about ten miles off the shore of Cape Vera. If we could push our canvas canoe through the channels of water as they opened, we might reach land. We quickly prepared the boat. With trepidation we pushed it into the black, frigid waters. We hesitated to leave the sheltering berg which had saved our lives. Still, it had served its purpose. To remain might mean our being carried out to sea. The ultimate time had come to seek a more secure refuge on *terra firma*.

Leaping into the frail, rocking canoe, we pushed along desperately through a few long channels to reach a wide, open space of water landward. Paddling frantically, we made a twisting course through opening lanes of water, ice on both sides of us, visible bergs bearing down at times on us, invisible bergs with spear-points of ice beneath the water in which our course lay. We sped forward at times with quick darts. Suddenly, and to our horror, an invisible piece of ice jagged a hole in the port quarter. Water gushed into the frail craft. In a few minutes it would be filled; we should sink to an icy death! Fortunately, I saw a floe was near, and while the canoe rapidly filled we pushed for the floe, reaching it not a moment too soon.

A boot was sacrificed to mend the canoe. Patching the cut, we put again into the sea and proceeded.

The middle pack of ice was separated from the land pack, leaving much free water. But now a land breeze sprang up and gave us new troubles. We could not face the wind and sea, so we took a slant and sought the lee of the pans coming from the land.

Our little overloaded canoe weathered the seas very well, and we had nothing to gain and everything to lose by turning back. Again we were drenched with spray, and the canoe was sheeted with ice above water. The sun was passing over Hell Gate. Long blue shadows stretched over the pearl-gray sea. By these, without resort to the compass, we knew it was about midnight.

As we neared the land-ice, birds became numerous. The waters rose in easy swells. Still nearer, we noted that the entire body of land-ice was drifting away. A convenient channel opened and gave us a chance to slip behind. We pointed for Cape Vera, dashed over the water, and soon, to our joy, landed on a ledge of lower rocks. I cannot describe the relief I felt in reaching land after the spells of anguish through which we had passed. Although these barren rocks offered neither food nor shelter, still we were as happy as if a sentence of death had been remitted.

Not far away were pools of ice water. These we sought first, to quench our thirst. Then we scattered about, our eyes eagerly scrutinizing the land for breakfast. Soon we saw a hare bounding over the rocks. As it paused, cocking its ears, one of my boys secured it with a sling-shot. It was succulent; we cut it with our knives. Some moss was found among the rocks. This was a breakfast for a king. I returned to prepare it. With the moss as fuel, we made a fire, put the dripping meat in a pot, and, with gloating eyes, watched it simmering. I thrilled with the joy of sheer living, with hunger about to be satisfied by cooked food.

Before the hare was ready the boys came along with two eider-ducks, which they had secured by looped lines. We therefore had now an advance dinner, with a refreshing drink and a stomach full, and solid rocks to place our heads upon for a long sleep. These solid rocks were more delightful and secure than pillows of down. The world had indeed a new aspect for us. In reality, however, our ultimate prospect of escape from famine was darker than ever.

ARCTIC HARE

UNDER THE WHIP OF FAMINE

XXIV

Imprisoned by the Hand of Frost

No time was lost in our onward course. Endeavoring at once to regain the distance lost by the drifting berg, we sought a way along the shores. Here, over ice with pools of water and slush, we dragged our sledge with the canvas boat ever ready to launch. Frequent spaces of water necessitated constant ferrying. We found, however, that most open places could be crossed with sledge attached to the boat. This saved much time.

We advanced from ten to fifteen miles daily, pitching the tent on land or sleeping in the boat in pools of ice water, as the conditions warranted. The land rose with vertical cliffs two thousand feet high, and offered no life except a few gulls and guillemots. By gathering these as we went along, a scant hand-to-mouth subsistence daily was obtained.

Early in August we reached the end of the land-pack, about twenty-five miles east of Cape Sparbo. Beyond was a water sky, and to the north the sea was entirely free of ice. The weather was clear, and our ambitions for the freedom of the deep rose again.

At the end of the last day of sledge travel, a camp was made on a small island. Here we saw the first signs of Eskimo habitation. Old tent circles, also stone and fox traps in abundance, indicated an ancient village of considerable size. On the mainland we discovered abundant grass and moss, with signs of musk ox, ptarmigan, and hare, but no living thing was detected. After a careful search, the sledge was taken apart to serve as a floor for the boat. All our things were snugly packed. For breakfast, we had but one gull, which was divided without the tedious process of cooking.

As we were packing the things onto the edge of the ice, we espied an oogzuk seal. Here was a creature which could satisfy for a while our many needs. Upon it one of our last cartridges was expended. The seal fell. The huge carcass was dragged ashore. All of its skin was jealously taken. For this would make harpoon lines which would enable the shaping of Eskimo implements, to take the place of the rifles, which, with ammunition exhausted, would be useless. Our boots could also be patched with bits of the skin, and new soles could be made. Of the immense amount of oogzuk meat and blubber we were able to take only a small part; for, with three men and our baggage and sledge in the little canvas boat, it was already overloaded.

The meat was cached, so that if ultimate want forced our retreat we might here prolong our existence a few weeks longer. There was little wind, and the night was beautifully clear. The sun at night was very close to the horizon, but the sparkle of the shimmering waters gave our dreary lives a bright side. On the great unpolished rocks of the point east of Cape Sparbo a suitable camping spot was found, a prolonged feed of seal was indulged in, and with a warm sun and full stomachs, the tent was unnecessary. Under one of the rocks we found shelter, and slept with savage delight for nine hours.

Another search of the accessible land offered no game except ducks and gulls far from shore. Here the tides and currents were very strong, so our start had to be timed with the outgoing tide.

Starting late one afternoon, we advanced rapidly beyond Cape Sparbo, in a sea with an uncomfortable swell. But beyond the Cape, the land-ice still offered an edge for a long distance. In making a cut across a small bay to reach ice, a walrus suddenly came up behind the canoe and drove a tusk through the canvas. E-tuk-i-shook quickly covered the cut, while we pulled with full force for a pan of drift-ice only a few yards away. The boat, with its load, was quickly jerked on the ice. Already there were three inches of water in the floor. A chilly disaster was narrowly averted. Part of a boot was sacrificed to mend the boat.

While at work with the needle, a strong tidal current carried us out to sea. An increasing wind brought breaking waves over the edge of the ice. The wind fortunately gave a landward push to the ice. A sledge-cover, used as a sail, retarded our seaward drift. The leak securely patched, we pushed off for the land ice. With our eyes strained for breaking seas, the boat was paddled along with considerable anxiety. Much water was shipped in these dashes; constant bailing was necessary. Pulling continuously along the ice for eight miles, and when the leads closed at times, jumping on cakes and pulling the boat after us, we were finally forced to seek a shelter on the ice-field.

With a strong wind and a wet fall of snow, the ice-camp was far from comfortable. As the tide changed, the wind came from the west with a heavy, choppy sea. Further advance was impossible. Sleeping but a few minutes at a time, and then rising to note coming dangers, as does the seal, I perceived, to my growing dismay, a separation between the land and the sea ice. We were going rapidly adrift, with only interrupted spots of sea-ice on the horizon!

There were a good many reefs about, which quickly broke the ice, and new leads formed on every side. The boat was pushed landward. We pulled the boat on the ice when the leads closed, lowering it again as the cracks opened. By carrying the boat and its load from crack to crack, we at last reached the land waters, in which we were able to advance about five miles further, camping on the gravel of the first river which we had seen. Here we were storm-bound for two days.

There were several pools near by. Within a short distance from these were many ducks. With the sling-shot a few of these were secured. In the midst of our trouble, with good appetites, we were feeding up for future contests of strength.

With a shore clear of ice, we could afford to take some chance with heavy seas, so before the swell subsided, we pushed off. Coming out of Braebugten Bay, with its discharging glaciers and many reefs, the water dashed against the perpendicular walls of ice, and presented a disheartening prospect. These reefs could be passed over only when the sea was calm. With but a half-day's run to our credit, we were again stopped.

As we neared our objective point, on the fast ice inside of a reef, we were greeted with the glad sight of what we supposed to be a herd of musk ox. About three miles of the winter ice was still fast to the land. Upon this we landed, cleared the canvas boat, and prepared to camp in it. I remained to guard our few belongings, while the two Eskimo boys rushed over the ice to try to secure the musk ox with the lance. It was a critical time in our career, for we were putting to test new methods of hunting, which we had partly devised after many hungry days of preparation.

I followed the boys with the glasses as they jumped the ice crevasses and moved over the mainland with the stealth and ease of hungry wolves. It was a beautiful day. The sun was low in the northwest, throwing beams of golden light that made the ice a scene of joy. The great cliffs of North Devon, fifteen miles away, seemed very near through the clear air. Although enjoying the scene, I noted in the shadow of an iceberg a suspicious blue spot, which moved in my direction. As it advanced in the sunlight it changed from blue to a cream color. Then I made it out to be a Polar bear which we had attacked forty-eight hours previous.

The sight aroused a feeling of elation. Gradually, as bruin advanced and I began to think of some method of defense, a cold shiver ran up my spine. The dog and rifle, with which we had met bears before, were absent. To run, and leave our last bit of food and fuel, would have been as dangerous as to stay. A Polar bear will always attack a retreating creature, while it approaches very cautiously one that holds its position. Furthermore, for some reason, the bears always bore a grudge against the boat. None ever passed it without testing the material with its teeth or giving it a slap with its paw. At this critical stage of our adventure the boat was linked more closely to our destiny than the clothes we wore. I therefore decided to stay and play the rôle of the aggressor, although I had nothing—not even a lance—with which to fight.

Then an idea flashed through my mind. I lashed a knife to the steering paddle, and placed the boat on a slight elevation of ice, so as to make it and myself appear as formidable as possible. Then I gathered about me all the bits of wood, pieces of ice, and everything which I could throw at the creature before it came to a close contest, reserving the knife and the ice-ax as my last resort. When all was ready, I took my position beside the boat and displayed a sledge-runner moving rapidly to and fro.

The bear was then about two hundred yards away. It approached stealthily behind a line of hummocks, with only its head occasionally visible. As it came to within three hundred feet, it rose frequently on its hind feet, dropped its forepaws, stretched its neck, and pushed its head up, remaining motionless for several seconds. It then appeared huge and beautiful.

As it came still nearer, its pace quickened. I began to hurl my missiles. Every time the bear was hit, it stopped, turned about, and examined the object. But none of them proving palatable, it advanced to the opposite side of the boat, and for a moment stood and eyed

me. Its nose caught the odor of a piece of oogzuk
blubber a few feet beyond. I raised the sledge-runner
and brought it down with desperate force on the brute's
nose. It grunted, but quickly turned to retreat. I followed until it was well on the run.

Every time it turned to review the situation, I made
a show of chasing it. This always had the desired effect
of hastening its departure. It moved off, however, only
a short distance, and then sat down, sniffed the air, and
watched my movements. As I turned to observe the
boys' doings, I saw them only a short distance away,
edging upon the bear. Their group of musk oxen had
proved to be rocks, and they had early noted my troubles
and were hastening to enter the battle, creeping up behind hummocks and pressure ridges. They got to
within a few yards of the brute, and then delivered their
two lances at once, with lines attached. The bear
dropped, but quickly recovered and ran for the land.
He died from the wounds, for a month later we found
his carcass on land, placed near camp.

For two days, with a continuation of bad luck,
we advanced slowly. Belcher Point was passed at midnight of the 7th of August, just as the sun sank under
the horizon for the first time. Beyond was a nameless
bay, in which numerous icebergs were stranded. The
bend of the bay was walled with great discharging glaciers. A heavy sea pitched our boat like a leaf in a gale.
But, by seeking the shelter of bergs and passing inside
of the drift, we managed to push to an island for camp.

With moving glaciers on the land, and the sea
storming and thundering, sleep was impossible. Icebergs in great numbers followed us into the bay, and

later the storm-ground sea-ice filled the bay. On August 8, following a line of water along shore, we started eastward.

A strong wind on our backs, with quiet waters, sent the little boat along at a swift pace. After a run of ten miles, a great quantity of ice, coming from the east, filled the bay with small fragments and ensnared us.

Now the bay was jammed with a pack as difficult to travel over as quicksand. We were hopelessly beset. The land was sought, but it offered no shelter, no life, and no place flat enough to lie upon. We expected that the ice would break. It did not; instead, new winter ice rapidly formed.

The setting sun brought the winter storms and premonitions of a long, bitter night. Meanwhile we eked a meagre living by catching occasional birds, which we devoured raw.

Toward the end of August we pushed out on the ensnaring pack to a small but solid floe. I counted on this to drift somewhere—any place beyond the prison bars of the glaciers. Then we might move east or west to seek food. Our last meat was used, and we maintained life only by an occasional gull or guillemot. This floe drifted to and fro, and slowly took us to Belcher Point, where we landed to determine our fate. To the east, the entire horizon was lined with ice. Belcher Point was barren of game and shelter. Further efforts for Baffin's Bay were hopeless. The falling temperature, the rapidly forming young ice, and the setting sun showed us that we had already gone too long without finding a winter refuge.

Our only possible chance to escape death from

famine and frost was to go back to Cape Sparbo and
compel the walrus that ripped our boat to give up his
blubber, and then to seek our fortunes in the neighborhood. This was the only reachable place that had looked
like game country. With empty stomachs, and on a
heavy sea, we pushed westward to seek our fate. The
outlook was discouraging.

During all our enforced imprisonment we were
never allowed to forget that the first duty in life was to
provide for the stomach. Our muscles rested, but the
signals sent over the gastric nerve kept the gray matter
busy.

We were near to the land where Franklin and his
men starved. They had ammunition. We had none.
A similar fate loomed before us. We had seen nothing
to promise subsistence for the winter, but this cheerless
prospect did not interfere with such preparations as we
could make for the ultimate struggle. In our desperate
straits we even planned to attack bears, should we find
any, without a gun. Life is never so sweet as when its
days seem numbered.

The complete development of a new art of hunt-
ting, with suitable weapons, was reserved for the dire
needs of later adventures. The problem was begun by
this time. By an oversight, most of our Eskimo implements had been left on the returning sledges from
Svartevoeg.

We were thus not only without ammunition, but
also without harpoons and lances. We fortunately had
the material of which these could be made, and the boys
possessed the savage genius to shape a new set of weapons. The slingshot and the looped line, which had

served such a useful purpose in securing birds, continued to be of prime importance.   In the sledge was excellent hickory, which was utilized in various ways.   Of this, bows and arrows could be made.   Combined with the slingshot and the looped line snares, the combination would make our warfare upon the feathered creatures more effective.   We counted upon a similar efficiency with the same weapons in our hoped-for future attacks upon land animals.

The wood of the sledge was further divided to make shafts for harpoons and lances.   Realizing that our ultimate return to Greenland, and to friends, depended on the life of the sledge, the wood was used sparingly.   Furthermore, hickory lends itself to great economy.   It bends and twists, but seldom breaks in such a manner that it cannot be repaired.   We had not much of this precious fibre, but enough for the time to serve our purpose.   Along shore we had found musk ox horns and fragments of whale bone.   Out of these the points of both harpoon and lance were made.   A part of the sledge shoe was sacrificed to make metal points for the weapons.   The nails of the cooking-box served as rivets.   The seal skin, which we had secured a month earlier, was now carefully divided and cut into suitable harpoon and lassoo lines.   We hoped to use this line to capture the bear and the musk ox.   Our folding canvas boat was somewhat strengthened by the leather from our old boots, and additional bracing by the ever useful hickory of the sledge.   Ready to engage in battle with the smallest and the largest creatures that might come within reach, we started west for Cape Sparbo.   Death, on our journey, never seemed so near.

Apr. 21 '08 Est. Long 97 W.

Bar. 29.83 Temp 37.7 Cl. all St.

Wind — 1 May 8, Ice blue. Water Sky W

Noon Alt. ⊙ 23 - 3.3 - 25

OBSERVATION DETERMINING THE POLE—PHOTOGRAPH FROM
ORIGINAL NOTE

BACK TO LAND AND TO LIFE—AWAKENED BY A WINGED HARBINGER

BEAR FIGHTS AND WALRUS BATTLES

DANGEROUS ADVENTURES IN A CANVAS BOAT—ON THE
VERGE OF STARVATION, A MASSIVE BRUTE, WEIGHING
THREE THOUSAND POUNDS, IS CAPTURED AFTER A
FIFTEEN-HOUR STRUGGLE—ROBBED OF PRECIOUS
FOOD BY HUNGRY BEARS

XXV

GAME HAUNTS DISCOVERED

The stormy sea rose with heavy swells. Ocean-ward, the waves leaped against the horizon tumultu-ously. Pursuing our vain search for food along the southern side of Jones Sound, early in September, we had been obliged to skirt rocky coves and shelves of land on which we might seek shelter should harm come to the fragile craft in which we braved the ocean storms and the spears of unseen ice beneath water.

We had shaped crude weapons. We were pre-pared to attack game. We were starving; yet land and sea had been barren of any living thing.

Our situation was desperate. In our course it was often necessary, as now, to paddle from the near refuge of low-lying shores, and to pass precipitous cliffs and leaping glaciers which stepped threateningly into the sea. Along these were no projecting surfaces, and we passed them always with bated anxiety. A sudden storm or a mishap at such a time would have meant death in the frigid sea. And now, grim and suffering with hunger, we clung madly to life.

Passing a glacier which rose hundreds of feet out of the green sea, heavy waves rolled furiously from the distant ocean. Huge bergs rose and fell against the far-away horizon like Titan ships hurled to destruction. The waves dashed against the emerald walls of the smooth icy Gibraltar with a thunderous noise. We rose and fell in the frail canvas boat, butting the waves, our hearts each time sinking.

Suddenly something white and glittering pierced the bottom of the boat! It was the tusk of a walrus, gleaming and dangerous. Before we could grasp the situation he had disappeared, and water gushed into our craft. It was the first walrus we had seen for several weeks. An impulse, mad under the circumstances, rose in our hearts to give him chase. It was the instinctive call of the hungering body for food. But each second the water rose higher; each minute was imminent with danger. Instinctively Ah-we-lah pressed to the floor of the boat and jammed his knee into the hole, thus partly shutting off the jetting, leaping inrush. He looked mutely to me for orders. The glacier offered no stopping place. Looking about with mad eagerness, I saw, seaward, only a few hundred yards away, a small pan of drift-ice. With the desire for life in our arms, we pushed toward it with all our might. Before the boat was pulled to its slippery landing, several inches of water flooded the bottom. Once upon it, leaping in the waves, we breathed with panting relief. With a piece of boot the hole was patched. Although we should have preferred to wait to give the walrus a wide berth, the increasing swell of the stormy sea, and a seaward drift forced us away from the dangerous ice cliffs.

Launching the boat into the rough waters, we pulled for land. A triangle of four miles had to be made before our fears could be set at rest. A school of walrus followed us in the rocking waters for at least half of the distance. Finally, upon the crest of a white-capped wave, we were lifted to firm land. Drawing the boat after us, we ran out of reach of the hungry waves, and sank to the grass; desperate, despairing, utterly fatigued, but safe.

Now followed a long run of famine luck. We searched land and sea for a bird or a fish. In the boat we skirted a barren coast, sleeping on rocks without shelter and quenching our thirst by glacial liquid till the stomach collapsed. The indifferent stage of starvation was at hand when we pulled into a nameless bay, carried the boat on a grassy bench, and packed ourselves in it for a sleep that might be our last.

We were awakened by the glad sound of distant walrus calls. Through the glasses, a group was located far off shore, on the middle pack. Our hearts began to thump. A stream of blood came with a rush to our heads. Our bodies were fired with a life that had been foreign to us for many moons. No famished wolf ever responded to a call more rapidly than we did. Quickly we dropped the boat into the water with the implements, and pushed from the famine shores with teeth set for red meat.

The day was beautiful, and the sun from the west poured a wealth of golden light. Only an occasional ripple disturbed the glassy blue through which the boat crept. The pack was about five miles northward. In our eagerness to reach it, the distance seemed spread to leagues. There was not a square of ice for miles about which could have been sought for refuge in case of an attack. But this did not disturb us now. We were blinded to everything except the dictates of our palates.

As we advanced, our tactics were definitely arranged. The animals were on a low pan, which seemed to be loosely run into the main pack. We aimed for a little cut of ice open to the leeward, where we hoped to land and creep up behind hummocks. The splash of our paddles was lost in the noise of the grinding ice and the bellowing of walrus calls.

So excited were the Eskimos that they could hardly pull an oar. It was the first shout of the wilderness which we had heard in many months. We were lean enough to appreciate its import. The boat finally shot up on the ice, and we scattered among the ice blocks for favorable positions. Everything was in our favor. We did not for a moment entertain a thought of failure, although in reality, with the implements at hand, our project was tantamount to attacking an elephant with pocket knives.

We came together behind an unusually high icy spire only a few hundred yards from the herd. Ten huge animals were lazily stretched out in the warm sun. A few lively babies tormented their sleeping mothers. There was a splendid line of hummocks, behind which we could advance under cover. With a firm grip on harpoon and line, we started. Suddenly E-tuk-i-shook shouted *"Nannook!"* (Bear.)

We halted.   Our implements were no match for a bear.   But we were too hungry to retreat.   The bear paid no attention to us.   His nose was set for something more to his liking.   Slowly but deliberately, he crept up to the snoring herd while we watched with a mad, envious anger welling up within us.   Our position was helpless.   His long neck reached out, the glistening fangs closed, and a young walrus struggled in the air.   All of the creatures woke, but too late to give battle.   With dismay and rage, the walruses sank into the water, and the bear slunk off to a safe distance, where he sat down to a comfortable meal.   We were not of sufficient importance to interest either the bear or the disturbed herd of giants.

Our limbs were limp when we returned to the boat. The sunny glitter of the waters was now darkened by the gloom of danger from enraged animals.   We crossed to the barren shores in a circuitous route, where pieces of ice for refuge were always within reach.

On land, the night was cheerless and cold.   We were not in a mood for sleep.   In a lagoon we discovered moving things.   After a little study of their vague darts they proved to be fish.   A diligent search under stones brought out a few handfuls of tiny finny creatures. With gratitude I saw that here was an evening meal. Seizing them, we ate the wriggling things raw.   Cooking was impossible, for we had neither oil nor wood.

On the next day the sun at noon burned with a real fire—not the sham light without heat which had kept day and night in perpetual glitter for several weeks.   Not a breath of air disturbed the blue glitter of the sea.   Ice was scattered everywhere.   The central pack was farther away, but on it rested several suspicious black marks. Through the glasses we made these out to be groups of walruses. They were evidently sound asleep, for we heard no calls. They were also so distributed that there was a hunt both for bear and man without interference.

We ventured out with a savage desire sharpened by a taste of raw fish. As we advanced, several other groups were noted in the water. They gave us much trouble. They did not seem ill-tempered, but dangerously inquisitive. Our boat was dark in color and not much larger than the body of a full-sized bull. To them, I presume, it resembled a companion in distress or asleep. A sight of the boat challenged their curiosity, and they neared us with the playful intention of testing with their tusks the hardness of the canvas. We had experienced such love taps before, however, with but a narrow escape from drowning, and we had no desire for further walrus courtship.

Fortunately, we could maintain a speed almost equal to theirs, and we also found scattered ice-pans, about which we could linger while their curiosity was being satisfied by the splash of an occasional stone.

From an iceberg we studied the various groups of walruses for the one best situated for our primitive methods of attack. We also searched for meddlesome bears. None was detected. Altogether we counted more than a hundred grunting, snorting creatures arranged in black hills along a line of low ice. There were no hummocks or pressure lifts, under cover of which we might advance to within the short range required for our harpoons. All of the walrus-encumbered pans were

adrift and disconnected from the main pack.   Conflicting currents gave each group a slightly different motion.
We studied this movement for a little while.

We hoped, if possible, to make our attack from the
ice.   With the security of a solid footing, there was no
danger and there was a greater certainty of success.
But the speed of the ice on this day did not permit such
an advantage.   We must risk a water attack.   This is
not an unusual method of the Eskimo, but he follows it
with a kayak, a harpoon and line fitted with a float and
a drag for the end of his line.   Our equipment was only
a makeshift, and could not be handled in the same way.

Here was food in massive heaps.   We had had no
breakfast and no full meal for many weeks.   Something
must be done.   The general drift was eastward, but the
walrus pans drifted slightly faster than the main pack.
Along the pack were several high points, projecting a
considerable distance seaward.   We took our position
in the canvas boat behind one of these floating capes, and
awaited the drift of the sleeping monsters.

Their movement was slow enough to give us plenty
of time to arrange our battle tactics.   The most vital
part of the equipment was the line.   If it were lost, we
could not hope to survive the winter.   It could not be
replaced, and without it we could not hope to cope with
the life of the sea, or even that of the land.   The line was
a new, strong sealskin rawhide of ample length, which
had been reserved for just such an emergency.   Attached to the harpoon, with the float properly adjusted,
it is seldom lost, for the float moves and permits no
sudden strain.

To safeguard the line, a pan was selected only a few

yards in diameter.   This was arranged to do the duty
of a float and a drag.   With the knife two holes were
cut, and into these the line was fastened near its center.
The harpoon end was taken into the boat, the other end
was coiled and left in a position where it could be easily
picked from the boat later.   Three important purposes
were secured by this arrangement—the line was relieved
of a sudden strain; if it broke, only half would be lost;
and the unused end would serve as a binder to other ice
when the chase neared its end.

Now the harpoon was set to the shaft, and the bow
of our little twelve-foot boat cleared for action.   Peeping over the wall of ice, we saw the black-littered pans
slowly coming toward us.   Our excitement rose to a
shouting point.   But our nerves were under the disci-
pline of famine.   The pan, it was evident, would go by
us at a distance of about fifty feet.

The first group of walruses were allowed to pass.
They proved to be a herd of twenty-one mammoth creatures, and, entirely aside from the danger of attack, their
unanimous plunge would have raised a sea that must
have swamped us.

On the next pan were but three spots.   At a distance we persuaded ourselves that they were small—for
we had no ambition for formidable attacks.   One thousand pounds of meat would have been sufficient for us.
They proved, however, to be the largest bulls of the lot.
As they neared the point, the hickory oars of the boat
were gripped—and out we shot.   They all rose to meet
us, displaying the glitter of ivory tusks from little
heads against huge wrinkled necks.   They grunted and
snorted viciously—but the speed of the boat did not

slacken. E-tuk-i-shook rose. With a savage thrust he sank the harpoon into a yielding neck.

The walruses tumbled over themselves and sank into the water on the opposite side of the pan. We pushed upon the vacated floe without leaving the boat, taking the risk of ice puncture rather than walrus thumps. The short line came up with a snap. The ice pan began to plough the sea. It moved landward. What luck! I wondered if the walrus would tow us and its own carcass ashore. We longed to encourage the homing movement, but we dared not venture out. Other animals had awakened to the battle call, and now the sea began to seethe and boil with enraged, leaping red-eyed monsters.

The float took a zigzag course in the offing. We watched the movement with a good deal of anxiety. Our next meal and our last grip on life were at stake. For the time being nothing could be done.

The three animals remained together, two pushing the wounded one along and holding it up during breathing spells. In their excitement they either lost their bearings or deliberately determined to attack. Now three ugly snouts pointed at us. This was greatly to our advantage, for on ice we were masters of the situation.

Taking inconspicuous positions, we awaited the assault. The Eskimos had lances, I an Alpine axe. The walruses dove and came on like torpedo boats, rising almost under our noses, with a noise that made us dodge. In a second two lances sank into the harpooned strugglers. The water was thrashed. Down again went the three. The lances were jerked back by return lines, and in another moment we were ready for another·assault from the other side.   But they dashed on, and pulled the float-floe, on which we had been, against the one on which we stood, with a crushing blow.

Here was our first chance to secure the unused end of the line, fastened on the other floe.   Ah- ʋe-lah jumped to the floe and tossed me the line.   The spiked shaft of the ice-axe was driven in the ice and the line fixed to it, so now the two floes were held together. Our stage of action was enlarged, and we had the advantage of being towed by the animals we fought.

Here was the quiet sport of the fisherman and the savage excitement of the battle-field run together in a new chase.   The struggle was prolonged in successive stages.   Time passed swiftly.   In six hours, during which the sun had swept a quarter of the circle, the twin floes were jerked through the water with the rush of a gunboat.   The jerking line attached to our enraged pilots sent a thrill·of life which made our hearts jump. The lances were thrown, the line was shortened, a cannonade of ice blocks was kept up, but the animal gave no signs of weakening.   Seeing that we could not inflict dangerous wounds, our tactics were changed to a kind of siege, and we aimed not to permit the animal its breathing spells.

The line did not begin to slacken until midnight. The battle had been on for almost twelve hours.   But we did not feel the strain of action, nor did our chronic hunger seriously disturb us.   Bits of ice quenched our thirst and the chill of night kept us from sweating. With each rise of the beast for breath now, the line slackened.   Gently it was hauled in and secured.   Then a rain of ice blocks, hurled in rapid succession, drove the spouting animals down.   Soon the line was short enough to deliver the lance in the captured walrus at close range. The wounded animal was now less troublesome, but the others tore about under us like submarine boats, and at the most unexpected moments would shoot up with a wild rush.

We did not attempt to attack them, however.   All our attention was directed to the end of the line.   The lance was driven with every opportunity.   It seldom missed, but the action was more like spurs to a horse, changing an intended attack upon us to a desperate plunge into the deep, and depriving the walrus of oxygen.

Finally, after a series of spasmodic encounters which lasted fifteen hours, the enraged snout turned blue, the fiery eyes blackened, and victory was ours—not as the result of the knife alone, not in a square fight of brute force, but by the superior cunning of the human animal under the stimulus of hunger.

During all this time we had been drifting.   Now, as the battle ended, we were not far from a point about three miles south of our camp.   Plenty of safe pack-ice was near.   A primitive pulley was arranged by passing the line through slits in the walrus' nose and holes in the ice.   The great carcass, weighing perhaps three thousand pounds, was drawn onto the ice and divided into portable pieces.   Before the sun poured its morning beams over the ice, all had been securely taken ashore.

With ample blubber, a camp fire was now made between two rocks by using moss to serve as a wick.   Soon, pot after pot of savory meat was voraciously consumed.

We ate with a mad, vulgar, insatiable hunger. We spoke little.   Between gulps, the huge heap of meat and blubber was cached under heavy rocks, and secured—'so we thought—from bears, wolves and foxes.

When eating was no longer possible, sleeping dens were arranged in the little boat, and in it, like other gluttonous animals after an engorgement, we closed our eyes to a digestive sleep.   For the time, at least, we had fathomed the depths of gastronomic content, and were at ease with ourselves and with a bitter world of inhuman strife.

At the end of about fifteen hours, a stir about our camp suddenly awoke us.   We saw a huge bear nosing about our fireplace.   We had left there a walrus joint, weighing about one hundred pounds, for our next meal. We jumped up, all of us, at once, shouting and making a pretended rush.   The bear took up the meat in his forepaws and walked off, man-like, on two legs, with a threatening grunt.   His movement was slow and cautious, and his grip on the meat was secure.   Occasionally he veered about, with a beckoning turn of the head, and a challenging call.   But we did not accept the challenge.   After moving away about three hundred yards on the sea-ice, he calmly sat down and devoured our prospective meal.

With lances, bows, arrows, and stones in hand, we next crossed a low hill, beyond which was located our precious cache of meat.   Here, to our chagrin, we saw two other bears, with heads down and paws busily digging about the cache.   We were not fitted for a hand-to-hand encounter.   Still, our lives were equally at stake, whether we attacked or failed to attack.   Some defense

must be made.   With a shout and a fiendish rush, we
attracted the busy brutes' attention.   They raised their
heads, turned, and to our delight and relief, grudgingly
walked off seaward on the moving ice.   Each had a big
piece of our meat with him.

Advancing to the cache, we found it absolutely de-
pleted.   Many other bears had been there.   The snow
and the sand was trampled down with innumerable bear
tracks.   Our splendid cache of the day previous was entirely lost.   We could have wept with rage and disappointment.   One thing we were made to realize, and
that was that life here was now to be a struggle with the
bears for supremacy.   With little ammunition, we were
not at all able to engage in bear fights.   So, baffled, and
unable to resent our robbery, starvation again confront-
ing us, we packed our few belongings and moved westward over Braebugten Bay to Cape Sparbo.

A THIEF OF THE NORTH

BULL FIGHTS WITH THE MUSK OX

AN ANCIENT CAVE EXPLORED FOR SHELTER—DEATH BY
STARVATION AVERTED BY HAND-TO-HAND ENCOUN-
TERS WITH WILD ANIMALS

XXVI

To the Winter Camp at Cape Sparbo

As we crossed the big bay to the east of Cape
Sparbo, our eyes were fixed on the two huge Archæn
rocks which made remarkable landmarks, rising suddenly to an altitude of about eighteen thousand feet.
They appear like two mountainous island lifted out of
the water. On closer approach, however, we found the
islands connected with the mainland by low grassy
plains, forming a peninsula. The grassy lands seemed
like promising grounds for caribou and musk ox. The
off-lying sea, we also found, was shallow. In this, I
calculated, would be food to attract the seal and walrus.

In our slow movement over the land swell of the
crystal waters, it did not take long to discover that our
conjecture was correct.

Pulling up to a great herd of walrus, we prepared
for battle. But the sea suddenly rose, the wind increased, and we were forced to abandon the chase and
seek shelter on the nearest land.

We reached Cape Sparbo, on the shores of Jones

Sound, early in September. Our dogs were gone. Our ammunition, except four cartridges which I had secreted for use in a last emergency, was gone. Our equipment consisted of a half sledge, a canvas boat, a torn silk tent, a few camp kettles, tin plates, knives, and matches. Our clothing was splitting to shreds.

Cape Sparbo, with its huge walls of granite, was to the leeward. A little bay was noted where we might gain the rocks in quiet water. Above the rocks was a small green patch where we hoped to find a soft resting place for the boat, so that we might place our furs in it and secure shelter from the bitter wind.

When we landed we found to our surprise that it was the site of an old Eskimo village. There was a line of old igloos partly below water, indicating a very ancient time of settlement, for since the departure of the builders of these igloos the coast must have settled at least fifteen feet. Above were a few other ruins.

Shortly after arriving we sought an auspicious place, protected from the wind and cold, where later we might build a winter shelter. Our search disclosed a cave-like hole, part of which was dug from the earth, and over which, with stones and bones, had been constructed a roof which now was fallen in.

The long winter was approaching. We were over three hundred miles from Annoatok, and the coming of the long night made it necessary for us to halt here. We must have food and clothing. We now came upon musk oxen and tried to fell them with boulders, and bows and arrows made of the hickory of our sledge. Day after day the pursuit was vainly followed. Had it not been for occasional ducks caught with looped lines and sling shots, we should have been absolutely without any food.

By the middle of September, snow and frost came with such frequency that we omitted hunting for a day to dig out the ruins in the cave and cut sod before permanent frost made such work impossible. Bone implements were shaped from skeletons found on shore for the digging. Blown drifts of sand and gravel, with some moss and grass, were slowly removed from the pit. We found under this, to our great joy, just the underground arrangement which we desired; a raised platform, about six feet long and eight feet wide with suitable wings for the lamp, and footspace, lay ready for us. The pit had evidently been designed for a small family. The walls, which were about two feet high, required little alteration. Another foot was added, which leveled the structure with the ground. A good deal of sod was cut and allowed to dry in the sun for use as a roof.

While engaged in taking out the stones and cleaning the dungeon-like excavation, I suddenly experienced a heart-depressing chill when, lifting some debris, I saw staring at me from the black earth a hollow-eyed human skull. The message of death which the weird thing leeringly conveyed was singularly unpleasant; the omen was not good. Yet the fact that at this forsaken spot human hands had once built shelter, or for this thing had constructed a grave, gave me a certain companionable thrill.

On the shore not far away we secured additional whale ribs and with these made a framework for a roof. This was later constructed of moss and blocks of sod. We built a rock wall about the shelter to protect our-

selves from storms and bears.   Then our winter home
was ready.   Food was now an immediate necessity.
Game was found around us in abundance.   Most of it
was large.   On land there were bear and musk ox, in
the sea the walrus and the whale.   But what could we
do without either dogs or rifles?

The first weapon that we now devised was the bow
and arrow, for with this we could at least secure some
small game.   We had in our sledge available hickory
wood of the best quality, than which no wood could be
better; we had sinews and seal lashings for strings, but
there was no metal for tips.   We tried bone, horn and
ivory, but all proved ineffective.

One day, however, E-tuk-i-shook examined his
pocket knife and suggested taking the side blades for
arrow tips.   This was done, and the blade with its spring
was set in a bone handle.   Two arrows were thus tipped.
The weapons complete, the Eskimo boys went out on
the chase.   They returned in the course of a few hours
with a hare and an eider-duck.   Joy reigned in camp as
we divided the meat and disposed of it without the
process of cooking.

A day later, two musk oxen were seen grazing
along the moraine of a wasting glacier.   Now the musk
ox is a peace-loving animal and avoids strife, but when
forced into fight it is one of the most desperate and
dangerous of all the fighters of the wilderness.   It can
and does give the most fatal thrust of all the horned
animals.   No Spanish bull of the pampas, no buffalo
of the plains, has either the slant of horn or the intelligence to gore its enemies as has this inoffensive-looking
bull of the ice world.   The intelligence, indeed, is an

important factor, for after watching musk oxen for a time under varied conditions, one comes to admire their almost human intellect as well as their superhuman power of delivering self-made force.

Our only means of attack was with the bow and arrow. The boys crept up behind rocks until within a few yards of the unsuspecting creatures. They bent the bows, and the arrows sped with the force and accuracy as only a hungry savage can master. But the beasts' pelts were too strong. The musk oxen jumped and faced their assailants. Each arrow, as it came, was broken into splints by the feet and the teeth.

When the arrows were all used a still more primitive weapon was tried, for the sling shot was brought into use, with large stones. These missiles the musk oxen took good naturedly, merely advancing a few steps to a granite boulder, upon which they sharpened their horn points and awaited further developments. No serious injury had been inflicted and they made no effort to escape.

Then came a change. When we started to give up the chase they turned upon us with a fierce rush. Fortunately, many big boulders were about, and we dodged around these with large stones in hand to deliver at close range. In a wild rush a musk ox cannot easily turn, and so can readily be dodged. Among the rocks two legs were better than four. The trick of evading the musk ox I had learned from the dogs. It saved our lives.

After a while the animals wearied, and we beat a hasty retreat, with new lessons in our book of hunting adventures. The bow and arrow was evidently not the weapon with which to secure musk oxen.

The musk ox of Jones Sound, unlike his brother
farther north, is every ready for battle. He is often
compelled to meet the bear and the wolf in vicious contests, and his tactics are as thoroughly developed as his
emergencies require. Seldom does he fall the victim of
his enemies. We were a long time in learning completely his methods of warfare, and if, in the meantime,
we had not secured other game our fate would have been
unfortunate.

Harpoons and lances were next finally completed,
and with them we hastened to retrieve our honor in the
"ah-ming-ma" chase. For, after all, the musk ox alone
could supply our wants. Winter storms were coming
fast. We were not only without food and fuel, but without clothing. In our desperate effort to get out of the
regions of famine to the Atlantic, we had left behind
all our winter furs, including the sleeping bags; and our
summer garments were worn out. We required the fuel
and the sinew, the fat and the horn.

One day we saw a herd of twenty-one musk oxen
quietly grazing on a misty meadow, like cattle on the
western plains. It was a beautiful sight to watch them,
divided as they were into families and in small groups.
The males were in fur slightly brown, while the females
and the young ones were arrayed in magnificent black
pelts.

To get any of them seemed hopeless, but our appalling necessities forced us onward. There were no
boulders near, but each of us gathered an armful of
stones, the object being to make a sudden bombardment
and compel them to retreat in disorder and scatter
among the rocks.

We approached under cover of a small grassy hummock. When we were detected, a bull gave a loud snort and rushed toward his nearest companions, whereupon the entire herd gathered into a circle, with the young in the center.

We made our sham rush and hurled the stones. The oxen remained almost motionless, with their heads down, giving little snorts and stamping a little when hit, but quickly resuming their immobile position of watchfulness. After our stones were exhausted, the animals began to shift positions slightly. We interpreted this as a move for action. So we gave up the effort and withdrew.

The days were long and the nights still light enough to continue operations as long as we could keep our eyes open. The whip of hunger made rest impossible. So we determined to seek a less formidable group of oxen in a position more favorable. The search was continued until the sinking glimmer of the sun in the north marked the time of midnight—for with us at that time the compass was the timepiece.

When E-tuk-i-shook secured a hare with the bow and arrow, we ascended a rocky eminence and sat down to appease the calling stomach without a camp fire. From here we detected a family of four musk oxen asleep not far from another group of rocks.

This was a call to battle. We were not long in planning our tactics. The wind was in our favor, permitting an attack from the side opposite the rocks to which we aimed to force a retreat. We also found small stones in abundance, these being now a necessary part of our armament. Our first effort was based on the supposition of their remaining asleep. They were simply chewing their cud, however, and rose to form a ring of defence as we advanced. We stormed them with stones and they took to the shelter of the rocks. We continued to advance slowly upon them, throwing stones occasionally to obviate a possible assault from them before we could also seek the shelter of the rocks.

Besides the bow and arrow and the stones, we now had lances and these we threw as they rushed to attack us. Two lances were crushed to small fragments before they could be withdrawn by the light line attached. They inflicted wounds, but not severe ones.

Noting the immense strength of the animals, we at first thought it imprudent to risk the harpoon with its precious line, for if we lost it we could not replace it. But the destruction of the two lances left us no alternative.

Ah-we-lah threw the harpoon. It hit a rib, glanced to a rock, and was also destroyed. Fortunately we had a duplicate point, which was quickly fastened. Then we moved about to encourage another onslaught.

Two came at once, an old bull and a young one. E-tuk-i-shook threw the harpoon at the young one, and it entered. The line had previously been fastened to a rock, and the animal ran back to its associates, apparently not severely hurt, leaving the line slack. One of the others immediately attacked the line with horns, hoofs and teeth, but did not succeed in breaking it.

Our problem now was to get rid of the other three while we dealt with the one at the end of the line. Our only resource was a sudden fusilade of stones. This proved effective. The three scattered and ascended the

boulder-strewn foreland of a cliff, where the oldest bull
remained to watch our movements. The young bull
made violent efforts to escape but the line of sealskin
was strong and elastic. A lucky throw of a lance at
close range ended the strife. Then we advanced on the
old bull, who was alone in a good position for us.

We gathered stones and advanced, throwing them
at the creature's body. This, we found, did not enrage
him, but it prevented his making an attack. As we
gained ground he gradually backed up to the edge of
the cliff, snorting viciously but making no effort whatever either to escape along a lateral bench or to attack.
His big brown eyes were upon us; his sharp horns were
pointed at us. He evidently was planning a desperate
lunge and was backing to gain time and room, but each
of us kept within a few yards of a good-sized rock.

Suddenly we made a combined rush into the open,
hurling stones, and keeping a long rock in a line for
retreat. Our storming of stones had the desired effect.
The bull, annoyed and losing its presence of mind,
stepped impatiently one step too far backwards and fell
suddenly over the cliff, landing on a rocky ledge below.
Looking over we saw he had broken a fore leg. The cliff
was not more than fifteen feet high. From it the lance
was used to put the poor creature out of suffering. We
were rich now and could afford to spread out our
stomachs, contracted by long spells of famine. The bull
dressed about three hundred pounds of meat and one
hundred pounds of tallow.

We took the tallow and as much meat as we could
carry on our backs, and started for the position of our
prospective winter camp, ten miles away. The meat

left was carefully covered with heavy stones to protect
it from bears, wolves and foxes. On the following day
we returned with the canvas boat, making a landing
about four miles from the battlefield. As we neared
the caches we found to our dismay numerous bear and
fox tracks. The bears had opened the caches and removed our hard-earned game, while the foxes and the
ravens had cleared up the very fragments and destroyed even the skins. Here was cause for vengeance
on the bear and the fox. The fox paid his skin later,
but the bear out-generaled us in nearly every
maneuvre.

We came prepared to continue the chase but had
abandoned the use of the harpoon. Our main hope for
fuel was the blubber of the walrus, and if the harpoon
should be destroyed or lost we could not hope to attack
so powerful a brute as a walrus with any other device.
In landing we had seen a small herd of musk oxen at
some distance to the east, but they got our wind and
vanished. We decided to follow them up. One day
we found them among a series of rolling hills, where the
receding glaciers had left many erratic boulders. They
lined up in their ring of defence as usual when we were
detected. There were seven of them; all large creatures
with huge horns. A bitter wind was blowing, driving
some snow, which made our task more difficult.

The opening of the fight with stones was now a
regular feature which we never abandoned in our later
development of the art, but the manner in which we delivered the stones depended upon the effect which we
wished to produce. If we wished the musk oxen to retreat, we would make a combined rush, hurling the

stones at the herd. If we wished them to remain in position and discourage their attack, we advanced slowly and threw stones desultorily, more or less at random. If we wanted to encourage attacks, one man advanced and delivered a large rock as best he could at the head. This was cheap ammunition and it was very effective.

In this case the game was in a good position for us and we advanced accordingly. They allowed us to take positions within about fifteen feet, but no nearer. The lances were repeatedly tried without effect, and after a while two of these were again broken.

Having tried bow and arrow, stones, the lance and the harpoon, we now tried another weapon. We threw the lasso—but not successfully, owing to the bushy hair about the head and the roundness of the hump of the neck. Then we tried to entangle their feet with slip loops just as we trapped gulls. This also failed. We next extended the loop idea to the horns. The bull's habit of rushing at things hurled at him caused us to think of this plan.

A large slip loop was now made in the center of the line, and the two natives took up positions on opposite sides of the animal. They threw the rope, with its loop, on the ground in front of the creature, while I encouraged an attack from the front. As the head was slightly elevated the loop was raised, and the bull put his horns in it, one after the other. The rope was now rapidly fastened to stones and the bull tightened the loop by his efforts to advance or retreat. With every opportunity the slack was taken up, until no play was allowed the animal. During this struggle all the other oxen retreated except one female, and she was in-

offensive. A few stones at close range drove her off.
Then we had the bull where we could reach him with the
lance at arm's length, and plunge it into his vitals. He
soon fell over, the first victim to our new art of musk
ox capture.

The others did not run very far away. Indeed,
they were too fat to run, and two more were soon
secured in the same way. This time we took all the meat
we could with us to camp and left a man on guard.
When all was removed to the bay we found the load too
heavy for our boat, so, in two loads, we transported the
meat and fat and skins to our camp, where we built
caches which we believed impregnable to the bear,
although the thieving creatures actually opened them
later.

Our lances repaired, we started out for another adventure a few days later. It was a beautiful day. Our
methods of attack were not efficient, but we wished to
avoid the risk of the last plunge of the lance, for our
lives were in the balance every time if the line should
break, and with every lunge of the animal we expected
it to snap. In such case, we knew, the assailant would
surely be gored.

We were sufficiently independent now to proceed
more cautiously. With the bull's willingness to put his
head into the loop, I asked myself whether the line loop
could not be slipped beyond the horns and about the
neck, thus shutting off the air. So the line was lengthened with this effort in view.

Of the many groups of oxen which we saw we
picked those in the positions most to our advantage,
although rather distant. Our new plan was tried with

success on a female. A bull horned her vigorously when she gasped for breath, and which aided our efforts. A storming of stones scattered the others of the group, and we were left to deal with our catch with the knife.

Our art of musk ox fighting was now completely developed. In the course of a few weeks we secured enough to assure comfort and ease during the long night. By our own efforts we were lifted suddenly from famine to luxury. But it had been the stomach with its chronic emptiness which had lashed the mind and body to desperate efforts with sufficient courage to face the danger. Hunger, as I have found, is more potent as a stimulant than barrels of whiskey. Beginning with the bow and arrow we had tried everything which we could devise, but now our most important acquisition was our intimate knowledge of the animal's own means of offense and defense.

We knew by a kind of instinct when an attack upon us was ‹ bout to be made, because the animal made a forward move, and we never failed in our efforts to force a retreat. The rocks which the animals sought for an easy defense were equally useful to us, and later we forced them into deep waters and also deep snow with similar success. By the use of stones and utilizing the creatures' own tactics we placed them where we wished. And then again, by the animal's own efforts, we forced it to strangle itself, which, after all, was the most humane method of slaughter. Three human lives were thus saved by the invention of a new art of chase. This gave us courage to attack those more vicious but less dangerous animals, the bear and walrus.

The musk ox now supplied many wants in our "Robinson Crusoe" life. From the bone we made harpoon points, arrow pieces, knife handles, fox traps and sledge repairs. The skin, with its remarkable fur, made our bed and roofed our igloo. Of it we made all kinds of garments, but its greatest use was for coats with hoods, stockings and mittens. From the skin, with the fur removed, we made boots, patched punctures in our boat, and cut lashings. The hair and wool which were removed from the skins made pads for our palms in the mittens and cushions for the soles of our feet in lieu of the grass formerly used.

The meat became our staple food for seven months without change. It was a delicious product. It has a flavor slightly sweet, like that of horseflesh, but still distinctly pleasing. It possesses an odor unlike' musk but equally unlike anything that I know of. The live creatures exhale the scent of domestic cattle. Just why this odd creature is called "musk" ox is a mystery, for it is neither an ox, nor does it smell of musk. The Eskimo name of "ah-ming-ma" would fit it much better. The bones were used as fuel for outside fires, and the fat as both fuel and food.

At first our wealth of food came with surprise and delight to us, for, in the absence of sweet or starchy foods, man craves fat. Sugar and starch are most readily converted into fat by the animal laboratory, and fat is one of the prime factors in the development and maintenance of the human system. It is the confectionery of aboriginal man, and we had taken up the lot of the most primitive aborigines, living and thriving solely on the product of the chase without a morsel of civilized or vegetable food. Under these circumstances we especially delighted in the musk ox tallow, and more especially in the marrow, which we sucked from the bone with the eagerness with which a child jubilantly manages a stick of candy.

ARCTIC WOLF

WITH A NEW ART OF CHASE IN A NEW WORLD OF LIFE

THREE WEEKS BEFORE THE SUNSET OF 1908—REVELLING IN AN EDEN OF GAME—PECULIARITIES OF ANIMALS OF THE ARCTIC—HOW NATURE DICTATES ANIMAL COLOR—THE QUEST OF SMALL LIFE

XXVII

COMING OF THE SECOND WINTER

In two months, from the first of September to the end of October, we passed from a period of hunger, thirst and abject misery into the realm of abundant game. The spell for inactivity had not yet come. Up to this time we were too busy with the serious business of life to realize thoroughly that we had really discovered a new natural wonderland. The luck of Robinson Crusoe was not more fortunate than ours, although he had not the cut of frost nor the long night, nor the torment of bears to circumscribe his adventures. In successive stages of battle our eyes had opened to a new world of life.

In searching every nook and cranny of land we had acquired new arts of life and a new perspective of nature's wonders. We slept in caves in storm; in the lee of icebergs in strong winds and on the mossy cushions of earth concavities. Here we learned to study and appreciate primal factors of both animal and plant life.

In the Arctic, nature tries to cover its nakedness in places where the cruel winds do not cut its contour. The effort is interesting, not only because of the charm of the verdant dress, but because of the evidence of a motherly protection to the little life cells which struggle against awful odds to weave that fabric wherever a terrestrial dimple is exposed to the kisses of the southern sun. In these depressions, sheltered from the blasts of storms, a kindly hand spreads a beautiful mantle of colorful grass, moss, lichens and flowery plants.

Here the lemming digs his home under the velvet cover, where he may enjoy the roots and material protection from the abysmal frost of the long night. Here in the protected folds of Mother Earth, blanketed by the warm white robe of winter, he sleeps the peace of death while the warring elements blast in fury outside.

Here the Arctic hare plays with its bunnies during summer, and as the winter comes the young grow to full maturity and dress in a silky down of white. Under the snow they burrow, making long tunnels, still eating and sleeping on their loved cushions of frozen plants, far under the snow-skirts of Mother Earth, while the life-stilling blasts without expend their wintry force.

Here the ptarmigan scratches for its food. The musk ox and the caribou browse, while the raven, with a kind word for all, collects food for its palate. The bear and the wolf occasionally visit to collect tribute, while the falcon and the fox with one eye open are ever on the alert for the exercise of their craft.

In these little smiling indentations of nature, when the sun begins to caress the gentle slopes, while the snow melts and flows in leaping streams—the sea still locked by the iron grip of the winter embrace—the Arctic incubator works overtime to start the little ones of the snow wilds. Thus in these dimples of nature rocks the cradle of boreal life.

Relieved of the all-absorbing care of providing food, I now was often held spellbound as I wandered over these spots of nature's wonders. Phases of life which never interested me before now riveted my attention. Wandering from the softly cushioned gullies, the harsh ridge life next came under my eyes. While the valleys and the gullies become garden spots of summer glory, the very protection from winds which makes this life possible buries the vegetable luxuriousness in winter under unfathomable depths of snow. The musk ox and the caribou, dependent upon this plant life for food, therefore become deprived of the usual means of subsistence. But Mother Nature does not desert her children. The same winds which compel man and feebler animals to seek shelter from its death-dealing assault, afford food to the better fitted musk ox and caribou. In summer, plants, like animals, climb to ridges, hummocks and mountain slopes, to get air and light and warm sunbeams. But the battle here is hard, and only very strong plants survive the force of wind and frosts.

The plant fibre here become tenacious; with a body gnarled and knotty from long conflict the roots dig yards deep into the soil. This leaves the breathing part of the plant dwarfed to a few inches. Here the winter winds sweep off the snow and offer food to the musk ox and caribou. Thus the wind, which destroys, also gives means of life. The equalizing balance of nature is truly wonderful.

In small, circumscribed areas we thus found ourselves in a new Eden of primeval life.

The topography of North Devon, however, placed a sharp limit to the animated wilderness. Only a narrow strip of coast about Cape Sparbo, extending about twenty-five miles to the east and about forty miles to the west, presented any signs of land life. All other parts of the south shore of Jones Sound are more barren than the shores of the Polar sea.

Although our larder was now well stocked with meat for food and blubber for fuel, we were still in need of furs and skins to prepare a new equipment with which to return to the Greenland shores. The animals whose pelts we required were abundant everywhere. But they were too active to be caught by the art and the weapons evolved earlier in the chase of the walrus, bear and musk ox.

A series of efforts, therefore, was directed to the fox, the hare, the ptarmigan and the seal. It was necessary to devise special methods and means of capture for each family of animals. The hare was perhaps the most important, not only because its delicately flavored meat furnished a pleasing change from the steady diet of musk ox, but also because its skin is not equalled by any other for stockings. In our quest of the musk ox we had startled little groups of creatures from many centers. Their winter fur was not prime until after the middle of October. Taking notes of their haunts and

E-TUK-I-SHOOK WAITING FOR A SEAL AT A BLOW-HOLE

TOWARD CAPE SPARBO IN A CANVAS BOAT

WALRUS—PRIZE OF A FIFTEEN HOUR BATTLE—4,000 POUNDS OF
MEAT AND FAT

their habits, we had, therefore, reserved the hare hunt until the days just before sunset.

We had learned to admire this little aristocrat. It is the most beautiful, most delicate of northern creatures. Early in the summer we had found it grazing in the green meadows along the base of bird cliffs. The little gray bunnies then played with their mothers about crystal dens. Now the babes were full grown and clothed in the same immaculate white of the parents. We could distinguish the young only by their greater activity and their ceaseless curiosity.

In the immediate vicinity of camp we found them first in gullies where the previous winter's snow had but recently disappeared. Here the grass was young and tender and of a flavor to suit their taste for delicacies. A little later they followed the musk ox to the shores of lagoons or to the wind-swept hills. Still later, as the winter snows blanketed the pastures and the bitter storms of night swept the cheerless drifts, they dug long tunnels under the snow for food, and when the storms were too severe remained housed in these feeding dugouts.

An animal of rare intelligence, the hare is quick to grasp an advantage, and therefore as winter advances we find it a constant companion of the musk ox. For in the diggings of the musk ox this little creature finds sufficient food uncovered for its needs.

With a skeleton as light as that of the bird and a skin as frail as paper it is nevertheless as well prepared to withstand the rigors of the Arctic as the bear with its clumsy anatomy. The entire makeup of the hare is based upon the highest strain of animal economy. It expends the greatest possible amount of energy at the cost of the least consumption of food. Its fur is as white as the boreal snows and absorbs color somewhat more readily. In a stream of crimson light it appears red and white; in a shadow of ice or in the darkness of night it assumes the subdued blue of the Polar world. Nature has bleached its fur seemingly to afford the best protection against the frigid chill, for a suitable white fur permits the escape of less bodily heat than any colored or shaded pelt.

The fox is its only real enemy, and the fox's chance of success is won only by superior cunning. Its protection against the fox lies in its lightning-like movement of the legs. When it scents danger it rises by a series of darts that could be followed only by birds. Its expenditure of muscular energy is so economical that it can continue its run for an almost indefinite time. Shooting along a few hundred paces, it then rises to rest in an erect posture. With its black-tipped ears in line with its back it makes a fascinating little bit of nature's handiwork. Again, when asleep, it curls up its legs carefully in the long fur of its body, and its everactive nose, with the divided lip, is then pushed into the long soft fur of the breast where the frost crystals are screened from the breath when storms carry drift snow. It is a fluffy ball of animation which provokes one's admiration.

Deprived as we were of most of the usual comforts of life, many things were taught us by the creatures about. From the hare, with its scrupulous attention to cleanliness, we learned how to cleanse our hands and faces. With no soap, no towels and very little water, we had some difficulty in trying to keep respectable appearances. The hare has the same problem to deal with, but it is provided by nature with a cleansing apparatus. Its own choice is the forepaw, but with its need for snow shoes the hind legs serve a very useful purpose, and then, too, the surface is developed, a surface covered with tough fur which, we discovered, possessed the quality of a wet sponge and did not require, for efficiency, either soap or water. With hare paws, therefore, we kept clean. These paws also served as napkins. To take the place of a basin and a towel we therefore gathered a supply of hare paws, enough to keep clean for at least six months.

The hare was a good mark for E-tuk-i-shook with the sling shot, and many fell victims to his primitive genius. Ah-we-lah, never an expert at stone slinging, became an adept with the bow and arrow. Usually he returned with at least a hare from every day's chase. Our main success resulted from a still more primitive device. Counting on its inquisitiveness we devised a chain of loop lines arranged across the hare's regular lines of travel. In playing and jumping through these loops, the animal tightened the lines and became our victim automatically.

The ptarmigan chase was possible only for Ah-we-lah. The bird was not at all shy, for it often came close to our den and scattered the snow like a chicken. It was too small a mark for the sling shot and only Ah-we-lah could give the arrow the precise direction for these feathered creatures. Altogether, fifteen were secured in our locality, and all served as dessert for my special benefit. According to Eskimo custom, a young, unmarried man or woman cannot eat the ptarmigan, or *"ahr-rish-shah,"* as they call it. That pleasure is reserved for the older people, and I did not for a moment risk the sacrilege of trying to change the custom. It was greatly to my advantage, for it not only impressed with suitable force my dignity as a superior Eskimo, but it enabled me to enjoy an entire bird at a time instead of only a teasing mouthful.

To us the ptarmigan was at all times fascinating, but it proved ever a thing of mystery. Descending from the skies at unexpected times it embarks again for haunts unknown. At times we saw the birds in great numbers. At other times they were absent for months. In summer the bird has gray and brown feathers, mingled with white. It keeps close to the inland ice, making its course along the snowy coast of Noonataks, beyond the reach of man or fox. Late in September it seeks the lower ground along the sea level.

Like the hare and the musk ox, it delights in windy places where the snow has been driven away. There it finds bits of moss and withered plants which satisfy its needs. The summer plumage is at first sight like that of the partridge. On close examination one finds the feathers are only tipped with color—underneath, the plumage is white. In winter it retains only the black feathers of its tail, otherwise it is as white as the hare. Its legs often are covered with tough fur, like that of the hare's lower hind legs. The meat is delicate in flavor and tender. It is the most beautiful of the four birds that remain in the white world when all is bleak during the night.

We sought the fox more diligently than the ptarmi-

gan. We had a more tangible way of securing it.
Furthermore, we were in great need of its skin.
E-tuk-i-shook and Ah-we-lah regarded fox hams as
quite a delicacy—a delicacy which I never willingly
shared when there were musk tenderloins about. We
had no steel traps, and with its usual craft the fox usually managed to evade our crude weapons by keeping
out of sight. Bone traps were made with a good deal of
care after the pattern of steel traps. We used a musk-ox
horn as a spring. But with these we were only partially
successful. As a last resort, little domes were arranged
in imitation of the usual caches, with trap stone doors.
In these we managed to secure fourteen white and two
blue animals. After that they proved too wise for our
craft.

The fox becomes shy only in the end of October,
when its fur begins to be really worth taking. Before
that it followed us everywhere on the musk ox quest, for
it was not slow to learn the advantage of being near our
battle scenes. We frequently left choice bits for its
picking, a favor which it seemed to appreciate by a careful watchfulness of our camps. Although a much more
cunning thief than the bear, we could afford its plunder-
ings, for it had not so keen a taste for blubber and its
capacity was limited. We thus got well acquainted.

Up to the present we had failed in the quest of the
seal. During the open season of summer, without a
kayak, we could not get near the animal. As the winter
and the night advanced, we were too busy with the land
animals to watch the blow-holes in the new ice. When
the sea is first spread with the thin sheet of colorless ice,
which later thickens, the seal rises to the surface, makes

a breathing hole, descends to its feeding grounds on the sea bottom for about ten minutes, then rises and makes another hole. This line of openings is arranged in a circle or a series of connecting, oblong lines, marking that particular seal's favorite feeding ground. Before the young ice is covered with snow, these breathing holes are easily located by a ring of white frost crystals, which condense and fall as the seal blows. But now that the winter had sheeted the black ice evenly with a white cover, the seal holes, though open, could not be found. We were not in need of either fat or meat, but the seal skins were to fill an important want. We required for boots and sled lashing the thin, tough seal hide. How could we get it?

From our underground den we daily watched the wanderings of the bears. They trailed along certain lines which we knew to be favorable feeding grounds for seals, but they did not seem to be successful. Could we not profit by their superb scenting instinct and find the blow-holes? The bear had been our worst enemy, but unconsciously it also proved to be our best friend.

We started out to trail the bear's footprints. By these we were led to the blow-holes, where we found the snow about had been circled with a regular trail. Most of these had been abandoned, for the seal has a scent as keen as the bear, but a few "live" holes were located. Sticks were placed to locate these, and after a few days' careful study and hard work we harpooned six seals. Taking only the skins and blubber, we left the carcasses for bruin's share of the chase—to be consumed later. We did not hunt together with the bear—at least, not knowingly.

In these wanderings over game lands we were

permitted a very close scrutiny of the animals about, and it was at this time that I came to certain definite conclusions as to prevailing laws of color and dress of our co-habitants of the Polar wastes.

The animals of the Arctic assume a color in accordance to their need for heat transmission. The prevailing influence is white, as light furs permit the least escape of heat. It is evidently more important to confine the heat of the body, than to gather heat from the sun's feeble rays. The necessity for bleaching the furry raiment becomes most operative in winter when the temperature of the air is 150° below that of the body. In the summer, when the continued sunshine is made more heating by the piercing influence of the reflecting snow-fields, there is a tendency to absorb heat. Then nature darkens the skin, which absorbs heat accordingly.

The relative advantage of light and dark shades can be easily demonstrated by placing pieces of white and black cloth on a surface of snow, with a slope at right angles to the sun's rays. If, after a few hours, the cloth is removed the snow under the black cloth will be melted considerably, while that under the white cloth will show little effect.

Nature makes use of this law of physics to ease the hard lot of its creatures fighting the weather in the icy world. The laws of color protection as advocated in the rules of natural selection are not operative here, because of the vitally important demand of heat economy. If we now seek the problem of nature's body colored dyes, with heat economy as the key, our calculations will become easy. The serwah, a species of guillemot, which is as black as the raven in summer, is white in winter. The ptarmigan is light as pearl in winter, but its feathers become tipped with amber in summer. The hare is slightly gray in summer, but, in winter, becomes white as the snow under which it finds food and shelter.

The white fox is gray in summer, the blue fox darkens as the sun advances, while its under fur becomes lighter with increasing cold. The caribou is dark brown as it grazes the moss-colored fields, but becomes nearly white with the permanent snows. The polar bear, as white as nature can make it, with only blubber to mix its paints, basks in the midnight sun with a raiment suggestive of gold. The musk ox changes its dark under-fur for a lighter shade. The raven has a white under-coat in winter. The rat is gray in summer but bleaches to blue-gray in winter time. The laws of selection and heat economy are thus combined.

While thus preparing for the coming winter by seeking animals with furry pelts, the weather conditions made our task increasingly difficult. The storm of the descending sun whipped the seas into white fury and brushed the lands with icy clouds. With the descent of the sun, nature again set its seal of gloom on Arctic life. The cheer of a sunny heaven was blotted from the skies, and the coming of the winter blackness was signalled by the beginning of a warfare of the elements. All hostile nature was now set loose to expend its restive battle energy.

For brief moments the weather was quiet, and then in awe-inspiring silence we steered for sequestered gullies in quest of little creatures. This death-like stillness was in harmony with our loneliness. As the sea was stilled by the iron bonds of frost, as life sought protection under the storm-driven snows of land, the winds, growing even wilder, beat a maddening onslaught over the dead, frozen world. The thunder of elements shook the very rocks under which we slept. Then again would fall a spell of that strange silence—all was dead, the sun glowed no more, the creatures of the wilds were hushed. We were all alone—alone in a vast, white dead world.

LEMMING

A HUNDRED NIGHTS IN AN UNDER-
GROUND DEN

LIVING LIKE MEN OF THE STONE AGE—THE DESOLATION
OF THE LONG NIGHT—LIFE ABOUT CAPE SPARBO—
PREPARING EQUIPMENT FOR THE RETURN TO GREEN-
LAND—SUNRISE, FEBRUARY 11, 1909

XXVIII

LIFE ABOUT CAPE SPARBO

The coming night slowly fixed its seal on our field
of activity. Early in August the sun had dipped under
the icy contour of North Lincoln, and Jones Sound had
then begun to spread its cover of crystal. The warm
rays gradually melted in a perpetual blue frost. The
air thickened. The land darkened. The days shortened.
The night lengthened. The Polar cold and darkness
of winter came hand in hand.

Late in September the nights had become too dark
to sleep in the open, with inquisitive bears on every side.
Storms, too, increased thereafter and deprived us of the
cheer of colored skies. Thus we were now forced to
seek a retreat in our underground den.

We took about as kindly to this as a wild animal
does to a cage. For over seven months we had wandered
over vast plains of ice, with a new camp site almost

every day. We had grown accustomed to a wandering
life like that of the bear, but we had not developed his
hibernating instinct. We were anxious to continue our
curious battle of life.

In October the bosom of the sea became blanketed,
and the curve of the snow-covered earth was polarized
in the eastern skies. The final period for the death of
day and earthly glory was advancing, but Nature in her
last throes displayed some of her most alluring phases.
The colored silhouette of the globe was perhaps the most
remarkable display. In effect, this was a shadow of the
earth thrown into space. By the reflected, refracted
and polarized light of the sun, the terrestrial shadows
were outlined against the sky in glowing colors. Seen
occasionally in other parts of the globe, it is only in the
Polar regions, with its air of crystal and its surface of
mirrors, that the proper mediums are afforded for this
gigantic spectral show.

We had an ideal location. A glittering sea, with a
level horizon, lay along the east and west. The weather
was good, the skies were clear, and, as the sun sank, the
sky over it was flushed with orange or gold. This
gradually paled, and over the horizon opposite there
rose an arc in feeble prismatic colors with a dark zone
of purple under it. The arc rose as the sun settled; the
purple spread beyond the polarized bow; and gradually
the heavens turned a deep purple blue to the zenith,
while the halo of the globe was slowly lost in its own
shadow.

The colored face of the earth painted on the screen
of the heavens left the last impression of worldly charm
on the retina. In the end of October the battle of the

elements, storms attending the setting of the sun, began to blast the air into a chronic fury. By this time we were glad to creep into our den and await the vanishing weeks of ebbing day.

In the doom of night to follow, there would at least be some quiet moments during which we could stretch our legs. The bears, which had threatened our existence, were now kept off by a new device which served the purpose for a time. We had food and fuel enough for the winter. There should have been nothing to have disturbed our tempers, but the coming of the long blackness makes all Polar life ill at ease.

Early in November the storms ceased long enough to give us a last fiery vision. With a magnificent cardinal flame the sun rose, gibbered in the sky and sank behind the southern cliffs on November 3. It was not to rise again until February 11 of the next year. We were therefore doomed to hibernate in our underground den for at least a hundred double nights before the dawn of a new day opened our eyes.

The days now came and went in short order. For hygienic reasons we kept up the usual routine of life. The midday light soon darkened to twilight. The moon and stars appeared at noon. The usual partition of time disappeared. All was night, unrelieved darkness, midnight, midday, morning or evening.

We stood watches of six hours each to keep the fires going, to keep off the bears and to force an interest in a blank life. We knew that we were believed to be dead. For our friends in Greenland would not ascribe to us the luck which came after our run of abject misfortune. This thought inflicted perhaps the greatest pain of the queer prolongation of life which was permitted us. It was loneliness, frigid loneliness. I wondered whether men ever felt so desolately alone.

We could not have been more thoroughly isolated if we had been transported to the surface of the moon. I find myself utterly unable to outline the emptiness of our existence. In other surroundings we never grasp the full meaning of the word "alone." When it is possible to put a foot out of doors into sunlight without the risk of a bear-paw on your neck it is also possible to run off a spell of blues, but what were we to do with every dull rock rising as a bear ghost and with the torment of a satanic blackness to blind us?

With the cheer of day, a kindly nature and a new friend, it is easy to get in touch with a sympathetic chord. The mere thought of another human heart within touch, even a hundred miles away, would have eased the suspense of the silent void. But we could entertain no such hopefulness. We were all alone in a world where every pleasant aspect of nature had deserted us. Although three in number, a bare necessity had compressed us into a single composite individuality.

There were no discussions, no differences of opinion. We had been too long together under bitter circumstances to arouse each other's interest. A single individual could not live long in our position. A selfish instinct tightened a fixed bond to preserve and protect one another. As a battle force we made a formidable unit, but there was no matches to start the fires of inspiration.

The half darkness of midday and the moonlight still permitted us to creep from under the ground and seek a few hours in the open. The stone and bone fox traps and the trap caves for the bears which we had built during the last glimmer of day offered an occupation with some recreation. But we were soon deprived of this.

Bears headed us off at every turn. We were not permitted to proceed beyond an enclosed hundred feet from the hole of our den. Not an inch of ground or a morsel of food was permitted us without a contest. It was a fight of nature against nature. We either actually saw the little sooty nostrils with jets of vicious breath rising, and the huge outline of a wild beast ready to spring on us, or imagined we saw it. With no adequate means of defense we were driven to imprisonment within the walls of our own den.

From within, our position was even more tantalizing. The bear thieves dug under the snows over our heads and snatched blocks of blubber fuel from under our very eyes at the port without a consciousness of wrongdoing. Occasionally we ventured out to deliver a lance, but each time the bear would make a leap for the door and would have entered had the opening been large enough. In other cases we shot arrows through the peep-hole. A bear head again would burst through the silk covered window near the roof, where knives, at close range and in good light, could be driven with sweet vengeance.

As a last resort we made a hole through the top of the den. When a bear was heard near, a long torch was pushed through. The snow for acres about was then suddenly flashed with a ghostly whiteness which almost frightened us. But the bear calmly took advantage of the light to pick a larger piece of the blubber upon which our lives depended, and then with an air of superiority he would move into the brightest light, usually within a few feet of our peep-hole, where we could almost touch his hateful skin. Without ammunition we were helpless.

Two weeks after sunset we heard the last cry of ravens. After a silence of several days they suddenly descended with a piercing shout which cut the frosty stillness. We crept out of our den quickly to read the riddle of the sudden bluster. There were five ravens on five different rocks, and the absence of the celestial color gave them quite an appropriate setting. They were restless: there was no food for them. A fox had preceded them with his usual craftiness, and had left no pickings for feathered creatures.

A family of five had gathered about in October, when the spoils of the chase were being cached, and we encouraged their stay by placing food for them regularly. Some times a sly fox, and at other times a thieving bear, got the little morsels, but there were usually sufficient picking for the raven's little crop. They had found a suitable cave high up in the great cliffs of granite behind our den.

We were beginning to be quite friendly. My Eskimo companions ascribed to the birds almost human qualities and they talked to them reverently, thereby displaying their heart's desire. The secrets of the future were all entrusted to their consideration. Would the "too-loo-ah" go to Eskimo Lands and deliver their messages? The raven said "ka-ah" (yes).

E-tuk-i-shook said: "Go and take the tears from An-na-do-a's eyes; tell her that I am alive and well and will come to take her soon. Tell Pan-ic-pa (his father) that I am in Ah-ming-ma-noona (Musk Ox Land). Bring us some powder to blacken the bear's snout."

"Ka-ah, ka-ah," said the two ravens at once.

Ah-we-lah began an appeal to drive off the bears and to set the raven spirits as guardians of our blubber caches. This was uttered in shrill shouts, and then, in a low, trembling voice, he said: "Dry the tears of mother's cheeks and tell her that we are in a land of todnu (tallow)."

"Ka-ah," replied the raven.

"Then go to Ser-wah; tell her not to marry that lazy gull, Ta-tamh; tell her that Ah-we-lah's skin is still flushed with thoughts of her, that he is well and will return to claim her in the first moon after sunrise."

"Ka-ah, ka-ah, ka-ah," said the raven, and rose as if to deliver the messages.

For the balance of that day we saw only three ravens. The two had certainly started for the Greenland shores. The other three, after an engorgement, rose to their cave and went to sleep for the night as we thought. No more was seen of them until the dawn of day of the following year.

A few days later we also made other acquaintances. They were the most interesting bits of life that crossed our trail, and in the dying effort to seek animal companionship our soured tempers were sweetened somewhat by four-footed joys.

A noise had been heard for several successive days at eleven o'clock. This was the time chosen by the bears for their daily exercise along our foot-path, and we were usually all awake with a knife or a lance in hand, not because there was any real danger, for our house cemented by ice was as secure as a fort, but because we felt more comfortable in a battle attitude. Through the peep-hole we saw them marching up and down along the foot-path tramped down by our daily spells of leg-stretching.

They were feasting on the aroma of our foot-prints, and when they left it was usually safe for us to venture out. Noises, however, continued within the walls of the den. It was evident that there was something alive at close range.

We were lonely enough to have felt a certain delight in shaking hands even with bruin if the theft of our blubber had not threatened the very foundation of our existence. For in the night we could not augment our supplies; and without fat, fire and water were impossible. No! there was not room for man and bear at Cape Sparbo. Without ammunition, however, we were nearly helpless.

But noises continued after bruin's steps came with a decreasing metallic ring from distant snows. There was a scraping and a scratching within the very walls of our den. We had a neighbor and a companion. Who, or what, could it be? We were kept in suspense for some time. When all was quiet at the time which we chose to call midnight, a little blue rat came out and began to tear the bark from our willow lamp trimmer.

I was on watch, awake, and punched E-tuk-i-shook without moving my head. His eyes opened with surprise on the busy rodent, and Ah-we-lah was kicked. He turned over and the thing jumped into a rock crevasse.

The next day we risked the discomfort of bruin's interview and dug up an abundance of willow roots for our new tenant. These were arranged in appetizing display and the rat came out very soon and helped himself, but he permitted no familiarity. We learned to love the creature, however, all the more because of its shyness. By alternate jumps from the roots to seclusion it managed to fill up with all it could carry. Then it disappeared as suddenly as it came.

In the course of two days it came back with a companion, its mate. They were beautiful little creatures, but little larger than mice. They had soft, fluffy fur of a pearl blue color, with pink eyes. They had no tails. Their dainty little feet were furred to the claw tips with silky hair. They made a picture of animal delight which really aroused us from stupor to little spasms of enthusiasm. A few days were spent in testing our intentions. Then they arranged a berth just above my head and became steady boarders.

Their confidence and trust flattered our vanity and we treated them as royal guests. No trouble was too great for us to provide them with suitable delicacies. We ventured into the darkness and storms for hours to dig up savory roots and mosses. A little stage was arranged every day with the suitable footlights. In the eagerness to prolong the rodent theatricals, the little things were fed over and over, until they became too fat and too lazy to creep from their berths.

They were good, clean orderly camp fellows, always kept in their places and never ventured to borrow our bed furs, nor did they disturb our eatables. With a keen sense of justice, and an aristocratic air, they passed our plates of carnivorous foods without venturing a taste, and went to their herbivorous piles of sod delicacies. About ten days before midnight they went to sleep and did not wake for more than a month. Again we were alone. Now even the bears deserted us.

In the dull days of blankness which followed, few incidents seemed to mark time. The cold increased. Storms were more continuous and came with greater force. We were cooped up in our underground den with but a peep-hole through the silk of our old tent to watch the sooty nocturnal bluster. We were face to face with a spiritual famine. With little recreation, no amusements, no interesting work, no reading matter, with nothing to talk about, the six hours of a watch were spread out to weeks.

We had no sugar, no coffee, not a particle of civilized food. We had meat and blubber, good and wholesome food at that. But the stomach wearied of its never changing carnivorous stuffing. The dark den, with its walls of pelt and bone, its floor decked with frosted tears of ice, gave no excuse for cheer. Insanity, abject madness, could only be avoided by busy hands and long sleep.

My life in this underground place was, I suppose, like that of a man in the stone age. The interior was damp and cold and dark; with our pitiable lamps burning, the temperature of the top was fairly moderate, but at the bottom it was below zero. Our bed was a platform of rocks wide enough for three prostrate men. Its forward edge was our seat when awake. Before this was a space where a deeper hole in the earth permitted us to stand upright, one at a time. There, one by one, we dressed and occasionally stood to move our stiff and aching limbs.

On either side of this standing space was half a tin plate in which musk-ox fat was burned. We used moss as a wick. These lights were kept burning day and night; it was a futile, imperceptible sort of heat they gave. Except when we got close to the light, it was impossible to see one another's faces.

We ate twice daily—without enjoyment. We had few matches, and in fear of darkness tended our lamps diligently. There was no food except meat and tallow; most of the meat, by choice, was eaten raw and frozen. Night and morning we boiled a small pot of meat for broth; but we had no salt to season it. Stooped and cramped, day by day, I found occasional relief from the haunting horror of this life by rewriting the almost illegible notes made on our journey.

My most important duty was the preparation of my notes and observations for publication. This would afford useful occupation and save months of time afterwards. But I had no paper. My three note books were full, and there remained only a small pad of prescription blanks and two miniature memorandum books. I resolved, however, to try to work out the outline of my narrative in chapters in these. I had four good pencils and one eraser. These served a valuable purpose. With sharp points I shaped the words in small letters. When the skeleton of the book was ready I was surprised to find how much could be crowded on a few small pages. By a liberal use of the eraser many parts of pages were cleared of unnecessary notes. Entire lines were written between all the lines of the note books, the pages thus carrying two narrations or series of notes.

By the use of abbreviations and dashes, a kind of short-hand was devised. My art of space economy complete, I began to write, literally developing the very useful habit of carefully shaping every idea before an attempt was made to use the pencil. In this way my entire book and several articles were written. Charts, films and advertisement boxes were covered. In all 150,000 words were written, and absolute despair, which in idleness opens the door to madness, was averted.

Our needs were still urgent enough to enforce much other work. Drift threatened to close the entrance to our dungeon and this required frequent clearing. Blubber for the lamp was sliced and pounded every day. The meat corner was occasionally stocked, for it required several days to thaw out the icy musk ox quarters. Ice was daily gathered and placed within reach to keep the water pots full. The frost which was condensed out of our breaths made slabs of ice on the floor, and this required occasional removal. The snow under our bed furs, which had a similar origin, was brushed out now and then.

Soot from the lamps, a result of bad housekeeping, which a proud Eskimo woman would not have tolerated for a minute, was scraped from the bone rafters about once a week. With a difference of one hundred degrees between the breathing air of the den and that outside there was a rushing interchanging breeze through every pinhole and crevice. The ventilation was good. The camp cleanliness could almost have been called hygienic, although no baths had been indulged in for six months, and then only by an unavoidable, undesirable accident.

Much had still to be done to prepare for our home-going in the remote period beyond the night. It was necessary to plan and make a new equipment. The sledge, the clothing, the camp outfit, everything which had been used in the previous campaign, were worn out. Something could be done by judicious repairing, but nearly everything required reconstruction. In the new arrangement we were to take the place of the dogs at the traces and the sledge loads must be prepared accordingly. There was before us an unknown line of trouble for three hundred miles before we could step on Greenland shores. It was only the hope of homegoing, which gave some mental strength in the night of gloom. Musk ox meat was now cut into strips and dried over the lamps. Tallow was prepared and moulded in portable form for fuel.

But in spite of all efforts we gradually sank to the lowest depths of the Arctic midnight. The little mid-day glimmer on the southern sky became indiscernible. Only the swing of the Great Dipper and other stars told the time of the day or night. We had fancied that the persistent wind ruffled our tempers. But now it was still; not a breath of air moved the heavy blackness. In that very stillness we found reasons for complaint. Storms were preferable to the dead silence; anything was desirable to stir the spirits to action.

Still the silence was only apparent. Wind noises floated in the frosty distance; cracking rocks, exploding glaciers and tumbling avalanches kept up a muffled rumbling which the ear detected only when it rested on the floor rock of our bed. The temperature was low—

—48° F.—so low that at times the very air seemed to crack. Every creature of the wild had been buried in drift; all nature was asleep. In our dungeon all was a mental blank.

Not until two weeks after midnight did we awake to a proper consciousness of life. The faint brightness of the southern skies at noon opened the eye to spiritual dawn. The sullen stupor and deathlike stillness vanished.

Shortly after black midnight descended I began to experience a curious psychological phenomenon. The stupor of the days of travel wore away, and I began to see myself as in a mirror. I can explain this no better. It is said that a man falling from a great height usually has a picture of his life flashed through his brain in the short period of descent. I saw a similar cycle of events.

The panorama began with incidents of childhood, and it seems curious now with what infinite detail I saw people whom I had long forgotten, and went through the most trivial experiences. In successive stages every phase of life appeared and was minutely examined; every hidden recess of gray matter was opened to interpret the biographies of self-analysis. The hopes of my childhood and the discouragements of my youth filled me with emotion; feelings of pleasure and sadness came as each little thought picture took definite shape; it seemed hardly possible that so many things, potent for good and bad, could have been done in so few years. I saw myself, not as a voluntary being, but rather as a resistless atom, predestined in its course, being carried on by an inexorable fate.

Meanwhile our preparations for return were being

accomplished. This work had kept us busy during all of the wakeful spells of the night. Much still remained to be done.

Although real pleasure followed all efforts of physical labor, the balking muscles required considerable urging. Musk ox meat was cut into portable blocks, candles were made, fur skins were dressed and chewed, boots, stockings, pants, shirts, sleeping bags were made. The sledge was re-lashed, things were packed in bags. All was ready about three weeks before sunrise. Although the fingers and the jaws were thus kept busy, the mind and also the heart were left free to wander.

In the face of all our efforts to ward aside the ill effects of the night we gradually became its victims. Our skin paled, our strength failed, the nerves weakened, and the mind ultimately became a blank. The most notable physical effect, however, was the alarming irregularity of the heart.

In the locomotion of human machinery the heart is the motor. Like all good motors it has a governor which requires some adjustment. In the Arctic, where the need of regulation is greatest, the facilities for adjustment are withdrawn. In normal conditions, as the machine of life pumps the blood which drives all, its force and its regularity are governed by the never-erring sunbeams. When these are withdrawn, as they are in the long night, the heart pulsations become irregular; at times slow, at other times spasmodic.

Light seems to be as necessary to the animal as to the plant. A diet of fresh meat, healthful hygienic surroundings, play for the mind, recreation for the body, and strong heat from open fires, will help; but only the return of the heaven-given sun will properly adjust the motor of man.

As the approaching day brightened to a few hours of twilight at midday, we developed a mood for animal companionship. A little purple was now thrown on the blackened snows. The weather was good. All the usual sounds of nature were suspended, but unusual sounds came with a weird thunder. The very earth began to shake in an effort to break the seal of frost. For several days nothing moved into our horizon which could be imagined alive.

About two weeks before sunrise the rats woke and began to shake their beautiful blue fur in graceful little dances, but they were not really alive and awake in a rat sense for several days. At about the same time the ravens began to descend from their hiding place and screamed for food. There were only three; two were still conversing with the Eskimo maidens far away, as my companions thought.

In my subsequent strolls I found the raven den and to my horror discovered that the two were frozen. I did not deprive E-tuk-i-shook and Ah-we-lah of their poetic dream; the sad news of raven bereavement was never told.

The foxes now began to bark from a safe distance and advanced to get their share of the camp spoils. Ptarmigan shouted from nearby rocks. Wolves were heard away in the musk ox fields, but they did not venture to pay us a visit.

The bear that had shadowed us everywhere before midnight was the last to claim our friendship at dawn.

There were good reasons for this which we did not learn until later. The bear stork had arrived. But really we had changed heart even towards the bear. Long before he returned we were prepared to give him a welcome reception. In our new and philosophical turn of mind we thought better of bruin. In our greatest distress during the previous summer he had kept us alive. In our future adventures he might perform a similar mission. After all he had no sporting proclivities; he did not hunt or trouble us for the mere fun of our discomfort or the chase. His aim in life was the very serious business of getting food. Could we blame him? Had we not a similar necessity?

A survey of our caches proved that we were still rich in the coin of the land. There remained meat and blubber sufficient for all our needs, with considerable to spare for other empty stomachs. So, to feed the bear, meat was piled up in heaps for his delight.

The new aroma rose into the bleaching night air. We peeped with eager eyes through our ports to spot results. The next day at eleven o'clock footsteps were heard. The noise indicated caution and shyness instead of the bold quick step which we knew so well. There was room for only one eye and only one man at a time at the peep-hole, and so we took turns. Soon the bear was sighted, proceeding with the utmost caution behind some banks and rocks. The blue of the snows, with yellow light, dyed his fur to an ugly green. He was thin and gaunt and ghostly. There was the stealth and the cunning of the fox in his movements. But he could not get his breakfast, the first after a fast of weeks, without coming squarely into our view.

The den was buried under the winter snows and did not disturb the creature, but the size of the pile of meat did disturb its curiosity. When within twenty-five yards, a few sudden leaps were made, and the ponderous claws came down on a walrus shoulder. His teeth began to grind like a stone cutter. For an hour the bear stood there and displayed itself to good advantage. Our hatred of the creature entirely vanished.

Five days passed before that bear returned. In the meantime we longed for it to come back. We had unconsciously developed quite a brotherly bear interest. In the period which followed we learned that eleven o'clock was the hour, and that five days was the period between meals. The bear calendar and the clock were consulted with mathematical precision.

We also learned that our acquaintance was a parent. By a little exploration in February we discovered the bear den, in a snow covered cave, less than a mile west. In it were two saucy little teddies in pelts of white silk that would have gladdened the heart of any child. The mother was not at home at the time, and we were not certain enough of her friendship, or of her whereabouts, to play with the twins.

With a clearing horizon and a wider circle of friendship our den now seemed a cheerful home. Our spirits awakened as the gloom of the night was quickly lost in the new glitter of day.

On the eleventh of February the snow-covered slopes of North Devon glowed with the sunrise of 1909. The sun had burst nature's dungeon. Cape Sparbo glowed with golden light. The frozen sea glittered with hills of shimmering lilac. We escaped to a joyous freedom. With a reconstructed sled, new equipment and newly acquired energy we were ready to pursue the return journey to Greenland and fight the last battle of the Polar campaign.

GUILLEMOT

HOMEWARD WITH A HALF SLEDGE AND HALF-FILLED STOMACHS

THREE HUNDRED MILES THROUGH STORM AND SNOW AND
UPLIFTED MOUNTAINS OF ICE TROUBLES—DISCOVER
TWO ISLANDS—ANNOATOK IS REACHED—MEETING
HARRY WHITNEY—NEWS OF PEARY'S SEIZURE OF
SUPPLIES

XXIX

BACK TO GREENLAND FRIENDS

On February 18, 1908, the reconstructed sledge was taken beyond the ice fort and loaded for the home run. We had given up the idea of journeying to Lancaster Sound to await the whalers. There were no Eskimos on the American side nearer than Pond's Inlet. It was somewhat farther to our headquarters on the Greenland shores, but all interests would be best served by a return to Annoatok.

During the night we had fixed all of our attention upon the return journey, and had prepared a new equipment with the limited means at our command; but, traveling in the coldest season of the year, it was necessary to carry a cumbersome outfit of furs, and furthermore, since we were to take the place of the dogs in the traces, we could not expect to transport supplies for more than thirty days. In this time, however, we hoped to reach Cape Sabine, where the father of E-tuk-i-shook had been told to place a cache of food for us.

Starting so soon after sunrise, the actual daylight proved very brief, but a brilliant twilight gave a remarkable illumination from eight to four. The light of dawn and that of the afterglow was tossed to and fro in the heavens, from reflecting surfaces of glitter, for four hours preceding and following midday. To use this play of light to the best advantage, it was necessary to begin preparations early by starlight; and thus, when the dim purple glow from the northeast brightened the dull gray-blue of night, the start was made for Greenland shores and for home.

We were dressed in heavy furs. The temperature was —49°. A light air brushed the frozen mist out of Jones Sound, and cut our sooty faces. The sled was overloaded, and the exertion required for its movement over the groaning snow was tremendous. A false, almost hysterical, enthusiasm lighted our faces, but the muscles were not yet equal to the task set for them.

Profuse perspiration came with the first hours of dog work, and our heavy fur coats were exchanged for the sealskin *nitshas* (lighter coat). At noon the snows were fired and the eastern skies burned in great lines of flame. But there was no sun and no heat. We sat on the sledge for a prolonged period, gasping for breath and drinking the new celestial glory so long absent from our outlook. As the joy of color was lost in the cold purple of half-light, our shoulders were braced more vigorously into the traces. The ice proved good, but the limit of strength placed camp in a snowhouse ten miles from our winter den. With the new equipment, our camp life now was not like that of the Polar campaign. Dried musk ox meat and strips of musk fat made a steady diet. Moulded tallow served as fuel in a crescent-shaped disk of tin, in which carefully prepared moss was crushed and arranged as a wick. Over this primitive fire we managed to melt enough ice to quench thirst, and also to make an occasional pot of broth as a luxury. While the drink was liquefying, the chill of the snow igloo was also moderated, and we crept into the bags of musk ox skins, where agreeable repose and home dreams made us forget the cry of the stomach and the torment of the cold.

At the end of eight days of forced marches we reached Cape Tennyson. The disadvantage of manpower, when compared to dog motive force, was clearly shown in this effort. The ice was free of pressure troubles and the weather was endurable. Still, with the best of luck, we had averaged only about seven miles daily. With dogs, the entire run would have been made easily in two days.

As we neared the land two small islands were discovered. Both were about one thousand feet high, with precipitous sea walls, and were on a line about two miles east of Cape Tennyson. The most easterly was about one and a half miles long, east to west, with a cross-section, north to south, of about three-quarters of a mile. About half a mile to the west of this was a much smaller island. There was no visible vegetation, and no life was seen, although hare and fox tracks were crossed on the ice. I decided to call the larger island E-tuk-i-shook, and the smaller Ah-we-lah. These rocks will stand as monuments to the memory of my faithful savage comrades when all else is forgotten.

From Cape Tennyson to Cape Isabella the coast of Ellesmere Land was charted, in the middle of the last century, by ships at a great distance from land.   Little has been added since.   The wide belt of pack thrown against the coast made further exploration from the ship very difficult, but in our northward march over the sea-ice it was hoped that we might keep close enough to the shores to examine the land carefully.

A few Eskimos had, about fifty years previously, wandered along this ice from Pond's Inlet to the Greenland camps.   They left the American shores because famine, followed by forced cannibalism, threatened to exterminate the tribe.   A winter camp had been placed on Coburg Island.   Here many walruses and bears were secured during the winter, while in summer, from Kent Island, many guillemots were secured.   In moving from these northward, by skin boat and *kayak,* they noted myriads of guillemots, or "acpas," off the southeast point of the mainland.   There being no name in the Eskimo vocabulary for this land, it was called Acpohon, or "The Home of Guillemots."   The Greenland Eskimos had previously called the country "Ah-ming-mah Noona," or Musk Ox Land, but they also adopted the name of Acpohon, so we have taken the liberty of spreading the name over the entire island as a general name for the most northern land west of Greenland. In pushing northward, many of the Eskimos starved, and the survivors had a bitter fight for subsistence.   Our experience was similar.

Near Cape Paget those ancient Eskimos made a

PUNCTURED CANVAS BOAT IN WHICH WE PADDLED 1,000 MILES
FAMINE DAYS WHEN ONLY STRAY BIRDS PREVENTED STARVATION
DEN IN WHICH WERE SPENT 100 DOUBLE NIGHTS

BULL FIGHTS WITH THE MUSK OX ABOUT CAPE SPARBO

second winter camp. Here narwhals and bears were secured, and through Talbot's Fiord a short pass was discovered over Ellesmere Land to the musk ox country of the west shores. The Eskimos who survived the second winter reached the Greenland shores during the third summer. There they introduced the *kayak,* and also the bow and arrow. Their descendants are to-day the most intelligent of the most northern Eskimos.

To my companions the environment of the new land which we were passing was in the nature of digging up ancient history. Several old camp sites were located, and E-tuk-i-shook, whose grandfather was one of the old pioneers, was able to tell us the incidents of each camp with remarkable detail.

As a rule, however, it was very difficult to get near the land. Deep snows, huge pressure lines of ice, and protruding glaciers forced our line of march far from the Eskimo ruins which we wished to examine. From Cape Tennyson to Cape Clarence the ice near the open water proved fairly smooth, but the humid saline surface offered a great resistance to the metal plates of the sled. Here ivory or bone plates would have lessened the friction very much. A persistent northerly wind also brought the ice and the humid discomfort of our breath back to our faces with painful results. During several days of successive storms we were imprisoned in the domes of snow. By enforced idleness we were compelled to use a precious store of food and fuel, without making any necessary advance.

Serious difficulties were encountered in moving from Cape Clarence to Cape Faraday. Here the ice was tumbled into mountains of trouble. Tremendous

snowdrifts and persistent gales from the west made
traveling next to impossible, and, with no game and no
food supply in prospect, I knew that to remain idle
would be suicidal. The sledge load was lightened, and
every scrap of fur which was not absolutely necessary
was thrown away. The humid boots, stockings and
sealskin coats could not be dried out, for fuel was more
precious than clothing. All of this was discarded, and,
with light sleds and reduced rations, we forced along
over hummocks and drift. In all of our Polar march
we had seen no ice which offered so much hardship as
did this so near home shores. The winds again cut
gashes across our faces. With overwork and insufficient food, our furs hung on bony eminences over shriveled skins.

At the end of thirty-five days of almost ceaseless
toil we managed to reach Cape Faraday. Our food
was gone. We were face to face with the most desperate problem which had fallen to our long run of hard
luck. Famine confronted us. We were far from the
haunts of game; we had seen no living thing for a
month. Every fiber of our bodies quivered with cold
and hunger. In desperation we ate bits of skin and
chewed tough walrus lines. A half candle and three
cups of hot water served for several meals. Some
tough walrus hide was boiled and eaten with relish.
While trying to masticate this I broke some of my teeth.
It was hard on the teeth, but easy on the stomach, and
it had the great advantage of dispelling for prolonged
periods the pangs of hunger. But only a few strips of
walrus line were left after this was used.

Traveling, as we must, in a circuitous route, there

was still a distance of one hundred miles between us and Cape Sabine, and the distance to Greenland might, by open water, be spread to two hundred miles. This unknown line of trouble could not be worked out in less than a month. Where, I asked in desperation, were we to obtain subsistence for that last thirty days?

To the eastward, a line of black vapors indicated open water about twenty-five miles off shore. There were no seals on the ice. There were no encouraging signs of life; only old imprints of bears and foxes were left on the surface of the cheerless snows at each camp. For a number of days we had placed our last meat as bait to attract the bears, but none had ventured to pay us a visit. The offshore wind and the nearness of the open water gave us some life from this point.

Staggering along one day, we suddenly saw a bear track. These mute marks, seen in the half-dark of the snow, filled us with a wild resurgence of hope for life. On the evening of March 20 we prepared cautiously for the coming of the bear.

A snowhouse was built, somewhat stronger than usual; before it a shelf was arranged with blocks of snow, and on this shelf attractive bits of skin were arranged to imitate the dark outline of a recumbent seal. Over this was placed a looped line, through which the head and neck must go in order to get the bait. Other loops were arranged to entangle the feet. All the lines were securely fastened to solid ice. Peepholes were cut in all sides of the house, and a rear port was cut, from which we might escape or make an attack. Our lances and knives were now carefully sharpened. When all was ready, one of us remained on watch while the

others sought a needed sleep. We had not long to
wait.   Soon a crackling sound on the snows gave the
battle call, and with a little black nose extended from a
long neck, a vicious creature advanced.

Through our little eye-opening and to our empty
stomach he appeared gigantic.   Apparently as hungry
as we were, he came in straight reaches for the bait.
The run port was opened.   Ah-we-lah and E-tuk-i-
shook emerged, one with a lance, the other with a spiked
harpoon shaft.   Our lance, our looped line, our bow
and arrow, I knew, however, would be futile.

During the previous summer, when I foresaw a
time of famine, I had taken my four last cartridges and
hid them in my clothing.   Of the existence of these, the
two boys knew nothing.   These were to be used at the
last stage of hunger, to kill something—or ourselves.
That desperate time had not arrived till now.

The bear approached in slow, measured steps,
smelling the ground where the skin lay.

I jerked the line.   The loop tightened about the
bear's neck.   At the same moment the lance and the
spike were driven into the growling creature.

A fierce struggle ensued.   I withdrew one of the
precious cartridges from my pocket, placed it in my
gun, and gave the gun to Ah-we-lah, who took aim
and fired.   When the smoke cleared, the bleeding bear
lay on the ground.

We skinned the animal, and devoured the warm,
steaming flesh.   Strength revived.   Here were food
and fuel in abundance.   We were saved! With the
success of this encounter, we could sit down and live
comfortably for a month; and before that time should

elapse seals would seek the ice for sun baths, and when seals arrived, the acquisition of food for the march to Greenland would be easy.

But we did not sit down.   Greenland was in sight; and, to an Eskimo, Greenland, with all of its icy discomforts, has attractions not promised in heaven.   In this belief, as in most others, I was Eskimo by this time. With very little delay, the stomach was spread with chops, and we stretched to a gluttonous sleep, only to awake with appetites that permitted of prolonged stuffing.   It was a matter of economy to fill up and thus make the sled load lighter.   When more eating was impossible we began to move for home shores, dragging a sled overloaded with the life-saving prize.

A life of trouble, however, lay before us.   Successive storms, mountains of jammed ice, and deep snow, interrupted our progress and lengthened the course over circuitous wastes of snowdrifts and blackened our horizon.   When, after a prodigious effort, Cape Sabine was reached, our food supply was again exhausted.*

---

*The Tragedies of Cape Sabine.—Cape Sabine has been the scene of one of the saddest Arctic tragedies—the death by starvation of most of the members of the Greely Expedition. Several modern travelers, including Mr. Peary, have, in passing here, taken occasion to criticise adversely the management of this expedition. In his last series of articles in Hampton's Magazine, Peary has again attempted to throw discredit on General Greely. It is easy, after a lapse of forty years, to show the mistakes of our predecessors, and thereby attempt to belittle another's effort; but is it right? I have been at Cape Sabine in a half-starved condition, as General Greely was. I have watched the black seas of storm thunder the ice and rock walls, as he did; and I have looked longingly over the impassable stretches of death-dealing waters to a land of food and plenty, as he did. I did it, possessing the accumulated knowledge of the thirty years which have since passed, and I nearly succumbed in precisely the same manner as did the unfortunate victims of that expedition. The scientific results of the Lady Franklin Bay Expedition were so carefully and so thoroughly gathered that no expedition to the Arctic since has given value of equal

Here an old seal was found. It had been caught a year before and cached by Pan-ic-pa, the father of E-tuk-i-shook. With it was found a rude drawing spotted with sooty tears. This told the story of a loving father's fruitless search for his son and friends. The seal meat had the aroma of Limburger cheese, and age had changed its flavor; but, with no other food possible, our palates were easily satisfied. In an oil-soaked bag was found about a pound of salt. We ate this as sugar, for no salt had passed over our withered tongues for over a year.

The skin, blubber and meat were devoured with a relish. Every eatable part of the animal was packed on the sled as we left the American shore.

Smith Sound was free of ice, and open water extended sixty miles northward. A long detour was necessary to reach the opposite shores, but the Greenland shores were temptingly near. With light hearts and

importance. Greely's published record is an absolute proof of his ability as a leader and a vindication of the unfair insinuations of later rivals.

In passing along this same coast, E-tuk-i-shook called my attention to several graves, some of which we opened. In other places we saw human bones which had been left unburied. They were scattered, and had been picked by the ravens, the foxes and the wolves. With a good deal of sorrow and reserve I then learned one of the darkest unprinted pages of Arctic history. When the steamer *Erie* returned, in 1901, a large number of Eskimos were left with Mr. Peary near Cape Sabine. They soon after developed a disease which Mr. Peary's ship brought to them. There was no medicine and no doctor to save the dying victims. Dr. T. F. Dedrick, who had served Mr. Peary faithfully, was dismissed without the payment of his salary, because of a personal grudge, but Dedrick refused to go home and leave the expedition without medical help. He remained at Etah, living with the Eskimos in underground holes, as wild men do, sacrificing comfort and home interests for no other purpose except to maintain a clean record of helpfulness. As the winter and the night advanced, Dr. Dedrick got news that the Eskimos were sick and required medical assistance. He crossed the desperate reaches of Smith Sound at night, and offered Mr. Peary medical assistance to save the dying natives. Peary refused to allow Dedrick to attempt to cure the afflicted, crying people. Dedrick had been without civilized food for

cheering premonitions of home, we pushed along Bache Peninsula to a point near Cape Louis Napoleon. The horizon was now cleared of trouble. The ascending sun had dispelled the winter gloom of the land. Leaping streams cut through crystal gorges. The ice moved; the sea began to breathe. The snows sparkled with the promise of double days and midnight suns.

Life's buds had opened to full blossom. On the opposite shores, which now seemed near, Nature's incubators had long worked overtime to start the little ones of the wilds. Tiny bears danced to their mothers' call; baby seals sunned in downy pelts. Little foxes were squinting at school in learning the art of sight. In the wave of germinating joys our suppressed nocturnal passions rose with surprise anew. We were raised to an Arctic paradise.

As it lay in prospect, Greenland had the charm of Eden. There were the homes of my savage companions. It was a stepping-stone to my home, still very

---

months, and was not well himself after the terrible journey over the storm-swept seas of ice. Before returning, he asked for some coffee, a little sugar and a few biscuits. These Mr. Peary refused him. Dr. Dedrick returned. The natives, in fever and pain, died. Theirs are the bones scattered by the wild beasts. Who is responsible for these deaths?

"*Peary-tiglipo-savigaxua*" (Peary has stolen the iron stone), was now repeated with bitterness by the Eskimos. In 1897 it occurred to Mr. Peary that the museums would be interested in the Eskimos, and also in the so-called "Star Stone," owned by the Eskimos. It had been passed down from generation to generation as a tribal property; from it the natives, from the Stone Age, had chipped metal for weapons. This "meteorite" was, without Eskimo consent, put by Mr. Peary on his ship; without their consent, also, were put a group of men and women and children on the ship. All were taken to New York for museum purposes. In New York the precious meteorite was sold, but the profits were not divided with the rightful owners. The men, women and children (merchandise of similar value) were placed in a cellar, awaiting a marketplace. Before the selling time arrived, all but one died of diseases directly arising out of inhuman carelessness, due to the dictates of commercialism. Who is responsible for the death of this group of innocent wild folk?

far off.   It was a land where man has a fighting chance for his life.

In reality, we were now in the most desperate throes of the grip of famine which we had encountered during all of our hard experience.   Greenland was but thirty miles away.   But we were separated from it by impossible open water—a hopeless stormy deep.   To this moment I do not know why we did not sit down and allow the blood to cool with famine and cold.   We had no good reason to hope that we could cross, but again hope—"the stuff that goes to make dreams"—kept our eyes open.

We started.   We were as thin as it is possible for men to be.   The scraps of meat, viscera, and skin of the seal, buried for a year, was now our sole diet.   We traveled the first two days northward over savage uplifts of hummocks and deep snows, tripping and stumbling over blocks of ice like wounded animals.   Then we reached good, smooth ice, but open water forced us northward, ever northward from the cheering cliffs under which our Greenland homes and abundant supplies were located. No longer necessary to lift the feet, we dragged the ice-sheeted boots step after step over smooth young ice. This eased our tired, withered legs, and long distances were covered.   The days were prolonged, the decayed seal food ran low, water was almost impossible.   Life no longer seemed worth living.   We had eaten the strips of meat and frozen seal cautiously.   We had eaten other things—our very boots and leather lashings as a last resort.

So weak that we had to climb on hands and knees, we reached the top of an iceberg, and from there saw

Annoatok.   Natives, who had thought us long dead, rushed out to greet us.   There I met Mr. Harry Whitney.   As I held his hand, the cheer of a long-forgotten world came over me.   With him I went to my house, only to find that during my absence it had been confiscated.   A sudden bitterness rose within which it was difficult to hide.   A warm meal dispelled this for a time.

In due time I told Whitney: "I have reached the Pole."

Uttering this for the first time in English, it came upon me that I was saying a remarkable thing.   Yet Mr. Whitney showed no great surprise, and his quiet congratulation confirmed what was in my mind—that I had accomplished no extraordinary or unbelievable thing; for to me the Polar experience was not in the least remarkable, considered with our later adventures.

Mr. Whitney, as is now well known, was a sportsman from New Haven, Connecticut, who had been spending some months hunting in the North.   He had made Annoatok the base of his operations, and had been spending the winter in the house which I had built of packing-boxes.

The world now seemed brighter.   The most potent factor in this change was food—and more food—a bath and another bath—and clean clothes.   Mr. Whitney offered me unreservedly the hospitality of my own camp.   He instructed Pritchard to prepare meal after meal of every possible dish that our empty stomachs had craved for a year.   The Eskimo boys were invited to share it.

Between meals, or perhaps we had better call meals courses (for it was a continuous all-night performance—interrupted by baths and breathing spells to prevent spasms of the jaws)—between courses, then, there were washes with real soap and real cleansing warm water, the first that we had felt for fourteen months. Mr. Whitney helped to scrape my angular anatomy, and he volunteered the information that I was the dirtiest man he ever saw.

From Mr. Whitney I learned that Mr. Peary had reached Annoatok about the middle of August, 1908, and had placed a boatswain named Murphy, assisted by William Pritchard, a cabin boy on the *Roosevelt,* in charge of my stores, which he had seized. Murphy was anything but tactful and considerate; and in addition to taking charge of my goods, had been using them in trading as money to pay for furs to satisfy Mr. Peary's hunger for commercial gain. Murphy went south in pursuit of furs after my arrival.

For the first few days I was too weak to inquire into the theft of my camp and supplies. Furthermore, with a full stomach, and Mr. Whitney as a warm friend at hand, I was indifferent. I was not now in any great need. For by using the natural resources of the land, as I had done before, it was possible to force a way back to civilization from here with the aid of my Eskimo friends.

Little by little, however, the story of that very strange "Relief Station for Dr. Cook" was unraveled, and I tell it here with no ulterior notion of bitterness against Mr. Peary. I forgave him for the practical theft of my supplies; but this is a very important part of the controversy which followed, a controversy which can be understood only by a plain statement of the incidents which led up to and beyond this so-called "Relief Station for Dr. Cook," which was a relief only in the sense that I was relieved of a priceless store of supplies.

When Mr. Peary heard of the execution of my plans to try for the Pole in 1907, and before he left on his last expedition, he accused me of various violations of what he chose to call "Polar Ethics." No application had been filed by me to seek the Pole. Now I was accused of stealing his route, his Pole, and his people. This train of accusations was given to the press, and with the greatest possible publicity. A part of this was included in an official complaint to the International Bureau of Polar Research at Brussels.

Now, what are Polar ethics? There is no separate code for the Arctic. The laws which govern men's bearing towards each other in New York are good in any part of the world. One cannot be a democrat in civilized eyes and an autocrat in the savage world. One cannot cry, "Stop thief!" and then steal the thief's booty. If you are a member of the brotherhood of humanity in one place, you must be in another. In short, he who is a gentleman in every sense of the word needs no memory for ethics. It is only the modern political reformer who has need of the cloak of the hypocrisy of ethics to hide his own misdeeds. An explorer should not stoop to this.

Who had the power to grant a license to seek the Pole? If you wish to invade the forbidden regions of Thibet, or the interior of Siberia, a permit is necessary from the governments interested. But the Pole is a place no nation owned, by right of discovery, occupation, or otherwise.

If pushing a ship up the North Atlantic waters to the limit of navigation was a trespass on Mr. Peary's preserve, then I am bound to plead guilty. But ships had gone that way for a hundred years before Mr. Peary developed a Polar claim. If I am guilty, then he is guilty of stealing the routes of Davis, Kane, Greely and a number of others. But as I view the situation, a modern explorer should take a certain pride in the advantages afforded by his worthy predecessors. I take a certain historic delight in having followed the routes of the early pathfinders to a more remote destination. This indebtedness and this honor I do now, as heretofore, acknowledge. The charge that I stole Mr. Peary's route is incorrect. For, from the limit of navigation on the Greenland side, my track was forced over a land which, although under Mr. Peary's eyes for twenty years, was explored by Sverdrup, who got the same unbrotherly treatment from Mr. Peary which he has shown to every explorer who has had the misfortune to come within the circle he has drawn about an imaginary private preserve.

The charge of borrowing Peary's ideas, by which is meant the selection of food and supplies and the adoption of certain methods of travel, is equally unfounded. For Mr. Peary's weakest chain is his absolute lack of system, order, preparation or originality. This is commented upon by the men of every one of his previous expeditions. Mr. Peary early charged that my system of work and my methods of travel were borrowed from him. This was not true; but when he later, in a desperate effort to say unkind things, said that my system—the system borrowed from himself—was ineffi-

cient, the charge becomes laughable. As to the Pole—
if Mr. Peary has a prior lien on it—it is there still. We
did not take it away. We simply left our footprints there.

Now as to the charge of using Mr. Peary's supplies and his people—by assuming a private preserve of
all the reachable Polar wilderness of this section, he
might put up a plausible claim to it as a private hunting ground. If this claim is good, then I am guilty of
trespass. But it was only done to satisfy the pangs of
hunger.

This claim of the ownership of the animals of the
unclaimed North might be put with plausible excuses
to The Hague Tribunal. But it is a claim no serious
person would consider. The same claim of ownership,
however, cannot be said of human life.

The Eskimos are a free and independent people.
They acknowledge no chiefs among themselves and
submit to no outside dictators. They are likely to
call an incoming stranger "nalegaksook," which the
vanity of the early travelers interpreted as the "great
chief." But the intended interpretation is "he who has
much to barter" or "the great trader." This is what
they call Mr. Peary. The same compliment is given to
other traders, whalers or travelers with whom they do
business. Despite his claims Mr. Peary has been regarded as no more of a benefactor than any other
explorer.

After delivering, early in 1907, an unreasonable
and uncalled for attack, Mr. Peary, two months after
the Pole had been reached by me, went North
with two ships, with all the advantage that unlimited

funds and influential friends could give. At about the same time my companion, Rudolph Francke, started south under my instructions, and he locked my box-house at Annoatok wherein were stored supplies sufficient for two years or more.

The key was entrusted to a trustworthy Eskimo. Under his protection this precious life-saving supply was safe for an indefinite time. With it no relief expedition or help from the outside world was necessary.

Francke had a hard time as he pushed southward, with boat and sledge. Moving supplies to the limit of his carrying capacity, he fought bravely against storms, broken ice and thundering seas. The route proved all but impossible, but at last his destination at North Star was reached, only for him to find that he was too late for the whalers he had expected. Impossible to return to our northern camp at that time, and having used all of his civilized food en route, he was now compelled to accept the hospitality of the natives, in their unhygienic dungeons. For food there was nothing but the semi-putrid meat and blubber eaten by the Eskimos. After a long and desperate task by boat and sled he returned to Etah but he was absolutely unable to proceed farther. Francke's health failed rapidly and when, as he thought, the time had arrived to lay down and quit life, a big prosperous looking ship came into the harbor. He had not tasted civilized food for months, and longed, as only a sick, hungry man can, for coffee and bread.

Almost too weak to arise from his couch of stones, he mustered up enough strength to stumble over the rails of that ship of plenty. After gathering sufficient breath to speak, he asked for bread and coffee. It was breakfast time. No answer came to that appeal. He was put off the ship. He went back to his cheerless cave and prayed that death might close his eyes to further trouble. Somewhat later, when it was learned that there was a house and a large store of supplies at Annoatok, and that the man had in his possession furs and ivory valued at $10,000, there was a change of heart in Mr. Peary. Francke was called on board, was given bread and coffee and whiskey. Too weak to resist, he was bullied and frightened, and forced under duress to sign papers which he did not understand. To get home to him meant life; to remain meant death. And the ship before him was thus his only chance for life. Under the circumstances he would naturally have put his name to any paper placed under his feeble eyes. But the law of no land would enforce such a document.

In this way Mr. Peary compelled him to turn over $10,000 worth of furs and ivory, besides my station and supplies, worth at least $35,000, which were not his to turn over. The prized ivory tusks and furs were immediately seized and sent back on the returning ship.

One of the narwhal tusks, worth to me at least $1,000, was polished and sent as Peary's trophy to President Roosevelt. Under the circumstances has not the President been made the recipient of stolen goods?

When Francke, as a passenger, returned on the Peary supply ship, *Erik,* a bill of one hundred dollars was presented for his passage. This bill was presumably the bill for the full cost of his return. But the priceless furs and ivory trophies were confiscated without a murmur of conscious wrongdoing. This is what happened as the ship went south.

Now let us follow the ship *Roosevelt* in its piratic career northward. With Mr. Peary as chief it got to Etah. From there instructions were given to seize my house and supplies. This was done over the signature of Mr. Peary to a paper which started out with the following shameless hypocrisy:

"This is a relief station for Dr. Cook."

According to Mr. Whitney even Captain Bartlett quivered with indignation at the blushing audacity of this steal. The stores were said to be abandoned. The men, with Peary's orders, went to Koo-loo-ting-wah and forced from him the key with which to open the carefully guarded stores. The house was reconstructed.

Murphy, a rough Newfoundland bruiser, who had been accustomed to kick sailors, was placed in charge with autocratic powers. Murphy could neither read nor write, but he was given a long letter of instruction to make a trading station of my home and to use my supplies.

Now if Mr. Peary required my supplies for legitimate exploration I should have been glad to give him my last bread; but to use my things to satisfy his greed for commercial gain was, when I learned it, bitter medicine.

Because Murphy could not write, Pritchard was left with him to read the piratic instructions once each week. Pritchard was also to keep account of the furs bought and the prices paid—mostly in my coin. Murphy soon forbade the reading of the instructions, and also stopped the stock-taking and bookkeeping. The hypocrisy of the thing seemed to pinch even Murphy's narrow brain.

This same deliberate Murphy, accustomed to life in barracks, held the whip for a year over the head of Harry Whitney, a man of culture and millions. Money, however, was of no use there. Audacity and self-assumed power, it seems, ruled as it did in times of old when buccaneers deprived their victims of gold, and walked them off a plank into the briny deep.

Murphy and Pritchard, the paid traders, fixed themselves cosily in my camp. Mr. Whitney had been invited as a guest to stay and hunt for his own pleasure. The party lived for a year at my expense, but the lot of Whitney was very hard as an invited guest, a privilege for which I was told he had paid Mr. Peary two thousand dollars or more. His decision to stay had come only after a disappointment in a lack of success of hunting during the summer season. He was, therefore, ill-provided for the usual Polar hardships. With no food, and no adequate clothing of his own, he was dependent on the dictates of Murphy to supply him. As time went on, the night with its awful cold advanced. Murphy gathered in all the furs and absolutely prohibited Whitney from getting suitable furs for winter clothing. He, therefore, shivered throughout the long winter in his sheepskin shooting outfit. Several times he was at the point of a hand-to-hand encounter with Murphy, but with young Pritchard as a friend and gentlemanly instincts to soften his manner, he grit his teeth and swallowed the insults.

His ambition for a hunting trip was frustrated because it interfered with Murphy's plans for trading in skins. The worst and most brutal treatment was the almost inconceivable cruelty of his not allowing Mr.

Whitney enough food for a period of months, not even of my supplies, although this food was used eventually to feed useless dogs.

All of this happened under Mr. Peary's authority, and under the coarse, swaggering Murphy, whom Mr. Peary, in his book, calls "a thoroughly trustworthy man!" Mr. Peary's later contention, in a hypocritical effort to clear himself (see "The North Pole," page 76) that he placed Murphy in charge "to prevent the Eskimos from looting the supplies and equipment left there by Dr. Cook," is a mean, petty and unworthy slur upon a brave, loyal people, among whom thievery is a thing unknown. Unknown, yes, save when white men without honor, without respect for property or the ethics of humanity, which the Eskimos instinctively have, invade their region and rob them and fellow explorers with the brazenness of middle-aged buccaneers.

ANNOATOK TO UPERNAVIK

ELEVEN HUNDRED MILES SOUTHWARD OVER SEA AND
LAND—AT ETAH—OVERLAND TO THE WALRUS
GROUNDS—ESKIMO COMEDIES AND TRAGEDIES—A
RECORD RUN OVER MELVILLE BAY—FIRST NEWS FROM
PASSING SHIPS—THE ECLIPSE OF THE SUN—SOUTH-
WARD BY STEAMER GODTHAAB

XXX

ALONG DANISH GREENLAND

A few interesting days were spent with Mr. Whitney at Annoatok. The Eskimos, in the meantime, had
all gone south to the walrus hunting grounds at Nuerke.
Koo-loo-ting-wah came along with a big team of dogs.
Here was an opportunity to attempt to reach the Danish
settlements—for to get home quickly was now my all-
absorbing aim. Koo-loo-ting-wah was in my service.
He was guarding my supplies in 1908 when the ship
Roosevelt had come along. He had been compelled to
give up the key to my box-house. He had been engaged
to place supplies for us and search the American shores
for our rescue. Peary, making a pretended "Relief
Station," forced Koo-loo-ting-wah from his position as
guardian of my supplies, and forbade him to engage in
any effort to search for us, and absolutely prohibited

him and everybody else, including Murphy, Prichard and Whitney, from engaging in any kind of succor at a time when help was of consequence. Koo-loo-ting-wah was liberally paid to abandon my interests (by Mr. Peary's orders, from my supplies), but, like Bartlett and Whitney and Prichard later, he condemned Mr. Peary for his unfair acts. When asked to join me in the long journey to Upernavik, he said, *"Peari an-nutu"* (Peary will be mad.) Koo-loo-ting-wah was now in Peary's service at my expense, and I insisted that he enter my service, which he did. Then we began our preparations for the southern trip.

Accompanied by Whitney, I went to Etah, and for this part of the journey Murphy grudgingly gave me a scant food supply for a week, for which I gave him a memorandum. This memorandum was afterwards published by Mr. Peary as a receipt, so displayed as to convey the idea that all the stolen supplies had been replaced.

At Etah was a big cache which had been left a year before by Captain Bernier, the commander of a northern expedition sent out by the Canadian Government, and which had been placed in charge of Mr. Whitney. In this cache were food, new equipment, trading material, and clean underclothes which Mrs. Cook had sent on the Canadian expedition. With this new store of suitable supplies, I now completed my equipment for the return to civilization.*

---

*These supplies had, fortunately, been left in the care of Mr. Whitney. In the months that followed, Murphy several times threatened to take these things, but Whitney's sense of justice was such that no further pilfering was allowed.

The unbrotherly tactics which Mr. Peary had shown to Sverdrup and

To get home quickly, I concluded, could be done best by going to the Danish settlements in Greenland, seven hundred miles south, and thence to Europe by an early steamer. From Upernavik mail is carried in small native boats to Umanak, where there is direct communication with Europe by government steamers. By making this journey, and taking a fast boat to America, I calculated I could reach New York in early July.

Mr. Whitney expected the *Erik* to arrive to take him south in the following August. Going, as he planned, into Hudson Bay, he expected to reach New York in October. Although this would be the easiest and safest way to reach home, by the route I had planned I hoped to reach New York four months earlier than the *Erik* would.

The journey from Etah to Upernavik is about seven hundred miles—a journey as long and nearly as difficult as the journey to the North Pole. I knew it involved difficulties and risks—the climbing of mountains and glaciers, the crossing of open leads of water late in the season, when the ice is in motion and snow is falling, and the dragging of sledges through slush and water.

Mr. Whitney, in view of these dangers, offered to

---

other explorers were here copied by his representative. Captain Bernier was bound for the American coast, to explore and claim for Canada the land to the west. He desired a few native helpers. There were at Etah descendants of Eskimo emigrants from the very land which Bernier aimed to explore. These men were anxious to return to their fathers' land, and would have made splendid guides for Bernier. Murphy volunteered to ask the Eskimos if they would go. He went ashore, pretending that he would try to secure guides, but, in reality, he never asked a single Eskimo to join Bernier. Returning, he said that no one would go. Later he boasted to Whitney and Prichard of the intelligent way in which he had deceived Captain Bernier. Was this under Mr. Peary's instructions?

take care of my instruments, notebooks and flag, and take them south on his ship. I knew that if any food were lost on my journey it might be replaced by game. Instruments lost in glaciers or open seas could not be replaced. The instruments, moreover, had served their purposes. The corrections, notes, and other data were also no longer needed; all my observations had been reduced, and the corrections were valuable only for a future re-examination. This is why I did not take them with me. It is customary, also, to leave corrections with instruments.

In the box which I gave to Mr. Whitney were packed one French sextant; one surveying compass, aluminum, with azimuth attachment; one artificial horizon, set in a thin metal frame adjusted by spirit levels and thumbscrews; one aneroid barometer, aluminum; one aluminum case with maximum and minimum spirit thermometer; other thermometers, and also one liquid compass. All of these I had carried with me.

Besides these were left other instruments used about the relief station. There were papers giving instrumental corrections, readings, comparisons, and other notes; a small diary, mostly of loose leaves, containing some direct field readings, and meteorological data. These were packed in one of the instrument cases. By special request of Mr. Whitney, I also left my flag.

In addition, I placed in Mr. Whitney's charge several big cases of clothing and supplies which Mrs. Cook had sent, also ethnological collections, furs, and geological specimens. In one of these boxes were packed the instrument cases and notes.

Mr. Whitney's plans later were changed. His

ship, the *Erik,* not having arrived when Peary returned, Whitney arranged with Peary to come back to civilization on the latter's ship, the *Roosevelt.* As I learned afterwards, when the *Roosevelt* arrived Mr. Whitney took from one of my packing boxes my instruments and packed them in his trunk. He was, however, prohibited from carrying my things, and all my belongings were consequently left at the mercy of the weather and the natives in far-off Greenland. I have had no means of hearing from them since, so that I do not know what has become of them.

About Etah and Annoatok and on my eastward journey few notes were made. As well as I can remember, I left Annoatok some time during the third week of April. On leaving Whitney, I promised to send him dogs and guides for his prospective hunting trip. I also promised to get for him furs for a suitable winter suit— because, according to Mr. Peary's autocratic methods, he had been denied the privilege of trading for himself. He was not allowed to gather trophies, or to purchase absolutely necessary furs, nor was he accorded the courtesy of arranging for guides and dogs with the natives for his ambition to get big game. All of this I was to arrange for Whitney as I passed the villages farther south.

In crossing by the overland route, over Crystal Palace Glacier to Sontag Bay, we were caught in a violent gale, which buried us in drifts on the highlands. Descending to the sea, we entered a new realm of coming summer joys.

Moving along to Neurke, we found a big snow-house village. All had gathered for the spring walrus chase.　Many animals had been caught, and the hunters were in a gluttonous stupor from continued overfeeding.　It was not long before we, too, filled up, and succumbed to similar pleasures.

My boys were here, and the principal pastime was native gossip about the North Pole.

Arriving among their own people here, Ah-we-lah and E-tuk-i-shook recounted their remarkable journey. They had, of course, no definite idea of where they had been, but told of the extraordinary journey of seven moons; of their reaching a place where there was no game and no life; of their trailing over the far-off seas where the sun did not dip at night, and of their hunting, on our return, with slingshots, string traps, and arrows. These were their strong and clear impressions.*

---

*I now learned, also, that the Eskimos had told their tribesmen of their arrival at the mysterious "Big Nail," which, of course, meant less to them than the hardship and unique methods of hunting.

Among themselves the Eskimos have an intimate way of conveying things, a method of expression and meaning which an outsider never grasps. At most, white men can understand only a selected and more simple language with which the Eskimos convey their thoughts.　This partly accounts for the unreliability of any testimony which a white man extracts from them. There is also to be considered an innate desire on the part of these simple people to answer any question in a manner which they think will please. In all Indian races this desire to please is notoriously stronger than a sense of truth.　The fact that my Eskimos, when later questioned as to my whereabouts, are reported to have answered that I had not gone far out of sight of land, was due partly to my instructions and partly to this inevitable wish to answer in a pleasing way.

While they spoke among themselves of having reached the "Big Nail," they also said—what they later repeated to Mr. Peary—that they had passed few days beyond the sight of land, a delusion caused by mirages, in which, to prevent any panic, I had with good intentions encouraged an artificial belief in a nearness to land.

But we were for weeks enshrouded in dense fogs, where nothing could be seen.　The natives everywhere had heard of this, and inquired about it. Why has Mr. Peary suppressed this important information?　We traveled and camped on the pack for "seven moons."　Why was this omitted?　We reached a place where the sun did not dip at night; where there was not enough difference in the height of the day and night sun to give the Eskimo his usual sense of direction.　Why was this fact ignored?

From Neurke we crossed Murchison Sound, along the leads where the walrus was being hunted, and from there we set a course for the eastern point of Northumberland Island.

We next entered Inglefield Gulf. Our party had grown. Half of the natives were eager to join us on a pilgrimage to the kindly and beloved Danes of Southern Greenland; but, because of the advancing season, the marches must be forced, and because a large sled train hinders rapid advancement, I reduced the numbers and changed the personnel of my party as better helpers offered services.

From a point near Itiblu we ascended the blue slopes of a snow-free glacier, and after picking a dangerous footing around precipitous cliffs, we rose to the clouds and deep snows of the inland ice. Here, for twenty-four hours, we struggled through deep snow, with only the wind to give direction to our trail. Descending from this region of perpetual mist and storm, we came down to the sea in Booth Sound. From here, after a good rest, over splendid ice, in good weather, we entered Wolstenholm Sound. At Oomonoi there was a large gathering of natives, and among these we rested and fed up in preparation for the long, hazardous trip which lay before us.

In this locality, the Danish Literary Expedition, under the late Mylius Ericksen, had wintered. Their forced march northward from Uppernavik proved so desperate that they were unable to carry important necessaries.

But the natives, with characteristic generosity, had supplied the Danes with the meat for food and the fat for fuel, which kept them alive during dangerous and trying times.*

We now started for Cape York.   My-ah, Ang-ad-loo and I-o-ko-ti were accepted as permanent members of my party.   All of this party was, curiously enough, hostile to Mr. Peary, and the general trend of conversation was a bitter criticism of the way the people had been fleeced of furs and ivory; how a party had been left to die of cold and hunger at Fort Conger; how, at Cape Sabine, many died of a sickness which had been brought among them, and how Dr. Dedrick was not allowed to save their lives; how a number had been torn from their homes and taken to New York, where they had died of barbarous ill-treatment; how their great "Iron Stone," their only source of iron for centuries, the much-prized heritage of their nation, had been stolen from the point we were now nearing; and so on, throughout a long line of other abuses.   But, at the time, all of this bitterness seemed to soften my own resentment, and I began to cherish a forgiving spirit toward Mr. Peary.   After all, thought I, I have been successful; let us have an end of discord and seek a brighter side of life.

Now I began to think for the first time of the public aspect of my homegoing.   Heretofore my anticipations had been centered wholly in the joys of a family reunion, but now the thought was slowly forced as to the attitude

---

* In appreciation of this kind helpfulness, the Danes later sent a special ship loaded with presents, which were left for distribution among the good-natured Eskimos who had helped Ericksen. Mr. Peary came along after the Danes had turned their backs, and picked from the Danish presents such things as appealed to his fancy, thus depriving the Eskimos of the merited return for their kindness. What right had Mr. Peary to take these things? The Danes, who have since placed a mission station here, in continuation of their policy to guard and protect the Eskimos, are awaiting an answer to this question to-day.

which others would take towards me. In the wildest flights of my imagination I never dreamed of any world-wide interest in the Pole. Again I desire to emphasize the fact that every movement I have made disproves the allegation that I planned to perpetrate a gigantic fraud upon the world. Men had been seeking the North Pole for years, and at no time had any of these many explorers aroused any general interest in his expedition or the results.

Millions of money, hundreds of lives, had been sacrificed. The complex forces of great nations had been arrayed unsuccessfully. I had believed the thing could be done by simpler methods, without the sacrifice of life, without using other people's money; and, with this conviction, had gone north. I now came south, with no expectations of reward except such as would come from a simple success in a purely private undertaking.

I wish to emphasize that I regarded my entire experience as something purely personal. I supposed that the newspapers would announce my return, and that there would be a three days' breath of attention, and that that would be all. So far as I was personally concerned, my chief thought was one of satisfaction at having satisfied myself, and an intense longing for home.

We camped at Cape York. Before us was the great white expanse of Melville Bay to the distant Danish shores. Few men had ever ventured over this. What luck was in store for us could not be guessed. But we were ready for every emergency. We moved eastward to an island where the natives greeted us with enthusiasm, and then we started over treacherous ice southward. The snow was not deep; the ice proved fairly smooth. The seals, basking in the new summer sun, augmented our supplies. Frequent bear tracks added the spirit of the chase, which doubled our speed. In two days we had the "Devil's Thumb" to our left, and at the end of three and a half days the cheer of Danish cliffs and semi-civilized Eskimos came under our eyes.

The route from Annoatok to this point, following the circuitous twists over sea and land, was almost as long as that from Annoatok to the Pole, but we had covered it in less than a month. With a record march across Melville Bay, we had crossed a long line of trouble, in which Mylius Ericksen and his companions nearly succumbed after weeks of frosty torture. We had done it in a few days, and in comfort, with the luxury of abundant food gathered en route.

Behind the Danish archipelago, traveling was good and safe. As we went along, from village to village, the Eskimos told the story of the Polar conquest. Rapidly we pushed along to Tassuasak, which we reached in the middle of May. This is one of the small trading posts belonging to the district of Upernavik.

At Tassuasak I met Charles Dahl, a congenial Danish official, with whom I stayed a week. He spoke only Danish, which I did not understand. Despite the fact that our language was unintelligible, we talked until two or three o'clock in the morning, somehow conveying our thoughts, and when he realized what I told him he took my hand, offering warm, whole-souled Norse appreciation.

Here I secured for Mr. Whitney tobacco and other needed supplies. For the Eskimos, various presents were bought, all of which were packed on the returning sleds. Then the time arrived to bid the final adieu to my faithful wild men of the Far North. Tears took the place of words in that parting.

By sledge and oomiak (skin boat) I now continued my journey to Upernavik.

Upernavik is one of the largest Danish settlements in Greenland and one of the most important trading posts. It is a small town with a population of about three hundred Eskimos, who live in box-shaped huts of turf. The town affords residence for about six Danish officials, who live, with their families, in comfortable houses.

I reached there early one morning about May 20, 1909, and went at once to the house of Governor Kraul. The governor himself—a tall, bald-headed, dignified man, a bachelor, about fifty years of age, of genial manner and considerable literary and scientific attainments—answered my knock on the door. He admitted me hospitably, and then looked me over from head to foot.

I was a hard-looking visitor. I wore an old sealskin coat, worn bearskin trousers, stockings of hareskin showing above torn seal boots. I was reasonably dirty. My face was haggard and bronzed, my hair was uncut, long and straggling. However, I felt reassured in a bath and clean underclothing secured a week before at Tassuasak. Later these clothes were replaced by new clothes given me by Governor Kraul, some of which I wore on my trip to Copenhagen. My appearance was such that I was not surprised by the governor's question: "Have you any lice on you?"

Some years before he had entertained some Arctic

pilgrims, and a peculiar breed of parasites remained to plague the village for a long time. I convinced him that, in spite of my unprepossessing appearance, he was safe in sheltering me.

At his house I had all the luxuries of a refined home with a large library at my disposal. I had also a large, comfortable feather-bed with clean sheets. I slept for hours every day, devoting about four or five hours to my work on my notes.

At breakfast I told Governor Kraul briefly of my journey, and although he was polite and pleasant, I could see that he was skeptical as to my having reached the Pole. I remained with him a month, using his pens and paper putting the finishing touches on my narrative—on which I had done much work at Cape Sparbo. My notes and papers were scattered about, and Governor Kraul read them, and as he read them his doubts were dispelled and he waxed enthusiastic.

Governor Kraul had had no news of the inside world for about a year. He was as anxious as I was for letters and papers. I went over his last year's news with a good deal of interest. While thus engaged, early one foggy morning, a big steamer came into port. It was the steam whaler *Morning* of Dundee. Her master, Captain Adams, came ashore with letters and news. He recited the remarkable journey of Shackleton to the South Pole as his opening item in the cycle of the year's incidents. After that he gave it as his opinion that England had become Americanized in its politics, and after recounting the year's luck in whaling, sealing and fishing, he then informed me that from America the greatest news was the success of "The Merry Widow" and "The Dollar Princess." I was invited aboard to eat the first beefsteak and first fresh civilized food that I had eaten in two years. I then told him of my Polar conquest. He was keenly interested in my story, all of my reports seeming to confirm his own preconceived ideas of conditions about the Pole. When I went ashore I took a present of a bag of potatoes. To Governor Kraul and myself these potatoes proved to be the greatest delicacy, for to both the flavor and real fresh, mealy potatoes gave our meals the finishing touches of a fine dessert.

I gave Captain Adams some information about new hunting grounds which, as he left, he said would be tried.*

Life at Upernavik was interesting. Among other things, we noted the total eclipse of the sun on June 17. According to our time, it began in the evening at eighteen minutes past seven and ended ten minutes after nine.

For a number of days the natives had looked with anxiety upon the coming of the mysterious darkness attending the eclipse, for now we were in a land of anxiety and uneasiness. It was said that storms would follow each other, displaying the atmospheric rage; that

---

*When Captain Adams arrived off the haunts of the northernmost Eskimos, he sent ashore a letter to be passed along to Mr. Peary, as he was expected to return south during that summer. In his letter Captain Adams told of my attainment of the Pole. The letter got into Mr. Peary's hands before he returned to Labrador. With this letter in his pocket, Mr. Peary gave as his principal reason for doubting my success that nobody else had been told that I had reached the Pole. I told Whitney, I had told Pritchard—thus Peary's charge was proven false later. But why did he suppress the information which Captain Adams' letter contained? With this letter in his pocket, why did Mr. Peary say that no one had been told?

seals could not be sought, and that all good people should pray. Although a violent southwest gale did rush by, the last days before the eclipse were clear and warm.

Governor Kraul suggested a camp on the high rocks east. Mr. Anderson, the governor's assistant, and I joined in the expedition. We took smoked and amber glasses, a pen and paper, a camera and field glasses. A little disk was cut out of the northern side of the sun before we started. There was no wind, and the sky was cloudless. A better opportunity could not have been afforded. It had been quite warm. The chirp of the snow bunting and the buzz of bees gave the first joyous rebound of the short Arctic summer. Small sand-flies rose in clouds, and the waters glittered with midsummer incandescence. Small groups of natives, in gorgeous attire, gathered in many places, and occasionally took a sly glance at the sun as if something was about to happen. They talked in muffled undertones.

When one-third of the sun's disk was obscured it was impossible to see the cut circle with the unprotected eye. It grew perceptibly dark. The natives quieted and moved toward the church. The birds ceased to sing; the flies sank to the ground. With the failing light the air quickly chilled, the bright contour of the land blurred, the deep blue of the sea faded to a dull purple-blue seemingly lighter, but the midday splendor of high lights and shadows was lost. The burning glitter of the waters under the sun now quickly changed to a silvery glow. The alabaster and ultramarine blue of the icebergs was veiled in gray.

When a thread of light spread the cut out, we knew that the total eclipse was over. In what seemed like a

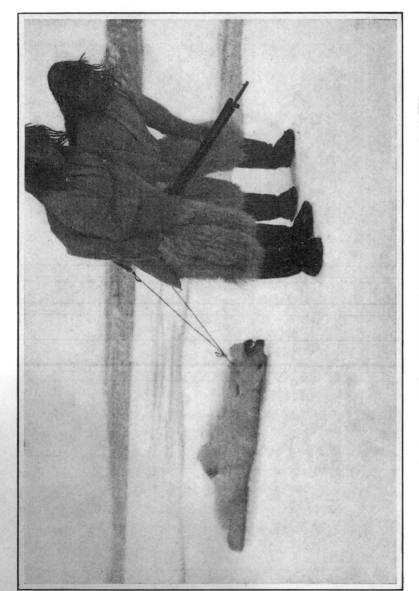

SAVED FROM STARVATION—THE RESULT OF ONE OF OUR LAST CARTRIDGES

"MILES AND MILES OF DESOLATION."
HOMEWARD BOUND
Copyright, 1909, "New York Herald Co."

few seconds the gloom of night brightened to the sparkle of noon.

At the darkest time the natives had called for open church doors, and a sense of immediate danger came over the savage horizon with the force of a panic. A single star was visible for about a minute before and after the total eclipse. A slight salmon flush remained along the western horizon; otherwise the sky varied in tones of purple-blue.

After the sea had brightened to its normal luster, Governor Kraul gave the entire native settlement a feast of figs.

About June 20, the Danish supply ship, *Godthaab*, with Captain Henning Shoubye in command, arrived from South Greenland. Inspector Dougaard Jensen and Handelschef Weche were aboard on a tour of inspection along the Danish settlements. A corps of scientific observers were also aboard. Among these were Professors Thompsen and Steensby and Dr. Krabbe. Governor Kraul asked me to accompany him aboard the *Godthaab*. Thus I first met this group of men, who afterwards did so much to make my journey southward to Copenhagen interesting and agreeable. The Governor told them of the conquest of the Pole. At the time their interest in the news was not very marked, but later every phase of the entire trip was thoroughly discussed.

In a few days the *Godthaab* sailed from Upernavik to Umanak, and I took passage on her. Captain Shoubye quietly and persistently questioned me as to details of my trip. Apparently he became convinced that I was stating facts, for when we arrived at Umanak, the social metropolis of North Greenland, the people enthusiastically received me, having been informed of my feat by the captain.

After coaling at a place near Umanak we started south.

At the "King's Guest House" in Eggedesminde, the only hotel in Greenland, I met Dr. Norman-Hansen, a scientist, with whom I talked. He questioned me, and a fraternal confidence was soon established.

Later the *Godthaab,* which took the missionary expedition to the northernmost Eskimo settlement at North Star Bay and then returned, arrived from Cape York with Knud Rassmussen and other Danes aboard They had a story that my two Eskimos had said I had taken them to the "Big Nail."

FROM GREENLAND TO COPENHAGEN

XXXI

AT THE DANISH METROPOLIS

At Eggedesminde was given the first banquet in
my honor. At the table were about twenty people.
Knud Rassmussen, the writer, among others spoke. In
an excited talk in Danish, mixed with English and German, he foretold the return of Mr. Peary and prophesied
discord. This made little impression at the time and
was recalled only by later events.

At this point I wish to express my gratitude and
appreciation of the universal courtesy of which I was the
recipient at every Danish settlement in my southward
progress along the coast of Greenland.

At Eggedesminde Inspector Daugaard-Jensen endeavored to secure an idle walrus schooner for me. By
this I hoped to get to Labrador and thence to New
York. This involved considerable official delay, and I

estimated I could make better time by going to Copenhagen on the *Hans Egede*. Although every berth on
this boat, when it arrived, was engaged, Inspector
Daugaard-Jensen, with the same characteristic kindness and courtesy shown me by all the Danes, secured
for me comfortable quarters.

On board were a number of scientific men and
Danish correspondents. As the story of my quest had
spread along the Greenland coast, and as conflicting
reports might be sent out, Inspector Daugaard-Jensen
suggested that I cable a first account to the world.

The anxiety of the newspaper correspondents on
board gave me the idea that my story might have considerable financial value. I was certainly in need of
money. I had only forty or fifty dollars and I needed
clothing and money for my passage from Copenhagen
to New York.

The suggestions and assistance of Inspector Daugaard-Jensen were very helpful. Iceland and the Faroe
Islands, frequent ports of call for the Danish steamers,
because of a full passenger list and the absence of commercial needs, were not visited by the *Hans Egede* on
this return trip. The captain decided to put into Lerwick, in the Shetland Islands, so that I could send my
message.

I prepared a story of about 2,000 words, and
went ashore at Lerwick. No one but myself and a representative of the captain was allowed to land. We
swore the cable operator to secrecy, sent several official
and private messages, and one to James Gordon Bennett briefly telling of my discovery. As the operator refused to be responsible for the press message, it was

left with the Danish consul. To Mr. Bennett I cabled: "Message left in care of Danish consul, 2,000 words. For it $3,000 expected. If you want it, send for it."

Our little boat pulled back to the *Hans Egede,* and the ship continued on her journey to Copenhagen. Two days passed. On board we talked of my trip as quite a commonplace thing. I made some appointments for a short stay in Copenhagen.

Off the Skaw, the northernmost point of Denmark, a Danish man-of-war came alongside us. There was a congratulatory message from the Minister of State. This greatly surprised me.

Meanwhile a motor boat puffed over the unsteady sea and a half dozen seasick newspaper men, looking like wet cats, jumped over the rails. They had been permitted to board on the pretext that they had a message from the American Minister, Dr. Egan. I took them to my cabin and asked whether the New York *Herald* had printed my cable. The correspondent of the *Politiken* drew out a Danish paper in which I recognized the story. I talked with the newspaper men for five minutes and my prevailing impression was that they did not know what they wanted. They told me Fleet Street had moved to Copenhagen. I confess all of this seemed foolish at the time.

They told me that dinners and receptions awaited me at Copenhagen. That puzzled me, and when I thought of my clothes I became distressed. I wore a dirty, oily suit. I had only one set of clean linen and one cap. After consulting with the Inspector we guessed at my measurements, and a telegram was written to a tailor at Copenhagen to have some clothing ready for me. At Elsinore cables began to arrive, and thence onward I became a helpless leaf on a whirlwind of excitement. I let the people about plan and think for me, and had a say in nothing. A cable from Mr. Bennett saying that he had never paid $3,000 so willingly gave me pleasure. There was relief in this, too, for my expenses at the hotel in Eggedesminde and on the *Hans Egede* were unpaid.

At Elsinore many people came aboard with whom I shook hands and muttered inanities in response to congratulations. Reporters who were not seasick thronged the ship, each one insisting on a special interview. Why should I be interviewed? It seemed silly to make such a fuss.

Cablegrams and letters piled in my cabin. With my usual methodical desire to read and answer all communications I sat down to this task, which soon seemed hopeless. I was becoming intensely puzzled, and a not-knowing-where-I-was-at sensation confused me. I did not have a minute for reflection, and before I could approximate my situation, we arrived at Copenhagen.

Like a bolt from the blue, there burst about me the clamor of Copenhagen's ovation. I was utterly bewildered by it. I found no reason in my mind for it. About the North Pole I had never felt such exultation. I could not bring myself to feel what all this indicated, that I had accomplished anything extraordinarily marvelous. For days I could not grasp the reason for the world-excitement.

When I went on deck, as we approached the city, I saw far in the distance flags flying. Like a darting army of water bugs, innumerable craft of all kind were leaping toward us on the sunlit water. Tugs and motors, rowboats and sailboats, soon surrounded and followed us. The flags of all nations dangled on the decorated craft. People shouted, it seemed, in every tongue. Wave after wave of cheering rolled over the water. Horns blew, there was the sound of music, guns exploded. All about, balancing on unsteady craft, their heads hooded in black, were the omnipresent moving-picture-machine operators at work. All this passed as a moving picture itself, I standing there, dazed, simply dazed.

Amidst increasing cheering the *Hans Egede* dropped anchor. Prince Christian, the crown prince, Prince Waldemar, King Frederick's brother, United States Minister Egan, and many other distinguished gentlemen in good clothes greeted me. That they were people who wore good clothes was my predominant impression. Mentally I compared their well-tailored garments with my dirty, soiled, bagged-at-the-knees suit. I doffed my old dirty cap, and as I shook hands with the Prince Christian and Prince Waldemar, tall, splendid men, I felt very sheepish. While all this was going on, I think I forgot about the North Pole. I was most uncomfortable.

For a while it was impossible to get ashore. Along the pier to which we drew, the crowd seemed to drag into the water. About me was a babel of sound, of which I heard, the whole time, no intelligible word. I was pushed, lifted ashore, the crown prince before me, William T. Stead, the English journalist, behind. I almost fell, trying to get a footing. On both sides the press of people closed upon us. I fought like a swimmer struggling for life, and, becoming helpless, was pushed and carried along. I walked two steps on the ground and five on the air. Somebody grabbed my hat, another pulled off a cuff, others got buttons; but flowers came in exchange. At times Stead held me from falling. I was weak and almost stifled. On both sides of me rushed a flood of blurred human faces. I was in a delirium. I ceased to think, was unable to think, for hours.

We finally reached the Meteorological building. I was pushed through the iron gates. I heard them slammed behind me. I paused to breathe. Somebody mentioned something about a speech. "My God!" I muttered. I could no more think than fly. I was pushed onto a balcony. I remember opening my mouth, but I do not know a word I said. There followed a lot of noise. I suppose it was applause. Emerging from the black, lonely Arctic night, the contrast of that rushing flood of human faces staggered me. Yes, there was another sensation—that of being a stranger among strange people, in a city where, however much I might be honored, I had no old-time friend. This curiously depressed me.

Through a back entrance I was smuggled into an automobile. The late Commander Hovgaard, a member of the Nordenskjöld expedition, took charge of affairs, and I was taken to the Phoenix Hotel. Apartments had also been reserved for me at the Bristol and Angleterre, but I had no voice in the plans, for which I was glad.

I was shown to my room and, while washing my face and hands, had a moment to think. "What the

devil is it all about?" I remember repeating to myself.
I was simply dazed. A barber arrived; I submitted to a
shave. Meanwhile a manicure girl appeared and took
charge of my hands. Through the bewildered days that
followed, the thought of this girl, like the obsession of a
delirious man, followed me. I had not paid or tipped
her, and with the girl's image a perturbed feeling persisted, "Here is some one I have wronged." I repeated
that over and over again. This shows the overwrought
state of my mind at the time.

Next the bedroom was a large, comfortable reception room, already filled with flowers. Beyond that was
a large room in which I found many suits of clothes,
some smaller, some bigger than the estimated size wired
from the ship. At this moment there came Mr. Ralph
L. Shainwald—an old friend and a companion of the
first expedition to Mt. McKinley. He selected for me
suitable things. Hastily I fell into one of these, and
mechanically put on clean linen—or rather, the clothing
was put on by my attendants.

Now I was carried to the American Legation,
where I lunched with Minister Egan, and I might have
been eating sawdust for all the impression food made on
me. For an hour, I have been told since, I was plied
with questions. It is a strange phenomenon how our
bodies will act and our lips frame words when the mind
is blank. I had no more idea of my answers than the
man in the moon.

Upon my brain, with the quick, nervous twitter of
moving-picture impressions, swam continually the
scenes through which I moved. I have a recollection, on
my return to the hotel, of going through hundreds of

telegrams. Just as a man looks at his watch and puts it in his pocket without noting the time, so I read these messages of congratulation. Tremendous offers of money from publishers, and for lecture engagements, and opportunities by which I might become a music-hall attraction excited no interest one way or another.

My desire to show appreciation of the hospitality of the Danes by returning to America on a Danish steamer prevented my even considering some of these offers. If I had planned to deceive the world for money, is it reasonable to believe I should have thrown away huge sums for this simple show of courtesy?

Having lunched with Minister Egan, I spent part of the afternoon of the day of my arrival hastily scanning a voluminous pile of correspondence. Money offers and important messages were necessarily pushed aside. I had been honored by a summons to the royal presence, and shortly before five o'clock repaired to the royal palace.

I still retain in my mental retina a picture of the king. It is a gracious, kindly memory. Surrounded by the queen and his three daughters, Princesses Ingeborg, Thyra, and Dagmar, he rose, a gray-haired, fatherly old man, and with warmness of feeling extended his hand. Out of that human sea of swirling white faces and staring eyes, in which I had struggled as a swimmer for life, I remember feeling a sense of security and rest. We talked, I think, of general topics.

I returned to the hotel. Into my brain came the words, from some one, that the newspaper correspondents, representing the great dailies and magazines of the world, were waiting for me. Would I see them? I went downstairs and for an hour was grilled with questions. They came like shots, in many tongues, and only now and then did familiar English words strike me and quiver in my brain cells.

I have been told I was self-possessed and calm. Had I gone through 30,000 square miles of land? Was I competent to take observations? Could I sit down and invent observations? Had I been fully possessed, I suppose, these sudden doubts expressed would have caused some wonderment; doubtless I was puzzled below the realm of consciousness, where, they say, the secret service of the mind grasps the most elusive things. I have since read my replies and marveled at the lucidity of certain answers; only my bewilderment, unless I were misquoted, can explain the absurdity of others.

My impression of the banquet that night in the City Hall is very vague. I talked aimlessly. There were speeches, toasts were drunk; I replied. The North Pole was, I suppose, the subject, but so bewildered was I at the time, that nothing was further from my mind than the North Pole. If an idea came now and then it was the feeling that I must get away without offending these people. I felt the atmosphere of excitement about me for days, pressing me, crushing me.

My time was occupied with consultations, receptions, lunches, and dinners, between which there was a feverish effort to answer increasingly accumulating telegrams. Mr. E. G. Wyckoff, an old friend, now came along and took from me certain business cares. By day there was excitement; by night excitement; there was excitement in my dreams. I slept no more than five hours a night—if I could call it sleep.

As a surcease from this turmoil came the evening at King Frederick's summer palace, where I dined with the royal family and many notable guests. All were so kindly, the surroundings were so unostentatious, that for a short while my confusion passed.

I remember being cornered near a piano after dinner by the young members of the family and plied with questions. I felt for once absolutely at ease and told them of the wild animals and exciting hunts of the north. Otherwise we talked of commonplace topics, and rarely was the North Pole mentioned.

Until after midnight, on my return to my hotel, I sat up with the late Commander Hovgaard and Professor Olafsen, secretary of the Geographical Society. I clearly recall an afternoon when Professor Torp, rector of the university, and Professor Elis Stromgren, informed me that the university desired to honor me with a decoration. Professor Stromgren asked me about my methods of observation and I explained them freely. He believed my claim. The question of certain, absolute and detailed proofs never occurred to me. I was sure of the verity of my claim. I knew I had been as accurate in my scientific work as anyone could be.

My first public account of my exploit was delivered before the Geographical Society on the evening of September 7, and in the presence of the king and queen, Prince and Princess George of Greece, most of the members of the royal family, and the most prominent people of Copenhagen. I had outlined my talk and written parts of it. With the exception of these, which I read, I spoke extempore. Because of the probability of the audience not understanding English, I confined myself to a brief narrative. The audience listened quietly and their credence seemed but the undemonstrative acceptance of an every-day fact.

Not knowing that a medal was to be presented to me at that time, I descended from the platform on concluding my speech. I met the crown prince, who was ascending, and who spoke to me. I did not understand him and proceeded to the floor before the stage. Embarrassed by my misunderstanding, he unfolded his papers and began a presentation speech. Confused, I remained standing below. Whether I ascended the stage and made a reply or received the medal from the floor, I do not now remember.

During the several days that followed I spent most of my time answering correspondence and attending to local obligations. An entire day was spent autographing photographs for members of the royal family. After much hard work I got things in such shape that I saw my way clear to go to Brussels, return to Copenhagen, and make an early start for home.

I had delivered my talk before the Geographical Society. The reporters had seen me, and assailed me with questions, and had packed their suit cases. Tired to death and exhausted with want of sleep, I viewed the prospect of a departure with relief. Because of my condition I refused an invitation to attend a banquet which the newspaper *Politiken* gave to the foreign correspondents at the Tivoli restaurant.

They insisted that I come, if only for five minutes, and promised that there would be no attempt at interviewing. I went and listened wearily to the speeches, made in different languages, and felt no stir at the applause. While the representative of the *Matin* was speaking in French, some one tiptoed up to me and placed a cablegram under my plate. From all sides attendants appeared with cables which were quietly placed under the plates of the various reporters. The *Matin* man stopped; we looked at the cables. A deadly lull fell in the room. You could have heard a pin drop. It was Peary's first message—"Stars and Stripes nailed to the Pole!"

My first feeling, as I read it, was of spontaneous belief. Well, I thought, he got there! On my right and left men were arguing about it. It was declared a hoax. I recognized the characteristic phrasing as Peary's. I knew that the operators along the Labrador coast knew Peary and that it would be almost impossible to perpetrate a joke. I told this to the dinner party. The speeches continued. No reference was made to the message, but the air seemed charged with electricity.

My feeling at the news, as I analyze it, was not of envy or chagrin. I thought of Peary's hard, long years of effort, and I was glad; I felt no rivalry about the Pole; I did feel, aside from the futility of reaching the Pole itself, that Peary's trip possibly might be of great scientific value; that he had probably discovered new lands and mapped new seas of ice. "There is glory enough for all," I told the reporters.

At the hotel a pile of telegrams six inches high, from various papers, awaited me. I picked eight representative papers and made some diplomatic reply, expressing what I felt. That Peary would contest my claim never entered my head. It did seem, and still seems, in itself too inconsequential a thing to make such a fuss about.   This may be hard to believe to those who have magnified the heroism of such an achievement, a thing I never did feel and could not feel.

While sitting at the farewell dinner of the Geographical Society the following day, Mr. Peary's second message, saying that my Eskimos declared I had not gone far out of sight of land, came to me.   Those about received it with indignation.   Many advised me to reply in biting terms.   This I did not do; did not feel like doing.

Peary's messages caused me to make a change in my plans.   Previously I had accepted an invitation to go to Brussels, but now, as I was being attacked, I determined to return home immediately and face the charges in person.   I took passage on the steamship *Oscar II,* sailing direct from Copenhagen to New York.

COPENHAGEN TO THE UNITED STATES

ACROSS THE ATLANTIC—RECEPTION IN NEW YORK—BE-
WILDERING CYCLONE OF EVENTS—INSIDE NEWS OF
THE PEARY ATTACK—HOW THE WEB OF SHAME WAS
WOVEN

XXXII

PEARY'S UNDERHAND WORK AT LABRADOR

It seemed that, coming from the companionless
solitude of the North, destiny in the shape of crowds
was determined to pursue me. I expected to transfer
from the *Melchior* to the *Oscar II* at Christiansaand,
Norway, quietly and make my way home in peace. At
Christiansaand the noise began. On a smaller scale
was repeated the previous ovation of Copenhagen.

On board the *Oscar II* I really got more sleep than
I had for months previous or months afterwards. After
several days of seasickness I experienced the joys of
comparative rest and slept like a child. My brain still
seemed numbed. There were on the boat no curiosity-
seekers; no crowds stifled me nor did applause thunder
in my ears.

Every few minutes, before we got out of touch with
the wireless, there were messages; communications
from friends, from newspapers and magazines; repeti-

tions of the early charges made against me; questions concerning Peary's messages and my attitude toward him. When the boat approached Newfoundland the wireless again became disturbing. Then came the "gold brick" cable.

At this time, every vestige of pleasure in the thought of the thing I had accomplished left me. Since then, and to this day, I almost view all my efforts with regret. I doubt if any man ever lived in the belief of an accomplishment and got so little pleasure, and so much bitterness, from it. That my Eskimos had told Mr. Peary they had been but two days out of sight of land seemed probable; it was a belief I had always encouraged. That Mr. Peary should persistently attack me did arouse a feeling of chagrin and injury.

I spent most of my time alone in my cabin or strolling on the deck. The people aboard considered Peary's messages amusing. I talked little; I tried to analyze the situation in my mind, but wearily I gave it up; mentally I was still dazed.

During the trip Director Cold, chief of the Danish United Steamship Company, helped me with small details in every way; Lonsdale, my secretary, and Mr. Cold's secretary were busy copying my notes and my narrative story, which I had agreed to give to the New York *Herald*. I had made no plans; my one object was to see my family.

As we approached New York the wireless brought me news of the ovation under way. This amazed and filled me with dismay. I had considered the exaggerated reception of Copenhagen a manifestation of local excitement, partly due to the interest of the Danes in the North.   New York, I concluded, was too big, too unemotional, too much interested in bigger matters to bother much about the North Pole.   This I told Robert M. Berry, the Berlin representative of the Associated Press, who accompanied me on the boat.   He disagreed with me.

Having burned one hundred tons of coal in order to make time, the *Oscar II* arrived along American shores a day before that arranged for my reception.   So as not to frustrate any plans, we lay off Shelter Island until the next day.   It was my wish to send a message to Mrs. Cook and ask her to come out.   But the sea was rough; and, moreover, she was not well.   Now tugs bearing squads of reporters began to arrive.   We agreed to let no one aboard.   The New York *Journal,* with characteristic enterprise, had brought Anthony Fiala on its tug with a note from Mrs. Cook.   So an exception had to be made.   An old friend and a letter from my wife could not be sent away.

That night I slept little.   Outside I heard the dull thud of the sea.   Voices exploded from megaphones every few minutes.   Mingled emotions filled me.   The anticipation of meeting wife and children was sweet; that again, after an absence of more than two years, I should step upon the shores of my own land filled me with emotions too strong for words.

The next morning I was up with the rising of the sun.   We arrived at Quarantine soon after seven. About us on the waves danced a dozen tugs with re- porters.   In the distance appeared a tug toward which I strained my eyes, for I was told it bore my wife and children.   With a feeling of delight, which only long separation can give, I boarded this, and in a moment they were in my arms. I was conscious of confusion about me; of whistling and shrieking; uncanny magnified voices thundering from scores of megaphones; of a band playing an American air. When the *Grand Republic,* thrilling a metallic salute, steamed toward us, and the cheers of hundreds rent the air, I remembered asking myself what it could be all about. Why all this agitation?

Again the contagion of excitement bewildered me; the big boat drew near to a tug, above me swirled a cloud of hundreds of faces; around me the sunlit sea, with decorated craft, whirled and danced. As I giddily ascended the gangplank and felt a wreath of roses flung about me I was conscious chiefly of an unsuitable lack of appreciation. I spoke briefly; friends and relatives greeted me; the shaking of thousands of hands began; and all the while a deep hurt, a feeling of soreness, oppressed me.

From that day on until after I left New York, my life was a kaleidoscopic whirl of excitement, for which I found no reason. I had no time to analyze or estimate public enthusiasm and any change of that enthusiasm into doubt. I had no sense of perspective; involuntarily I was swept through a cyclone of events. The bewilderment which came upon me at Copenhagen returned, and with it a feeling of helplessness, of puzzlement; I felt much as a child might when taking its first ride in a carousel. Each day thereafter, from morning until morning there was a continuous rush of excitement; at no time, until I fled from it, did I get more than four hours' sleep at night—disturbed sleep at that.

I had not a moment for reflection, and even now, after recovering from the lack of mental perception which inevitably followed, it is with difficulty that I recall my impressions at the time. I suppose there are those who think that I was having a good time, but it was the hardest time of my life.

I remember standing in the pilot house of the *Grand Republic,* my little ones by me, and watching thousands of men along the wharves of the East River, going mad. The world seemed engaged in some frantic revel. Factories became vocal and screamed hideously; boats became hoarse with shrieking; the megaphone cry was maddening. Drawing up to a gayly decorated pier, a thunder of voices assailed me. I felt crushed by the unearthly din.

I was involuntarily shoved along, and found myself in an automobile—one of many, all decorated with flags. Cameras clicked like rapid-fire guns. A band played; roaring voices like beating sound waves rose and fell; faces swam before me.

Through streets jammed with people we moved along. I hardly spoke a word to my wife, who sat near. Out of the scene of tumult, familiar faces peered now and again. I remember being touched by the sight of thousands of school children, assembled outside of public schools and waving American flags.

In the neighborhood of the new bridge, under the arch, I recall seeing the eager face of my favorite boyhood school-teacher. It struck me at the time that she hardly seemed aged a day. Something swelled up within me, and I was conscious of a desire to lean out through the crowd and draw her into the machine. Through the thick congestion it was difficult to move; even the police were helpless. Now and again people tried to climb into the machine and were torn away.

At the Bushwick Club I lunched in a small room with friends, and a feeling of pleasure warmed my heart. During the reception words of confidence were spoken and somehow filtered into my mind. I shook hands until my arms were sore, bowed my head until my neck ached. I was forced to retire. Later there was dinner at the club, after which I received seven hundred singers. By this time I felt like a machine. My brain was blank. About midnight, utterly exhausted, I arrived at the Waldorf-Astoria, where I fought through a crowd in the lobby. I think I sat and listened to Mrs. Cook telling me news of home and the family until night merged into morning.

Next day the storm through which I was being swept began again. During that and the days following I made many mistakes, did and said unwise things. I want to show you, in telling of these events, just how helpless I was; what a victim of circumstance; how unfitted to bear the physical and mental demands of a ceaseless procession of public functions, lectures, dinners, receptions, days and nights of traveling, and how unable to cope with the many charges. In sixty days there were not less than two hundred lectures, dinners, and receptions, not to mention the unremitting train of press interviews. With no club of friends or organization of any kind behind me, I stood the strain alone.

I was ignorant of much that was said about me. I had no one to gauge my situation at any time and advise me. About me was an unbearable pressure from friends and foes; I stood it until I could stand it no longer.   There was not a minute of relief, not a minute to think.   Coming after two years spent in the Arctic, at a time when nature was paying the debt of long starvation and hardship, the stress of events inevitably developed a mental strain bordering on madness. Where could I go to get rest from it all?   This was my last thought at night and my first thought in the morning.

During my second day at the Waldorf I had to read proofs of the narrative to be printed in the *Herald,* go over the plans of my book with the New York publishing house with whom I had signed a contract, and examine hundreds of films to select photographs.   There were hundreds of letters and telegrams; scores of reporters demanding interviews; hundreds of callers, few of whom I was able to see.   An army of publishers, lecture managers, and even vaudeville managers sent up their cards.

The chief event of the first day in New York was the inquisition by newspaper reporters.   They both interested and amused me.   I had gone through the same ordeal in Copenhagen, and I knew that American interviewers are famed for their wolfish propensities.

Before I saw the sensation-hungry press men, I got certain news that shocked my sense of the fairness of the American press.   Someone interested in my case had sent me unsolicited copies of all telegrams, cables and wireless messages passing between New York and the Peary ship.   These messages now continued to come daily, and thus I was afforded a splendid opportunity to watch an underhand game of deceit wherein Mr.

Peary was shown to be in league with a New York paper aiming secretly to further his claims and to cast doubt upon mine.

Among these was a message asking a certain editor to meet Peary at Bangor, Maine, to arrange for the pro-Peary campaign of bribery and conspiracy which followed.   In another, and the most remarkable message, Mr. Peary first showed the sneaking methods by which the whole controversy was conducted.   A long list of questions had been prepared by Mr. Peary at Battle Harbor, covering, as rival interests dictated, every phase of Polar work.   These questions were sent to the New York *Times* with instructions to compel answers from me on each of a series of catch phrases.

When the *Times* reporter came to me with these, I recognized the Peary phraseology at once.   I afterwards compared the copy of Peary's telegram with that of the *Times,* and found in it nearly every question asked by the reporters.   While the questions were being read off, it required a good deal of patience to conceal my irritation, as I knew Mr. Peary was talking through the smooth-faced, smiling press cubs, none of whom knew that he was Peary's mouthpiece.   Every one of the Peary questions, however, was amusing, for I had answered each a dozen times in Europe.   But if Mr. Peary must question me, why did he stoop to the hypocrisy of doing it through others?   The other reporters asked many questions, the reports of which I have not seen since.   But the duplicity of this little trick left a strong impression of unfairness.

At about this time I began to examine critically the many efforts which Mr. Peary had begun to make to discredit my achievement. In going over such of his reports of his own claims as had gotten to me, I was at once struck with the statements parallel to mine which he had sent out, and since these so thoroughly proved my case I felt that I could be liberal and patient with Mr. Peary's ill-temper.

I now learned that after Mr. Peary got the full reports of my attainment of the Pole at the wireless station at Labrador, he withdrew behind the rocks to a place where no one was looking, and digested that report. His own report came after the digestion of mine. In the meantime, his delay in proceeding to Sydney, Nova Scotia, and his silence, were explained by the official announcement that the ship was being washed and cleaned. This was manifestly absurd. No seaman returning from a voyage of a year, where sailors have no occupation whatever except such work, waits until he gets to port before cleaning his decks. Furthermore, this hiding behind the rocks of Labrador continued for weeks. What was the mysterious occupation of Mr. Peary? The *Roosevelt,* as described by visitors when she arrived at Sydney, was still very dirty. When Mr. Peary's much-heralded report was finally printed, every Arctic explorer at once said the astonishing parallel statements in Mr. Peary's narrative either proved my case or convicted Mr. Peary of plagiarism. My story, by this time, had got well along in the New York *Herald.* To help Mr. Peary out of his position, McMillan later rushed to the press. He was under contract not to write or talk to the press, nor to lecture, write magazine articles or books, as were all of Peary's men. But this prohibition was waived temporarily.

Then McMillan made the statement that Dr. Cook must have gotten the "parallel data" and inside information from Mr. Peary's Eskimos.   Everyone acquainted with Greenland, including McMillan, knows that such inter-communication was impossible.   I had left for Uper-navik by the time Peary returned to Etah.   Therefore, McMillan and Peary both were caught in a deliberate lie, as were also Bartlett* and Borup later.   These were Mr. Peary's witnesses in the broadside of charges with which I was to be annihilated.

A few days after my arrival in America I learned for the first time of the strange death of Ross Marvin. We were asked by Mr. Peary to believe that this young man of more than average intelligence, a graduate of Cornell University and of the New York Nautical School, a man of experience on the Polar seas, stepped over young ice alone, without a life-line, and sank through a film of ice to a grave in the Arctic waters.

An idiot might do that; but Marvin, unless he went

---

*Captain Robert A. Bartlett, of the Peary ship *Roosevelt,* has fig-ured much in this controversy. Most of his reported statements, I am inclined to believe, are distorted. But he has allowed the words attrib-uted to him to stand; therefore, the harm done is just as great as if the charges were true. He allowed Henry Rood, in *The Saturday Evening Post,* to say that my expedition was possible only through the advice of Bartlett. Every statement which Rood made, as Bartlett knows, is a lie. He has allowed this to stand, and he thereby stands convicted as party to a faked article written with the express purpose of inflicting an injury.

Bartlett cross-questioned my Eskimos about instruments. By showing them a sextant and other apparatus he learned that I not only had a full set, but he also learned how I used them. Peary, although having Bart-lett's report on this, insinuated that I had no instruments, and that I made no observations. Bartlett knew this to be a lie, but he remained silent. He is therefore a party to a Peary lie.

In the early press reports Bartlett is credited with saying that "Cook had no instruments." A year later, after Bartlett returned from another trip north, faked pictures and faked news items were printed with the Bartlett interviews and reports. There was no protest, and at the same time Bartlett said that books, instruments, and things belonging to me had been destroyed. In the following year Bartlett announced that he was

suddenly mad, would not do it. To cross the young ice of open leads, like that in which Marvin is said to have perished, is a daily, almost hourly, experience in Arctic travel. To safeguard each other's lives, and to save sledges and dog teams, life-lines are carried in coils on the upstanders of the sled. When about to risk a crossing, a line is always fixed from one to the other and from sled to sled. When this is done, and an accident happens such as that which is alleged to have befallen Marvin, the victim is saved by the pull of his companions on the line. This is done as unfailingly as one eats meals. Would a man of Marvin's experience and intelligence neglect such a precaution? I knew such an accident might have happened to the inexperienced explorers of the days of Franklin, but to-day it seemed incredible. Furthermore, Peary was boasting of what he styled the "Peary system," for which is claimed such thoroughness that without it no other explorer could reach the Pole. If Marvin's death was natural, then he is a victim of this system.

"going after Cook's instruments." Has the press lied, or has Bartlett lied? Next to Henson, Mr. Peary's colored servant, Captain Bartlett is Peary's star witness.

George Borup, in "A Tenderfoot With Peary," after repeating in his book many pro-Peary lies, tried to prove his assertion by an alleged study of my sledge (P. 300): "Except for its being shortened, the sledge was the same as when it had left Annoatok. It weighed perhaps thirty pounds, and was very flimsy."

This is a deliberate lie, for it was only a half-sled, reassembled and repaired by old bits of driftwood. After this first lie he says, in the same paragraph: "Yet it had only two cracks in it." The upstanders had been cracked in a dozen places, the runners were broken, and every part was cracked.

Borup shows by his orthography of Eskimo words that he knows almost nothing of the Eskimo language. Therefore he may be dismissed as incompetent where Eskimo reports are to be interpreted. He is committed to the Peary interests, which also eliminates him from the jury. But in his report of my sled he has stooped to lies which forever deprive him of being credited with any honest opinion on the Polar controversy.

But let us read between the lines of this harrowing tragedy. After learning of my attainment of the Pole, Peary rushed to the wireless. With a letter in his pocket from Captain Adams which gave the news that started the ire of envy, and which also gave the news that convicted Peary of a lie, he thereafter for a week or more kept the wires busy with the famous "gold brick" messages.

Marvin's death, and the duty to a bereaved family, which ordinary humanity would have dictated, were of no consequence to one making envious, vicious attacks. For a week all the world blushed with shame because of the dishonor thus brought upon our country and our flag. In New York there was a happy home, a loving mother, a fond sister; anxious friends were all busy in preparing surprises for the happy homecoming of the one beloved by all. It was a busy week, with joyous, heart-stirring anticipation. There was no news from the Peary ship. Not a word came to indicate that their expected returning hero had been lost in the icy seas. To that mother's yearning heart her boy was nearing home—but alas! no news came! A week passed, and still no news!

At last, after Peary had digested my narrative, the carefully prepared press report was put on the wires. Ross Marvin's family, engrossed in preparations for a reception with flowers and flags, was about to see, in cold, black print, that he for whom their hearts beat expectantly was no more. At the last moment, Peary's conscience seemingly troubled him. A long message was sent to a friend to break the news and to soften the effects of the press reports on that poor

mother and sister.   That message was sent "Collect."
A man who had given years of his time and his life to
glorify Peary was not worthy of a prepaid telegram!

Later, an important letter from Marvin reached his
own home.   In it the stealing of my supplies is referred
to in a way to show that Marvin condemned Peary.
The public ought to know the wording of this part of the
letter.   Why has it been suppressed?   Marvin's death,
to my understanding, does not seem natural.   With a
good deal of empty verbiage the sacrifice of this unfortunate young man is explained; but two questions
are forced at once: Why was Marvin without a life-
line?   Why were conveniently lost with him certain
data that might disprove Peary's case?

If Marvin sank into the ice, as Peary said he did,
then Peary is responsible for the loss of that life, for he
did not surround him with proper safeguards.   The
death of this man points to something more than
tragedy.   Since Marvin's soundings were made under
the authority of the Coast and Geodetic Survey, the
American Government is, therefore, answerable for this
death.

Mr. Peary's treatment of Marvin wearied me of
all the Peary talk at the time; and, furthermore, all of
Mr. Peary's charges, of which so much fuss was made,
carried the self-evident origin of cruel envy and selfishness.   First, the Eskimos, put through a third degree
behind closed doors, were reported to have said that I
had not been more than two sleeps out of sight of land.
This was easily explained.   They had been instructed
not to tell Mr. Peary of my affairs, and they had been
encouraged to believe themselves always near land.

Then this charge was dropped, and the next was made, the one about my not reporting the alleged cache at "Cape Thomas Hubbard." That assertion, instead of injuring me, convicted Peary of trying to steal from Captain Sverdrup the honor of discovering and naming Svartevoeg. For it was shown that by deception "Cape Thomas Hubbard" had been written over a point discovered years earlier by another explorer. For this kind of honor Hubbard had contributed to Peary's expeditions. But is not the obliteration of a geographic name for money a kind of geographic larceny?

Then was forced the charge that I had told no one of my Polar success in the North, and therefore the entire report was an afterthought. Whitney and Prichard later cleared this up, but at the very time when Peary made this charge he had in his possession a letter from Captain Adams, of the whaler *Morning,* which he had received in the North, wherein my attainment of the Pole was stated. When Peary got the Adams letter he put on full steam, abandoned his plan to visit other Greenland ports, and came direct to Labrador, to the wireless. Why was the Adams letter suppressed, when it was charged that I had told no one? And, furthermore, why had Mr. Peary told no one on his ship of his own success until he neared Battle Harbor?

All of these charges betrayed untruthful methods on the part of Mr. Peary in his own method of presentation. Automatically, without a word of defence on my part, each charge rebounded on the charger.

Then there came the page broadside of rearranged charges printed by every American paper. It contained nothing new in the text, but with it there was a faked map, copied from Sverdrup, which was made to appear as though drawn by Eskimos. The best answer to this whole problem is that from the same tongues with which Mr. Peary tried to discredit me has come a much more formidable charge against Mr. Peary. For these same Eskimos have since said, without quizzing from me, that Mr. Peary never got to the Pole and that he never saw Crocker Land.

This part of the controversy was thoroughly analyzed by Professor W. F. Armbruster and Dr. Henry Schwartz in the St. Louis *Mirror**.

While this controversy early began to rage, the tremendous offers of money which came in every hour contributed to my bewilderment. They seemed fabu-

---

*Professor Armbruster and Dr. Schwartz, of St. Louis, at a time when few papers had the courage to print articles in my defence, appealed to W. R. Reedy, of the *Mirror*, for space to uncover the unfair methods of the Pro-Peary conspiracy. This space was liberally granted, and the whole controversy was scientifically analyzed by the *Mirror* in an unbiased manner. Here is shown an important phase of the Peary charges, from the *Mirror*, April 21, 1910. As it clearly reveals the facts, I present part of it as follows:

The point made by Dr. Schwartz, that there is a contradiction between Peary's statements of September 28 and October 13, is well taken. The statement of October 13 is a point-blank contradiction of the previous one. Dr. Schwartz notes that when Peary made, on September 28, what Peary called his strongest indictment of Dr. Cook, Peary must have had with him at Bar Harbor the chart with the trail of Cook's route, and infers that, as the later charge was by far the stronger indictment of the two, there must be some other explanation of the contradiction.

Analysis of this contradiction develops one of the most serious propositions of the whole Polar controversy. Mr. Peary might now say that he was holding his strongest point in reserve, but such explanation would not be sufficient, for he stated that the indictment of September 28 is "the strongest that has been advanced in Arctic exploration ever since the great expedition was sent there," and no child is so simple as to believe that the indictment of September 28 is at all comparable in magnitude to the one of October 13. Upon analysis, we find that there is indeed another explanation, and only one, and that is, that *when the indictment of September 28 was made, the one of October 13 had not been conceived or concocted*, and it will show that Peary, Bartlett, McMillan, Borup and Henson, *all* who signed the statement of October 13, perpetrated a gross falsehood and imposition upon the public. All are caught in the one net.

If this coterie had received from the Eskimos such information as is

lous; the purport was beyond me. I imagined this as part of a dream from which I should awake. Were I the calculating monster of cupidity which some believe me, I suppose I should have been more circumspect in making my financial arrangements.

I should hardly, for instance, have sold my narrative story to Mr. James Gordon Bennett for $25,000 when there were single offers of $50,000, $75,000, $100,000, and more, for it. While I was in Copenhagen, and before the *Herald* offer was accepted, Mr. W. T. Stead had come with a message from W. R. Hearst with instructions to double any other offer presented for my narrative. Had I accepted Mr. Hearst's

---

claimed by them in their statement of October 13, then they must have received it from the Eskimos *before Peary and his party left Etah on their return to America.* If they had the information when they left the Eskimos at Etah, on their return to America, then they had it when they arrived at Indian Harbor, and before their statement of September 28 was made.

In their statement of October 13, 1909, Peary, Bartlett, McMillan, Borup and Henson state, and sign their names to the statement made to the world and copyrighted, that they had a map on which E-tuk-i-shook and Ah-we-lah, Dr. Cook's two Eskimos, had traced for them the route taken by Dr. Cook, and that this was also supported by the verbal statements of the two Eskimos, *that Dr. Cook had reached the northern point of Heiberg Land, or Cape Thomas Hubbard; that he had gone two sleeps north of it, had then turned to the west or southwest, and returned to the northern headland of Heiberg Land, but on the west or northwest side, and had sent back one of the Eskimos to the cache left on the headland, but on the east side of the point, and remained at this new place on the west side of the point for four or five sleeps.* Then, all the time that Peary was challenging and impugning that Dr. Cook had reached even the northern point of Heiberg Land, according to their own statement of October 13, *they had in their pockets the map and information from the Eskimos that Dr. Cook had not only reached the northern point of Heiberg Land, but traveled above it and turned around the point.* In so challenging that Dr. Cook had reached even the northern point of said land, and thereby discrediting Dr. Cook with all the force and influence at their command, when, according to their own later statement, they had then and at that time, and before such time (since they left Etah on their return to America), the statements, trail of route and testimony of the Eskimos entirely to the contrary, *Peary and his coterie deliberately and knowingly prepetrated on the public the grossest of falsehoods and impositions.*

There are several other contradictions in the statement of October 13.

bid he would have paid $400,000 for what I sold for $25,000. Here is a sacrifice of $375,000. Does that look as if I tried to hoax the world for sordid gain, as my enemies would like the public to believe? What Mr. Bennett asked and offered $25,000 for was a series of four articles on adventures in the North, for use in the Sunday supplement of the *Herald*. I had no such articles prepared at the time, nor, as I knew, should I have time to write these. I did have the narrative story of my trip, which consisted of twenty-five thousand to thirty thousand words, complete. I decided, when I heard the first reports of doubt cast on my claim, to publish my narrative story as an honest and sincere proof of my claim as soon as possible. So I gave this to Mr. Bennett for the sum offered purely for Sunday articles.

One is the statement that Pan-ic-pa (the father of E-tuk-i-shook), was familiar with the first third and last third of the journey of Dr. Cook and his two Eskimos. Pan-ic-pa may be familiar with the territory of the last third of the route, but not with the journey made by Dr. Cook and E-tuk-i-shook and Ah-we-lah over this part of the route, for these three alone made the journey from Cape Sparbo to Annoatok. Pan-ic-pa went only as far as the northern point of Heiberg Land, and returned from there nearly a year before Dr. Cook and his two Eskimos arrived from Cape Sparbo. This is shown by Peary and his party themselves in their statement that Pan-ic-pa, the father of E-tuk-i-shook, a very intelligent man, *who was in the party of Eskimos that came back from Dr. Cook from the northern end of Nansen's Strait* (Sound), came in and indicated the same localities and details as the two boys. Of course Pan-ic-pa could only indicate the localities that he had himself journeyed to with Dr. Cook, and not any after he had left Dr. Cook and the two Eskimos at the norther point of Heiberg Land, or the northern end of Nansen's Sound, which is the same thing.

Another contradiction, a very serious one indeed, as important as the first of the foregoing contradictions is, that if Peary and his party had such information from the Eskimos as they claimed in their statement of October 13, then they knew that the little sledge of Dr. Cook which they saw at Etah was not the sledge that made the trip to the Pole. The printed reports show that long before October 13 Peary and all his henchmen were challenging and charging to the public that the little sled in question left with Whitney, could not possibly have made the trip to the Pole. In the statement of October 13, Peary and his party state that,

GOVERNOR KRAUL IN HIS STUDY
ARRIVAL AT UPERNAVIK

POLAR TRAGEDY—A DESERTED CHILD OF THE SULTAN OF THE
NORTH AND ITS MOTHER

Mr. Bennett offered me $5,000 additional for the European rights of this story. To this offer I made no reply, giving Mr. Bennett the sole news rights of the story for the entire world.

When I reached New York, needing ready money, I wired Mr. Bennett for an advance on my story. He cabled back an immediate order for the entire sum of $25,000. This gave me a sudden glow, a feeling of pleasure at what I regarded as a display of confidence.

With my lecture work and traveling I was kept so busy that I did not have time to go over the story, type-written from my almost illegible notes, which was sent to the New York *Herald*. When I did go over the proofs and found many grievous errors, the *Herald* had

---

according to the Eskimos, Dr. Cook and his two Eskimos started from the northern point of Heiberg Land with only two sledges. Further on in the statement, that the dogs and one sledge were abandoned in Jones Sound, and that at Cape Vera—western end of Jones Sound—Peary and his party say that E-tuk-i-shook and Ah-we-lah, Dr. Cook's two Eskimos, informed them that (quoting Peary and his party's statement verbatim), "here they cut the remaining sledge off—that is, shortened it, as it was awkward to transport with the boat, and near here they killed a walrus."

During all the time then, before October 13, that Peary and his party were belittling this sled, and referring to its character as a positive proof that Dr. Cook could not have reached the Pole, and stating that it would have been knocked to pieces in a few days, they, according to their own statement of October 13, knew, even while using such argument against Dr. Cook, that the little sled was not the original sled, but only a part of one which the desperate and fearfully hard-pressed wanderers had themselves—having no dogs—dragged their food for three hundred miles over one of the roughest and most terrible strectches of the frozen zone, never before traveled by man. According to their own statement of October 13, Peary and his clique convict themselves of boldly and deliberately perpetrating gross falsehoods against Dr. Cook and upon the people. Then shall we believe anything further from them?

There is only one rational view to take of their statement of October 13. That, knowing their first charges were certain to fail, the statement of October 13 was concocted for their own base purposes. *No sane person can believe that if they had had such exceedingly damaging information as is claimed by them in their statement of October 13, they could have instead made use of charges far less damaging and known to them to be false.*

W. J. ARMBRUSTER.

ST. LOUIS, Mo., April 13, 1910.

already syndicated the story. It was too late for any corrections, and thus many errors appeared.

I made a contract with a New York publishing house, while in Copenhagen, with the idea of getting out my book and all proofs possible as soon as the presses would allow, in view of the imminent controversy. For the English and American rights to my book I was to receive $150,000 in a lump sum and an additional $150,000 in royalties. Although papers were signed for this, later on, when things seemed turning against me and I saw the publishers were getting "cold feet," I voluntarily freed them from the contract.

By the time I left Copenhagen, as I figured later, offers for book and magazine material and lectures had aggregated just one and one-half million dollars. A prominent New York manager made me an offer of $250,000 for a series of lectures. During the first few days I had absolutely no system of caring for this correspondence, hundreds of important cablegrams remained unopened, and huge offers of money were ignored. It was only after Minister Egan sent Walter Lonsdale, in response to my request for a competent secretary, that some intelligible information was gleaned from the mass of correspondence. Most of it, as a matter of fact, was read only when we were on the *Oscar II,* bound for home.

After making my arrangement with Mr. Bennett, the *Matin* of Paris had sent me an offer of $50,000 for the serial rights of a French translation of the story to appear in the *Herald.* This included a lecture under the auspices of the paper in Paris. My anxiety to get home prevented a consideration of this; and it was only after I sailed on the *Oscar II* that I realized I could have gone to Paris, delivered the lecture, and returned to New York by a fast boat.

On the *Oscar II* a wireless had reached me of a large offer for a lecture during the convention in St. Louis. This I decided to accept, the simple reason being that I needed money.

Much criticism has been hurled at me because I started on a lecture campaign when I should have prepared my data and submitted proof. At that time I was in no position to anticipate or understand this criticism. Every explorer for fifty years had done the same thing, all had delivered lectures and written articles about their work after a first preliminary report. Supplementary and detailed data were usually given long afterwards, not as proof but as a part of the plan of recording ultimate results. I had the precedents of Stanley, Nordenskjöld, Nansen, Peary, and others.

Had I anticipated the furore that was being raised about proofs, I probably should have taken public opinion into my consideration. So firm was my own conviction of achievement that the difficulty of supplying such absolute proof as the unique occasion afterwards demanded never occurred to me. My feeling at the time was that I was under no obligation to patrons, to the Government, to any society, or anyone, and that I had a right to deliver lectures at a time when public interest was keyed up, and to prepare my detailed reports at a time when I should have more leisure.

My family needed money. Huge sums were offered me hourly; I should have been unwise indeed had I not accepted some of the offers. I am advised that stories of enormous lecture profits have been told. I am informed that the newspapers said I was to receive $25,000 for going to .St. Louis. The truth is that I got less than half that, though I believe St. Louis probably spent more than $25,000 in preparing for my appearance there. All told, I delivered about twenty lectures in various large cities, receiving from $1,000 to $10,000 per lecture. My expenses were heavy, so that in the end I netted less than $25,000. When I determined to stop the lecture work and prepare my data, I canceled $140,000 worth of lecture engagements.

Each day there was a routine of lunches with speeches, dinners with speeches, suppers with speeches. The task of devising speeches was ever present; with me it did not come easy. But speeches must be made, and I felt a tense strain, as if something were drawing my mentality from me.

Everywhere I went crowds pressed about me. I shook hands until the flesh of one finger was actually worn through to the bone. Hundreds of people daily came to see me.

About this time, too, my bewildered brain began to realize that I was also the object of most ferocious attacks from many quarters. I had no time to read the newspapers, and these charges and suspicions filtered in to me through reporters and friends. Usually they reached me in an exaggerated or a distorted form.

There began at this time the publication of innumerable fake interviews and stories misrepresenting me.* One interviewer quoted me as saying that

---

*One of the meanest and pettiest charges concocted for Mr. Peary at a time when personal veracity was regarded as the test of rival claims was

Dagaard Jensen had seen my records, and therefore confirmed my claim to the people in Copenhagen; another that I said Governor Kraul of Greenland had reported talking with my Eskimos, who had confirmed my report. Dagaard Jensen justly denied this by cable, as I had made no such statement. That about Governor Kraul was absurd on the face of it, as he was a thousand miles away from my Eskimos. I have no means of knowing the embarrassing statements attributed to me—things which were variously denied, and which hurt me. There was not time for me to consider or answer them.

Then came the blow which almost stunned me—the news that Harry Whitney had not been allowed by Peary to bring my instruments and notes home with him.

During the long night at Cape Sparbo I had carefully figured out and reduced most of my important observations. The old, rubbed, oily, and torn field

---

that I had attempted to steal the scientific work of a missionary while I was on the Belgica Antarctic Expedition. Director Townsend, of the New York Aquarium, who, like Mr. Peary, was drawing a salary from the taxpayers while his energies were spent in another mission, declared I had taken a dictionary, compiled by Thos. Bridges, of Indian words, and had put it forth as my own work. Dalenbagh, of the American Geographical Society, and of the "Worm Diggers' Union," polly-like, also repeated this charge. "Of the other charges against Dr. Cook we are at sea," he said, "but here is something that we know about." By expending five cents in stamps, five minutes with the pen, both Townsend and Dalenbaugh might have learned that the dishonor which they were trying to attach to some one else was on themselves.

Under big headlines, "Dr. Cook Steals a Missionary's Work," the New York *Times* and other pro-Peary papers printed columns of absolute lies in what purported to be interviews with Townsend. Dalenbaugh, pointing to this gleefully, said "Dr. Cook has been guilty of wrong-doing for many years."

Now what were the facts? Among the scientific collections of the Belgian Expedition, was a series of notes, embodying a Yahagan Indian Dictionary, made by the missionary, Thomas Bridges. Although this was of little use to anybody, it was a scientific record worthy of preservation.

notes, the instrumental corrections and the direct readings were packed with the instruments, and these were mostly left with Mr. Whitney. The figures were important for future recalculation, but otherwise had not seemed materially important to me, for they had served their purpose. I had with me all the important data, such as is usually given in a traveler's narrative. No more had ever been asked before.

Under ordinary circumstances, these instruments and papers would not have been of great value, but under the public excitement their importance was immensely enhanced.

I had publicly announced that Mr. Whitney would bring these with him on the boat in which he was to return. Had there been no notes and no instruments, I hardly should have said this were I perpetrating a fraud, for I should have known that the failure of Mr. Whitney to supply these would provoke widespread suspicion.

In a friendly spirit toward the late Mr. Bridges and his Indians, I persuaded the Belgians at great expense to publish the work. It was written in the old Ellis system of orthography, which is not generally understood. Working on this material for one year without pay, I changed it to ordinary English orthography, but made few other alterations. The book is not yet printed, but part of it is in press. The introduction was printed five years ago, and among the first paragraphs appear these words:

"My visit among the tribe of Fuegians was not of sufficient length to make a thorough study, nor had I the opportunity to collect much data from Indians, but I was singularly fortunate in being in the company of Mr. Thomas Bridges and Mr. John Lawrence, men who have made these people their life study. The credit of collecting and making this Yahagan Grammar and Vocabulary belongs solely to Mr. Bridges, who devoted most of his time during thirty-seven years to recording this material. My work is limited to a slight re-arrangement of the words, a few additions of notes and words, and a conversion of the Ellis phonetic characters in which the native words were written into ordinary English orthography. It is hoped that this study of Yahagan language, with a few of their tales and traditions, will, with a report of the French Expedition, make a fitting end to an important record of a vanishing people."

Then follows a short favorable biography of the man whose work I was accused of stealing.

This is just what happened.   Had I foreseen the trouble that resulted, I should have taken my instruments with me to Upernavik, and have supplied my observations and notes at once.

As I have said before, I believed in an accomplishment which I felt was largely personal, for which a world excitement was not warranted and in which I had such a sure confidence that I never thought of absolutely accurate proof.   This was my folly—for which fate made me pay.   Imagine my dismay, the heart-sickness which seized me when, through the din of tumult and excitement, in the midst of suspicion, came the news that Mr. Whitney had been forced by Mr. Peary to take from the *Roosevelt* and bury the very material with which I might have dispelled suspicion and quelled the storm of unmerited abuse.

The instruments carried on my northern trip, and left with Mr. Whitney, and which he had seen, consisted of one French sextant; one aluminum surveying compass, with azimuth attachment, bought of Keuffer & Essen, New York; one glass artifical horizon, set in a thin metal frame, adjusted by spirit levels and thumb-screws, bought of Hutchinson, Boston; one aneroid barometer, aluminum, bought of Hicks; an aluminum case with maximum and minimum spirit thermometer; other thermometers, and one liquid compass.

Other instruments used about stations were also left.   With these were papers giving some instrumental corrections, readings, and comparisons, and other occasional notes, and a small diary, mostly loose leaves, containing some direct field reading of instruments and meteorological data.   These took up very little space;

and, if I remember correctly, all were snugly packed in one of the instrument cases.

Mr. Whitney especially asked, as a personal favor, the honor of caring for my flag. Later, after his return, he said that as Mr. Peary had refused to let him take aboard my things, he had no alternative but to bury them at Etah. I have no complaint to make against Mr. Peary about this. He was at liberty to pick the freight of his own ship. But he later said: "His [Dr. Cook's] leaving of his records at Etah was a scheme by which he could claim that they were lost." If Mr. Peary knew this, why did he not bring them?

At the time I felt crippled; my feeling of disgust with the problem, with myself, and with the situation began. It would be impossible to give in my report a continuous line of observations. I had no corrections for the instruments. I knew they might vary. I had no means of checking them. I had some copies of the original data, but they were not complete. I should have to rest my whole case on a report with reduced observations, for I knew it would not be possible to send a ship to Etah until the following year. And I also knew that if Eskimos were not given strong explicit instructions all would be lost.

Meanwhile, many apparently trivial accusations against me were being widely discussed, which, never refuted, had their weight in the long run in discrediting my good faith. On every side I was attacked, not so much for unintentional error, as for deliberate false-hood.

In the bewildering days that followed—during which I traveled to various cities to fulfill lecture engagements—I felt alone, a victim of such pressure as, I believe, has seldom been the fate of any human being.

Friends confused me as much as the attacks of foes. Some advised one thing; others another; my brain staggered with their well-meaning advice. Most of them wanted me to "light out," as they expressed it, and attack Mr. Peary. A number suggested the formation of an organization, the work of which would be to issue counter attacks on Mr. Peary, to be written by various men, and to reply systematically to charges made against me. Such a course was distasteful to me, and, furthermore, the selfish, envious origin of all of Mr. Peary's charges seemed evident.

Many of the other attacks seemed so ridiculous that I felt no one would believe them—which was another of my many mistakes. The more serious charges I believed could wait until I had time to sit down and reply to them at length. I felt the futility of any fragmentary retorts. At no time did I have an intelligent grasp of the situation, of the excited and exaggerated interest of the public, or of the fluctuating state of public opinion.

In my many years of Arctic work I had gathered pictures of almost every phase of Arctic life and scene; on subsequent trips, unless for some special reason, I did not duplicate photographs of impregnable, unmeltable headlands, or of walrus, or icebergs which I considered typical. In the early rush for illustrative material I gave a number of these to the *Herald,* stating they were scenes I had passed, but which had been taken on an earlier expedition. By · some mistake, which is not unusual in newspaper offices, one of these pictures was put under a caption, "Pictures of Dr. Cook's Polar Trip," or something to this effect. Whereupon, Mr. Herbert Bridgman, secretary of the Peary Arctic Club, shouted aloud, "Fraud!" and others took up the cry. A further charge that these pictures were not mine at all, but had been stolen or borrowed from Herbert Berri, was advanced—an absolute untruth, as I had the negatives, from which these pictures were made, in my possession.

What, in those early days, had seemed a serious criticism offered against my claim, was that I had exceeded possible speed limits by asserting an average of about fifteen miles a day. The English critics were particularly severe. According to their reading, this had never been done before. Admiral Melville had taken this up in America before my arrival; by the time I got to New York, Mr. Peary had made a report of twenty to forty-five miles daily under similar conditions, and I asked myself the reason of the sudden hush.

Much space was now given to the criticism by learned men of my giving seconds in observations. The point was taken that as you near the Pole the degrees of longitude narrow, and seconds are of no consequence. Therefore I was charged with trying to fake an impossible accuracy. I always regarded seconds as of little consequence, put them down as a matter of routine—for in that snow-blinding, bewildering North I worked more like a machine than a reasoning being—and now the inadvertent use of these was used to cast suspicion upon me.

With this attack, like echoes from many places, came reiterations of the criticism, which, polly-like, was taken up by Rear-Admiral Chester. Professor Stockwell of Cleveland had earlier brought out this academic discussion. Because I had seen the midnight sun for the first time on April 7 it was claimed I must have been at a more southern point of the globe than I believed. At the time it seemed the only serious scientific criticism of my reports which was used against me.

Whether I was on a more southerly point of the globe than I believed or not, I had not used the midnight sun, seen through a mystic maze of unknowable refraction, to determine position; to do so would have been impossible. With a constant moving and grinding of the ice, causing opening lanes of water, from which the inequality of temperature drew an evaporation like steam from a volcano, it is impossible at this season to see a low sun with a clear horizon. One looks through an opaque veil of blinding crystals. Every Arctic traveler knows that even when the sun is seen on a clear horizon, as it returns after the long night, his eyes are deceived—he does not see the sun at all, but a refracted image caused by the optical deception of atmospheric distortions. For this reason, as I knew, all observations of the sun when very low are worthless as a means of determining position. The assumption that I had done this seemed mere foolishness to me at the time.

Staggered by the blow that Whitney had buried my instruments in the North, the recurring thoughts of these harassing charges certainly had no soothing effect.

Alone, I was unable to cope with matters, anyway. I under-estimated the effect of the cumulating attacks. Oppressed by the undercurrent feeling that it was all a fuss about very little, a thing of insignificant worth, and disturbed by the growing uncertainty of proving such a claim to the point of hair-breadth accuracy by any figures, despair overcame me.

I was so busy I could not pause to think, and was conscious only of the rush, the labor, the worry. I no longer slept; indigestion naturally seized me as its victim. A mental depression brought desperate premonitions.

I developed a severe case of laryngitis in Washington; it got worse as I went to Baltimore and Pittsburg. At St. Louis, where I talked before an audience said to number twelve thousand persons, I could hardly raise my voice above a whisper. The lecture was given with physical anguish. I was feverish and mentally dazed. Thereafter, day by day, my thoughts became less coherent; I, more like a machine.

I do not exaggerate when I say that there was practically not one hour of pleasure in those troubled days. The dinner which was given by the Arctic travelers at the Waldorf-Astoria pleased me more than anything during the entire experience. I felt the close presence of hundreds of warm friends; I was conscious of their good will.

I can recall the ceremony of presenting the keys of the City of New York to me, but I was so confused and half ill that I was not in a condition to appreciate the honor.

After I had been on my lecture tour for a few weeks, I began to feel persecuted. On every side I sensed hostility; the sight of crowds filled me with a growing sort of terror. I did not realize at the time that I was passing from periods of mental depression to

dangerous periods of nervous tension. I was pursued
by reporters, people with craning necks, good-natured
demonstrations of friendliness that irritated me. In the
trains I viewed the whirling landscape without, and felt
myself part of it—as a delirious man swept and hurtled
through space.

I suppose I answered questions intelligently; like
an automaton delivered my lectures, shook hands. I
have been told I smiled pleasantly always—mentally I

Author's Note.—I have never attempted to disprove Mr. Peary's
claim to having reached the North Pole. I prefer to believe that Mr.
Peary reached the North Pole.

So avid have been my enemies, however, to cast discredit upon my
own achievement, by such trivial and petty charges, that it seems curious
they have never noticed or have remained silent about many striking and
staggering discrepancies in Mr. Peary's own published account of his
journey.

In Mr. Peary's book, entitled "The North Pole; Its Discovery, 1909,"
published by Frederick A. Stokes Company, on page 302, appears the
following:

"We turned our backs upon the Pole at about four o'clock of the
afternoon of April 7."

According to a statement made on page 304, Mr. Peary took time on
his return trip to take a sounding of the sea five miles from the Pole.

On page 305, Mr. Peary says: "Friday, April 9, was a wild day. All
day long the wind blew strong from the north-northeast, increasing finally
to a gale." And on page 306: "We camped that night at 87° 47′."

Mr. Peary thus claims to have traveled from the Pole to this point, a
distance of 133 nautical miles, or 153 statute miles, in a little over two
days. This would average 76½ statute miles a day. Could a pedestrian
make such speed? During this time Mr. Peary camped twice, to make
tea, eat lunch, feed the dogs, and rest—several hours in each camp.

Why I should never have gone out of sight of land for more than
two days, as he has charged, when such miraculous speed can be made on the
circumpolar sea, is something Mr. Peary might find interesting reasons to
explain.

On page 310, Mr. Peary says: "We were coming down the North
Pole hill in fine shape now, and another double march, April 16-17, brought
us to our eleventh upward camp at 85° 8′, one hundred and twenty-one
miles from Cape Columbia."

According to this, Mr. Peary covered the distance from 87° 47′, on
April 9, to 85° 8′, on April 17—a distance of 159 nautical miles in eight
day. This averaged twenty miles a day.

On page 316, he says: "It was almost exactly six o'clock on the
morning of April 23 when we reached the igloo of 'Crane City,' at Cape
Columbia, and the work was done."

was never conscious of a smile. It is strange how, machine-like, a man can conduct himself like a reasonable being when, mentally, he is at sea. I have read a great deal about the subconscious mind; on no other theory can I account for my rational conduct in public at the time. Really, as I view myself from the angle of the present, I marvel that a man so distraught did not do desperate things.

Mr. Peary left 85° 8' on April 17, according to his statement, and traveled 121 miles to Cape Columbia in six days, arriving on April 23. This last stretch was at the rate of twenty miles a day. To sum up, he traveled from the North Pole, according to his statements, to land, as follows:

The first 133 nautical miles southward in two days, at the rate of 66 nautical miles, or 76½ statute miles, a day; the last 279 nautical miles in fourteen days, an average of 20 miles a day.

According to Peary's book, Bartlett left him at 87° 46', and Mr. Peary started on his final spurt to the Pole a little after midnight on the morning of April 2. By arriving at the point where he left Bartlett on the evening of \April 9, he would have made the distance of 270 miles to the Pole from this point and back, in a little over seven days.

In the New York *World* of October 3, 1910, page 3, column 6, Matthew Henson makes the following statement: "On the way up we had to break a trail, and averaged only eighteen to twenty miles a day. On the way back we had our own trail to within one hundred miles of land, and then Captain Bartlett's trail. We made from twenty to forty miles a day."

At the rate of twenty miles a day on the way up, which Henson claims was made, it would have taken 6 days and 18 hours to cover the distance of 135 miles from 87° 47' to the Pole. Adding the thirty hours Mr. Peary claims he spent at the Pole for observations, eight days would have elapsed before they started back. Peary says the round trip of 270 miles from 87° 47' N. to the Pole and the return to the same latitude was done in seven days and a few hours.

Why has Mr. Peary never been asked to explain his miraculous speed and the discrepancy between his statement and Henson's?

Henson was Mr. Peary's sole witness. When Mr. Peary, in a framed-up document, endeavors to disprove my claim by quoting my Eskimos, it would be just as fair to apply Henson's words to disprove Peary.

Moreover, inasmuch as Mr. Peary's partisans attacked my speed limits when I made my first reports, does it not seem curious indeed that they now accept as infallible, and *ex cathedra,* the published reports of the almost supernatural feat in covering distance made by Mr. Peary?

THE KEY TO THE CONTROVERSY

PEARY AND HIS PAST—HIS DEALING WITH RIVAL EXPLOR-
ERS—THE DEATH OF ASTRUP—THE THEFT OF THE
"GREAT IRON STONE," THE NATIVES' SOLE SOURCE OF
IRON

XXXIII

ACTIONS WHICH CALL FOR INVESTIGATION

Aiming to be retired from the Navy as a Captain, with a comfortable pension; aiming eventually to wear the stripes of a Rear-Admiral, which necessitated a promotion over the heads of others in the normal line of advancement, a second Polar victory, which was all that Peary could honestly claim, was not sufficient. Something must be done to destroy in the public eye the merits of my achievement for the first attainment of the Pole. I had reached the Pole on April 21, 1908. Mr. Peary's claims were for April 6, 1909, a year later. To destroy the advantage of priority of my conquest, and to establish himself as the first and only one who had reached the Pole, was now the one predominant effort to which Mr. Peary and his coterie of conspirators set themselves. To this end the cables were now made to burn with an abusive campaign, which the press, eager for sensations, took up from land's end to land's end, even to the two worlds. The wireless operators picked up messages that were being thrown from ship to ship and from point to point. Each carried unkind insinuations coming from the lips of Mr. Peary. The press and the public were induced to believe that Peary's words came from one who was himself above the shadow of suspicion. Their efforts, however, as we will see later, did not differ from the battle of envy forced against others before me, but it was now done more openly.

It was difficult to remain silent against such world-wide slanders. But I reasoned that truth would ultimately prevail, and that the rebound of the American spirit of fair play would quell the storm.

I had known for nearly a quarter of a century the man for whom the press now attacked me. I had served on two of his expeditions without pay; I had watched his successes and his failures; I had admired his strong qualities, and I had shivered with the shocks of his wrongdoings. But still I did not feel that anything was to be gained by retaliative abuse; and the truth about him, out of charity, I hesitated to tell. No, I argued, this warfare of the many against one, under the dictates of envy, must ultimately bring to light its own injustice.

I had always reasoned that a quiet, dignified, non-assailing bearing would be most effective in a battle of this kind. Contrary to the general belief at the time, this was not done out of respect for Mr. Peary; it seemed the best means to a worthier end. But I did not know at this time that the press, dog-like, jumps upon him who maintains a non-attacking attitude. In modern times, the old Christian philosophy of turning the other cheek, as I have found, does not give the desired results.

The press, which, at my home-coming, had lavished praise and glowing panegyric, now, as promptly, swung completely around and heaped upon my head terms of opprobrium and obloquy. Faked news items were issued to discredit me by Peary's associates; editors devoted space to jibes and sarcasms at my expense; clever writers and cartoonists did their best to make my name a humorous byword with my countrymen. Much of this I did not know until long after.

The suddenness of all this—the terrible injustice and unreasonableness of it—simply overwhelmed me. Arriving from the cruel North, completely spent in body and in mind, the rest that I was urgently in need of had been constantly denied me. Instead, I had been caught up and held within a perfect maelstrom of excitement. That excitement still ran like fever in my veins. The plaudits of the multitude were still ringing in my ears when this horror of a world's contumely burst on my head. I could only bow my head and let the storm spend itself about me. Sick at heart and dazed in mind, conscious only of a vague disgust with all the world and myself, I longed for respite and forgetfulness within the bosom of my family.

So, quietly, I decided to retire for a year, out of reach of the yellow papers; out of reach of the grind of the pro-Peary mill of infamy, still maintaining silence rather than stoop to the indignity of showing up the dark side of Mr. Peary's character. Having returned, I hesitate to do it now; but the weaving of the leprous blanket of infamy with which Peary and his supporters attempted to cover me cannot be understood unless we look through Mr. Peary's eyes—regard other explorers as he regarded them; regard the North as his inalienable property as he did, and regard his infamous, highhanded injustices as right.

I have now decided to uncover the incentive of this one-sided fight to which I have so long maintained a non-attacking attitude. I had hoped, almost against hope, that the public would ultimately understand, without a word from me, the humbug of the mudslingers who were attempting to defame my character. I had felt sure that the hand which did the besmearing was silhouetted clearly against the blackness of its own making. But the storm of a sensation-seeking press later so thickened the atmosphere that the public, from which one has a sure guarantee of fair play, was denied a clear view.

Now that the storm has spent its force; now that the hand which did the mudslinging has within its grasp the unearned gain which it sought; now that a clear point of observation can be presented, I am compelled, with much reluctance and distaste, to reveal the unpleasant and unknown past of the man who tried to ruin me; showing how unscrupulous and brutal he was to others before me; with evidence in hand, I shall reveal how he wove his web of defamation and how his friends conspired with him in the darkest, meanest and most brazen conspiracy in the history of exploration.

In doing this, my aim is not to challenge Mr. Peary's claim, but to throw light on unwritten pages of history, which pages furnish the key to unlock the long-closed door of the Polar controversy and the pro-Peary conspiracy.

From the earliest days, Mr. Peary's effort to reach the Pole was undertaken primarily for purposes of personal commercial gain. For twenty years he has passed the hat along lines of easy money. That hat would be passing to-day if the game had not been, in the opinion of many, spoiled by my success.

For nearly twenty years he sought to be promoted over the heads of stay-at-home but hardworking naval officers. During all of this time, while on salary as a naval officer, he was away engaged in private enterprises from which hundreds of thousands of dollars went into his pockets. By wire-pulling and lobbying he succeeded in having the American Navy pay him an unearned salary. Such a man could not afford to divide the fruits of Polar attainment with another.

In 1891, as the steamer *Kite* went north, Mr. Peary began to evince the brutal, selfish spirit which later was shown to every explorer who had the misfortune to cross his trail. Nansen had crossed Greenland; his splendid success was in the public eye. Mr. Peary attempted to belittle the merited applause by saying that Nansen had borrowed the "Peary system." But Peary had borrowed the Nordenskiold system, without giving credit. A few months later, Mr. John M. Verhoeff, the meteorologist of the *Kite* expedition, was accorded such unbrotherly treatment that he left his body in a glacial crevasse in preference to coming home on the same ship with Mr. Peary. This man had paid $2,000 for the privilege of being Peary's companion.

Eivind Astrup, another companion of Peary, a few

years later was publicly denounced because he had written a book on his own scientific observations and did work which Peary had himself neglected to do. This attempt to discredit a young, sensitive explorer was followed by his mental unbalancement and suicide.

About 1897, Peary took from the people of the Farthest North the Eskimos' treasured "Star Stone." At some remote period in the unknown history of the frigid North, thousands of years ago, when, possibly, the primitive forefathers of the Eskimos were perishing from inability to obtain food in that fierce war waged between Nature and crude, blindly struggling, aboriginal life because of a lack of weapons with which to kill, there swiftly, roaringly, descended from the mysterious skies a gigantic meteoric mass of burning, white-hot iron. Whence it came, those dazed and startled people knew not; they regarded it, as their descendants have regarded it, with baffled mystified terror; later, with reverence, gratitude, and a feeling akin to awe. Gazing skyward, in the long, starlit nights, there undoubtedly welled up surgingly in the wild hearts of these innocent, Spartan children of nature, a feeling of vague, instinctive wonder at the Power which swung the boreal lamps in heaven; which moves the worlds in space; which sweeps in the northern winds, and which, for the creatures of its creation, apparently consciously, and often by means seemingly miraculous, provides methods of obtaining the sources of life. As the meteor and its two smaller fragments cooled, the natives, by the innate and adaptive ingenuity of aboriginal man, learned to chip masses from it, from which were shaped knives and arrows and spearheads. It became their mine of treasure, more precious than gold; it was their only means of making weapons for obtaining that which sustained life. With new weapons, they developed the art of spear-casting and arrow-throwing. As the centuries passed, animals fell easy prey to their skill; the starvation of elder ages gave way to plenty.

The arm of God, it is said in the Scriptures, is long. From the far skies it extended to these people of an ice-sheeted, rigorous land, that they might survive, this miraculous treasure. It seemed, however, that the arm of man, in its greed, proved likewise long; and as the strange providence which gave these people their chief means of killing was kind, so the arm of man was cruel.

In 1894, R. E. Peary, regarding the Arctic world as his own, the people as his vassals, came north, and a year later took from these natives, without their consent, the two smaller fragments. In 1897 he took "The Tent," or Great Iron Stone, the natives' last and one source of mineral wealth and ancestral treasure. That it was these people's great source of securing metal meant nothing to him; that it was a scientific curio, whereby he might secure a specious credit from the well-fed armchair gentlemen of science at home, meant much to the man who later did not hesitate to employ methods of dishonor to try to secure exclusive credit of the achievement of the Pole. Just as he later tried to rob me of honor, so he ruthlessly took from these people a thing that meant abundance of game—and game there meant life.

The great "Iron Stone" was hauled aboard the S. S. *Hope,* and brought to New York. Today it reposes in the Museum of Natural History—a bulky, black heap of metal, which can be viewed any day by the well-fed and curious. In the North, where he will not go again to give his mythical "abundance of guns and ammunition," the Eskimos need the metal which was sold to Mrs. Morris K. Jesup (who presented it to the museum) for $40,000. That money went into Mr. Peary's pockets. In a land where laws existed this act would be regarded as a high-handed, monumental and dishonorable theft. One who might attempt now to purloin the ill-gotten hulk from the museum would be prosecuted. Taken from the people to whose ancestors it was sent, as if by a providence that is divine, and to whom it meant life, it gave Mr. Peary so-called scientific honors among his friends. In the name of religion, it has been said, many crimes have been committed. It remained for this man to reveal what atrocious things could be done in the fair name of science.

At about the same time a group of seven or eight Eskimos were put aboard a ship against their will and brought to New York for museum purposes. They were locked up in a cellar in New York, awaiting a market place. Before the profit-time arrived, because of unhygienic surroundings and improper food, all but one died. When in the grip of death, through a Mrs. Smith, who ministered to their last wants, they appealed with tears in their eyes for some word from Mr. Peary. They begged that he extend them the attention of visiting them before their eyes closed to a world of misery and trouble. There came no word and no responsive call from the man who was responsible for their suffering. Of seven or eight innocent wild people, but one little child survived. That one—

Mene—was later even denied a passage back to his fathers' land by Mr. Peary.

A few years later, the Danish Literary Expedition visited the northernmost Eskimos in their houses. The splendid hospitality shown the Danes by the Eskimos saved their lives. The Danish people, aiming to express their gratitude for this unselfish Eskimo kindness, sent a ship to their shores on the following year, loaded with presents, at an expenditure of many thousands of kroner. That ship, under the direction of Captain Schoubye, left at North Star great quantities of food, iron and wood. After the Danes had turned their backs, Mr. Peary came along and deliberately, highhandedly, took many of the things. This story is told today by every member of the tribe whom Peary claims to have befriended, whom he calls "my people."

The sad story of the unavoidable deaths by starvation of the members of General Greely's Expedition has for years been issued and reissued to the press by Mr. Peary and his press agents, in such form as to discredit General Greely and his co-workers. His own inhuman doings about Cape Sabine and the old Greely stamping-grounds have been suppressed.

In 1901 the ship *Erik* left Mr. Peary, with a large group of native helpers, near Cape Sabine. An epidemic, brought by the Peary ship, soon after attacked the Eskimos. Many died; others survived to endure a slow torture. Peary had no doctor and no medicine. In the year previous, Peary had shown the same spirit to the ever faithful Dr. Dedrick that he had shown to Verhoeff, to Astrup, and to others. Although Dedrick could not endure Peary's unfairness, he remained, against instructions, within reach for just such an emergency as this epidemic presented. He offered his services when the epidemic broke out, but Peary refused his offer, and allowed the natives to die rather than permit a competent medical expert to attend the afflicted.

Near the same point, a year later, Captain Otto Sverdrup wintered with his ship. His mission was to explore the great unknown to the west. This unexplored country had been under Mr. Peary's eye for ten years; but instead of exploring it, his time was spent in an easy and comparatively luxurious life about a comfortable camp. When Sverdrup's men visited the Peary ship, they were denied common brotherly courtesy and were refused the hospitality which is universally granted, by an unwritten law, to all field workers. Mr. Peary even refused to send him, on his returning ship, important letters and papers which Sverdrup desired taken back. He also refused to allow Sverdrup to take native guides and dogs—which did not belong to Mr. Peary. This same courtesy was later denied to Captain Bernier, of the Canadian Expedition.

Thus attempting to make a private preserve of the unclaimed North, he attempted to discredit and thwart every other explorer's effort. In line with the same policy, every member of every Peary expedition has been muzzled with a contract which prevented talking or writing after the expedition's return—contracts by which Mr. Peary derived the sole credit, the entire profit, and all the honor of the results of the men who volunteered their services and risked their lives. This same spirit was shown at the time when, at 87° 45″, he turned Captain Bartlett back, because he (Peary), to use his own words, "wanted all the honors."

In profiting by his long quest for funds for legitimate exploration, we find Peary engaged in private enterprises for which public funds were used. Much of this money was, in my judgment, used to promote a lucrative fur and ivory trade, while the real effort of getting to the Pole was delayed, seemingly, for commercial gain. I believe the Pole might have been reached ten years earlier. But delay was profitable.

After being thus engaged for years in a propaganda of self-exploitation, in assailing other explorers whom he regarded as rivals, in committing deeds in the North unworthy of an American and officer of the Navy, Peary, knowing that I had started Poleward, knowing that relief must inevitably be required, ultimately appropriated my supplies, and absolutely prevented any effort to reach me, which even the natives themselves might have made. Peary knew he was endangering my life. He knew that he was getting ivory and furs in return for supplies belonging to me, and which I should need. He knew, also, that it would not coincide with his selfish purposes of appropriating all honor and profit if I reached the Pole and should return and tell the world. His deliberate act was in itself—whether so designed or not—an effort to kill a brother explorer. The stains of at least a dozen other lives are on this man.

The property which Peary took from Francke and myself, with the hand of a buccaneer and the heart of a hypocrite, was worth thirty-five thousand dollars. This was done, not to insure expedition needs, but to satisfy a hunger for commercial gain, and to inflict a cowardly, underhanded injury on a rival. All of my caches, my camp equipment, my food, were taken; and under his own handwriting he gave the orders which deprived me of all relief efforts at a time when relief was of vital importance. Certainly to all appearances this was a deliberate, preconceived plan to kill a rival worker by starvation. Here we find an American naval officer stooping to a trick for which he would be hanged in a mining camp.

Many members of his expeditions, some rough seamen, speak with shuddering of his actions in that faraway North. In my possession are affidavits, voluntarily made and given to me by members of Mr. Peary's expeditions, revealing gross actions, which, in an officer of the Navy, call for investigation. Mention has been made of certain facts, because, only by knowing these things, can people understand the spirit and character of the man and the unscrupulous attacks made upon me, and understand, also, why, out of a sense of delicacy and dislike for mudslinging, I remained silent so long. It is only because the public has been misled by a sensational press, because I realize I have suffered by my own silence, in order that history may know the full truth and accord a just verdict, that with reluctance, with a sense of shuddering distaste, I have been compelled to present these unpleasant pages of unwritten Arctic history.

When Mr. Peary and his partisans attacked me they hesitated at nothing that was untrue, cruel and dishonorable—forgery and perjury even seemed justifiable to them in their effort to discredit me. I still hesitate to speak of certain unworthy, unblushing and utterly cruel acts of which Mr. Peary is guilty. I would have preferred to remain silent about the actions of which I have told.

Assuming the attitude of one above reproach, Peary, upon his return, assailed me as a dishonest person who tried to rob him of honor. Had the actual and full truths been told at the time about Peary's life in the North, his charges would have rebounded annihilatingly upon himself. For certain things the people of this country, who are clean, honest and fair, will not stand. The facts told about Peary in the affidavits given me make his charges of dishonor and dishonesty against me a travesty, indeed. Yet, at a time when 1 might have profited by revealing phases of Mr. Peary's personal character, I preferred to remain silent. Of certain things men do not care to speak. Although Mr. Peary and his friends endeavored to make the Polar controversy a personal one, I regarded Mr. Peary's personal actions as having no bearing upon his, or my, having attained the Pole. He and his friends forced a personal fight; they tried to injure my veracity, my reputation for truth-telling, my personal honor. I had hoped against hope that the truth would resolve itself without any necessity of my revealing elements of Mr. Peary's character. I have herein recited pages from his past, known to Arctic explorers but not to the general public, so that his attitude toward me may be understood. Yet all, indeed, has not been told. Although Mr. Peary did not scruple to lie about me, I still hesitate to tell the full truth about him.

In the white, frozen North a tragedy was enacted

which would bring tears to the hearts of all who possess human tenderness and kindness.   This has never been written.   To write it would still further reveal the ruthlessness, the selfishness, the cruelty of the man who tried to ruin me.   Yet here I prefer the charity of silence, where, indeed, charity is not at all merited.

The knowledge of these facts tempered the shocks I felt when the Peary campaign of defamation was first made against me.   I told myself that a man who had done these things would, in the nature of things, be branded by the truth, as he deserved.

I was not so greatly surprised that Peary tried to steal my honor.   I knew that he had stolen tangible things.   Yet the theft of food, even though a man's life depends upon it, is not so awful as the attempt to steal the good name a father hopes to bequeath his children. Yet Peary has attempted to do this.

He has attempted to blacken me in the eyes of my family; but, with the conscience of a brute, he has deserted two of his own children—left them to starve and freeze in the cheerless north.   They are there today crying for food and a father, while he enjoys a life of luxury at the expense of the American taxpayers.   This statement calls for an investigation by the Secretary of the Navy.   See photograph of the deserted child of the Sultan of the North, facing page 493.

THE MT. McKINLEY BRIBERY

THE BRIBED, FAKED AND FORGED NEWS ITEMS—THE PRO-
PEARY MONEY POWERS ENCOURAGE PERJURY—MT.
M'KINLEY HONESTLY CLIMBED—HOW, FOR PEARY,
A SIMILAR PEAK WAS FAKED

XXXIV

How a Man's Soul Was Marketed.

After Mr. Peary had done his utmost to try to disprove my Polar attainment; after the chain of newspapers which, for him, in conjunction with the New York *Times,* had printed the same egregious lies on the same days, from the Atlantic to the Pacific; after they had expended all possible ammunition, the damages inflicted were still insufficient. My narrative, as published in the New York *Herald,* was still more generally credited than Mr. Peary's. To gain his end, something else had to be done. Something else *was* done. The darkest page of defamation in the world's history of exploration was now written by the hands of bribers and perjurers.

The public suddenly turned from the newspaper-inculcated idea of "proof" in figures to a more sane examination of personal veracity. To destroy my reputation for truth in the public mind was the next unscrupulous effort decided upon. The selfish and self-evident press campaign, obviously managed by the Peary cabal, to that end had given unsatisfactory results. Some vital blow must be delivered by fair means or otherwise.

The climb of Mt. McKinley was now challenged.

I had made a first ascent of the great mid-Alaskan peak in 1906. The record of that conquest was published during my absence in the North, under the title, "To the Top of the Continent." The book, being printed at a time when I was unable to see the proofs, contained some mistakes; but in it was all the data that could be presented for such an undertaking.

The Board of Aldermen of the City of New York decided to honor me by offering the keys and the freedom of the metropolis on October 15. This was to be an important event. The pro-Peary conspiracy aiming to deliver striking blows through the press, their propaganda was so planned that the bribed, faked and forged news items were issued on days which gave them dramatic and psychologic climaxes. Two days before the New York demonstration in my favor, the pretentious full-page broadside of distorted Eskimo information was issued. This fell flat; for it was instantly seen to be a pretentious rearrangement of old charges. But it was so played up as to fill columns of newspaper space and impress readers by its magnitude. This was followed by the Barrill affidavit, similarly played up so as to fill a full newspaper page, which I shall analyze later. All this was done to draw a black cloud over the day of honor in New York, the 15th day of October.

Since the published affidavit of my old associate, Barrill, was a document which proved him a self-confessed liar; since the affidavit carried with it the earmarks of pro-Peary bribery and perjury, I reasoned again that fair-minded people would in time see through this moneyed campaign of dishonor. In all history it has been shown that he who seeks to besmear others usually leaves the greatest amount of mud on himself. But again I had not counted on the unfairness of the press.

The only reason given that I should have faked the climb of Mt. McKinley is that, in some vague way, I was to profit mightily by a successful report. The expedition was to have been financed by a rich Philadelphia sportsman. He did advance the greater portion of the sum required. We were to prepare a game trail for him. Something interfered, he relinquished his trip, and did not send the balance of money promised.

The result was that many checks I had given out went to protest. Harper & Brothers had agreed, before starting, to pay me $1,500 for an account of the expedition, whether successful or not. On my return this was paid, and went to meet outstanding debts—debts to pay which I embarrassed myself. Instead of "profits" from this alleged "fake," I suffered a loss of several thousand dollars.

As is quite usual in all exploring expeditions, some of the members of my Mt. McKinley expedition, who did not share in the final success, were disgruntled. Chief among these was Herschell Parker. Owing to ill-health and inexperience, Parker had proved himself inefficient in Alaskan work. Climbing a little peak forty miles from the great mountain, when he was with me, he had pronounced Mt. McKinley unclimbable. Climbing a similar hill, four years later, he stooped to the humbug of offering a photograph of it as a parallel to my picture of the top of Mt. McKinley. This man was so ill-fitted for such work that two men were required to help him mount a horse. But I insisted that we continue at least to the base of the mountain. At the first large glacier, Parker and his companion, Belmore Brown, balked, halting in front of an insignificant ice-wall. The ascent of Mt. McKinley, still thirty-five miles off, they said, was impossible. Parker returned, and in a trail of four thousand miles to New York told every press representative how impossible was the ascent of Mt. McKinley. By the time Parker reached New York a cable went through that the thing was done. At a point four thousand miles from the scene of action, he again cried, "Impossible!" When I returned to New York, however, a month later, and Parker learned the details, he publicly and privately credited my ascent of Mt. McKinley. Nothing further was said to doubt the climb until two years later, when he lined up with the Peary interests.

Using Parker as a tool, Peary's Arctic Club, through him, first forced the side-issue of Mt. McKinley. With the Barrill affidavit, made later, were printed other affidavits by Barrill's friends, who had not been within fifty miles of the mountain when it was climbed. This act, to me, was a bitter climax of injustice. But I have since learned that Printz got $500 of pro-Peary money; that both Miller and Beecher were promised large amounts, but were cheated at the "showdown." Printz afterwards wrote that he would make an affidavit for me for $300, and at Missoula he made an affidavit in which he attempted to defend me.* This he offered to sell to Roscoe Mitchell for $1,000.

While easy pro-Peary money was passing in the West, Parker came forward with his old grudge. His chief contention was that, because he had taken home with him in deserting the object of the expedition a hypsometer, I could not have measured the high altitudes claimed. The altitude had been measured by triangulation by the hydrographer of the expedition, but I had other methods of measuring the ascent.

I had two aneroid barometers, specially marked for very high climbing, thermometers, and all the usual Alpine instruments. The hypsometer was not at that time an important instrument. Parker also showed unfair methods by allowing the press repeatedly to print that he had been the leader and the organizer of the expedition. This he knew to be false. I had organized two expeditions to explore Mt. McKinley, at a cost of $28,000. Of this Parker had furnished $2,500. Parker took no part in the organization of the last expedition, had given no advice to help supply an adequate equipment, and in the field his presence was a daily handicap to the progress of the expedition. Heretofore, this was

---

*Letter from Barrill's associate:
                                        MISSOULA, MONT., Oct. 12, 1909.
    Friend Cook—I am sorry that I can't come at present. But will come and see you in about fifteen days if you will send me Three Hundred and Fifty ($350.00), and I will say that the report in the papers (that Dr. Cook did not ascend Mt. McKinley), from what I have, is not true.
    Hoping to see you soon.
                                        Your friend,
                                        (Signed) FRED PRINTZ.

never indicated. But when he allows himself to be quoted as the leader of an expedition upon which he attempts to throw discredit, then it is right that all the facts be known.

In the press reports, when Parker was first heard from, came the news that on the Pacific coast, at Tacoma, a lawyer by the name of J. M. Ashton was retained by someone. To the press Ashton said he was engaged "to look into the McKinley business," but he did not know by whom—whether by Cook or Peary. He was "engaged" in a business too questionable to tell who furnished the money.

In the final ascent of Mt. McKinley there was with me Edward Barrill, the affidavit-maker. He was a good-natured and hard-working packer, who had proved himself a most able climber. Together we ascended the mountain in September, 1906. To this time (1909) there was not the slightest doubt about the footprints on the top of the great mountain. Barrill had told everybody that he knew, and all who would listen to him, that the mountain was climbed. He went from house to house boastfully, with my book under his arm, telling and retelling the story of the ascent of Mt. McKinley. That anyone should now believe the affidavit, secured and printed for Peary, did not to me seem reasonable.

Parker, filling the position of betrayer and traitor to one who had saved his life many times, had decided, as the Polar controversy opened, to direct the Mt. McKinley side-issue of the pro-Peary effort.

The first news of bribery in the matter came from Darby, Montana. This was Barrill's home town. A

Peary man from Chicago was there. He frankly said that he would pay Barrill $1,000 to offer news that would discredit the climb of Mt. McKinley. Other news of the dishonest pro-Peary movement induced me to send Roscoe Mitchell, of the New York *Herald,* to the working ground of the bribers. Mitchell was working under the direction of my attorneys, H. Wellington Wack, of New York, Colonel Marshal, of Missoula, and General Weed, of Helena, Montana.

Mitchell secured testimony and evidence regarding the buying of Barrill, but was unable to put the conspirators in jail. At Hamilton, Montana, there had appeared a man with $5,000 to pass to Barrill. Barrill's first reply was that he had climbed the mountain; that Dr. Cook had climbed the mountain; that to take that $5,000, in his own words, he "would have to sell his own soul." Barrill's business partner, Bridgeford, was present. He later made an affidavit for Mr. Mitchell covering this part of the pro-Peary perjury effort.

A little later, however, Barrill said to his partner he "might as well see what was in it." Five thousand dollars to Barrill meant more than five million dollars to Mr. Peary or his friends. To Barrill, ignorant, poor, good-natured, but weak, it was an irresistible temptation.

Barrill now went to Seattle. He visited the office of the Seattle *Times.* In the presence of the editor, Mr. Joe Blethen, he dickered for the sale of an affidavit to discredit me. He knew such an affidavit had news value. Indefinite offers ranging from $5,000 to $10,000 were made. Not getting a lump sum off-hand, Barrill, dissatisfied, then went over to Tacoma, to the mysterious Mr. Ashton. That all this was done, was told me on my trip west shortly afterward, by Mr. Blethen himself.

After visiting Ashton, Barrill was seen in a bank in Tacoma. Barrill had said to his partner that to make an affidavit denying my climb would be "selling his soul." Barrill, ill at ease, reluctant, appeared. It is a terrible thing to lure a weak man to dishonor; it is still more tragic and awful when that man is bought so his lie may hurt another. The time for the parting of his soul had arrived in the bank. With the sadness of a funeral mourner Barrill was pushed along. The talk was in a muffled undertone. But it all happened. In the presence of a witness, whose evidence I am ready to produce, $1,500 was passed to him. This money was paid in large bills, and placed in Barrill's money-belt. There were other considerations, and I know where some of this money was spent. His soul was marketed at last. The infamous affidavit was then prepared.

This affidavit was printed first in the New York *Globe*. The *Globe* is partly owned and entirely controlled by General Thomas H. Hubbard, the President of the Peary Club. With General Hubbard, Mr. Peary had consulted at Bar Harbor immediately after his return from Sydney. Together they had outlined their campaign. General Hubbard is a multi-millionaire. A tremendous amount of money was spent in the Peary campaign. In the Mt. McKinley affidavit of Barrill we can trace bribery, a conspiracy, and black dishonor, right up to the door of R. E. Peary.

If Peary is not the most unscrupulous self-seeker in the history of exploration, caught in underhand, surreptitious acts too cowardly to be credited to a thief, caught in the act of bartering for men's souls and honor in as ruthless a way as he high-handedly took others' property in the North; if he, drawing an unearned salary from the American Navy, has not brindled his soul with stripes that fit his body for jail, let him come forward and reply. If Peary is not the most conscienceless of self-exploiters in all history, caught in the act of stealing honor by forcing dishonor, let him come forward and explain the Mt. McKinley perjury.

Now let us examine the others who were lined up in this desperate black hand movement. In New York there is a club, at first organized to bring explorers together and to encourage original research. It bore the name of Explorers' Club; but, as is so often the case with clubs that monopolize a pretentious name, the membership degenerated. It is now merely an association of museum collectors. Among real explorers, this club to-day is jocularly known as the "Worm Diggers' Union." In 1909 Mr. Peary was president. His press agent, Bridgman, was the moving spirit, and one of Colonel Mann's muck-rakers was secretary. Of course, such a society, committed to Peary, had no use for Dr. Cook.

In a spirit of helping along the pro-Peary conspiracy, and after the Barrill affidavit was secured, the Explorers' Club took upon itself the superrogatory duty of appointing a committee to pass on my ascent of Mt. McKinley. There was but one real explorer on this committee. The others were kitchen geographers, whose honor and fairness had been bartered to the Peary interests before the investigation began. Without a line of data before them, they decided, with glee and gusto, that Mt. McKinley had not been climbed. This was what one would expect from such an honor-blind group of meddlers. But Mr. Peary's press worker, Bridgman, who himself had engineered the investigation, used this seeming verdict of experts to Mr. Peary's advantage.*

Still all these combined underhanded efforts failed to reach vital spots and to turn the entire public Mr. Peary's way. Something more must still be done. Peary's press agent offered $3,000, and the cowardly Ashton, of Tacoma, offered another $3,000, to send an expedition to Alaska, to further the pro-Peary effort to down a rival. The traitor, Parker, responded. He was joined by the other quitter, Belmore Brown, who has conveniently forgotten to return borrowed money to me. This Peary-Parker-Brown combination went to Alaska in 1910, engaged in mining pursuits and hunting adventures. They returned with the expected and framed report that Mt. McKinley had not been climbed, and that they had climbed a snow-hill, had photographed it, and that the photograph was similar to mine of the topmost peak of Mt. McKinley. Mt. McKinley has a base twenty-five miles wide; it has upon the various slopes of its giant uplift hundreds of peaks, all glacial, polished, and of a similar contour. No one peak towers gigantically above the others. On the top are many peaks, no par-

---

*While this book was going through the press, several chapters of the proof-sheets, stolen from the printers, Messrs. Lent & Graff, were found on the table of the Explorers' Club on June 27, 1911. It is important to note that this pro-Peary repository of bribed, faked and forged writings, which were issued to defame me, is also the den for stolen goods. Who are the thieves who congregate there to deposit their booty? Why the theft of a part of my book? What humbug has this club and its shameless president next to offer?

ticular one of which can with any accuracy of inches be decided arbitrarily as the very highest. The top of a mountain does not converge to a pin-point apex. One looks out, not into immediate space on all sides, but over an, area, as I have said, of many peaks. My photograph of the peak, which loomed highest among the others on the top, possesses a profile not unsual among ice-cut rocks. The Peary-Parker-Brown seekers tried hard to duplicate this photograph, so as to show I had faked my picture. The thing might have been done easily in the Canadian Rockies. It could be done in a dozen more accessible places in Alaska; but, without real work, it could be only crudely done near Mt. McKinley. The photograph which Peary's friends offered to discredit the first ascent is one of a double peak, part of which vaguely suggests but a poor outline of Mt. McKinley, and in which a rock has been faked. Who is responsible for this humbug? Where is the negative? The photograph bears no actual semblance to my picture of the top of Mt. McKinley whatever. But why was the negative faked? Parker excuses the evident unfairness of the dissimilar photograph by saying that he could not get the same position as I must have had. But is laziness or haste an excuse when a man's honor is assailed.†

---

†Letter from an onlooker when Mt. McKinley was climbed:
To Dr. Cook's Friends:
 Professor Parker says "regretfully" that Dr. Cook's evidence as to the ascent of Mt. McKinley was unconvincing.
 I was located in the foothills of Mt. McKinley, and had been for about a year, when Dr. Cook, Professor H. C. Parker, Mr. Porter, the topographer of the party, and Mr. Miller, Fred Printz and the rest of the party, landed at the head-waters of the Yentna River, in the foothills of Mt. McKinley.
 I met Professor Parker and the rest of the party, and saw a great

Let us follow the Peary high-handed humbugs further. To the southeast of Mt. McKinley is a huge mountain, which I named Mt. Disston in 1905. This peak was robbed of its name, and over it Parker wrote Mt. Huntington. To the northeast of Mt. McKinley is another peak, charted on my maps, to which Peary gave the name of the president of the Peary Arctic Trust. To this peak was given the same name, by the same methods of stealing the credit of other explorers, as that adopted by Peary when, in response to $25,000 of easy money, he wrote the same name, "Thomas Hubbard," over Sverdrup's northern point of Heiberg

deal of them while they were up there, as I had three mining camps in the foothills from which they made their try for the top of the mountain. I let Dr. Cook have one of my Indian hunters, who knew every foot of the country around there, for a guide. Dr. Cook also had some of his caches in my camps, leaving supplies which he did not take along with his pack-trains. Some of Dr. Cook's party were in our camps nearly every day or so, and consequently I became very well posted in regard to Dr. Cook's affairs, and very well acquainted with him. Dr. Parker should be the last one to say anything about mountain-climbing or anything else connected with the expedition, or anything where it takes a man and pluck to accomplish results—good results; as he showed himself to be the rankest kind of a tenderfoot while in the foothills of Mt. McKinley, and was the laughing stock of the country. Mt. McKinley and the country around there was too rough for him. He got "cold feet," and started back for the States, before he had even seen much of the country around there.

Looking over my memoranda, I find that Dr. Cook had given up his attempt to climb Mt. McKinley for the time being, and had sent Printz and Miller on a hunting expedition, and the rest of the party was scattered out to hunt up something new.

At that time I came into Youngstown, and the boys were getting ready to strike out on their different routes, and Dr. Cook was going down to Tyonic, in Cook's Inlet, with his launch, to meet a friend, Mr. Disston, who expected to go on a hunting trip with him. The friend did not arrive, so Dr. Cook returned to the head-waters of the Yentna River, to Youngstown, arriving there on Monday, August 27. On Sunday, August 28, he started down to the Sushitna River. I went down with him as far as the Sushitna Station, and he told me he was going to run up the river and strike Fish Creek, which ran up on another side of Mt. McKinley, and see what the chances were to make the top of the continent from that side. He made it. I was one of the last to see him start on the ascent, and one of the first to see him when he returned after he had made the ascent.

Dr. Cook proved to be a man in every respect, as unselfish as he was

Land. Can it be doubted that the Peary-Parker-Brown propaganda of hypocrisy and dishonor in Alaska is guided by no other spirit than that of Mr. Peary?

Many persons say: "We will credit Dr. Cook's attainment of the Pole if this Mt. McKinley matter is cleared up." I have heard this often. I have offered in my book proofs of the climb—the same proofs any

courageous, always giving the other fellow a thought before thinking of himself.

Upon his arrival from the ascent of the mountain, although tired and worn and in a bad physical condition himself, he gave his unlimited attention to a party of prospectors who had been picked up from a wreck in the river, and brought into camp in an almost dying condition just before his arrival. He spent hours working over these men, and did not give himself a thought until they were properly cared for.

Evidence? No man who has known Dr. Cook, been with him, worked with him, and learned by personal experience of his courage, energy and perseverance, would ask for evidence beyond his word.

Dr. Cook is one of the most daring men, and can stand more hardships than any man I have ever met, and I believe I have met some of the most able men of the world when it comes to roughing it over the trails in Alaska and the North.

Dr. Cook climbed Mt. McKinley. Of course there are always skeptics—men who have a wishbone instead of a backbone, and who, when wishing has brought to them no good results, their last effort is pushed forth in criticism of the things which have been constructed or accomplished by men, their superiors.

If Professor Parker wants evidence to convince him, I think he can find it, provided he will put himself to as much trouble in looking for evidence as he has in criticising such evidence as he has obtained.

Respectfully yours,

J. A. MacDonald.

Vontrigger, California.

Author's Note.—It is a curious fact that most men who have assailed me are themselves sailing under false colors. Herschell Parker was an assistant professor and instructor in the Department of Physics in Columbia University. This gave him the advantage of using the title, "Professor," but, like many others, his university association was mostly for the prestige it gave him. His professorship assumption was, therefore, a deception. Instead of devoting himself conscientiously to university interests, he was, like Peary, engaged in private enterprises—such as the Parker-Clark light, and other ventures—and employed substitute instructors to do the work for which he drew a salary, and for which he claimed the honor and the prestige. A man who thus sails falsely under the banner of a professorship is just the man to try to steal the honor of other men. Here is a make-believe professor who is not a professor; whose dwarfed conscience is eased by drippings from the Arctic Trust; who has stooped to a photographic humbug. He is a fitting exponent of the bribing pro-Peary propaganda.

mountain-climber offers.   To discredit these, my enemies stooped to bribery.   I have in my possession, and
have stated here, proofs of this.   Such proofs are even
more tangible than the climbing of a far-away mountain.   Is any other clarifier or any other evidence
required to prove the pro-Peary frauds?

THE PEARY-PARKER-BROWN HUMBUG UP TO DATE

This chapter is best closed by an analysis of the second effort of Parker
and Brown. It will be remembered that in their first venture as hirelings of the
Peary propaganda, they balked at the north-east ridge, without making a serious
attempt. This ridge—(the ridge upon which I had climbed to the top of Mt.
McKinley) was pronounced impossible and therefore my claim in their judgment was false, for such a statement $3,000.00 had been paid. During the spring
of 1912, again with $5,000 of Pro-Peary money to discredit me—The same hire-
lings went through the range, attacked the same ridge from the west and by the
really able efforts of their guide, La Voy, a point near the top was reached. The
Associated Press report of this effort said that the principal result of the expedition was to show that the north-east ridge (the ridge which I had climbed), was
climbable. The very men sent out and paid, therefore, by my enemies to disprove my work have proven, against their will, my first ascent of Mt. McKinley.
Two other exploring parties were about the slopes of Mt. McKinley during
the time of the Peary-Parker defamers. The first, a group of |hardy Alaskan
pioneers, whose report is written in the Overland Magazine for February, 1913,
by Ralph H. Cairns—after an unbiased study of reports both for and against,
Cairns credits my first ascent. The well known Engineer R. C. Bates, who as a
U. S. revenue inspector of mines and an explorer and mountain climber, did much
pioneer work about Mt. McKinley. He also goes on record in the Los Angeles
Tribune of February 13th, 1913, as saying: "Dr. Cook really succeeded in ascending the north-east ridge of Mt. McKinley as claimed in 1906." Bates confirms
the charge of $5,000 being paid the Parker-Brown expedition to refute my 1906
ascent, and says: "In 1906 Dr. Cook claimed he climbed Mt. McKinley by the
north-east ridge. In the account of the 1910 expedition, Parker claimed that
'the north-east ridge, the one used by Dr. Cook, was absolutely unsurmountable'.
I, with a party of two, explored the mountain in 1911 and selected the north-east
ridge as the only feasible route to the top. I ascended to 11,000 feet, according
to barometric measure. I told of the exploit to members of the Parker party,
who took the same course in 1912. Mr. Parker now contradicts his former statement by saying, 'The north-east ridge is the only feasible ridge, and whoever
goes up will follow in my footsteps.' " It is important to note that Dr. Cook's
previous footsteps were eliminated, $5,000 had been paid for that very purpose.
In a personal interview Mr. Bates made the very grave change that one
of the leaders of the very expedition sent out to discredit me, had offered him
a bribe to swear falsely to certain assessment work on claims which had not been
done. The Peary-Parker-Brown movement is therefore from many sources a
proven propaganda of bribery, conspiracy and perjury. That such men can escape
the doom of prison cells is a parody upon human decency, and yet such are the
men who are responsible for the distrust which has been thrown on my work.

THE DUNKLE-LOOSE FORGERY

XXXV

The Last Perjured Defamation

With the bitterness of the money-bought document to shatter my veracity regarding the ascent of Mt. McKinley ever before me, I canceled in November all my lecture engagements. Mr. William M. Grey, then managing my tour, broke contracts covering over $140,000. But, for the time being, these could not be filled. I was nearing a stage of mental and physical exhaustion, and required rest. Seeking a quiet retreat, my wife and I left the Waldorf-Astoria and secured quarters at the Gramatan Inn, in Bronxville, N. Y. Here was prepared my report and data to be sent to Copenhagen.

At this time, as if again destined by fate, innocently I made my greatest error, opened myself to what became the most serious and damaging charge against my good faith, and the misstated account of which, published later, was used by my enemies in their efforts to brand me as a conscious faker and deliberate fraud.

When I now think of the incidents leading up to the acquaintance of Dunkle and Loose, it does seem that I had lost all sense of balance, and that my brain was befogged. Shortly before I had started West, Dunkle was brought to me by Mr. Bradley on the pretext of wanting to talk life insurance.

During my lecture tour threats from fanatics reached me, and in my nervous condition it was not hard for me to believe that my life was in danger. Then, too, it seemed that all the money I had made might be spent in efforts to defend myself. I decided to protect my wife and children by life insurance. How Dunkle guessed this—if he did—I do not know. But at just the right moment he appeared, and I fell into the insurance trap.

At the time I did not know that Dunkle had been a professional "subscription-raiser," who, while I was in the North, had volunteered to raise money for a relief expedition—provided he was given an exorbitant percentage.

For this reason both Anthony Fiala and Dillon Wallace had refused to introduce him to me before he secured the introduction by Mr. Bradley. When Mrs. Cook first saw him, with feminine intuition she said:

"Don't have anything to do with that man. I don't like his looks."

I did not heed this, however. After some futile life insurance talk, he surprised me by saying irrelevantly:

"By the way, I have an expert navigator, a friend of mine, who can prove that Peary was not at the Pole."

"I have not challenged Mr. Peary's claim," I replied, "and do not wish to. The New York *Herald,* however, may listen to what you have to say." That was all that was said at the time.

After my return from the western lecture tour, Dunkle seemed to be always around, and at every opportunity spoke to me.   He gained a measure of confidence by criticising the press campaign waged against me.   I naturally felt kindly toward anyone who was sympathetic.   At this time, when the problem of accurate observations was worrying me, when my mind was beginning to weigh the problem of scientific accuracy— again just at the psychological moment—Dunkle brought Loose out to the Gramatan Inn and introduced him to me, saying that he was an expert navigator.

Pretending a knowledge of the situation in Europe, Loose told me the Danes were becoming impatient.   I replied that I was busy preparing my report.

"Something ought to be done in the meantime," he said.   "Now, I have connections with some of the Scandinavian papers, and I think some friendly articles in the meantime would allay this unrest."

The idea seemed reasonable; anything that would help me was welcome, and I told Loose, if he wanted to, that he might go ahead.   He visited me several times, and broached the subject of the possible outcome of the Copenhagen verdict.   By this time I felt fairly friendly with him.   Finally he brought me several articles. They seemed weak and irrelevant.   Lonsdale read them, said there was not much to them, but that they might help.   Loose mailed the articles—or said he did. Then, to my amazement, he made the audacious suggestion that I let him go over my material.   I flatly refused.

He pointed out, what I myself had been thinking

about, that all observations were subject to extreme inaccuracy. He suggested his working mine out backward to verify them. As I regarded him as an experienced navigator, I thought this of interest. I was not a navigator, and, moreover, had had no chance of checking my figures. So, desiring an independent view, and thinking that another man's method might satisfy any doubts, I told him to go ahead, using the figures published in my story in the New York *Herald*.

At the time I told him to purchase for me a "Bowditch Navigator," which I lacked, and any other almanacs and charts he needed for himself. He came out to the Gramatan to live. Arrangements for his stay had been made by Dunkle—under the name of Lewis, I have been told since—but I knew nothing of this at the time. I gave Loose $250, which was to compensate him in full for the articles and his running expenses. It struck me that he took an unnecessarily long time to finish his work of checking my calculations.

Late one night, returning from the city, I went to his room. Dunkle was there. Papers were strewn all over the room.

"Well," said Loose, "I think we have this thing all fixed up."

Dunkle, smooth-tongued and friendly as ever, said, "Now, Doctor, I want to advise you to put your own observations aside. *Send these to Copenhagen!*"

I looked up amazed, incredulous. I felt stunned for the moment, and said little. I then took the trouble to look over all the papers carefully. There was a full set of faked observations. The examination took me an hour. During that time Dunkle and Loose were talking in a low tone. I did not hear what they said. I saw at once the game the rascals had béen playing. The insinuation of their nefarious suggestion for the moment cleared my mind, and a dull anger filled me.

"Gentlemen," I said, "pack up every scrap of this paper in that dress-suit case. Take all of your belongings and leave this hotel at once."

I stood there while they did so. Not a word was spoken. Sheepish and silent, they shuffled from the room, ashamed and taken aback. Sick at heart at the thought that these men should have considered me unscrupulous enough to buy and use their faked figures, I went to my room. From that day—November 22—I have not received a letter or telegram from either.

Months later, in South America, I read with horrified amazement a summary of the account of this occurrence, sold by Dunkle and Loose to the New York *Times*. Distorted and twisted as it was I doubt if even the *Times* would have used it had Dunkle and Loose not forced the lie that these faked figures were sent to Copenhagen. They knew, as God knows, that every scrap of paper on which they wrote was packed in a suit-case as dirty as the intent of their sin-blotted paper.

If my report to the Copenhagen University proved anything, it was, by comparison, figure by figure, with the affidavits published, that in this at least I was guilty of no fraud.

In a re-examination later, a handwriting expert has come to the conclusion that the name of Loose was forged, and Loose was later put in jail for another offense. To the city editor of a New York evening paper Loose offered to sell a story retracting the charges published in the *Times*. Dunkle admitted to witnesses that he had been paid for the affidavit published in the New York *Times*. Loose, willing to discredit the *Times* story, said, however, he "wanted big money" for a retraction. One question that is forced in the interest of fair-play is, Why did the New York *Times,* without investigation, print a news item by which a man's honor is attacked, which is not only a perjury but a forgery? The managing editor was shown the evidence of this forgery, admitted its force, but not a word was printed to counteract the harm done by printing false news.

Captain E. B. Baldwin, a year later, discovered that this pro-Peary faked stuff was in possession of Professor James H. Gore, one of Mr. Peary's friends in the National Geographic Society, which prostituted its name for Peary by passing upon valueless "proofs." From the methods pursued by this society later, I am inclined to the belief that the Dunkle-Loose fake was concocted for members of this society. If not, how does it happen that Professor Gore is in possession of this faked, forged, and perjured stuff?

HOW A GEOGRAPHIC SOCIETY PROSTITUTED ITS NAME

XXXVI

THE WASHINGTON VERDICT—THE COPENHAGEN VERDICT

While one group of pro-Peary men were early-engaged in various conspiracies, extending from New York to the Pacific coast, fabricating false charges, faking, and forging news items designed to injure me, men higher up in Washington were planning other deceptions behind closed doors. The Mt. McKinley bribery and the Dunkle-Loose humbug had the desired effect in reducing the opposition in Washington, and by December of 1909 the controversy was settled to Mr. Peary's satisfaction by a group of men who, by deception, betrayed public trust.

The National Geographic Society very early assumed a meddlesome air in an effort to dictate the distribution of Polar honors. With the excuse that they would give a gold medal to him who could prove priority to the claim of Polar discovery, they began a series of movements that would put a dishonorable political campaign to shame. In the light of later developments, medals from this society are regarded by true scientific workers as badges of dishonor. By way

of explanation, one of the officers said that they made
it a rule to examine all original field observations before
the society honored an explorer.   This was a deliberate
falsehood, for no explorer going to Washington had
previously packed his field papers and instruments for
inspection.   If so, then this society again convicts itself
of a humbug, as it did later.   Mr. Peary had been given
a gold medal for his claim of having reached the farthest north in 1906.   Peary admitted that his position
rested on one imperfect observation.   I happened,
quite by accident, to be in a position, soon after Peary's
return, to examine the instruments with which the
farthest north observations had been made.   Every
apparatus was so bent and bruised that further observations were impossible.   Of course Peary will say that
the instruments were injured en route on the return.
But this does not excuse the idle boast of the members
of the National Geographic Society, who said that they
always examined a returning explorer's field notes and
apparatus, when in this case they did not see Mr.
Peary's observations nor his instruments.

As a matter of fact, the National Geographic, like
every other geographic society, had previously rated the
merits of an explorer's work by his published reports.
Their tactics were now changed to bring about a position
where they might focus the controversy to Mr. Peary's
and their advantage.   There would have been no harm
in this effort, if it had been honest; but, as we will see
presently, falsehood and deception were evident in
every move.

The position of the National Geographic Society
is very generally misunderstood because of its preten-

tious use of the word "National." In reality, it is neither national nor geographic. It is a kind of self-admiration society, which serves the mission of a lecture bureau. It has no connection with the Government and has no geographic authority save that which it assumes. As a lecture bureau it had retained Mr. Peary to fill an important position as its principal star for many years. To keep him in the field as their head-line attraction they had paid $1,000 to Mr. Peary for the very venture now in question. This so-called "National" Geographic Society was, therefore, a stock owner in the venture upon which they passed as an unbiased jury.

Of course Mr. Peary consented to rest his case in their hands; but, for reasons above indicated and for others given below, I refused to have any dealings with such an unfair combination. The Government was appealed to, and every political and private wire was pulled to compel me to submit my case to a packed jury. During all the time when this was done, its moving spirits, Gilbert Grosvenor and Admiral Chester, were publicly and privately saying things about me and my attainment of the Pole that no gentleman would utter. That Mr. Peary was a member of this society; that his friends were absolute dictators of the power of appointment; that they were stock owners in Mr. Peary's enterprise—all of this, and a good many other facts, were carefully suppressed. To the public this society declared they were "neutral, unbiased and scientific"—no more deliberate lie than which was ever forced upon the public.

Of course I refused to place my case in dishonest

pro-Peary hands. With shameless audacity this society helped Mr. Peary carry along his press campaign by disseminating the cowardly slurs of Grosvenor, Chester, and others. They watched and encouraged the McKinley bribery; they closed their eyes to the Kennan lies. Through Chester and others, they faked pages of sensational pseudo-scientific news, all with the one centered aim of forcing doubt on opposing interests before the crucial moment, when, behind closed doors, the matter could be settled to their liking.

Thus, when Peary, his club, and his affiliated boosters at Washington were carrying their press slanders to a focus, there came a loud cry from the National Geographic Society for proofs.

With some wrangling, and a good deal of protest from half-hearted men, like Professor Moore, a jury was appointed to pass upon Mr. Peary's claims and mine. My claims were to be passed upon against my will. Unbiased and real Arctic explorers like General Greely and Admiral Schley were carefully excluded from this jury. Instead, armchair geographers, who were closely related to the Peary interests, were appointed as a "neutral jury," as follows:

Henry Gannett, a close personal friend of Mr. Peary.

C. M. Chester, related to Mr. Peary's fur trader, a member of a coterie that divided the profits of fleecing the Eskimos.

O. H. Tittman, chief of a department under which part of Mr. Peary's work was done.

With a flourish of trumpets, including pages of self-boosting news distributed by Mr. Peary's press agents, this commission began its important investigation. At the time, it was said that all of Mr. Peary's original field papers and instruments were under careful scrutiny. Later it was shown that one of the jury saw only COPIES. On November 4, 1909, was issued the verdict of this jury: "That Commander Peary reached the North Pole on April 6, 1909."

This verdict, at its face value, was fair; but the circumstances which surrounded it before and after were such as to raise a doubt that can never be removed. With the verdict came the insinuation that no one else had reached the Pole before Peary; that my claim of priority was dishonest. A nagging press campaign continued to emanate from Washington.

I have no objection to Mr. Peary's friends endorsing him—a friend who will stretch a point is not to be condemned. But when such friends stoop to dishonorable methods to inflict injury upon others, then a protest is in order. My aim here is not to deny that Mr. Peary reached the Pole near enough for all practical purposes, but to show how men sacrificed their word of honor to boost Mr. Peary and to discredit me.

The verdict of this jury which was to settle the controversy for all time was sent out on wires that encircled the globe. Soon after there was a call for the data upon which that jury passed. The public called for it; the Government called for it; foreign geographical societies asked for it. No one was allowed to see the wonderful "proofs." Why?

Officially, that commission said that Mr. Peary's contract with a magazine prevented the publication of the "proofs." But every member of the commission was on the Government pay-roll. Why, may we ask, should a Government official be muzzled with a bid for commercial gain?   This contract was held by Benjamin Hampton, of *Hampton's Magazine*.   If Hampton's contract muzzled the Government officials, Mr. Hampton thought so little of the so-called "proofs" that he did not print them.   For, in *Hampton's* installment, with the eye-attracting title, "Peary Proofs Positive," the real data upon which the Peary case rests were eliminated. Why? In Mr. Peary's own book that material is again suppressed. Why? For the same reason that the jury was muzzled. *The material would not bear public scrutiny!*

The real difficulty is that, in the haste to floor rival claims, Mr. Peary and all his biased helpers fixed as the crucial test of Polar attainment an examination of field observations.   Mr. Peary had his; he had refused to let Whitney bring part of mine from the North; and, therefore, he and his friends supposed that I was helpless, by assuming this false position. But when Mr. Peary's own material was examined, it was found that his position rested on a set of worthless observations— calculations of altitudes of the sun so low that it is questionable if the observation could have been made at all.   So long as three men, behind closed doors, could be made to say "Yes, Peary reached the Pole," and so long as this verdict came with the authority of a Geographic Society and the seeming endorsement of national prestige, the false position could be impressed upon the pubic as a *bona-fide* verdict.   But, with publicity, the whole railroading game would be spoiled. These three men could be influenced.   But there are a hundred thousand other men in the world whose lives depend upon their knowledge of just such observations as were here involved. They knew publicity would bring the attention of these men to the fact that Mr. Peary's polar claim rests upon the impossible observations of a sun at an altitude less than 7° above the horizon. The three armchair geographers, seldom out of reach of dusty book-shelves, passed upon these worthless observations. Not one of one hundred thousand honest sextant experts would credit such an observation as that upon which Mr. Peary's case rests— not even in home regions, where for centuries tables for corrections have been gathered.

*A year later, at the Congressional investigation of the Naval Committee in Washington, Mr. Peary and two of his jurors admitted that in the much-heralded Peary proofs "there was no proof." Members of the Geographic Society acknowledged their "examination" of Peary's instruments was made in the Pennsylvania

---

*When Mr. Peary first returned from the North, and began his attacks upon me, he caused a demand for "proofs" through the New York *Times* and its affiliated papers; he had them call for my instruments; he insinuated that I had had no instruments with me in the North (despite the fact that Captain Bartlett had informed him that my own Eskimos had testified that I had); he declared that any Polar claim must be established by an examination of observations and an examination of the explorer's instruments.

In view of the unwarranted newspaper call for "proofs," I was embarrassed by having left my instruments with Whitney. Mr. Peary had his, however. But were they carefully examined by the august body who so eagerly decided he reached the Pole? Was the verdict of the self-appointed arbiters of the so-called National Geographic Society based upon such examination as Mr. Peary—concerning my case—had declared necessary?

Testifying before the subcommittee of the Committee on Naval Affairs, when the move was on to have Peary made a Rear-Admiral, Henry Gannett, one of the three members of the National Geographic Society, who had passed on Peary's claim, admitted that their examination of Mr. Peary's instruments was casually and hastily made in the Pennsylvania Station at

Station, when they opened Mr. Peary's trunk and casually looked over its contents. Therefore, Mr. Peary's claim for a second victory now rests upon his book.

In forcing the controversy, the press and the public have come to the conclusion that one or the other report must be discredited. This is an incorrect point of view. Each case must be judged upon its own merits. To prove my case, it is not necessary to disprove Peary's; nor, to prove Peary's, should it have been necessary to try to disprove mine.

Much has been said about my case resting in foreign hands. This came about in a natural way. It was

---

Washington. When Peary later appeared in person before the committee, he admitted having come to Washington from Portland, Maine, to consult with the members of the National Geographic Society who were to examine his proofs, and that he had brought his instruments with him in a trunk, which was left at the station. The following took place (See official Congressional Report, Private Calendar No. 733, Sixty-first Congress, Third Session, House of Representatives, Report No. 1961, pages 21 and 22):

"Mr. Roberts—How did the instruments come down?

"Captain Peary—They came in a trunk.

"Mr. Roberts—Your trunk?

"Captain Peary—Yes.

"Mr. Roberts—After you reached the station and found the trunk, what did you and the committee do regarding the instruments?

"Captain Peary—I should say that we opened the trunk there in the station.

"Mr. Roberts—That is, in the baggage-room of the station?

"Captain Peary—Yes.

"Mr. Roberts—Were the instruments all taken out?

"Captain Peary—*That I could not say. Members of the committee will probably remember better than I.*

"Mr. Roberts—Well, do you not have any recollection of whether they took them out and examined them?

"Captain Peary—Some were taken out, I should say; whether all were taken out I could not say.

"Mr. Roberts—Was any test of those instruments made by any member of the committee to ascertain whether or not the instruments were inaccurate?

"Captain Peary—*That I could not say. I should imagine that it would not be possible to make tests there.*

"Mr. Roberts—Were those instruments ever in the possession of the committee other than the inspection at the station?

not intended to convey the idea that my own countrymen were incompetent or dishonest. In the case of the
National Geographic Society they have irretrievably
prostituted their name; but the same is not true of other
American authorities.

When I came to Copenhagen, the Danish Geographic Society gave me a first spontaneous hearing.
The Copenhagen University honored me. It was,
therefore, but proper that the Danes should be the first
to pass upon the merits of my claim. While these
arrangements were in progress, I met Professor Thorp,
the Rector of the University of Copenhagen, at the
American Legation. I did not know the purport of
that meeting, nor of his detailed, careful questions; but
on the 6th of September appeared an official statement
in the press reports. In these it was stated that the

"Captain Peary—NOT TO MY KNOWLEDGE."

NOTE.—This, then, was the basis of the glorious verdict of the packed
jury which assailed me; which demanded as necessary instruments of me
which had been left in the North, and which posed as a fair body of
experts!

All important questions asked of Peary, Tittman and Gannett were
hedged, their aim being to avoid publicity. In substance, they admitted
that in the "Peary Proofs," passed upon a year before, there was no
proof. They admitted that their favorable verdict was reached upon an
examination of COPIES of Mr. Peary's observations, and that the examination and decision occurred at a sort of social gathering in the house of
Admiral Chester, who had attacked me. Chairman Roberts, commenting
on the testimony, wrote (see page 15):

"From these extracts from the testimony it will be seen that Mr.
Gannett, after his careful examination of Captain Peary's proofs and
records, did not know how many days it took Captain Peary from the
time he left Bartlett to reach the Pole and return to the *Roosevelt*, that
information being supplied by a Mr. Grosvenor. It will be also observed
that Mr. Gannett, as a result of his careful examination of Captain
Peary's proofs and records, gives Captain Peary, in his final dash to the
Pole, the following equipment: Two sledges, 36 or 32 dogs, 2 Eskimos,
and Henson. It will be seen later from Captain Peary's testimony, that
he had on that final dash 40 dogs, 5 sledges, and a total of six men in
his party. This discrepancy on so vital a point must seem quite con-
clusive that the examination of the Geographic Society's committee was
anything but careful."

meeting had been arranged to satisfy the University authorities as to whether the Pole had been reached. Among other things, Professor Thorp said:

"As there were certain questions of a special astronomical nature with which I myself was not sufficiently acquainted, I called in our greatest astronomical scientist, Professor Stromgren, who put an exhaustive series of mathematical, technical and natural scientific questions to Dr. Cook, based particularly on those of his contentions on which some doubts had been cast.

"Dr. Cook answered all to our full satisfaction. He showed no nervousness or excitement at any time. I dare say, therefore, that there is no justification for anybody to throw the slightest doubt on his claim to have reached the Pole and the means by which he did it. Professor Stromgren and I are entirely satisfied with the evidence."

I have always maintained that the proof of an explorer's doings was not to be found in a few disconnected figures, but in the continuity of his final book which presents his case. To this end I prepared a report, accompanied by the important part of the original field notes and a complete set of reduced observations. These were submitted to the University of Copenhagen in December of 1909. The verdict on this was that in such material there was no absolute proof of the attainment of the Pole.

The Peary press agents were in Copenhagen, and sent this news out so as to convey the idea that Copenhagen had denounced me; that, in their opinion, the Pole had not been reached as claimed, and that I had hoaxed the world for sordid gain; all of which was untrue. But the press flaunted my name in big head-lines as a faker.

"In the Cook data there is no proof," they repeated as the verdict of Copenhagen.

A year later Mr. Peary and his jurors confessed unwillingly in Congress that in the Peary data there was no proof.

This was reported in the official Congressional pamphlets, but, so far as I know, not a single newspaper displayed the news. The two cases, therefore, so far as verdicts go, are parallel.

Wearied of the whole problem of undesirable pub-licity; mentally and physically exhausted; disgusted with the detestable and slanderous campaign, which, for Mr. Peary, the press forced unremittingly, I decided to go away for a year, to rest and recuperate. This could not be done if I took the press into my confidence; and, therefore, I quietly departed from New York, to be joined by my family later. Out of the public eye, life, for me, assumed a new interest. In the meantime, the public agitation was stilled. Time gave a better per-spective to the case; Mr. Peary got that for which his hand had reached. He was made a Rear-Admiral, with a pension of $6,000 under retirement.

By the time I had resolved my case, I received through my brother, William L. Cook, of Brooklyn, and my London solicitor, various offers from news-papers and magazines for any statement I desired to make. Because I had gone away quietly and remained in seclusion, the newspapers had inflamed the public with an abnormal curiosity in my so-called mysterious disappearance. This fact imparted a great sensational

value to any news of my public reappearance or to any
statement which I might make. Eager to secure a
"beat," newspapers were offering my brother as high as
one thousand dollars merely for my address. The
New York newspaper which had led the attack against
me sent an offer, through my London solicitor, of any
figure which I might make for my first exclusive statement to the public. One magazine offered me ten
thousand dollars for a series of articles.

While in London I received a message from Mr.
T. Everett Harry, of *Hampton's Magazine,* concerning the publication of a series of articles explaining my
case. Mr. Harry came to London and talked over
plans for these. The opportunity of addressing the
same public, through the same medium, as Mr. Peary
had in his serial story, strongly influenced me—in fact,
so strongly that, while I had a standing offer of ten
thousand dollars, I finally gave my articles to *Hampton's* for little more than four thousand dollars.

In order that *Hampton's Magazine* might benefit
by the publicity attaching to my first statement, and in
response to the editor's request, I came quietly to the
United States with Mr. Harry, by way of Canada, to
consult with the editor before making final arrangements. Mr. Harry and I had agreed upon the outline
for the articles. They were to be a series of heart-to-
heart talks, embodying the psychological phases of the
Polar controversy and my own actions. In these I
determined fully to state my case, explain the ungracious controversy, and analyze the impossibility of
mathematically ascertaining the Pole or of proving such
a claim by figures. The articles that eventually

appeared in *Hampton's,* with the exception of unauthorized editorial changes and excisions of vitally important matter concerning Mr. Peary, were practically the same as planned in London.

Coming down from Quebec, I stopped in Troy, New York, to await Mr. Hampton, who was to come from New York. While there, a sub-editor, with all a newspaper man's sensational instincts, came to see me. He communicated, it seems, a brilliant scheme for a series of articles. As he outlined it, I was to go secretly to New York, submit myself to several employed alienists who should pronounce me insane, whereupon I was to write several articles in which I should admit having arrived at the conclusion that I reached the Pole while mentally unbalanced! This admission was to be supported by the alienists' purchased report! This plan, I was told, would "put me right" and make a great sensational story!

When I was told of this I felt staggered. Did people—could they—deem me such a hoax that, in order to obtain an unwarranted sympathy, or to make money, I should be willing to admit to such a shameful, mad, atrocious and despicable lie? I said nothing when the suggestion was made. At heart, I felt achingly hurt. I felt that this newspaper man, not hesitating at deceiving the public in order to get a sensation, regarded me as a scoundrel. I was learning, too, as I had throughout the heart-bitter controversy, the duplicity of human nature.

After a talk with Mr. Hampton, who finally arrived, and who, I am glad to say, had no such suggestion himself to offer, I got to work on my articles after the general plan spoken of in London. These were written at the Palatine Hotel, in Newburgh. The articles finished, I returned to London to settle certain business matter prior to my public return to America by Christmas.

Imagine my amazed indignation when, shortly before sailing, the cables brought the untrue news, "Dr. Cook Confesses." Imagine my heart-aching dismay when, on reaching the shores of my native country, I found the magazine which was running the articles in which I hoped to explain myself, had blazoned the sensation-provoking lie over its cover—"Dr. Cook's Confession."

I had made no confession. I had made the admission that I was uncertain as to having reached the exact mathematical Pole. That same admission Mr. Peary would have to make had he been pinned down. He did make this admission, in fact, while his own articles, a year before, were being prepared, in the *Hampton's* office.

In order to advertise itself, the magazine employed the trick of construing a mere admission of uncertainty as to the exact pin-point attainment of the Pole as a "confession." To the public I had apparently authorized this. The misrepresentation hurt me, and for a time placed me in an unhappy dilemma.

Before the appearance of the January *Hampton's,* in which the first instalment of my articles appeared, a series of press stories supposedly based upon my forthcoming articles were prepared and sent out by the sub-editor who had suggested the insanity plan. These were prepared during the absence of Mr. Harry in Atlantic

City. By picking garbled extracts from my articles about the impossibility of a pin-point determination of the Pole, and the crazy mirage-effects of the Arctic world, these news-stories were construed to the effect that I admitted I did not know whether I had been at the North Pole or whether I had not been at the North Pole, and also that I admitted to a plea of insanity. These stories were printed on the first pages of hundreds of newspaper all over the country, under scareheads of "Dr. Cook Admits Fake!" and "Dr. Cook Makes Plea of Insanity!"

In these reports, written by the sub-editor, he gave himself credit for the "discovery" of Dr. Cook and the securing of his articles for *Hampton's*. This claim for the magazine "beat" was as dishonest as his handling of the press matter for *Hampton's*. My dealings with the magazine were entirely through Mr. Harry, whose frankness and fair-dealing early disposed me to give my story to the publication he represented.

The widespread dissemination of the untrue and cruelly unfair "confession" and "insanity-plea" stories dazed me. I felt impotent, crushed. In my very effort to explain myself I was being irretrievably hurt. I was being made a catspaw for magazine and newspaper sensation.

But misrepresentations do not make history. The American people cannot always be hoodwinked. The reading public soon realized that my story was no more a confession than the "Peary Proof Positive" instalment in Hampton's had been the embodiment of any real Polar proofs.

Finding that it was impossible, in magazines and

newspapers, to tell the full truth; finding that what I did say was garbled and distorted, I concluded to reserve the detailed facts for this book. There were truths about Mr. Peary which, I suppose, no paper would have dared to print. I have told them here. There were truths about myself which, because they explain me, the papers, preferring to attack me, would not have printed. I have told them here.

I climbed Mt. McKinley, by my own efforts, without assistance; I reached the Pole, save for my Eskimos, alone. I had spent no one's money, lost no lives. I claimed my victory honestly; and as a man believing in himself and his personal rights, at a time when I was nervously unstrung and viciously attacked, I went away to rest, rather than deal in dirty defamation, alone. At a time when the tables seemed turned, when the wolves of the press were desirous of rending me, I came back to my country—alone.

I have now made my fight; I have been compelled to extreme measures of truth-telling that are abhorrent to me. I have done this because, otherwise, people would not understand the facts of the Polar controversy or why I, reluctant, remained silent so long. I have done this single-handedly. I have confidence in my people; more than that, I have implicit and indomitable confidence in—Truth.

RETROSPECT

Returning from the North, in September, 1909, while being honored in Copenhagen for my success in reaching the North Pole, there came, by wireless from Labrador, messages from Robert E. Peary, claiming the attainment exclusively as his own, and declaring that in my assertion I was, in his vernacular, offering the world a "gold brick."

On April 21, 1908, I had reached a spot which I ascertained, with as scientific accuracy as possible, to be the top of the axis around which the world spins—the North Pole.

On April 6, 1909, a year later, Mr. Peary claimed to have reached the same spot.

To substantiate his charge of fraud, Peary declared that my Eskimo companions had said I had been only two sleeps from land. Why, he further asked, had I not taken reputable witnesses with me on such a trip?

I had taken, on my final dash, two expert Eskimos. Mr. Peary had four Eskimos and a negro body servant.

Before launching further charges, Mr. Peary delayed his ship, the *Roosevelt,* at Battle Harbor, on the pretext of cleaning it, that he might digest my New York *Herald* story, compare it with his own, and fabricate his broadside of abuse. There he was in constant communication with the New York *Times,* General Thomas Hubbard—president of the Peary Arctic Club and financial sponsor of the "trust"—and Herbert L. Bridgman. The *Times,* eager to "beat" the *Herald,* was desirous of descrediting me and launching Peary's as the *bona-fide* North Pole discovery story. General Hubbard, Mr. Bridgman, and the "trust" were eager for a publicity and acclaim greater than that which might attach to any honorable second victor. Dishonor and perjury, to secure first honors, were not even to be weighed in the balance.

When I arrived in New York, I was confronted by a series of technical questions, designed to baffle me. These questions, I learned, had been sent to the *Times* by Mr. Peary with instructions that the *Times* "get after" me.

I answered these questions. I had answered them in Europe. Mr. Peary, when he arrived at Sydney, and afterward, refused to answer any questions. He continued simply to attack me, to make insinuations asperging my honesty, playing the secret back-hand game of defamation conducted by his friends of his Arctic Club.

Why had I not, on my return from my Polar trip, told anyone of the achievement, Mr. Peary asked in an interview, aiming to show that my Polar attainment was an afterthought.

On my return to Etah I had told Harry Whitney and Pritchard. They, in turn, told Captain Bob Bartlett. Captain Bartlett, as well as the Eskimos, in turn told Peary at Etah that I claimed to have reached the Pole. At the very moment when this charge was made, Peary had in his pocket Captain Adams' letter which gave the same information. Why did Mr. Peary suppress this information, convicting himself of insinuating an untruth from three different sources to challenge my claim. Returning from the North with the negro, Henson, and Eskimos, Mr. Peary himself had not told his own companions on the *Roosevelt* of his own success. Why was this?

In a portentous statement Mr. Peary and his party declared my Eskimos said I had not been more than two sleeps from land.

I had instructed my companions not to tell Peary of my achievement. He had stolen my supplies. I felt him unworthy of the confidence of a brother explorer. I had encouraged the delusion of E-tuk-i-shook and Ah-we-lah that almost daily mirages and low-lying clouds were signs of land, so as to prevent the native panic and desertion on the circumpolar sea. They had possibly told this to Peary in all honesty; but other natives also told him that we had reached the "Big Nail."

Why was the news to Mr. Peary's liking given, while that which he did not like was ignored?

Not long ago, Matthew Henson, interviewed in the south, was quoted as saying that Peary did not get to the Pole. In another interview he said that Peary, like a tenderfoot, rode in a fur-cushioned sledge until they got to a place which was "far enough." I still prefer to believe Peary rather than Henson. Peary's Eskimo companions of a former trip positively deny Peary's claimed discovery of Crocker Land. I still prefer to believe that Crocker Land does deserve a place on the map. Peary's last Eskimo companions say that he did not reach the Pole. But I prefer to credit his claim. Mr. Peary's spirit has never been that of fairness to others when a claim impignes upon his own. He has always adopted the tactics of the claim-jumper.

In a like manner, and with similar intent, Mr. Peary had attacked many explorers before me. To prevent his companions from profiting by their own work, members of each expedition were forced to sign contracts that barred press interviews, eliminated cameras, prohibited lecturing or writing, or even trading for trophies. To insure Mr. Peary all the honor, his men were made slaves to his cause.

In a quarrel which resulted from these impossible conditions, Eivind Astrup was assailed. Broken-hearted, he committed suicide. Captain Otto Sverdrup was made to feel the sting of the same grasping spirit. General A. W. Greely has been unjustly attacked. All of this detestable selfishness culminated in the treatment of Captain Bob Bartlett. When the Pole, to Peary, seemed within reach, and the glory of victory was within grasp, the ever-faithful Bartlett was turned back and his place was taken by a negro, that Peary might be, to quote his own words, "the only white man at the Pole."

When, on my return to New York, I found myself attacked by a man of this caliber, I decided that the public, without any counter-defamation on my part, would read him aright and see through the unscrupulous and dishonest campaign. So I remained silent.

Coming down to Portland from Sydney, where he had landed, Mr. Peary gave out an interview insinuating that I had had no instruments with which to take observations. "Would Dr. Cook," he asked, "if he had had instruments, have left them in the hands of a stranger (Harry Whitney), when upon these depended his fame or his dishonor?"

On his return to this country, Mr. Whitney corroborated my statement of leaving my instruments with him. Mr. Peary's own captain, who had cross-questioned my Eskimos for Mr. Peary, later stated to two magazine editors that my companions had described to him the instruments I had had. Is it reasonable to suppose that Mr. Peary did not know of this? I know that he knew. If he is an honest man, why did he stoop to this dishonesty? Even if he believed me to be dishonest, dishonest methods only placed him in the class of the one he attacked as dishonest.

By using the same underhand methods, as when he got the New York *Times* to cross-question me for himself, Peary now got his friends of the Geographic Society, who had boosted him, to call for "proofs." Such proofs, it appeared, should always be presented before public honors were accepted or the returns of a lecture tour considered. But Peary had engaged in exploration for twenty years, and had always given lectures at once, without ever offering proofs. I was asked to cancel lecture engagements and furnish what Peary knew neither he nor anybody else could furnish offhand. For the proof of an explorer's doings is his final book, which requires months and years to prepare.

With much blaring of trumpets, the Peary "proofs" were submitted to his friends of the National Geographic Society. With but a casual examination of copies of data, claimed at the time to be original field notes, with no explanation of the wonderful instruments upon which it had been earlier claimed Polar honors rested, an immediate and favorable verdict was rendered.

A huge picture was published, showing learned, bewhiskered gentlemen examining the Peary "proofs," and reaching their verdict. Mr. Peary's case for a rediscovery of the Pole was won—for the time. The public were deceived into believing that positive proofs had been presented; that the society, acting as a competent and neutral jury, was honest. Later it was shown that its members were financially interested in Mr. Peary's expedition, and still later it was admitted that the Peary proofs contained no proof. All of this later development has had no publicity.

In the meantime, I was attacked for delay. My data was finally sent to the University of Copenhagen. A verdict of "Unproven" was rendered.

Thereupon, Mr. Peary and his friends at once shouted "Fraud!" The press parrot-like re-echoed that shout. With this unfair insinuation there came to me the biting sting of a burning electric shock as the wires quivered all around the world. At the Congressional investigation, a year later, the Peary data was shown to be useless as proof. It was a verdict precisely like that of Copenhagen on mine, but the press did not print it. Did the Peary interests have any control over the American press or its sources of news distribution?

After the call for "proof" came charges, from members of the Peary cabal, that I was unable to take observations. Mr. Peary was so much better equipped than I to do so! Moreover, he had had the able scientific assistance of Bartlett and—the negro.

When I was at the Pole the sun was 12° above the

horizon. At the time Peary claims he was there it was less than 7°. Difficult as it is to take observations at 12°, because of refracted light, any accurate observation at 7° is impossible. It is indeed, questionable if an observation could be made at all at the time when Peary claims to have been at the Pole.

Finding that, despite all charges, the public believed in me, Mr. Peary, through his coöperators, attempted to discredit my veracity. An affidavit, which was bought, as I have evidence to prove, was made by Barrill to the effect that I had not climbed Mt. McKinley. The getting of this affidavit is placed at the door of Mr. Peary.

Do honest men, with honest intentions, buy perjured documents?

Do honest men, believing in themselves, besmirch their own honor by deliberate lying?

Dunkle and Loose came to me, offered to look over the observations in my *Herald* story, and—suddenly— to my amazement—offered a set of faked observations, manufactured at the instigation of someone. I refused the batch of faked papers, and turned the two nefarious conspirators out of my hotel.

A comparison of my Copenhagen report with the Dunkle perjured story, later printed in the New York *Times,* proves I used not one of their figures. Mr. R. J. McLouglin later proved that the hand which signed "Dunkle" also signed "Loose" to that lying document. It is, therefore, not only a perjury, but a forgery.

Recently, Professor J. H. Gore, a member of the National Geographic Society, and one of Peary's

friends, acknowledged to Evelyn B. Baldwin that he
had in his possession the faked observations which were
made by Dunkle and Loose.

How did he come by them? Why does he have
them? What were the relations between Dunkle and
Loose, Peary's friends, the New York *Times,* and the
National Geographic Society? Do honest men, with
honest intentions, conspire with men of this sort, men
who offered to sell me faked figures—most likely to
betray me had I been dishonest enough to buy them—
and who, failing, perjured themselves?

Disgusted, I decided to let my enemies exhaust
their abuse. I knew it eventually would rebound. Determined to retire to rest, to resolve my case in quietude
and secrecy, I left America. My enemies gleefully proclaimed this an admission of imposture.

Yet, after they had turned almost every newspaper in the country against me, having rested, having
resolved my case, having secured damaging proofs of
the facts of the conspiracy against me, I returned to
America.

Realizing my error in so long remaining silent;
realizing the power of a sensation-seeking press, which
has no respect for individuals or of truth, I determined,
painful as would be the task, to tell the unpleasant,
distasteful truth about the man who tried to besmirch
my name. This may seem unkind. But I was kind too
long. Truth is often unpleasant, but it is less malicious than the sort of lies hurled at me.

After I had left America, the newspapers, desirous of sensation, had played into the hands of those
who, with seeming triumph, assailed me. But mean-

while, however, I was taking advantage of the opportunity to rest and gain an accurate perspective of the situation. I thought out my case, considered it pro and con, puzzled out the reasons for, and the source of, the newspaper clamor against me. Through friends in America who worked quietly and effectively, I secured evidence, which is embodied in affidavits, which laid bare the methods employed to discredit me in the Mt. McKinley affair. I learned of the methods used, and just what charges were made, to discredit my Polar claim. Damaging admissions were secured concerning Mr. Peary's fabricated attacks from the mouths of Mr. Peary's own associates. Knowing these facts, at the proper time, I returned to my native country to confront my enemies. I have proceeded in detail to state my case and reveal the hitherto unknown inside facts of the entire Polar controversy. I have stated certain facts before the public. Neither Mr. Peary nor his friends have replied. One point in the Polar controversy has never reached the public. Both Mr. Peary and many of his friends asserted that I left the country just in time to escape criminal prosecution. They said the charge was to be that I had obtained money on a false pretence by accepting fees for lecturing on my discovery. I returned to America. I have been lecturing for fees on my discovery since; I have not yet been prosecuted.

Were Mr. Peary not the sort of man who would stoop to dishonor, to discredit a rival in order to gain an unfair advantage for himself, were he not guilty of the gross injustice I have stated, he would have had all the opportunity in the world for effectively coming back at me.   But he has remained silent.   Why?

I have, as I have said, absolute confidence in the good sense, spirit of fair-play, and ability of reasoning judgment of my people.   My case rests, not with any body of armchair explorers or kitchen geographers, but with Arctic travelers who can see beyond the mist of selfish interests, and with my fellow-countrymen, who breathe normal air and view without bias the large open fields of honest human endeavor.

In this book I have stated my case, presented my proofs.   As to the relative merits of my claim, and Mr. Peary's, place the two records side by side.   Compare them.   I shall be satisfied with your decision.

FREDERICK A. COOK.

APPENDIX

COPY OF THE FIELD NOTES

The following copy of the daily entries in one of my original note-books takes the expedition step by step from Svartevoeg to the Pole and back to land.

As will be seen by those here reproduced, the original notes are mostly abbreviations and suggestions, hasty tabulations and reminders, memoranda to be later elaborated. The hard environment, the scarcity of materials, and cold fingers did not encourage extensive field notes. Most of these field notes were rewritten while in Jones Sound, and some were also copied and elaborated in Greenland.

In planning this expedition, every article of equipment and every phase of effort was made subordinate to the one great need of covering long distances. We deliberately set out for the Pole, with a desperate resolution to succeed, and although appreciating the value of detail scientific work, I realized that such work could not be undertaken in a pioneer project like ours. We therefore did not burden ourselves with cumbersome instruments, nor did we allow ourselves to be side-tracked in attractive scientific pursuits. Elaborate results are not claimed, but the usual data of Arctic expeditions were gathered with fair success.

(Notes usually written at end of day's march.)

Date.	Miles Covered.	OBSERVATIONS, ETC. (Exact copy from original Field Papers)
March 1908. 18	26	Svartevoeg. Made cache here for return. Supporting party goes back. Noon start; 4 men, 46 dogs, 4 sleds; 26 miles. Ice heavy, wavy; little snow; crystals hard; land screened by drift. Camp on old field. Night uncomfortable; air humid, penetrating. Snowhouse of hard snow imperfectly made. (Other notes of this date so dim that they cannot be read. *Compass directions, unless otherwise noted, are true.*)

Date.	Miles Covered.	OBSERVATIONS, ETC. (Exact copy from original Field Papers)
March 1908. 19	21	Clearer, overland thick; —56° F.; Wind 2 W.; sun feeble; blue haze. On march, ice smaller; use of axe; crossings troublesome. Camp lee of big hummock. Cannot send supply back; must follow for another day.
20	16	Land more clearly visible; sky overcast; wind W. S. W. 1; ice worse. Small igloo. The last feed men return.
21	29	Awoke, sun N. E.; orange glow; —63° F.; bar. 30.10, steady; no clouds; sky pale purple. More snow (on ice); groaning sledges; mirages, lands, mountains, volcanoes. Air light; wind sky N.; Grant Land a mere line; —46°. Torture of light snow; march 14 hours.
22	22	A. M.; wind E. 3; —59°. Start 12 (noon); sky clearer; wind 2; water sky N. Grant Land visible P. M. (Later) Temp. rose to —46°. Wind tolerably high; pressure lines; the big lead. Camp on old field on bank; ice noises; search for the crossing. Young, elastic ice.
23	17	Cross the big lead. Young ice elastic and dangerous; western sky again threatening; ice movement east; fields small; narrow open lanes. Course for 85th on 97th; —40°; march 11 hours; 23 miles, credit 17 miles. Ice noises; night beautiful; sun sank into pearly haze. (Later) Orange glow; pack violet and pale purple blue; sky late—partly cl. appearance of land W.
24	18	Observations 83.31—96.27; —41°; bar. 29.70. West bank of fog and haze. Start afternoon; no life; old seal hole and bear tracks; long march; ice improving. 10 h.; pedometer 21 m.; camp in coming storm; rushing clouds; signs of land W. 18 m. (credited on course).
25	18	Early awakened by dogs. Storm spent soon; sunrise temp. —26°, later —41°; west again smoky. Back to the bags; cracking ice; the breaking and separating ice and the crevasse episode; in a bag and in water; ice-water and pemmican; masks of ice. Good march over newly-fractured ice; ice in motion.
26	17	Still windy; some drift snow; another storm threatening. How we need rest! Strong wind during the night. Position D. R. 84.24—96.53.
27	16	In camp until noon. Strong winds all night; eased at noon; clearing some; sun; weather unsettled. Short run; squally en route; made early camp. Bar. 29.05.

Date.	Miles Covered.	OBSERVATIONS, ETC. (Exact copy from original Field Papers)
March 1908. 28	0	Weather still unsettled. Temp. —41°; Bar. 29.15; west ugly. No progress. The drift. In camp. Anxious about stability of igloo. The collapsed camp. Midnight; north cloudy, but ice bright; many hummocks.
29	9	Start early P. M. A little blue in the west; sun bursts; pack disturbed; hard traveling, due to fresh crevasses. Camp midnight; only 9 miles.
30	10	Land, 9 A. M., cleared; land was seen; westerly clouds settled over it. Observations 84.50, 95.36; bearing of land, southern group, West by South to West by North true. Other bearings taken later place a coast line along the 102 meridian from lat. 84° 20′ to 85° 10′. There must be much open water about the land, for banks of vapor persistently hide part. A low fog persistent; cannot see shore; for days we have expected to see something W., but never a clear horizon. Probably two island S. like Heiberg, 1,800 ft. high, valleys, mountains, snow N., table 1,000, thin ice sheet, bright nights. From observation paper: Bar. 30.10, had risen from 29.50 in 2 hours; wind 2-3 mag. S.; clouds mist, East, water-bands W.; shadow (of 6 ft. pole) 39 ft.
31	10	Land screened by mist; wind W. 2-0. Ice fracture; no sign of life—none since 83.
April 1908. 1	18	(Time of traveling) 9 to 6; ice better; fields larger; crevasses less troublesome; temp. —32°. There is no more darkness at night.
2	12	(Start) 9.30; (stop) 8. Smooth ice; hard snow; ice 28 ft. and 32. Night bright but cloudy. Temp. —35°; bar. 30.10; leads difficult.
3	10	8.30 to 6.30. Temp. —39°; bar. 30.12; sky clearing at noon, but low clouds and frosty haze persist in the W. and N. Night bright; sun at midnight under cloud and haze.
4	14	8.45 to 6.10. Snow softer; used snowshoes; have crossed 11 crevasses; much chopping; brash and small hummocks.
5	14	9 (A. M.) to 5.45 (P. M.). Snow better. Ice larger. Oh, so tired! Snowshoes.
6	14	8.10 (A. M.) to 6.15 (P. M.). Snow hard. Ice flat. Few hummocks. Less wavy. Snow (shoes). Sun faces.

Date.	Miles Covered.	OBSERVATIONS, ETC. (Exact copy from original Field Papers)
April 1908.	7	14	11 to 10. Beautiful clear weather; even the night sky clear. Midnight sun first seen. Ice 36 ft. (thick). (Another measurement gave 21 feet.)
	8	9	Observation before starting, 86.36, 94.2. In spite of what seemed like long marches we made only 106 miles in 9 days. Much distance lost in crossings. (From field paper) bar. 29.50, rising; temp. —37°; wind mag. N. E., 2; clouds St. 3; shadow (6 ft. pole), 32 feet.
	9	14	9 A. M. to 5.30 P. M.; snow hard; ice about the same; wind cutting; frost bites. Clothes humid.
	10	16	10 P. M. to 7 A. M. Working hours changed; big marches and long hours no longer possible; snow good; ice steadily improving; bodily fatigue much felt; wind 1—28 W.
	11	15	10.30 to 8 A. M. Observation end of March, 87.20, 95.19; the pack disturbance of B. Ld. lost; farthest north; little crushed ice; old floes less irregular; anxious about food; wind 3 W. (true); 300 miles in 24 days; work intermittent; too tired to read instruments. (From other field notes, Temp. —39°; bar. 29.90°.)
	12	21	11 P. M. to 7 A. M. Thoughts of return. Food supply reduced. Hope to economize in warmer weather. Very heavy ice. Much like land ice. Wind 2 W. S. W. The awful monotony!
	13	17	12 P. M. to 7 A. M. The same heavy glacier-like ice. . . . . . . The occasional soup. Hummocks 15-20 ft. Ahwelah in tears at start. W. black. Sun under rushing vapors. Ice changes. Leads.
	14	23	11 P. M. to 7.10 A. M. 88.21, 95.52. Wind light but penetrating. Off the big field, ice smaller. Some open leads. Little sign of pressure. Snow soft, but less precipitation. Dogs get up better speed. 100 miles from Pole. (From other observation papers: Bar. 29.90, falling; temp., —44°; shadow (6 ft. pole) 30½ feet.)
	15	14	10 P. M. to 7 A. M. Ice same. Wind —1, S. W. Working to the limit of muscle capacity. So tired and weary of the never ceasing tread!
	16	15	10.30 to 8 A. M. Ice passed. Several heavy old floes. Made 6 crossings. Wind 1—3, W. S. W.

Date.	Miles Covered.	OBSERVATIONS, ETC. (Exact copy from original Field Papers)
April 1908. 17	13	10.15 to 8 A. M. Ice same. Crevasses new. 7 crossings. Saw several big hummocks. Ice less troublesome. Temp., —40°; bar., 30.00. Sled friction less.
18	14	9 P. M. to 6. Ice, though broken, smooth. The horizon line not so irregular as that of more S. ice. Sky and ice of a dark purple blue. (Bar. 30.02.)
19	16	11 P. M. to 8 A. M. (Position) 89.31. D. R. 94.03. Camp on an old field—the only one on the horizon with big hummocks. Ice in very large fields; surface less irregular, but in other respects not different from farther S. Eskimos told that in two average marches Pole would be reached. Extra rations served. Camp in tent. (Bar., 29.98; Temp., —46°.)
20	15½	8 P. M. to 4 A. M. An exciting run; ice aglow in purple and gold; Eskimos chanting. Wind, S. 1 89; 46.45. (D. R.) 94.52. New enthusiasm; good march. Temp., —36°; bar. (not legible on notes); course set for 97th.
21	13½	1 A. M. to 9 A. M. Observations noon: 89; 59.45; ped. 14. Camp; sleep in tent short time; after observations advance; pitch tent; (also) made camp—snow—prepared for two rounds of observations. Temp., 37.7°; bar., 29.83. Nothing wonderful; no Pole; a sea of unknown depth; ice more active; new cracks; open leads; but surface like farther south. Overjoyed but find no words to express pleasure. So tired and weary! How we need a rest! 12, night. Sun seems as high as at noon, but in reality is a little higher, owing to its spiral ascent. The mental elation—the drying of furs, and (making) photos—Eskimos' ideas and disappointment of no Pole—thoughts of home and its cheer. But oh, such monotony of sky, wind and ice! The dangers of getting back. (From other observation papers: Temp. ranged from —36° by mercury thermometer to —39° by spirit thermometer; clouds Alt. St., 1; wind mag. S., 1; ice blink E.; water sky, W.; shadow (of 6 ft. pole) 28 feet.)
22	0	Moved camp 4 m. magnetic S. Made 4 observations for altitude; S. at noon, W. at 6, N. at 12M, E. at 6 A. M. Ice same; more open water; wind 2-3; temp., —41°; (from field paper) W. S. W., 1 to 2. There are only two big hummocks in sight. (Made a series of observations for the sun's altitude, 2 on the 21st at the first camp, 4 on the 22nd at W. M. camp, and another midnight 22-23. Before we left deposited tube.)

Date.	Miles Covered.	OBSERVATIONS, ETC. (Exact copy from original Field Papers)
April 1908. 23	20	Start for home. 12.30 to noon. Fairly clear—ice smooth, but many new crevasses. Temp., —41°. Course for 100 mer.
24	16	11 P. M. to 9 A. M. These records, being made at the end of the day's journey, give the doings of the day previous—this note for the 24th is in reality written on the morning of the 25th, when comfortable in camp. Wind 1-2 W. Temp., —36°. Ice smooth—fields larger; 5 crossings; the pleasure of facing home.
25	15	8-8. Temp., —37°; Wind 1-2 W. S. W.; ice same. The worry of ice breaking up for me, signs of joy for the Eskimo.
26	14	9 to 7. Still much worried about return; possibility of ice disruption and open water near land; wind light; ice shows new cracks, but few have opened; seems to be little pressure; few hummocks; snow hard and traveling all that could be desired.
27	14	9.30 to 8. Ice same; wind S. E. 1; good going; crossings not troublesome; dogs in good spirits; Eskimos happy; but all very tired. Temp., —40°.
28	14	9.15 to 7.45. Ice same; wind 1 W.; snow moderately hard; few hummocks and no pressure lines.
29	13	Midnight to 8.45 A. M. Ice more active; fresh cracks; some open cracks but no leads. Wind 1 S.
30	15	Midnight to 8 A. M. Ped. registered 121 m. from Pole; camp by D. R., 87.59—100; observations 88.01, 97.42. Course half point more W. Temp., —34°. Start more westerly.
May 1908. 1	18	12.30 to 9 A. M. Much color to the sunbursts, but the air humid; the temperature persistently near —40°, but considerable range with the direction of the light winds and mists when they come over leads. Much very heavy smooth ice—undulating, not hummocky like S.
2	12	2 A. M. to 11 A. M. Fog, clouds and wet air. Temp., —15°. Hard to strike a course.
3	13	1 A. M. to 10 A. M. Thick weather; wind E. 2; ice friction less; occasional light snow fall.
4	14	3 to 11 A. M. Air clear but sky obscured; ice very good, but hummocks appearing on the horizon.

Date.	Miles Covered.	OBSERVATIONS, ETC. (Exact copy from original Field Papers)
May 1908. 5	11	11 P. M. to 6 A. M. Strong wind; occasional breathing spell behind hummocks; squally with drifts.
6	0	In camp. Stopped by signs of storm; tried to build igloo but wind prevented; in a collapsed tent for 24 hours; eat only half ration of pemmican.
7	10	8 A. M. to 3 P. M. Wind detestable; ice bad; life a torture; sky persistently obscured; no observations; pedometer out of order, only time to gauge our distance.
8	12	2 A. M. to 10. Weather bad; windy, S. W.; some drift; heavy going.
9	13	1 to 8 A. M. (Weather) thick; wind easier; ice in big fields; snow a little harder, snowshoes steady.
10	13	11 P. M. of the 9th to 6 A. M. Heavy going but little friction on sled; some drift; see more hummocks.
11	0	May 11. In camp. Strong wind; heavy drift; encircle tent with snow blocks.
12	11	12.30 to 8.30 A. M. Wind still strong; cestrugi troublesome, but temperature moderate; sled loads getting light.
13	12	11 P. M. of 12th, to 7.30 A. M. of 13th. Wind easier, S. S. W.; snow harder; ice very thick and very large fields; fog.
14	9	3 A. M. to 9 A. M. No sky; strong wind compelled to camp early.
15	13	1 A. M. to 10. Fog; ice much crevassed; passed over several cracks—some opening.
16	14	May 16. 11 P. M. of the 15th to 6 A. M. Cl. 10; wind again troublesome; light diffused, making it difficult to find footing.
17	11	2 A. M. to 10. Thick; ice more and more broken; smaller and more cracked—cracks give much trouble.
18	11	1 A. M. to 9.30. Wind more southerly and strong; ice separating; some open water in leads.
19	12	11 P. M. to 7.30. Wind veering east; fog thicker; ice very much broken, but snow surface good.

Date.	Miles Covered.	OBSERVATIONS, ETC. (Exact copy from original Field Papers)
May 1908.	20	6	Midnight to 9 A. M. Open water; active pack; almost impossible.
	21	8	11 P. M. to 9. Conditions the same; our return seems almost hopeless; no observations—cannot even guess at the drift.
	22	0	In camp. Gale N. E.; temp. high; air wet; ice breaking and grinding; worried about the ultimate return; food low.
	23	5	3 A. M. to 7 A. M. Still squally, but forced a short march.
	24	12	12 noon to 8 A. M. Short clearing at noon; the first clear mid-day sky for a long time; west still in haze. Water sky W. and S. W.; no land in sight—though the boys saw the land later when I was asleep; ice much broken. 84° 02'—97° 03'.
	25	14	10 P. M. to 6 A. M. Ice better; no wind; thick fog; snow hard. Temp., —10°.
	26	12	11 P. M. to 7.45 A. M. Ice in fields of about 1 M. somewhat hummocky; crossings hard; no wind.
	27	11	11.30 P. M. to 9.30 A. M. Ice same; thick fog.
	28	13	12 m. night to 10 A. M. Ice still same; fog; wind 3, shifting E. S. E. and S. W.
	29	11	11.30 P. M. to 9.30 A. M. As we came here the water sky in the southwest to which we had aimed, gradually working west, led to a wide open lead, extending from north to south, and almost before knowing it, in the general plan of the ice arrangement, we found ourselves to the east of this lead. Temp. rose to zero. Ice much broken; air thick; light vague; impossible to see irregularities. Food ¾ rations; and straight course for Nansen Sound.
	30	10	12 to 11 A. M. Ice in heaps; open water; brash the worst trouble; little fog.
	31	11	11.15 P. M. to 9 A. M. Ice little better; snow hard; sleds go easy; much helping required (over pressure lines).
June 1908.	1	12	10.45 to 8. Ice in large fields; many hummocks; few heavy fields.

Date.	Miles Covered.	OBSERVATIONS, ETC. (Exact copy from original Field Papers)
June 1908. 2	12	10 P. M. to 9 A. M. Ice steadily improving.
3	11	10 P. M. to 8 A. M. Ice begins to show action of sun. Temperature occasionally above freezing.
4	10	9.30 P. M. to 7.30 A. M. Fog; ice offering much trouble, but friction little and load light.
5	11	9.45 P. M. to 7 A. M. Hummocks exposed to sun have icicles.
6	0	In camp. Strong N. W. gale.
7	0	In camp. Gale continues, with much snow; the ice about breaks up; anxious about map. (Not knowing either drift or position, were puzzled as to proper course to set.)
8	14	1 A. M. to noon. Ice bad, but snow hard, and after rest progress good; wind still blowing west.
9	10	11 P. M. to 9 A. M. With thick ice and this kind of traveling it is hard to guess at distances.
10	0	10.30 P. M. to 8. Bad ice; open leads; still no sun.
11	14	10 P. M. to 8 A. M. Large smooth ice; little snow; wind S. W., 1; no fog, but sky still of lead.
12	15	10.30 to 5. Small fields but good going; sky black to the east.
13	14	10 to 8 A. M. Fog cleared first time since last observation. Land in sight south and east. Heiberg and Ringnes Land; water sky; small ice; brash and drift eastward. We have been carried adrift far to the south and west, and examination of ice eastward proves that all is small ice and open water. Heiberg Island is impossible to us. What is our fate? Food and fuel is about exhausted, though we still have 10 bony dogs. Upon these and our little pemmican we can possibly survive for 20 days. In the meantime we must go somewhere. To the south is our only hope.

Note.—*June* 14 and thereafter to *September* 1, all notes were briefly jotted down in another diary, a collection of loose leaves in which the observations of the return were made. This diary was left with the instruments at Etah with Mr. Whitney. The data, however, had been re-written at Cape Sparbo, so that the notes had served their purpose and were of no further value when no pretentious publication was anticipated.

Other notes were made on loose sheets of paper or on leaves of the note books. Many of these were destroyed, others were rubbed out to make room for recording what was regarded as more important data, and a few were retained quite by accident.

QUESTIONS THAT ENTER CALCULATIONS FOR POSITION OF THE NORTH POLE.

By Frederick A. Cook.

Much abstruse, semi-scientific and academic material has been forced into the polar discussions about proofs by observation. The problem presented is full of interesting points, and to elucidate these I will ask the reader to go back with me to that elusive imaginary spot, the North Pole. Here we find no pole—and absolutely nothing to mark the spot for hundreds of miles. We are in the center of a great moving sea of ice and for 500 miles in every direction it is the same hopeless desert of floating, shifting crystal. I believed then that we had reached the Pole, and it never occurred to me that there would be a cry for absolute proof. Such a demand had never been presented before. The usual data of the personal narrative of the explorers had always been received with good faith. But let us reopen the question and examine the whole problem.

Is there any positive proof for a problem of this kind? Is there any one sure shoulder upon which we can hang the mantle of polar conquest? We are deprived of the usual landmarks of terrestrially fixed points. The effort to furnish proof is like trying to fix a point in Mid-Atlantic. But here you have the tremendous advantage of known compass variation, sure time, reasonably accurate corrections. Not only by careful observation at sea of fixed stars and other astronomical data, but by an easy and quick access to and from each shore, and by reliable tables for reductions gathered during scores of years of experience.

All this is denied in the mid-polar basins at the time when it is possible to arrive there. There is no night, there are no stars, and the sun, the only fixed object by which a position can be calculated, is not absolutely fixable. It is low on the horizon. Its rays are bent in getting to the recording instruments while passing through the thick maze of floating ice mist. This mist always rests on the pack even in clear days. The very low temperature of the atmosphere and the distorting, twisting mirage effect of different strata of air, with radically different temperatures, wherein each stratum has a different density, carry different quantities of frosted humidity.

All of this gives to the sunbeam, upon which the calculation for latitude and longitude is based, the deceptive appearance of a paddle thrust into clear water. The paddle in such case seems bent. The sunbeam is bent in a like manner, since it passes through an unknown depth of refractory air for the correction of which no law can be devised until modern aerial navigation brings to a science that very complex problem of the geography of the atmosphere. For this reason, and for others which we will presently show, this whole idea of proof by figures as devised by Mr. Peary and the armchair geographers, falls to pieces.

Let us take the noon observation—a fairly certain method to determine latitude in most zones of the earth where for hundreds of years we have learned to make certain corrections, which by use have been incorporated as laws in the art of navigation. About five minutes before local noon the sea captain goes to the bridge with sextant in hand. His time is certain, but even if it were not, the sun rises and sets and therefore changes its altitude quickly. The captain screws the sun down to a fixed angle on his sextant; he puts the instrument aside; then takes it up again, brings the sun to the horizon, examines his instrument. The sun has risen a little further; it is not yet noon. This is repeated again and again, and at last the sun begins to descend. It is now local noon. This gives a rough check for his time. There is a certain sure moment for his observation at just the second when it is accurate,—when the sun's highest ascent has been reached. Such advantages are impossible when nearing the Pole. The chronometers have been shooting the shoots of the pack for weeks. The sudden changes of temperature also disturb the mechanism, and therefore time, that very important factor upon which all astronomical data rest, is at best only a rough guess. For this reason alone, if for no other, such as unknown refraction and other optical illusions, the determination of longitude when nearing the Pole becomes difficult and unreliable. All concede this, but latitude, we are told by the armchair observer, is easy and sure. Let us see.

The time nears to get a peep of the sun at noon, but what

is local noon? The chronometers may be, and probably are, far off. And there is no way to correct even approximately. I do not mean on hours, but there may be unknowable differences of minutes, and each minute represents a mile. Let us see how this affects our noon observation. Five or ten minutes before local noon the observer levels his artificial horizon and with sextant in hand lies down on the snow. A little drift and nose bleaching wind complicate matters. The fingers are cold; the instrument must be handled with mittens; the cold is such that at best a shiver runs up the spine, the eye blinks with snow glitter and frost. The arms, hands and legs become stiff from cold and from inaction. He tries exactly what the sea captain does in comfort on the bridge, but his time is a guess, he watches the sun, he tries to catch it when it is highest, but this is about as difficult as it is to catch a girl in the act of winking when her back is turned.

The sun does not rise and set as it does in temperate climes—it circles the horizon day and night in a spiral ascent so nearly parallel to the line of the horizon that it is a practical impossibility to determine by any possible means at hand when it is highest. One may lie on that snow for an hour, and though steadied with the patience of Job, the absolute determination of the highest point of the sun's altitude or the local noon is almost a physical impossibility.

This observation is not accurate and gives only results of use in connection with other calculations. These results at best are also subject to that unknown allowance for really great atmospheric refraction. The geographic student will, I am sure, agree that against this the magnetic needle will offer some check, for if you can be certain that when the needle points to a positive direction, then it is a simple matter to get approximate time with it and the highest noon altitude; but since the correction for the needle, like that of latitude and longitude, is based on accurate time, and since it is further influenced by other local and general unknown conditions— therefore even the compass, that sheet anchor of the navigator, is as uncertain as other aids to fixing a position in the polar basin.

In making such observations an artificial horizon must be used. This offers an uncontrollable element of inaccuracy in all Arctic observations when the sun is low.

My observations were made with the sun about 12° above the horizon. At this angle the image of the sun is dragged over the glass or mercury with no sharp outlines, a mere streak of light, and not a perfect, sharp-cut image of the sun which an important observation demands.

Mr. Peary's altitudes were all less than 7°. I challenge any one to produce a clear cut image of the sun on an artificial horizon with the sun at that angle. All such observations therefore are unreliable because of imperfect contact, for which there can be no correction.

The question of error by refraction is one of very great importance. In the known zones the accumulated lesson of ages has given us certain tables for correction, but even with these advantages few navigators would take an observation when the sun is but 7° above the horizon and count it of any value whatever.

In the Arctic the problem of refraction presents probable inaccuracies, not of seconds or minutes, but possibly of degrees. Every Arctic traveler has seen in certain atmospheric conditions a dog enlarged to the image of a bear. A raven frequently looks like a man, and a hummock, but 25 feet high, a short distance away, will at times rise to the proportions of a mountain. Mirages turn things topsy-turvy, and the whole polar topography is distorted by optical illusions. Many explorers have seen the returning sun over a sea horizon after the long night one or two days before the correct time for its reappearance. This gives you an error in observations which can be a matter of 60 miles.

Here is a tangle in optics, which cannot under the present knowledge of conditions be elucidated, and yet with all these disadvantages, the group of armchair geographers of the National Geographic Society pronounces a series of sun altitudes less than 7° above the horizon as proof positive of the attainment of the Pole. Furthermore these men are personal friends of Mr. Peary, and the society for whom they act is financially interested in the venture which they indorsed.

Is this verdict based upon either science or justice, or honor?

In response to a public clamor for a peep at these papers, a more detestable unfairness was forced on the public. The venerable director of the Coast and Geodetic Survey, who was one of Mr. Peary's jurors, instead of showing his hand, and thus freeing himself from a dishonest entanglement, asked his underlings, H. C. Mitchell and C. R. Duval, to stoop to a dishonor to veil the humbug previously perpetrated. Under the instruction of their chief, the first figures of Mr. Peary's sextant readings have been taken, and by manipulating these they have helped Mr. Peary by saying that their calculation placed Mr. Peary within two miles of the Pole.

Perhaps Mr. Peary was at the pin-point of the Pole, but when he allows his friends to use questionable methods to give a false security to his claim, then his claim is insecure indeed.

Mitchell and Duval took the sextant readings at face value. If Mr. Peary or his computers had frankly admitted the uncertainty of the grounds upon which these sextant readings rested, then one would be inclined to grant the benefit of doubt; but as was the case regarding the verdict of the National Geographic Society, the public was carefully excluded from a knowledge of the shaky grounds upon which these calculations are based. The impossibility of correct time and adequate allowance for refraction render such figures useless as proof of a position. But what about the image of the sun upon the artificial horizon?

An important observation demands that this should be sharp and clear, otherwise the observation is worthless. Mitchell and Duval have surely thought of this. Perhaps they have tried an experiment. As real scientific students they should have experimented with the figures with which they played. If the experiment has not been made they are incompetent. In either case a trick has been used to bolster up the deceptive verdict of the National Geographic Society.

A dish of molasses, a bull's eye lantern and a dark room are all that is necessary to prove how the public has been deceived by men in the Government pay as scientific computers. With the bull's eye as the sun, the molasses or any other reflecting surface as a horizon, with the light striking the surface at less than 7 degrees, as Mr. Peary's sun did, it will be found that the sun's image is an oblong streak of light with ill-defined edges. Such an image cannot be recorded on a sextant with sufficient accuracy to make it of any use as an observation. Mitchell and Duval must know this. If so, they are dishonest, for they did not tell the public about it. If they did not know it they are incompetent and should be dismissed from the Government service.

With all of these uncertainties a course which gives a workable plan of action can be laid over the blank charts, but there always remains the feebly guarded mystery of the ice drift. When the course is set, the daily run of distance can be checked by estimating speed and hourly progress with the watches. Against this there is the check of the pedometer or some other automatic measure for distance covered. The shortening night shadows and the gradual coming to a place where the night and day shadows are of about equal length is a positive conviction to him who is open to self-conviction, as a polar aspirant is likely to be. But frankly and candidly, when I now review one and all of these methods of fixing the North Pole, or the position of a traveler en route to it, I am bound to admit that all attempt at proof represented by figures is built on a foundation of possible and unknowable inaccuracy. Figures may convince an armchair geographer who has a preconceived opinion, but to the true scientist with the many chances for mistakes above indicated there is no real proof. The verdict on such data must always be "not proven" if the evidence rests on a true scientific examination of material which at best and in the very nature of things is not checked by the precision which science demands. The real proof—if proof is possible—is the continuity of the final printed book that gives all the data with the consequent variations.

FROM A CRITICAL REVIEW OF THE POLAR CLAIMS IN A FORTHCOMING BOOK
By CAPTAIN THOMAS F. HALL of Omaha, Neb.

DR. COOK'S VALID CLAIM.

Cook's narrative has been before the public nearly two years. It has been subject to the most minute scrutiny that invention, talent and money could give. It is to-day absolutely unscathed. Not one item in it from beginning to end has been truthfully discredited. It stands unimpeached. Mud enough has been thrown. Bribery and conspiracy have done their worst. A campaign of infamy has been waged, and spent its force; but not one solitary sentence has been proven wrong. Musk-ox fakes, starved dogs, fictitious astronomical or other calculations may have some effect on popular opinion; but they have none on the actual facts. They do not budge the truth a hair's breadth and they do not make history.

Cook's claim to the Discovery of the North Pole is as sound and as valid as the other claims of discovery, or the achievement of any one preceding him in the Arctic or the Antarctic.

VERDICT OF GEN. A. W. GREELY, REAR ADMIRAL W. S. SCHLEY AND OTHER ARCTIC EXPERTS

Dr. Cook is the discoverer of the North Pole.—GENERAL A. W. GREELY.

No one familiar with the Polar problem doubts Dr. Cook's success. Peary never tried to get to the Pole. He copied Cook's data and then, by official intrigue tried to "put it over." A study of Peary's deception on compass variation will prove that.—CLARK BROWN.

You can prove the discovery of Northermost Land. The Eskimo talk is nonsense. The Polar discussion should be settled by an International Commission—PROF. OTTO NORDENSKJOLD.

Dr. Cook was the first and only man to reach the North Pole—CHAS. E. RILLIET.

I have gone over all of Dr. Cook's data, and, in spite of the statements to the contrary, I believe he reached the Pole.—MAURICE CONNELL.

It has always been my pleasure to support Dr. Cook. I can see no reason for doubting his success. Who are his accusers, surely not Arctic Explorers?—CAPTAIN OTTO SVERDRUP.

I am convinced that if anyone reached the Pole, Dr. Cook got there.—ANDREW J. STONE.

From first to last I have championed Dr. Cook's cause, and after going over the printed records of both claimants I am doubly convinced that he reached the Pole.—CAPTAIN EDWARD A. HAVEN.

Dr. Cook reached the Pole, I doubt Peary, his observations bear the stamp of inexcusable inaccuracy and bunglesome carelessness. One cannot read Peary's book and believe in him.—CAPTAIN JOHN MENANDER.

                                                 Washington, D. C.,
                                                      Jan. 7th, 1911.
Dear Dr. Cook:
    .   .   .   .   I would assure you that I have never varied in the belief that you reached the Pole. After reading the published accounts, daily and critically, of both claimants, I was forced to the conclusion from their striking similarity that each of you was the eye witness of the other's success.

Without collusion it would have been impossible to have written accounts so similar, and yet in view of the ungracious controversy that has occurred since that view (collusion) would be impossible to imagine.

While I have never believed that either of you got within a pin-point of the Pole, I have steadfastly held that both got as near the goal as was possible to ascertain considering the imperfections of the instruments used and the personal errors of individuals under circumstances as adverse to absolute accuracy.

Again I have been broad enough in my views to believe that there was room enough at the Pole for two; and never narrow enough to believe that only one man got there.

I believe that both are entitled to the honor of the achievement.

                              Very truly yours,

                                      (Signed)   W. S. SCHLEY.

POSITIVE PROOF OF DR. COOK'S ATTAIN-
MENT OF THE POLE

By CAPTAIN EVELYN BRIGGS BALDWIN

METEOROLOGIST PEARY EXPEDITION, 1893-4, SECOND-IN-COM-
MAND WELLMAN EXPEDITION 1898-9, AND ORGANIZER AND
LEADER OF THE BALDWIN-ZIEGLER POLAR EXPEDITION,
1901-2, ETC.

I can prove the truth of Dr. Cook's statements in regard
to his discovery of the North Pole from Peary's own official
record of his last dash to the Northward.

So far as I can learn, Dr. Cook has never made a "confession" in regard to his trip to the Pole in the sense that he
denied his first statements. He has merely said that, in view of
the great difficulty in determining the exact location of the
Pole, he may not have been exactly upon the northernmost
pin-point of the world. Peary, under pressure at the Congressional investigation, was forced to admit the same.

For three hundred years there has been a rivalry among
civilized men to be the first to reach the North Pole. I believe
that the honor of having succeeded in the attempt should go—
not to Peary—but to the man who reached the Pole a year
before Peary claims to have been there.

Dr. Cook is now in New York City, and I have talked with
him several times recently. With the information that I myself have gathered, I believe that he really did reach the Pole,
or came so close to that point that he is entitled to the credit
of the Pole's discovery.

Bradley Land is located between latitude 84 and 85.
It was discovered by Cook in his Poleward march. The land
ice, or glacial ice, which Cook also discovered, is located be-

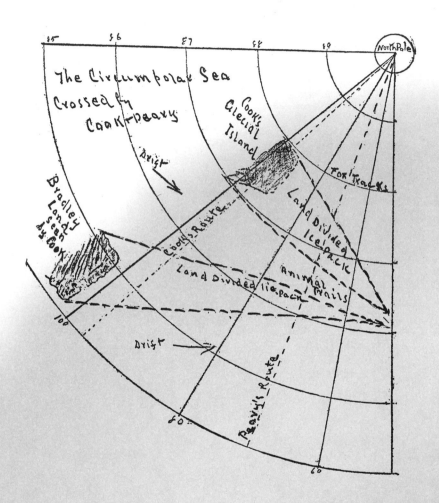

THE LAND-DIVIDED ICE-PACK REPORTED BY PEARY·
PROVES COOK'S ATTAINMENT OF THE POLE

tween latitude 87 and latitude 88. Cook's line of march carried him thirty or forty miles to the east of Bradley Land and then upon the glacial ice. The proximity to the new land gave Cook a favorable land-protected surface upon which to travel, and also afforded him protection from gales and from the consequent movements of the pack-ice westward of the new lands. Cook traveled in the lee of the groups of islands and over ice floes more stationary than the ice farther to the east, over which Peary traveled.

EVIDENCE OF COOK'S TRAVELS

A critical examination of Peary's book not only reveals a remarkable corroboration of Cook's discovery of Bradley Land and the glacial island north of it, but also seems to indicate the existence of islands farther west between the same parallels of latitude.

Referring to page 250, when beyond the 86th parallel, Peary says: "In this march there was some pretty heavy going. Part of the way was over some old floes, which had been broken up by many seasons of unceasing conflict with the winds and tides. Enclosing these more or less level floes were heavy pressure ridges over which we and the dogs were obliged to climb." In other words, the floes which Peary describes in this part of his journey clearly indicate that they were just such floes as one would expect to find after having passed through a group of islands, and, therefore, contrasting naturally with the immense size of the floes which both Cook and Peary traversed north of the 88th parallel.

Beginning with page 258, we have a most instructive description by Peary of the ice between the parallels wherein Cook locates the glacial ice and upon which he traveled for two days. It is such ice as one would expect to find after having passed around the north and south ends of an island from forty to sixty miles to the westward. This particular area Peary designates as a veritable "Arctic Phlegethon," and it is inconceivable to believe in this Phlegethon without also believing in the existence of the glacial ice, as located and described by Dr. Cook. Let us, therefore, examine Peary's narrative minutely. He says, on page 259, "When I awoke the following day, March 28, the sky was apparently clear; but, ahead of us, was a thick, smoky, ominous haze drifting low over the ice, and a bitter northeast wind, which, in the orthography of the Arctic, plainly spelled 'Open Water'. . . ."

Also, on the same page: "After traveling at a good rate for six hours along Bartlett's trail, we came upon his camp beside a wide lead, with a dense black, watery sky to the north-west, north and northeast."

Again, on page 260: ". . . The break in the ice had occurred within a foot of the fastening of one of my dog teams, . . . Bartlett's igloo was moving east on the ice raft, which had broken, and beyond it, as far as the belching fog from the lead would let us see, there was nothing but black water."

Finally, on page 262, Peary says: "This last march had put us well beyond my record of three years before, probably 87° 12'. The following day, March 29, was not a happy one for us. Though we were all tired enough to rest, we did not enjoy picnicing beside this Arctic Phlegethon which, hour after hour, to the north, northeast and northwest, seemed to belch black smoke like a prairie fire. . . . Bartlett made a sounding of one thousand two hundred and sixty fathoms, but found no bottom."

In the foregoing we have positive proof that this almost open water area was not caused by shoals at that immediate point.

Peary's concern as regards this big hole in the ice-pack is set forth further on page 265, as follows: "The entire region through which we had come during the last four marches was full of unpleasant possibilities for the future. Only too well we knew that violent winds, for only a few hours, would send the ice all abroad in every direction. Crossing such a zone on a journey north is only half the problem, for there is always the return to be figured on. Though the motto of the Arctic must be 'Sufficient unto the day is the evil thereof,' we ardently hoped there might not be violent winds until we were south of this zone again on the return."

From this it is apparent that Peary realized fully the permanent character of this Phlegethon over which he was traveling. With astonishing persistency, he refers again and again to this particular locality. Quoting from page 303, when on his return march, he says: "There was one region just above the 87th parallel, a region about fifty-seven miles wide, which gave me a great deal of concern until we had passed it. Twelve hours of strong wind blowing from any quarter excepting the north would have turned that region into an open sea. I breathed a sigh of relief when we left the 87th parallel behind."

And, as though the Phlegethon had not already been sufficiently described, on page 307 we find recorded: "Inspired by our good fortune we pressed on again completing two marches, and when we camped we were very near the 87th parallel. The entry that I made in my diary that night is perhaps worth quoting: "'Hope to reach the Marvin Igloo (86° 38') tomorrow. I shall be glad when we get there on to the big ice again. This region here was open water during February and the early part of March and is now covered with young ice which is thoroughly unreliable as a means of return. A few hours of a brisk wind east, west, or south, would make this entire region open water for some fifty to sixty miles north and south, and an unknown extent east and west. Only calm weather or a northerly wind keeps it practicable.'"

ABSOLUTE PROOF OF COOK'S CLAIM

From the foregoing it is self-evident that Peary's observations by sextant could not be more corroborative of Cook's latitude than that the Phlegethon is proof of the existence of a glacial island between the same two parallels traversed by both explorers. Cook had discovered the *cause*, and Peary followed to discover the *effect* of that cause. To one familiar with the conditions of ice-floes in the vicinity of islands in the Arctic the reasons for this are as clear as it would be to the lay mind should it be suddenly announced that on a certain date an astronomer had discovered the head of a comet, which being doubted by rival investigators, might lead to the unhappy discrediting of the original discoverer; but should it be as suddenly announced that a rival astronomer had observed the tail of a comet in the same locality there would quite certainly follow a reversal of public sentiment.

EVIDENCE OF HIS TRAVELS

Of first importance also in proving the existence of new lands discovered by Cook is the evidence derived from the existence of animal life, since Arctic game clings close to the shore line in its search for food. Birds must find their nesting places on lands. Foxes live upon birds and the refuse left in the trails of polar bears and seals. Seals feed upon shrimps and find the chief source of food in waters close to the land. Polar bears in turn feed upon seals, and necessarily are found more numerously about lands or islands.

For this reason we will examine Peary's official narrative of his journey north for evidence of Dr. Cook's discovery of land to within 2° of the North Pole. Having noted Dr. Cook's statement relative to the blow hole of a seal near Bradley Island, we will follow in Peary's trail for corroboration of Cook's journey eleven months previous, and a comparatively short distance westward of Peary's line of march. Referring to Peary's "North Pole" on page 249, while in latitude 85° 48' he records:

"While we were engaged in this business we saw a seal disporting himself in the open water of the lead."

Still farther along, when in latitude 86° 13', Peary states, on page 252: "Along the course of one of those leads we saw the fresh tracks of a polar bear going west."

ANIMAL TRAILS VERIFY COOK'S REPORT

Arctic travelers will well appreciate the force of this statement relative to the polar bear, who, scenting the land a few miles to the westward, was in search of seals. The freshness of the bear's tracks is proof that it had not drifted on some ice floe from remote parts of the Arctic basin.

Again, referring to page 257, we find that Peary while traveling through deep snow March 28, records: "During the day we saw the tracks of two foxes in this remote and icy wilderness, nearly two hundred and forty nautical miles beyond the northern coast of Grant Land."

It is worthy of note that Peary does not state just how far from the glacial or land ice upon the submerged island over which Cook traveled the fox tracks were. But it is evident that the foxes were less than two sleeps from land, since Peary states that Marvin's observation placed them in about latitude 86° 38', the very latitude in which Cook traveled upon the stationary land ice.

Still again, page 307, while on his return march and near the 88th parallel Peary observes: "Here we noticed some fox tracks that had just been made. The animal was probably disturbed by our approach. These are the most northerly animal tracks ever seen."

Certainly. Why not? Since they were so near the northern termination of the land ice discovered by Dr. Cook. In this connection it is also important to remark that between latitude 88 and his approximate approach to the Pole, Dr. Cook makes no mention of animal life, and this is corroborated by Peary's own statement that he observed no tracks of animals beyond the 88th parallel. Thus Peary corroborated Cook by the very absence of animal life in the very region where Cook states he saw no land.

PEARY'S STATEMENTS PROVE COOK'S

On Peary's return journey he states that as they approached Grant Land the fresh tracks of foxes and other evidences of animal life were very numerous. And if the nearness of land was evidenced in this case it is also clear that the tracks and appearance of animals on his journey in the high latitudes should be given equal weight as evidence of the lands discovered by Cook.

The line of deep sea soundings taken by Peary from Cape Columbia northward indicates a steady increase in depth to latitude 84° 24', where the lead touched bottom at eight hundred and twenty-five fathoms, until, in latitude 85° 23', the sounding showed a depth of but three hundred and ten fathoms. Referring to this, we find that Peary says, on page 338 of his narrative: "This diminution in depth is a fact of considerable interest in reference to the possible existence of land to the westward."

It seems to me that it is not impertinent to remark that this land to the westward was scarcely two sleeps distant, as Dr. Cook has steadfastly maintained. Finally, on page 346, Peary says: "Taking various facts into consideration it would seem that an obstruction (lands, islands or shoals) containing.nearly half a million square statute miles probably exists, and another at or near Crocker Land."

More Accurate Observations by Cook Than by Peary

And this is all that Dr. Cook claims in his location of land to the northward of the very Crocker Land to which Peary alludes.

As to Dr. Cook's and Peary's observations when in the immediate vicinity of the Pole, I would call attention to the following facts: Cook's determination by the sextant of the sun's altitude was made April 21, 1908; Peary's final observations were taken April 7 of the following year. The sun being thus two weeks higher at the time Cook made his observations, he was able to secure a more accurate series of altitudes, and this will have an important bearing in substantiation of his claims.

Considering the difficulty which Peary has had in proving whether he was at 1.6 miles from the Pole on the Grant Land side or the Bering Strait side, and whether he was ten or fifteen miles away, I think Dr. Cook was justified in saying that, al-

though he believed he was at the North Pole, he is not claiming
that he had been exactly at the pin-point of the North Pole.
At any rate, it places Dr. Cook in the position of endeavoring
to tell the truth.

In this connection I feel like replying to a criticism which
Mr. Grosvenor, editor of the National Geographic Magazine,
published over his own signature immediately following Dr.
Cook's return from the Pole. "Cook's story reads like that of a
man who had filled his head with the contents of a few books on
polar expeditions and especially the writings of Sverdrup."

ARMCHAIR CRITICISMS UNFAIR

Now, since Sverdrup is a real navigator, having accompanied Nansen during his three years' drift on the Fram, and,
following this, having himself organized and led an expedition
during three years to the westward of Grinnell Land, in the
course of which he discovered and charted, in 1902, Heiberg
Land and contiguous islands (which, however, Peary charted
four years later and named Jessup Land), I do not consider
Mr. Grosvenor's armchair criticism of the writings of Capt.
Sverdrup and of Dr. Cook quite in keeping with the principles
of a square deal and fair play.

Among the reasons which Peary assigns for doubting
Dr. Cook is one pertaining to the original records which Dr.
Cook unwillingly left at Etah. The leaving behind of these
papers, according to Peary, was merely a scheme on Cook's
part, so that he might claim they had been lost or destroyed
and thus escape being forced to produce them in substantiation
of his claim. Recently, when I asked Dr. Cook about this, his
reply was: "This does not sound very manly. If this was
so in Peary's belief, why did he not bring them back? Here
was absolute proof in his own hands. Why did he bury it?"

Armchair geographers and renegades may endeavor to
discredit Dr. Cook, but the seals and polar bears and little foxes
will bear testimony of unimpeachable character to substantiate
his claims as the discoverer of the North Pole. The reading

public will not forget that when Paul Du Chaillu, returning from his expedition to Africa, reported the discovery of the pigmies, he was denounced as a faker and a liar. For three years Du Chaillu, as he has told me himself, sought in vain to reestablish his credibility, and when at the end of that time he succeeded in bringing some of the pigmies and exhibiting them before the scientific bodies of the world, then the "doubting Thomases" were obliged to give him credit as the discoverer of the African dwarfs. The yellow press and sensation mongers will decry Dr. Cook as they did Du Chaillu, for some years to come, but Arctic explorers endorse him to-day.

Rear Admiral W. S. Schley, General A. W. Greely, Captain Otto Sverdrup, Captain Roald Amundsen, and all the world's greatest explorers have indorsed Dr. Cook.

I have seen Dr. Cook's original field notes, his observations, and the important chapters of his book, wherein his claim is presented in such a way that the scientific world must accept it as the record and the proof of the greatest geographic accomplishment of modern times.

Putting aside the academic and idle argument of pin-point accuracy—the North Pole has been honestly reached by Dr. Cook 350 days before anyone else claimed to have been there.

(Signed) EVELYN BRIGGS BALDWIN.

VERDICT OF THE GEOGRAPHIC HISTORIAN

DR. COOK'S RECORD IS ACCURATE
IT IS CERTIFIED—IT IS CORROBORATED

HE IS THE DISCOVERER OF
THE NORTH POLE

By Edwin Swift Balch

(From the N. Y. Tribune, April 14, 1913)

Which was it: Cook or Peary? Who discovered the North Pole? Everybody thought the question had been settled long ago, but now comes an eminent geographer and explorer, who says, over his name, that both got to the "Big Nail," and that it was the Brooklyn doctor who did it first. And in defense of his belief he cites chapter and verse, and uses Peary's own story to prove that his hated rival it was who first stood at the top of the earth, "where every one of the cardinal points is South."

The intrepid defender of Cook is Edwin Swift Balch, fellow of the Association for the Advancement of Science, member of the Wyoming Historical and Geological Society, the Franklin Institute, American Philosophical, American Geographical and Royal Geographical Societies, writer on arctic, antarctic geographical and ethnological topics for the learned societies of the world. Dr. Balch lives at No. 1412 Spruce street, Philadelphia, and the title of his book, just published by Campion & Co., of Philadelphia, is "The North Pole and Bradley Land."

"All Travellers Called Liars"

"From time immemorial travellers have been called liars," says Mr. Balch in a chapter devoted to "travellers who were first doubted and afterward vindicated," and it is on this general assumption of their Munchausen-like proclivities that much of

the weight of argument depends.   But most of all the truthfulness of the doctor's assertion that on April 21, 1908, he and his
two Eskimo boys, E-tuk-i-shook and Ah-we-lah, reached the
goal and "were the only pulsating creatures in a dead world of
ice," is shown by the fact that conditions reported by Cook as
existing there were corroborated by Peary.

"The man who breaks into the unknown may say what
he chooses and present such astronomical observations as he
sees fit, says Mr. Balch, "but his proof rests on his word.   But
if the next traveller corroborated the discoverer, instantly the
first man's statements are immeasurably strengthened.

"To solve such a problem as that of who discovered the
North Pole, this comparative method seems to the writer the
only one available.   It is not a matter of belief, it is a matter
of comparison and reasoning.   It is not the evidence which Cook
produces *which in itself alone could prove Cook's claims*.   It is
the geographical evidence offered by both Cook and Peary,
which, when carefully compared, affords, in the writer's judgment, the only means of arriving at a conclusion.   It is Peary's
statements and observations which prove, as far as can be proved
at present, Cook's statements."

All Discoverers First Doubted

The writer then mentions a score of the great discoverers
and explorers of history who have been defamed and berated
by their contemporaries, yet whose achievements have in time
proved them to be truth tellers.   Marco Polo, "greatest of medi-
aeval travellers, was generally discredited."   Amerigo Vespucci
"to this day remains under a cloud for things he did not do."
Fernao Mendes Pinto, Nathaniel B. Palmer, Robert Johnson,
James Weddell, von Drygalski, Nordenskjold, Bruce, Charcot,
Dr. Krapf, Dr. Robmann, Du Chaillu, Stanley, Livingstone,
Colter, all have been reviled as fabricators, yet all have been
honored by those who came later, he says.

"There are three records of Dr. Cook's journey of 1908,"
says the writer.   "Cook's first announcement was a long cable-

gram sent from Lerwick, Shetland Islands, and published in the 'New York Herald' of September 2, 1909. The full original narrative was sent immediately after this and published in the 'New York Herald' between September 15 and October 7, 1909, with the title 'The Conquest of the Pole.'

"Both of these were written and sent before Cook could, by any possibility, have seen or heard of any of the results of Peary's last expedition.

The third record is Cook's book "My Attainment of the Pole," which is simply an enlargement on the earlier story.

COOK MUST HAVE BEEN FIRST

The point here emphasized is that Cook could not have had anything on which to base his description of conditions north of 83:20 north latitude, and as his description agreed with that later given by Peary, there could be no doubt that Cook was there first.

"The reason for this is that these statements can be based on nothing but Cook's own observations," says Mr. Balch, "for Cook started for Denmark from South Greenland before Peary started for Labrador from North Greenland, and therefore everything Cook stated or wrote or published immediately after his arrival in Europe must be based on what Cook observed or experienced himself.

"Cook's original narrative stands on its own merits; it is the first and most vital proof of Cook's veracity, and yet it has passed almost unnoticed.

The points on which the two accounts, Cook's and Peary's, of conditions at 90 degrees north agree most fundamentally, and hence most definitely establish the truthfulness of Cook, are first the "account of the land sighted in 84:20 north to 85:11 north (Bradley Land). The second is the glacial land ice in 87-88 degrees north. The third is the account of the discovery of the North Pole and the description of the ice at the North Pole."

Cook's Three Achievements

Cook's first great discovery, the writer holds, was Bradley Land, named after his friend and backer. This land, Cook declared, had a great crevasse in it, making it appear like two islands, the southerly one starting at 84:20 north. Peary made no mention of land north of 83:20 north.

"Whether there is land or water in the intervening sixty geographical miles is a problem," says the writer, "but in order to be perfectly fair to both explorers and to allow for errors in observation one might split the difference at 83:50 north and consider that latitude as a dividing line between the lands discovered respectively by Cook and Peary."

"The second important discovery of Cook's is the glacial land ice in 87 north to 87 north-88 north," says the writer. "A closely similar occurrence was observed by Peary on his 1906 trip in about 86 north, 60 west."

But the most important particular in which the two men agree, in the mind of Mr. Balch, is in their description of the ice at the pole. Cook reported that it was "a smooth sheet of level ice." The writer adds: "if that description of the North Pole is accurate, the writing of it by Cook, first of all men, on the face of it is proof that Cook is the discoverer of the North Pole."

The Snow Was Purple

But not only was the ice at the pole smooth and level, but the snow there was "purple" in the story of Cook, a detail in which he is again borne out by Peary.

"Purple snow," says the writer, "is a linguistic expression, an attempt to suggest with words what Frank Wilbert Stokes has done with paints in his superb pictures of the polar regions. Hence," he says, "the use of the word 'purple' by Dr. Cook, who is not a trained artist, proves that he has the eye of an impressionist painter and that he is an extremely accurate observer of his surroundings. . . . .

That Cook's description is accurate is in the next place certified to by Peary. Peary corroborates Cook absolutely about conditions enroute to the North Pole; and Cook is corroborated by Peary, not only by what Peary saw, but by what Peary did. If there was anything in the Western Arctic between the North Pole and 87:47 north but 'an endless field of purple snows,' smooth and slippery, Peary could not have covered the intervening 133 geographical miles in two days and a few hours. Peary, therefore, from observation and from actual physical performance proves that Cook's most important statement is true."

The evidence is thus examined, step by step. The statements of the two men are compared, word by word, and this is the conclusion reached:

"In view of all these facts it becomes certain that Cook must have written his description of the North Pole from his own observations, for until Cook actually traversed the Western Arctic between 88 degrees north and the North Pole, and told the world the facts, no one could have said whether in that area there was land or sea, nor have stated anything of the conditions of its ice, with its unusual, perhaps unique, flat surface.

"But Cook, in his first cable dispatch, stated definitely and positively and finally that at the North Pole there was no land, but sea, frozen over into smooth ice, and Peary confirmed Cook's statements.

"Cook was accurate, and the only possible inference is that Cook was accurate because Cook knew; and the further inevitable conclusion is that since Cook knew, Cook had been at the North Pole"

(*Ed.*) In personal letters Balch further says, "I have tried to look at it as if this were the year 2013, and all of us in heaven. . . . . . It is only a question of time till Dr. Cook is recognized as the discoverer of the North Pole."

FOR A NATIONAL INVESTIGATION

A REQUEST

By Dr. Frederick A. Cook

For three years I have sought in various ways to bring about a National investigation of the relative merits of the Polar Attainment and the unjust propaganda of distrust which followed. Such an investigation would do no harm if the original work and the later criticism has been done in good faith. Why has it been refused? To take the ground that it is a private matter and that the Government has taken no official part in the Polar race is to assume a false position. The injustice of this evasive policy is brought out in my telegram to former President Taft—and again in my letter to President Wilson. To compel such an investigation and to appoint Arctic explorers as National experts has been my main mission on the platform. Much against my will I have been forced to adopt the usual political tactics of getting to the voters to force action by Congress and the official circles of Washington.

When in 1911 the bill was introduced in Congress to retire Peary as a Rear Admiral with a pension, I supposed that this would automatically bring about a thorough scientific examination of the merits of the rival Polar claims. And such an investigation I then believed would surely bring about the only reward I have ever claimed—The appreciation of my fellow countrymen. It was however, as I learned later, a bold Pro-Peary movement fostered by lobbyists whose conscience was eased by drippings from the Hubbard-Bridgeman Arctic Trust, but I still believed that the dictates of National prestige were such that the usual white-washing and rail-roading process could not be adopted in a question of such International importance. I did not begrudge Mr. Peary a pension if honest methods were pursued to adjust the bitterly fought contention in the eyes of the world. My friends made no protest in Congress. As matters progressed, however, I saw that such men as Prof. Willis Moore and others of his kind—men I had previously trusted as honest, really proved themselves, double-faced, political back-scratchers. Then I changed my tactics. When one's honor is bartered by thieves under the guise of friends—and when these thieves are part of a government from which justice is expected—Then one is bound to uncover the leprous spots of one's accusers. I am glad to note that Prof. Moore, the President of the National Geographic Society, has since been exposed as being too crooked to fit into a berth of the present administration. There are others whose long fingers have been in the Polar-pie who will also meet their fate as time exposes their flat-heads.

To call a halt on this National Humbug where only official chair-warmers and political crooks served as experts, I sent the following telegram to former President Taft:

COPY OF TELEGRAM SENT TO FORMER PRESIDENT TAFT

Omaha, Neb., March 4, 1911

The President—The White House,
Washington, D. C.

When you sign the Peary bill you are honoring a man with sin-soiled hands who has taken money from our innocent school children. A part of this money I believe was used to make Arctic concubines comfortable. I am ready to produce others of the same opinion. Thus for twenty years while in the pay of the navy, supplied with luxuries from the public purse, Peary has enjoyed, apparently with National consent, the privilege denied the Mormons.

There are at least two children now in the cheerless north crying for bread and milk and a father. These are growing witnesses of Peary's leprous character. Will you endorse it?

By endorsing Peary you are upholding the cowardly verdict of Chester, Tittman and Gannett, who bartered their souls to Peary's interests by suppressing the worthlessness of the material upon which they passed. These men on the Government pay-roll have stooped to a dishonor that should make all fair-minded people blush with shame. This underhanded performance calls for an investigation. Will you close these dark chamber doings to the light of justice?

In this bill you are honoring one, who in seeking funds for legitimate exploration, has passed the hat along the line of easy money for twenty years. Much of this money was in my judgment used to promote a lucrative fur and ivory trade, while the real effort of getting to the pole was delayed seemingly for commercial gain. Thus engaged in a propaganda of hypocrisy he stooped to immorality and dishonor and ultimately when his game of fleecing the public was threatened, he tried to kill a brother explorer. The stain of at least two other lives is on this man. This bill covers a page in history against which the spirits of murdered men cry for redress.

Peary is covered with the scabs of unmentionable indecency, and for him your hand is about to put the seal of clean approval upon the dirtiest campaign of bribery, conspiracy and black-dishonor that the world has ever known.

If you can close your eyes to this, sign the Peary bill.

(Signed) FREDERICK A. COOK

The telegram was received but not acknowledged—the Peary bill was signed. But the false assumption of Peary's "Discovery of the Pole" was eliminated from the bill. There is therefore no National endorsement of Peary; though he was given an evasive Old Age Pension which the newspapers quoted incorrectly as an official recognition of Peary's claim to polar priority.

I now appeal to President Wilson and the present administration to make some official endeavor to clear our National emblem of the stain of the envious Polar contention. To that end I have written the following letter:

AN APPEAL TO PRESIDENT WILSON
(COPY OF A LETTER)

Chicago, May 1, 1913

Honored Sir:

I appeal to you to forward a movement which will adjust in the eyes of the world the contention regarding the rival Polar claims. The American Eagle has spread its wings of glory over the world's top. It would seem to be a National duty to determine officially whether there is room for one or two under those wings.

The graves of our worthy ancestors are marks in the ascent of the ladder of latitudes. Hundreds of lives, millions of dollars, have been sacrificed in the quest of the Pole. The success at last attained has lifted the United States to the first ranks as a Nation of Scientific Pioneers. Every true American has quivered with an extra thrill of pride with the knowledge that the unknown boreal center has been pierced and that the stars and stripes have been put to the virgin breezes of the North Pole. The unjustified and ungracious controversy which followed has wounded our National honor; it has left a stain upon our flag. Is it not, therefore, our duty as a Nation to dispel the cloud of contention resting over the glory of Polar attainment?

I have given twenty years to the life-sapping task of Polar exploration—all without pay—all for the benefit of future man. Returning—asking for nothing, expecting only brotherly appreciation of my fellow countrymen, I am compelled to face an unjust battle of political intrigues by men in the pay of the Government. My effort now is not for money nor for a pension, but to defend my honor and that of my family. The future of my children demands an exposition of the unfair methods of the arm-chair geographers in Washington. However, I do not ask the administration to defend me or my posterity, but do ask that the men who draw a salary from the National treasury be made answerable for a propaganda of character assassination, among these is Prof. Willis Moore and others of the so-called National Geographic Society.

The National Geographic Society with Prof. Moore as President is responsible for the false interpretation of the rival Polar claims. This society is a private organization used mostly for political purposes; for two dollars per year a college professor or a street-sweeper becomes with equal facility a "national geographer." It is, therefore, not "national" nor "geographic," and when this society poses as a scientific body, it is an imposition upon American intelligence, and yet it is this society, with the well-known political trickery of Prof. Moore, which has attempted to decide for the world the merits of Polar attainment. An investigation of the wrong doings of this society will quickly bring to light the injustice of the Polar controversy.

A commission of Polar explorers appointed by National authority will end for all times the problem of the rival Polar claims. There is an abundance of material on both sides by which such a commission could come to a reasonable conclusion. The general impression that the Polar contention has been scientifically determined is not true. There has been no real investigation into either claim. Such an investigation could only be made by Arctic explorers, and to bring about this end I would suggest the appointment of an International Commission of such men as General A. W. Greely, U. S. A., Captain Otto Sverdrup of Norway and Professor Georges Lecointe of Belgium. Their decision would be accepted everywhere. Greely and Sverdrup have each spent four years in the very region under discussion, and Lecointe is the Secretary of the International Bureau for Polar Research and also director of the Royal Observatory of Belgium. Such men will render a decision free from personal bias, free from National prejudice and their verdict will be accepted by the Nations of the world.

Though I am an interested party I insist that my appeal is not altogether a personal one. In the interest of that deep-seated American sense of fair play, in the interest of National honor, in the interest of the glory of our flag, it would seem to be a National duty to have the distrust of the Polar attainment cleared by an International commission.

Respectfully submitted,
(Signed) FREDERICK A. COOK

To the President,
    The White House,
        Washington, D. C.

Thousands of requests similar to those reproduced below have gone to various officials in Washington. Such appeals demand action.

Chicago, May 7, 1913

Mr. Josephus Daniels, Secretary of the Navy,
        Washington, D. C.
Dear Sir:

Rear Admiral Peary wears the stripes of the Navy, he is drawing a pension of $6,000.00 per year from the tax-payers—The National dictates of honor compel such a man to be clean morally—honest and upright officially. Dr. Cook has publicly made charges against Peary which relegate this Naval Officer to the rank of a common thief and degenerate. In his book, "My Attainment of the Pole," (Mitchell-Kennedy, N. Y.) there are specific charges made which call for an investigation. These charges have remained unanswered for three years—Why?

In the Polar controversy the flag has been dragged through muck, and this dishonor seems to rest upon a man for whose actions you are responsible.

The American people have a right to demand an investigation into the intrigue of the Peary Polar Propaganda, and as one believing in justice at the bar of public opinion, I ask that you take steps to clear this cloud in the eyes of the world.

Respectfully,

FRED HIGH

Editor of *The Platform*,

The Lyceum and Chautauqua Magazine,

Steinway Hall, Chicago.

Chicago, May 22, 1913.

To Congressman James R. Mann,
          Washington, D. C.

Dear Sir:

The conquest of the North Pole has lifted the United States to a first position as a Nation of scientific pioneers.   The controversy which followed is a blot on our flag and it is a slur at our National honor.   From the Government purse and from private resources we have spent millions to reach the top of the earth; it would appear therefore to be our duty as a Nation to adjust the Polar contention in the eyes of the world.

If Dr. Cook has reached the Pole, a year earlier than Peary, as most Arctic explorers believe, then the seeming endorsement and the pension of the Naval officer is an injustice to Dr. Cook and an imposition on the public; if both have reached the Pole then there should be a suitable recognition and reward extended to each.   As one of thousands of American citizens, I beg of you to forward a movement which will bring about a National investigation into this problem, with a suitable provision for a proper recognition.

Respectfully,

CHARLES W. FERGUSON,

Pres.,

The Chautauqua Managers Association,

Orchestra Bldg., Chicago.

CAN THE GOVERNMENT ESCAPE THE RESPONSIBILITY?

By FRED HIGH

While the Danes were royally entertaining Dr. Cook on September 4th, 1909, telegrams were being showered upon him by all the world. The King of Sweden sent this message:

"A BRILLIANT DEED, OF WHICH THE AMERICAN PEOPLE MAY RIGHTLY BE PROUD."

The American minister to Denmark made Dr. Cook's visit state business and joined in the effort to share Cook's honors. Dr. Cook paused in the midst of all this splendor to cable the following message to our President:

Copenhagen, Sept. 4, 1909.

President,
  The White House, Washington.
    I have the honor to report to the chief magistrate of the United States that I have returned, having reached the North Pole."

To which President Taft cabled the following reply:

Beverly, Mass., Sept. 4, 1909.

Frederick A. Cook,
  Copenhagen, Denmark,
    Your dispatch received. Your report that you have reached the North Pole calls for my heartiest congratulations, and stirs the pride of all Americans that this feat which has so long baffled the world has been accomplished by the intelligent energy and wonderful endurance of a fellow countryman."
                                        WILLIAM H. TAFT.

Was President Taft speaking for the American people when he called Dr. Cook's achievement the pride of all Americans? Were we ready to share Cook's joys? Share his honors? If so, then in all fairness, should we not share in his trials and tribulations? Are we like the crazy base ball fan who cheers a pitching hero when he wins and insults him with all kinds of vile epithets when he loses?

For one I shared in that thrill of pride and was glad to know that I had had dealings with Dr. Cook before he went in search of the Pole, consequently, I felt in honor bound to withhold any hasty criticisms that I might feel tempted to hurl at Dr. Cook. All who joined in his praises should insist upon it that he be given a chance to disprove every charge that has been brought against him, that he be given a chance to explain his every act before we join in the cry to crucify him. "Crucify him, or give us the most contemptible coward, moral leper and political crook that has lived in our time," if Dr. Cook's charges are true.

Believing that this is a matter that ought to be fairly settled by competent and orderly methods, I have written to several congressmen and senators, and the following correspondence speaks for itself:

Hon. Wooda N. Carr,   Chicago, Illinois, May 7, 1913.
    Washington, D. C.
Dear Sir:
    I wish to ask a personal favor of you, one that I think the public is interested in and one that I think the world ought to know more about. It is the Cook-Peary controversy. I have given this considerable thought and study. I have heard Dr. Cook lecture a number of times and have talked to him personally and tried to find out from every angle the facts as to whether or not his story is true. So far I have been unable to find a flaw in any of his statements, and Mr. Peary by his actions has given every evidence that Dr. Cook is telling the truth. Therefore, as a citizen who is interested in the larger affairs of this country, and as the editor of The Platform, which is devoted to the Lyceum and Chautauqua movement, I am asking whether or not it would be compatible with fair play and our sense of justice and real national dignity to take this controversy out of the hands of individuals and settle it by an official tribunal, or by a commission of arctic explorers.
    I shall be very glad, indeed, if you will inform me of what steps could best be taken to bring about the settlement of this controversy. If there are any authoritative facts developed along this line, I will be glad to know where to locate them as my sole object is to learn the truth.
    Under separate cover I am sending you copy of The Platform which contains Doctor Cook's letter to President Wilson, which I hope you will read.
                                        Yours very truly,
                                            (Signed) FRED HIGH.

                            House of Representatives, U. S.
Mr. Fred High,   Washington, D. C., May 13, 1913.
    602 Steinway Hall,
        Chicago, Ill.
Dear Sir:
    Your letter of the 7th inst., regarding the Cook-Peary controversy, received. I do not think it would be possible to get Congress to interfere in this matter. It is a question of little concern to many who discovered the Pole, or whether it was discovered at all. It seems to be a personal matter, the settlement of which should be determined by the persons interested.
                                        Very truly yours,
                                            (Signed) WOODA N. CARR.

Is it a matter of no concern whether or not the North Pole has been discovered? Is it a matter of no concern whether a man can fake a story about having discovered the North Pole, receive the homage of the world, fleece the American public out of thousands of dollars for fees to hear his lecture and go unpunished? If Dr. Cook has hoaxed the world as so many have charged him with having done, this is more than a private matter.

If Dr. Cook has discovered the North Pole, are we acting the part of fellow countrymen by shirking our duty? Shall Congress say that the clique at Washington either make good its charges against Dr. Cook, or be made to retract and stand disgraced in the eyes of the world? We shared Cook's honors. Will we shirk when he calls upon his countrymen for a square deal?

The following letter was received from Senator Miles Poindexter and should be carefully studied:

United States Senate, Committee on Expenditures in the War Department.

Washington, D. C. May 9, 1913.

Mr. Fred High, Editor,
   The Platform, 602 Steinway Hall,
     64 E. Van Buren St.,
      Chicago, Illinois.
My dear Mr. High:

I have yours of 7th inst., and was very much pleased to know that you are interested in securing a fair examination, officially if possible, into Dr. Cook's claims of discovery.

Ever since the Cook-Peary controversy began, I have paid more or less close attention to the questions involved therein. I have talked with a number of residents around the neighborhood of Mt. McKinley, Alaska, some of whom are friendly and some unfriendly to Dr. Cook; have read with great care Dr. Cook's book describing his polar expedition; and have followed through the newspapers and otherwise the various phases of the controversy and happenings in connection therewith. As a lawyer, I have always been especially interested in the study of the credibility of witnesses, the weight of evidence; and in deducing logical conclusions therefrom. From the careful consideration of the comparative character of the witnesses for and against Dr. Cook, their motives, and the attitude and hearing throughout the controversy of Cook and Peary themselves, I have a very fixed and firm conviction that Dr. Cook's story is true. I believe the majority of the people of the country who are interested in the subject are of the same opinion.

From my observation of the miserable petty cliques and factional squabbles in official circles of the Government, such for instance as the Sampson-Schley controversy and innumerable smaller disputes, I have long ago ceased to accept, as necessarily correct, official evidence merely because it is official.

I have not yet seen a copy of The Platform containing Dr. Cook's letter to President Wilson which you say you are forwarding me under separate cover, and when received will read it with much interest. Not having read it, I do not know just what plan Dr. Cook proposes for an official investigation. I will be glad however, to learn the basis upon which it is proposed to make the test an official investigation. It occurs to me that it is entirely a private matter and that the Government officially has nothing to do with it. Every man has as much right as any other man to form a conclusion in the case; public opinion, if the facts can be presented to the public, is the best judgment. I would be apprehensive of submitting the absolute determination of the question to an official tribunal for the reasons, among others, which I have mentioned above. However, will be glad to learn further as stated of the proposal.

With kind regards.

Very truly yours,
(Signed) MILES POINDEXTER.

Senator Poindexter's letter is a stricture on official Washington that ought to cause every true patriot to blush with shame. Are we at the point where even an impartial investigation can not be had into the controversy as to who discovered the North Pole?

There are thousands who believe this is a question that touches our national honor and therefore is a rightful subject for a Congressional Investigation. Those who believe this, ought to write to their representatives at Washington and urge such action as will lay the facts before the world.

The following letter from Hon. Champ Clark is worthy of much consideration as it reveals the real status of this controversy as it exists in official circles.

Dr. Cook is a private citizen with no Cook Arctic club to back him and share his gains. No National Geographical Society helped to finance his venture with the hope of managing his lectures as a sort of bureau graft. He is a private citizen.

Speaker Clark's letter furnishes us with the reason for asking Congress to take a hand in this affair for it shows how ready our statesmen are to give ear when the people speak:

THE SPEAKER'S ROOM

HOUSE OF REPRESENTATIVES

WASHINGTON, D. C.

May 10, 1913.

Mr. Fred High,
    Editor of The Platform,
        Chicago, Illinois.
My dear Mr. High:
    I have your letter touching the Cook-Peary controversy. I note what you say. I do not see clearly what it is that you are suggesting. That is, whether you want Congress to formulate some plan to determine the matter by appointing a commission of Arctic explorers, or exactly what it is that you do want.
    Of course, I do not know very much about Arctic explorations and do not set a very high store on them as I never could understand what sort of good would come of locating the North Pole. I am a good deal of a utilitarian, and am a disciple of the Baconian philosophy rather than of the philosophy of Aristotle and the Greek school. To tell the truth, I have always had a hazy sort of an idea that both Cook and Peary discovered the North Pole. I have not valued my opinion highly enough to undertake to exploit it or to induce anybody else to believe it as I have enough other matters on hand to employ the time and attention of one man.
    Wishing you success, I am

                            Your friend,
                                (Signed) CHAMP CLARK

The following opinion of the men on the Chautauqua platform is attributed to our good friend from Missouri:

> "The Chautauqua has been a powerful force in directing the political thought of the country, which is largely sociological in these latter days. I approve the Chautauqua lecturers, with whom I have been associated, because they constitute as fine a group of men and women as can be found among the splendid citizenship of America. I have a deep and abiding interest in them, and bid them a hearty godspeed in their work."

Dr. Cook is perhaps the leading Chautauqua lecturer of the present season. He is now booked to appear at seventy Chautauquas this Summer and it is certain that even the genial Speaker of the House wouldn't want to associate with a man who would hoax the world for gain. Certainly he wouldn't want "The greatest liar of the Century to be one of the powerful forces directing the political thoughts of the Century. If Dr. Cook discovered the North Pole he should be given the credit for that great achievement.

We certainly have a right to see to it that neither Dr. Cook nor Mr. Peary are treated as though they were the scum of the earth. Dr. Cook has brought charges against Mr. Peary as a Naval officer. He still brings these charges, and he should be made to prove them. Peary, an officer of the Navy, has brought charges against Cook and he should be made to prove them.

Mr. Peary is an officer of our navy, drawing an old age pension. His position is such that he cannot ignore Dr. Cook's open charges. He is honor bound to protect the good name of this great country by asking an investigation of these charges. To remain silent, is to stand to be branded as the arch-degenerate of our day. Don't forget it was he who opened up the mud batteries and caused this undignified controversy.

No honorable man can allow such open charges of gross immorality as Dr. Cook preferred against Mr. Peary in his telegram to President Taft. These have been printed in magazines and newspapers as well as appearing in Dr. Cook's books, now in the sixtieth thousand edition.

Here in Illinois press stories of improper conduct implicating Lieutenant-Governor Barrett O'Hara were circulated and he immediately asked the state legislature to investigate them. The legislature appointed a committee that took testimony and reported these stories were groundless and false.

Is a retired Admiral less important in the eyes of the world than the Lieutenant-Governor of Illinois, or has the "old tar" taken an immunity bath?

Are we any farther along than were those who put Columbus in chains and stoned the Prophets and nailed the Christ to the Cross? Are we so engrossed in the material things that all questions of honor are of no concern to us?

It is true that the bar of public opinion is the court of last resort in a real democracy, but it is equally true that it is essential to see that the source of public opinion be not polluted. Should our school children be taught that Peary discovered the Pole if Dr. Cook was there first?

Senator Robert M. LaFollette says: "You can't buy, you can't subsidize the Lyceum. At least, it never has been done. The Press has been subsidized. Papers and magazines which were printing the bad records of public officials and political parties have, in many instances, been forced out of the field or silenced. Special privilege organized as a System has its own press.

But the Lyceum platform is free. Really, I sometimes think that, from the days of Wendell Phillips to now, the Lyceum has pretty nearly been the salvation of the country."

The Lyceum and the Chautauqua have given Dr. Cook a fair hearing, and it is now a matter of National pride that when the press was silent or hostile, Congress indifferent, the Chautauqua, the one distinctively American institution, gave him an honest, impartial hearing.

I write as I do because, being the editor of The Lyceum and Chautauqua Magazine, I have tried to give Dr. Cook the same opportunity to present his case as I would expect him to do by me were I in his place and he in mine.

AFTER YOU HAVE READ THIS BOOK KINDLY WRITE YOUR CONGRESSMAN CALLING FOR AN INVESTIGATION.

INDEX

INDEX

INDEX

INDEX

INDEX

INDEX

INDEX

INDEX

INDEX TO 1913 EDITION

OTHER COOPER SQUARE PRESS TITLES OF INTEREST

THE NORTH POLE
Robert Peary
New introduction by Robert M. Bryce
480 pp., 109 b/w illustrations, 1 map
0-8154-1138-3
$22.95

THE SOUTH POLE
An Account of the Norwegian Antarctic Expedition
in the *Fram*, 1910–1912
Captain Roald Amundsen
Foreword by Fridtjof Nansen
New introduction by Roland Huntford
960 pp., 155 b/w illustrations
0-8154-1127-8
$29.95

THE *KARLUK*'S LAST VOYAGE
An Epic of Death and Survival in the Arctic, 1913–1916
Captain Robert A. Bartlett
New introduction by Edward E. Leslie
378 pp., 23 b/w photos, 3 maps
0-8154-1124-3
$18.95

CARRYING THE FIRE
An Astronaut's Journeys
Michael Collins
Foreword by Charles Lindbergh
512 pp., 32 pp. of b/w photos
0-8154-1028-6
$19.95

THROUGH THE BRAZILIAN WILDERNESS
Theodore Roosevelt
New introduction by H. W. Brands
448 pp., 3 maps
0-8154-1095-6
$19.95

AFRICAN GAME TRAILS
An Account of the African Wanderings of
an American Hunter-Naturalist
Theodore Roosevelt
New introduction by H. W. Brands
600 pp., 210 b/w illustrations
0-8154-1132-4
$22.95

ANTARCTICA
Firsthand Accounts of Exploration and Endurance
Edited by Charles Neider
468 pp.
0-8154-1023-9
$18.95

MAN AGAINST NATURE
Firsthand Accounts of Adventure and Exploration
Edited by Charles Neider
512 pp.
0-8154-1040-9
$18.95

GREAT SHIPWRECKS AND CASTAWAYS
Firsthand Accounts of Disasters at Sea
Edited by Charles Neider
256 pp.
0-8154-1094-8
$16.95

THE FABULOUS INSECTS
Essays by the Foremost Nature Writers
Edited by Charles Neider
288 pp.
0-8154-1100-6
$17.95

Available at bookstores; or call 1-800-462-6420

Cooper Square Press

150 Fifth Avenue
Suite 911
New York, NY 10011